KD1554 GRI.

CONTRACTING WITH COMPANIES

This book surveys the main rules of Company Law governing the making of contracts with companies. It adopts an economic perspective, examining these rules in terms of the risks they apportion between companies and parties contracting with them. It reviews the use that has been made of economics in the analysis of Company Law and considers what guidance this can provide in analysing corporate contracting. The book then examines the relevant law and the issues raised by this law, covering the role of corporate constitutions as the source of the authority of corporate agents, the mechanisms of corporate activity and decision-making, the identification of corporate contracting parties, pre-incorporation contracts and other contracts with non-existent companies, the contractual power of a company's board, the protection of parties dealing with subordinate corporate agents and the regulation of contracts in which a director has a conflict of interest.

CONTEMPORARY STUDIES IN CORPORATE LAW

Edited by John Parkinson (d. 2004),
formerly Professor of Law, University of Bristol

Corporate law scholarship has a relatively recent history despite the fact
that corporations have existed and been subject to legal regulation for
three centuries. The modern flourishing of corporate law scholarship has
been matched by some broadening of the field of study to embrace insolvency, corporate finance, corporate governance and regulation of the
financial markets. At the same time the intersection between other
branches of law such as, for example, labour, contract, criminal law, competition, and intellectual property law and the introduction of new inter-
disciplinary methodologies affords new possibilities for studying the
corporation. This series seeks to foster intellectually diverse approaches to
thinking about the law and its role, scope and effectiveness in the context
of corporate activity. In so doing the series aims to publish works of high
intellectual content and theoretical rigour.

Titles in this series

Working Within Two Kinds of Capitalism: Corporate Governance and
Employee Stakeholding: US and EC Perspectives
Irene Lynch Fannon

Contracting with Companies
Andrew Griffiths

The Jurisprudence of the Takeover Panel
Tunde Ogowewo

To the memory of John Edward Parkinson

Futuram Civitatem Inquirimus

Published in North America (US and Canada) by
Hart Publishing
c/o International Specialized Book Services
5804 NE Hassalo Street
Portland, Oregon
97213-3644
USA

Hart Publishing is a specialist legal publisher based in Oxford, England.
To order further copies of this book or to request a list of other
publications please write to:

Hart Publishing, Salters Boatyard, Folly Bridge,
Abingdon Rd, Oxford, OX1 4LB
Telephone: +44 (0)1865 245533 Fax: +44 (0) 1865 794882
email: mail@hartpub.co.uk
WEBSITE: http//:www.hartpub.co.uk

British Library Cataloguing in Publication Data
Data Available

ISBN 1–84113–154–7 (hardback)

Typeset by Datamatics Technologies Ltd, India
Printed and bound in Great Britain by
MPG Books, Bodmin, Cornwall

Contracting with Companies

Andrew Griffiths
School of Law
University of Manchester

·HART·
PUBLISHING

OXFORD AND PORTLAND, OREGON
2005

Preface

The aim of this book is to survey and analyse those areas of Company Law concerned with the making of contracts. In keeping with the spirit of 'Contemporary Studies in Corporate Law', it examines this law in its economic context. The DTI's 'Company Law Review', which produced its Final Report in 2001, has acknowledged the economic role of Company Law and identified improving the 'competitiveness' of companies as a goal of Company Law reform. This book argues that reforming the law of corporate contracting can contribute to the pursuit of this goal.

John Parkinson encouraged me to write this book for the series. His untimely and unexpected death in February 2004 has been a great loss to academic law and to Company Law in particular. His reputation and influence spread far beyond the legal community and his leading role in the steering group of the Company Law Review and in the aftermath of that project has been widely acknowledged and commended. I am grateful for his advice during the writing of this book and for his comments on the draft manuscript.

In writing this book, I have been helped by many friends and colleagues. I am grateful in particular to David Milman for his comments and advice and to Simon Baughen, Gerard McCormack and Anthony Ogus for commenting on various draft chapters. I would also like to thank Laura Short and Myra Knutton for their help and Richard Hart for his patience and support.

Whilst I have attempted to state the law as at the end of April 2004, I have been able to take some account of subsequent developments, in particular the judgments of the Court of Appeal in *EIC Services v Phipps* and the House of Lords in *Criterion Properties v Stratford Properties*.

Table of Contents

Table of Cases

Table of Legislation

UNITED KINGDOM – STATUTORY INSTRUMENTS

1

Attribution and Risk Assignment: An Introduction to the Legal and Economic Dimensions of Contracting with Companies

1 ATTRIBUTION

THIS BOOK WILL analyse a number of legal issues that can arise when a company (as opposed to a natural person) enters into a contract or other transaction with another party. In practice, both parties to a contract may be companies, but for ease of analysis parties (or 'third parties') contracting with companies will be treated as a uniform class. This book will focus on contracting with companies that are formed by incorporation under the Companies Act 1985, in particular on companies that are limited by a share capital.[1] It will examine the relevant law of England and Wales (although this is largely analogous to company law in the rest of the United Kingdom) and will emphasise the economic context and economic implications of this law. The role of this law is to strike a balance between facilitating commerce with companies and maintaining respect for the formalities of company law. It will be argued that economic concepts can help to analyse and judge this balance.

A company is a form of corporation and as such has a legal personality of its own.[2] However, it is an artificial legal person and a creature of the relevant law. A company can be party to a contract, but cannot actually 'make' or 'enter' a contract. A company cannot itself engage in the necessary acts

---

[1] On the various kinds of company and the other legal structures that may be used by a firm, see P Davies, *Gower and Davies' Principles of Modern Company Law* 7th ed (London, Sweet & Maxwell, 2003) ('Gower & Davies') at 3–10.

[2] For an historical analysis of the evolution of the company into its modern form and of its antecedents, see R Harris, *Industrializing English Law* (Cambridge, Cambridge University Press, 2000) ('Harris') and the early chapters in previous editions of Gower & Davies: for example, P Davies, *Gower's Principles of Modern Company Law* (London, Sweet & Maxwell, 1997) 6th edn ('Gower') at 18–48. See also J Baskin and P Miranti, *A History of Corporate Finance* (Cambridge, Cambridge University Press, 1997).

of offer or acceptance and 'its' actions are legal fictions. The law has to provide a basis on which the actions of natural persons can be deemed to be those of a company.

Lord Hoffmann emphasised the artificial nature of a company's actions in giving the Privy Council's advice in *Meridian Global Funds v Securities Commission*:[3]

> Any proposition about a company necessarily involves a reference to a set of rules. A company exists because there is a rule (usually in a statute) which says that a *persona ficta* shall be deemed to exist and to have certain of the powers, rights and duties of a natural person. But there would be little sense in deeming such a *persona ficta* to exist unless there were also rules to tell one what acts were to count as acts of the company. It is therefore a necessary part of corporate personality that there should be rules by which acts are attributed to the company. These may be called the rules of attribution.

Such 'rules of attribution' govern the ability of companies to make or enter into contracts and the ability of third parties to enforce contracts against companies. They have to perform the balancing act noted above and will form the subject matter of this book.

1.1 The Attribution of Contracts to a Company: An Historical Perspective

The law governing the attribution of contracts to companies reflects the various antecedents of the company as a legal form for business firms. Prior to the Joint Stock Companies Act 1844, incorporation was only possible for firms through the grant of a charter under the royal prerogative or by an Act of Parliament. The former had become rare and the latter was prohibitively expensive for most firms.[4]

Most joint stock companies at this time were therefore unincorporated and took the legal form of a partnership, although they mitigated the practical difficulties entailed by having large numbers of 'partners' by delegating management to directors and by vesting the company's property in a body of trustees.[5] This was achieved through a constitution or 'deed of settlement'. The law of partnership, which drew upon the laws of contract and agency, governed the relationship between these unincorporated

---

[3] *Meridian Global Funds Management Asia Ltd v Securities Commission* [1995] 2 AC 500 (PC) at 506. See generally HLA Hart, 'Definition and Theory in Jurisprudence' (1954) 70 *Law Quarterly Review* 37.

[4] See Gower at 36.

[5] See Gower at 28–35 and Harris at 137–167. See also R Grantham and C Rickett (eds), *Corporate Personality in the 20th Century* (Oxford, Hart Publishing, 1998) ('Grantham & Rickett') at 8–10.

companies and third parties.[6] In particular, all the members of such companies faced the prospect of being treated as partners and thus of having unlimited personal liability for the company's debts and liabilities.[7] Further, although a company's deed of settlement might include provisions limiting the authority of those actually running its affairs to incur debts or liabilities for which the members might be personally liable, these limits could only affect the members' liability to a third party if the third party had had notice of them.[8]

The Joint Stock Companies Act 1844 limited the size of partnerships and required all new companies to take the form of a corporation, but enabled them to do this through registration.[9] This was much simpler and much less expensive than the alternative mechanisms for incorporation. Companies that registered in the required manner now had a separate legal personality in accordance with the law of corporations.[10] However, the members of a registered company still faced the risk of unlimited personal liability because of their potential liability to the company itself to provide it with the funds needed to enable it to meet its own liabilities.[11] Like any other legal person, a company has unlimited liability for its own debts and liabilities. The Limited Liability Act 1855 limited this remaining exposure of a company's members by limiting their liability to contribute to its funds to any outstanding amount due on their shares, subject to certain conditions. At the end of the nineteenth century, the House of Lords in *Salomon v Salomon* confirmed the extent of the limited liability that the members of a registered company now enjoyed when it held that a company could have no further recourse to its members even where one person was exercising effective control over the company.[12]

---

[6] *Ernest v Nicholls* (1857) 6 HLC 401 at 417–9 (HL), per Lord Wensleydale.

[7] It has been suggested that the practical difficulties involved in suing the members of a large and fluctuating body and the even greater difficulties of levying execution made their personal liability 'largely illusory': see Gower at 32. However, it has also been suggested that the unlimited liability faced by members of unincorporated companies was a significant disadvantage for this form of organisation since the laws of insolvency and bankruptcy remained at the 'pre-industrial' stage until their reform in the mid nineteenth century: see Harris at 130–2. In practice, efforts were made to achieve limited liability contractually through standard notices to third parties, but the effectiveness of such devices was unclear and in any event could not eliminate the risk entirely: see Gower at 31–2. See also H Butler, 'General Incorporation in Nineteenth Century England: Interaction of Common Law and Legislative Processes' (1986) 6 *Int Rev Law & Econ* 169.

[8] *Ernest v Nicholls* (1857) 6 HLC 401 at 417–9 (HL), per Lord Wensleydale.

[9] See Gower at 38–9 and Harris at 282–5.

[10] On the legal nature of corporations, see Harris at 16–19.

[11] On limited liability, see Harris at 127–32 and 143–4.

[12] *Salomon v A Salomon & Co Ltd* [1897] AC 22 (HL). See also *Rayner v DTI* [1989] Ch 77 (CA) and [1990] 2 AC 418 (HL) and *Carlton Communications and Granada Media v The Football League* [2002] EWHC 1650. There are, however, various legal devices that a company or its creditors can use to reach the assets of those involved in the management of a company's affairs such as the personal liability of directors (and shadow directors) for breach of duty and for 'wrongful trading' under s 214 of the Insolvency Act 1986. See generally D Goddard, 'Corporate Personality—Limited Recourse and its Limits' in Grantham & Rickett.

The 1844 Act required registered companies to register their deeds of settlement as part of the incorporation process, which meant that their constitutions now became public documents. The Joint Stock Companies Act 1856, which consolidated the earlier legislation governing registered companies, replaced the deed of settlement with a constitution consisting of a separate memorandum and articles of association. This remains the required form of the constitution of a registered company limited by shares, although it is now proposed to replace it with a single document.[13]

A registered company limited by its share capital is therefore a corporation in legal nature, but is also still subject to rules derived from the laws of partnership and trusts. Until 1989, a company was obliged to have a common seal, this being a unique feature of incorporation.[14] At common law, this provided the basic rule for the attribution of contracts to corporations:[15]

> A corporation aggregate, being considered as an indivisible body, cannot manifest its intentions by any personal act or oral discourse … the law, therefore, has established an artificial mode, by which the general assent of the corporation to any act which affects their property may be expressed. This is by affixing the common seal.

In fact, in the absence of any provision to the contrary, a corporation could only make or enter into a contract through the affixing of its common seal.[16]

In the case of companies incorporated under the 1844 Act, it was established relatively early on that they could incur contractual liabilities through the actions of their agents, as had been the case when they were unincorporated.[17] However, there was a key change in the application of partnership law to registered companies, stemming from the fact that they now had to register their constitutions and thereby make them available

---

[13] See chapter 3.

[14] See Harris at 19. The Companies Act 1989 and the Law of Property Act 1989 abolished the requirement to have a common seal, although companies can still have one.

[15] S Kyd, *A Treatise on the Law of Corporations*, 2 vols (London, 1793–4) vol I at 267–8, cited in The Law Commission, *The Execution of Deeds and Documents by or on behalf of Bodies Corporate* (Law Commission Consultation Paper No 143, The Stationery Office, London, 1996 ('Execution of Deeds (CP)') at 2.3. See also on the law governing contracting with corporations, The Law Commission, *The Execution of Deeds and Documents by or on behalf of Bodies Corporate* (Law Commission Report No 253, The Stationery Office, London, 1998) ('Execution of Deeds (Rep)'); Lord Chancellor's Department, *The Execution of Deeds and Documents: A Consultation Paper on the Implementation of the Law Commission's Report 'The Execution of Deeds and Documents by or on behalf of Bodies Corporate'* by way of a Regulatory Reform Order (September 2002) and Department for Constitutional Affairs, *Response to the Consultation Paper* (January 2004) ('Execution of Deeds (Response)').

[16] *Ernest v Nicholls* (1857) 6 HLC 401 at 418; *Wright & Son v Romford BC* [1957] 1 QB 431. See also F Reynolds, *Bowstead & Reynolds on Agency* (London, Sweet & Maxwell, 2001) 17th ed ('Bowstead & Reynolds') at 2–038 and Execution of Deeds (CP) at 7.2. The Corporate Bodies' Contracts Act 1960 finally abolished this basic rule.

[17] *Smith v Hull Glass Co* (1852) 11 CB 897; *Ernest v Nicholls* (1857) 6 HLC 401 at 418–419.

for public inspection. The House of Lords held that this gave third parties dealing with such a company notice of any limits that its constitution placed on the authority of its directors or other agents to incur liabilities on its behalf.[18] This notice included any restrictions on the affixing of a company's common seal since this procedure is also subject to the provisions of a corporation's constitution.[19]

The registration of the constitutions of companies pursuant to the 1844 Act and its successors was therefore the basis of the so-called 'doctrine of constructive notice' in company law whereby third parties dealing with companies were deemed to know all information that could have been discerned from an inspection of the company's public file.[20] This doctrine originated in a case concerning a company registered under the 1844 Act, the members of which therefore faced unlimited liability for the actions of its directors.[21] However, the doctrine continued after members' liability was limited and still persists, although statutory reform in 1972 and 1989 has substantially mitigated its effect.[22] Whilst the doctrine provided some additional protection for the members of companies, it presented third parties with a burden and potential trap. It is ironic that it came about as part of the process leading to limited liability, which marked a general transfer of risk from members to third parties.

The reforms of 1844 and 1855 moved the arrangements for a company's management and governance from the domain of private law into the public arena. The doctrine of constructive notice reflected this shift. However, those responsible for drafting the constitutions of companies still enjoyed great freedom over their terms and thus over the precise level of authority vested in their companies' directors and other agents, as they had done when operating under the law of partnership. Thus, whilst third parties dealing with companies now had formal notice of the terms of a company's constitution, they could not presume that it would set the authority of the company's agents at any particular level.[23] The implications of this

---

[18] *Ernest v Nicholls* (1857) 6 HLC 401; *Royal British Bank v Turquand* (1855) 5 E & B 248; (affirmed) (1856) 6 E & B 327.

[19] *Clarke v The Imperial Gas Light and Coke Co* (1832) 4 B & Ad 315; *Ernest v Nicholls* (1857) 6 HLC 401; *TCB v Gray* [1986] Ch 621 at 636. See Execution of Deeds (CP) at 4.3.

[20] *Irvine v Union Bank of Australia* (1876–7) LR 2 App Cas 366 (PC) at 379–80. See further on the doctrine of constructive notice D Prentice, *Reform of the* Ultra Vires *Rule: A Consultative Document* (London, DTI, 1986) ('the Prentice Report') at 21–4 and Execution of Deeds (CP) at 5.10. This doctrine, which is also known as 'deemed notice', will be examined further in chapters 5 and 6 of this book.

[21] *Ernest v Nicholls* (1857) 6 HLC 401.

[22] *Irvine v Union Bank of Australia* (1876–77) LR 2 App Cas 366 (PC) at 379–80; *Mahony v East Holyford Mining* (1875) LR 7 HL 869; *Rama v Proved Tin and General Investments* [1952] 2 QB 147. On the statutory mitigation of the doctrine of constructive notice, see chapters 5 and 6.

[23] The 1856 Act included a model set of articles of association, appended as Table B, which became the familiar Table A in the Companies Act 1862: see Gower at 45. See now Table A in the Companies (Tables A to F) Regulations 1985 SI 1985/805 ('Table A').

unpredictability will be explored further in this book. It is one symptom of a tension in company law between (on the one hand) treating a company in much the same way as an unincorporated joint stock company, as the creature and property of its members, and (on the other hand) recognising its status as a separate legal person, standing between its members and third parties and shielding its members from personal liability.[24]

1.2 The Attribution of Contracts to a Company: The Current Position

The Companies Act 1985 provides that a company can become party to a contract in two ways:[25]

(a) by a company, by writing under its common seal, or
(b) on behalf of a company, by any person acting under its authority, express or implied …

The former method derives from the company's legal nature as a corporation. It also reflects a common tendency to treat a company as if it were a real person and could somehow act on its own behalf.[26] It obscures the fact that it is the company's officers who must physically sign or execute a contract made under a company's common seal. Their authority to do this is governed by and therefore can be limited by the terms of the company's constitution. A contract made by writing under a company's common seal therefore raises the same kind of legal issues as one made by the officers of a company acting as its agents.

Contracts can be of two types. First, there are contracts executed as deeds or 'in solemn form', which must be in writing and executed in a prescribed manner.[27] Secondly, there are contracts made 'in simple form' or 'under hand'.[28] A deed is necessary for certain transactions such as conveyances and other dealings in real property. A deed also has some different legal effects compared to a simple contract. Thus, a party can be bound by a deed without giving consideration (though such 'volunteers' are subject only to legal and not equitable remedies) and liability under a

---

[24] On the various conflicting visions or models of the company and their role in the development of company law, see M Horwitz, '*Santa Clara* Revisited: The Development of Corporate Theory' (1985) 88 *West Virginia Law Rev* 173, M Stokes, 'Company Law and Legal Theory' in W Twining (ed.), *Legal Theory and Common Law* (Oxford, Basil Blackwell, 1986), J Hill, 'Changes in the Role of the Shareholder' in Grantham & Rickett above n 5.

[25] Companies Act 1985, s 36. The Companies Act 1989 inserted this version of the provision with effect from 31st July 1990: SI 1990/1392.

[26] See Gower & Davies at 178–79. The affixing of the common seal has been portrayed as a company's own signature: see *Northside Developments v Registrar-General* (1990) 64 ALJR 427 at 430–31 (per Mason CJ)

[27] See generally Execution of Deeds (CP).

[28] *Ibid.*

deed is subject to a much longer limitation period.[29] Further, a person who is not party to a deed can enforce an undertaking in the deed given for their benefit, thereby overcoming the doctrine of privity.[30]

Prior to the reform of the law governing the execution of deeds by the Companies Act 1989 and the Law of Property Act 1989, the two ways in which a company could enter into a contract corresponded to the two types of contract. Thus, a company had to execute a deed through the affixing of its common seal and all contracts made in this way took effect as deeds.[31] Section 36A of the Companies Act 1985 (which was inserted retrospectively) now prescribes two ways in which companies can execute deeds.[32] The first is through the affixing of the common seal, if a company has one.[33] Secondly, it provides that a document signed by a director and the secretary of a company or by two directors and which is 'expressed (in whatever form of words) to be executed by the company' has the same effect as a document executed under the company's common seal.[34] A company is therefore no longer obliged to have a common seal, but is still free to have one.[35]

The 1989 reforms did not, however, make it entirely clear whether a contract made through the affixing of a company's common seal would still always take effect as a deed.[36] The Law Commission has recommended that the relevant law should be amended to make it clear that a contract made through affixing a company's seal can only take effect as a deed if it is expressly executed as a deed.[37] Such an amendment is likely to be made through a Regulatory Reform Order.[38] This means that a contract made

---

[29] Execution of Deeds (CP) at 2.8–2.9.

[30] See *OTV Birwelco v Technical & General Guarantee* [2002] EWHC 2240 at 11–13. Such persons also have a limited right to enforce undertakings in simple form contracts made for their benefit under the Contracts (Rights of Third Parties) Act 1999.

[31] See generally Execution of Deeds (CP) at 11.6. It is also possible for a company to appoint an attorney to execute documents on its behalf: Execution of Deeds (CP) at 8.16–8.24. The position changes in the case of insolvency when a liquidator, administrator or administrative receiver has powers to act on behalf of an insolvent company: Execution of Deeds (CP) at 8.25–8.41.

[32] The reform took effect as from 31 July 1990: SI 1990/1393.

[33] Companies Act 1985, s 36A(2): 'A document is executed by a company through the affixing of its common seal'. The Law Commission has taken the view that this means affixing the seal in accordance with the relevant provisions in a company's constitution: Execution of Deeds (CP) at 4.9 and 11.25.

[34] Companies Act 1985, s 36A(4).

[35] S 350 of the Companies Act 1985 provides that, where a company does have a common seal, it 'shall have its name engraved in legible characters on the seal; and if it fails to comply with this subsection it is liable to a fine'. In *OTV Birwelco v Technical & General Guarantee*, it was held that where a company executed a deed through the affixing of a seal with an incorrect name and which therefore did not comply with s 350, this did not render the deed void or unenforceable: [2002] EWHC 2240 at 55–8.

[36] Execution of Deeds (CP) at 11.7–11.10.

[37] Execution of Deeds (Rep) at 2.34 and 2.44.

[38] Execution of Deeds (Response).

through affixing a company's common seal, but not expressly executed as a deed, has the same effect as a contract made by an agent.

The second way in which a company can enter into a contract is through an agent acting under its authority.[39] Agency has been defined as:[40]

> the fiduciary relationship which exists between two persons, one of whom expressly or impliedly consents that the other should act on his behalf so as to affect his relations with third parties, and the other of whom similarly consents so to act or so acts.

A company can therefore make a contract through an agent if it has consented to the agent acting on its behalf. As an artificial legal person, a company cannot physically give or express such consent. In effect, the law has to attribute the giving of consent to a company in the same way as it has to attribute other actions such as making or entering into contracts.

Consent can be attributed to a company if it can be discerned from the terms of the company's constitution. In effect, the founding members of a company (or those members entitled to vary the terms of the constitution from time to time) act as the company in this respect, reflecting its roots in partnership law. As will be seen in chapter 3, it is through its constitution that a company consents to its board of directors having general powers to manage its affairs and enter into contracts on its behalf. Otherwise, the consent of a company has to be discerned from the actions of its board or from the actions of someone to whom the board has delegated the power to act on the company's behalf.[41]

A key feature of the ability of a company to make a contract through an agent is that the agent should have been duly authorised to act on behalf of the company in accordance with the company's internal governance mechanisms and, in particular, in accordance with the terms of its constitution. The validity of contracts made in this way therefore raises the same basic legal issues as contracts made through affixing the company's seal. However, agency covers a much wider range of possibilities since any member of a company's management can act as an agent on its behalf and not just its officers. In practice, therefore, the rules of law governing contracting through agents have much greater practical significance.

---

[39] Companies Act 1985, s 36(b).
[40] Bowstead & Reynolds, Art 1.
[41] See generally *Freeman & Lockyer v Buckhurst Park Properties* [1964] 2 QB 480 (CA). An agent's legal ability to make a contract can be referred to as 'power' or as 'authority'. However, the latter term has particular significance in agency law. See generally Bowstead & Reynolds, Art 1 and the discussion of the 'concepts of power and authority' in B Markesinis and R Munday, *An Outline of the Law of Agency* (London, Butterworths, 1998) 4th ed ('Markesinis & Munday') at 1–11.

1.3 The Approach of this Book

In the *Meridian Global Funds* case,[42] Lord Hoffmann identified the constitution of a company as the foundation of its rules of attribution. The constitution is the source of the authority of a company's board of directors to approve the affixing of its common seal to a document (or to approve the document's due execution in the alternative manner), to act as the company's agent in entering into a contract on its behalf and to delegate to others the authority to act as the company's agent. Chapter 3 of this book will therefore examine this foundational role of the constitution.

Chapter 3 will also consider the significance in this respect of the unitary board structure of companies under English law. This means that if the founding members of a company (or their successors) wish to set limits on the authority of their company's board of directors to make contracts on its behalf or authorise other agents to do so, then only the members can extend these limits or approve the overriding of them. For some companies, especially public companies, this can be a time consuming and expensive process. Chapter 3 will show that the legal nature of the limits on the board's powers can vary and that this legal nature determines the nature of the members' power to alter or override them. This adds to the complexity of the relevant law and the importance to third parties of there being rules of law that can override these limits in some circumstances and ensure the validity of contracts that have not been properly authorised in accordance with a company's constitution. This book will refer to such rules of law as 'overriding rules of attribution'.

Chapter 4 will examine two preconditions that must be satisfied before the law can attribute a particular contract to a particular company. First, the law must recognise the particular company as the true or 'intended' party to the contract. The artificial nature of a company's existence can make the task of identification much more difficult than when the contractual party is a natural person. Before the time of King James I, it appears that a corporation was treated as having no identity apart from its name and that 'if it does not act by its name, the act is not its act'.[43] However, it is now accepted that a company has characteristics other than its name by which it can be identified.[44] Chapter 4 will therefore examine the rules that govern the process of identification.

The second precondition is that the law must recognise the particular company as a legal person in existence at the time of contracting. Again,

---

[42] *Meridian Global Funds Management Asia Ltd v Securities Commission* [1995] 2 AC 500 (PC) at 506.
[43] J Grant, *A Practical Treatise on the Law of Corporations in General As well Aggregate as Sole* (London, 1850) at 145, which Stamp J noted in his judgment in *F Goldsmith (Sicklemere) v Baxter* [1970] Ch 85 at 92.
[44] [1970] Ch 85 at 92.

this issue is much more complex than in the case of natural persons. In the case of corporations, it has long been acknowledged that 'every corporation must have a legal creation'.[45] Further, the separate legal personality of a corporation does not 'terminate with the death of any human individual', but is 'potentially immortal and subject to dissolution only in a strictly defined manner'.[46] In the case of a registered company, this depends on the rules governing its entry on and removal from the register. Chapter 4 will consider the legal effect of a contract made by or on behalf of a company that proves not to exist in accordance with these rules.

Chapters 5 and 6 will examine the rules of law governing the attribution of contracts to a company, looking respectively at contracts made (or approved) by a company's board of directors and those made (or approved) by other agents. The constitution of a company determines the contractual power of its board and thus the board's actual authority to bind the company to a contract. The actual authority of other agents is determined both by the company's constitution and by the terms of any relevant acts of delegation. These two sources of actual authority can be viewed as a company's 'internal rules of attribution' and provide the initial reference point for the rules of law governing attribution.

However, the key feature of the law to be examined in chapters 5 and 6 will be the relevant overriding rules of attribution. Overriding rules have much greater significance to third parties than do a company's internal rules because the latter may vary widely in practice and can prove hard for third parties to discover or discern. The European First Directive on Company Law ('the First Directive') required that the law of Member States protect third parties from the risk of invalidity due to constitutional limits on the contractual power of the company's 'organs'.[47] Accordingly, the Companies Act 1985 now includes an overriding rule of attribution that protects third parties where a contract is made (or approved or authorised) by a company's board.[48] There is also a specific overriding rule entitling third party 'purchasers' to presume that a deed executed by a company in one of the two prescribed ways will bind the company as a deed.[49] Chapter 5 will examine these statutory rules of attribution. Chapter 6 will examine the overriding rules of attribution that protect third parties dealing with other corporate agents, which are still largely drawn from the common law of agency.

Chapter 7 of this book will examine the special rules of law that determine the validity of contracts with a company in which a director has a conflicting interest or duty of some kind (which will be referred

[45] M Hale, *The Prerogatives of the King* (London, Seldon Society, 1976), vol 92, ch 19, cited in Harris at 18.
[46] Harris at 19.
[47] EEC/68/151. See Gower & Davies at 111 and 135–36 and V Edwards, *EC Company Law* (Oxford, Oxford EC Law Library, 1999) at 33–7.
[48] Companies Act 1985, ss 35–35B and 322A.
[49] Companies Act 1985, s 36A(6).

to as contracts involving 'self-dealing'). The European Court of Justice has confirmed that the First Directive does not apply to such contracts and that their validity is subject to national laws.[50] In England and Wales, the relevant law derives from the rules of equity governing self-dealing by trustees, but these have been supplemented by statutory rules, currently set out in Part X of the Companies Act 1985. Under these rules, a self-dealing contract may not bind a company even though it would otherwise be validated by an overriding rule of attribution and even though it has otherwise been duly authorised in accordance with the company's internal rules of attribution.

This book will focus on the general law applicable to all companies on the assumption that they are solvent at the time of contracting and that they do not subsequently go into administration or insolvent liquidation. It will not, therefore, examine the special rules of law that can affect the validity of a contract with a company when the company does subsequently go into administration or liquidation.[51] For example, under the Insolvency Act 1986, the administrator or liquidator of an insolvent company can apply to the court to have a contract set aside on the basis that it amounts to a 'transaction at an undervalue' or a 'preference', provided that it was made within a specified time before the company went into administration or liquidation.[52] Further, the liquidator of a company in insolvent liquidation can disclaim 'onerous property', which includes 'any unprofitable contract'.[53] And a third party to a contract with a company which later goes into insolvent liquidation can apply to the court for an order rescinding the contract and the court has the power to make such an order on such terms 'as the court thinks just'.[54]

2 SOME GENERAL OBSERVATIONS ON THE LAW GOVERNING ATTRIBUTION

2.1 Lack of Focus on the Artificial Nature of Corporate Personality

The law governing contracting with companies is drawn from the general law of contract and agency in which a natural person is the model contracting party and the model principal. In applying this law to companies,

---

[50] *Cooperative Rabobank v Erik Aarnoud Minderhoud* (Case C–104/96) [1998] 2 CMLR 270.
[51] On the law governing the impact of insolvency on the validity of contracts with a company, see generally R Parry, *Transaction Avoidance in Insolvencies* (Oxford, OUP, 2001) and J Armour and H Bennett (eds), *Vulnerable Transactions in Corporate Insolvency* (Oxford, Hart Publishing, 2003).
[52] Insolvency Act 1986, ss 238 and 239.
[53] Insolvency Act 1986, s 178.
[54] Insolvency Act 1986, s 186.

the courts have tended to view them as analogous to natural persons and in effect as entities that exist separately from the agents acting on their behalf.[55] This attitude is reflected in the idea that certain acts performed on behalf of a company should be treated as the acts of the company itself and not as the acts of an agent or agents acting on behalf of the company that the law attributes to the company. Attempts to distinguish and privilege certain acts on this basis have made the relevant law unnecessarily complicated.

The treatment of documents executed under a company's common seal as executed directly by the company itself is an example of this tendency. This special treatment led to complication in the application of the common law overriding rules of attribution when those affixing a company's common seal to a document had not been duly authorised to do so under the company's constitution.[56] The courts' willingness to draw a distinction between the acts of a company itself and acts performed by an agent on its behalf also affected the common law rules governing the validity of contracts made with non-existent companies, which will be examined in chapter 4. Here, the distinction could prove crucial to such a contract having any legal effect at all, but it was an artificial one and thus the law was seen as arbitrary in its impact. Again, drawing the distinction complicated the law unnecessarily.

The relevant law has in many places failed to attach much weight to the fact that a corporate agent does not have a real and tangible principal that can act as a reference point for third parties. In reality, there are significant differences between a third party dealing with a corporate agent and a third party dealing with an agent acting for a human principal. These differences are likely to affect the third party's perception of the agent and should be taken into account in determining the burden that the law places on a third party who wishes to ensure the validity of a contract. Thus, third parties dealing with many kinds of corporate agent (especially those with an apparently senior position within a company's management hierarchy) are likely to view the agent as the external face of the company and as a key source of information about its affairs. They are unlikely therefore to have a clear awareness of a separate principal who can act as a superior reference point and a superior source of information in the same way as they would when dealing with an agent acting for a natural person.

In terms of the general policy considerations that should influence the development of the law, it is arguable that the factors used to justify the law's recognition of a company as a legal person in its own right should

---

[55] On the problems arising from applying rules of law to artificial legal persons in this way, see HLA Hart, (1954) 70 *Law Quarterly Review* 37. See also R Grantham, 'Commentary on Goddard' in Grantham & Rickett, above n 5.

[56] See *Ruben v Great Fingall Consolidated* [1906] AC 439 (HL), *Kreditbank Cassel v Schenkers* [1927] 1 KB 826 (CA) and *Northside Developments v Registrar-General* (1990) 64 ALJR 427.

be taken into account in determining the legal rules of attribution applicable to corporate agency. Unlike a natural person, a company exists for the benefit of its members. Its members, however, no longer face unlimited personal liability for actions that are attributed to the company. Further, as will be seen in chapter 3, it is the directors and other agents of a company rather than its members who conduct its affairs and are therefore likely to be the best source of information about its affairs. All these factors affect the nature of the risks associated with corporate agency and this book will argue that they should be taken into account in setting the legal burden faced by third parties dealing with corporate agents. This argument will be developed in chapter 2.

It is therefore arguable that the common law failed to give adequate weight to the special circumstances of corporate agency in setting the burden that the rules of attribution place on third parties, but it is also arguable that it evolved to give undue weight to the special features of a company designed to protect its members from the danger of mismanagement. This observation applies in particular to the doctrine of constructive notice, which evolved in response to the requirement that companies incorporated through registration had to file their constitutions.[57] In effect, as well as dealing with entities whose members were protected by limited liability, third parties had to assume a burden of responsibility for enforcing an additional safeguard for these members. As a consequence of this approach, which will be examined in chapters 3, 5 and 6, the common law rules of attribution came to be viewed as unduly harsh on third parties in practice and overly protective of companies and their members.[58] This created a general case for reform, which was given urgency by the need to comply with the First Directive and its requirement that third parties be given 'security of transaction'.[59]

2.2 Statutory Reform

Despite the shortcomings of the relevant law, there has been no systematic attempt to restructure it to reflect the practicalities of corporate personality and corporate agency. Reform so far has been piecemeal, targeting certain features of the law that were unduly prejudicial to third

---

[57] *Ernest v Nicholls* (1857) 6 HLC 401 (HL); *Mahony v Liquidator of the East Holyford Mining Co* (1875) LR 7 HL 869 (HL); *Irvine v Union Bank of Australia* (1876–77) LR 2 App Cas 366 (PC); *Re Jon Beauforte* [1953] Ch 131.

[58] See generally the Prentice Report.

[59] This term is used to refer the general objective of the First Directive, as stated in its recitals, that 'the protection of third parties must be ensured by provisions which restrict to the greatest possible extent the grounds on which obligations entered into in the name of the company are not valid.' See generally N Green, 'Security of Transaction after Phonogram' (1984) 47 *Modern Law Review* 671 on the philosophy underlying the First Directive.

parties dealing with companies. The First Directive led to the reform of the law governing pre-incorporation contracts (see chapter 4), to the effective abolition of the 'ultra vires' doctrine (see chapter 5) and to changes in the law governing contracts made or approved by a company's board of directors (see chapter 5).

The DTI's Company Law Review ('the Company Law Review') recommended a fundamental overhaul of company law,[60] which provides an opportunity for reforming the law governing contracting with companies. The Company Law Review advocated that company law be simplified and made more accessible as far as possible. It also stated that the 'main driver' in this exercise should be to make sure that British companies are 'competitive, in the sense that they exploit resources in the most efficient way possible to generate such wealth, and that they contribute to an internationally competitive economy'.[61]

As regards international competitiveness, the Company Law Review commented as follows:[62]

> Our company law needs to be internationally competitive, to ensure that we retain our existing companies and attract new ones ... we need attractive conditions not only for company management and operation, but also for investment. Companies are both direct users of company law and affected as trading bodies by its application to others.

[60] The DTI's Company Law Review Steering Group was set up in March 1998 and published its final report in June 2001: *Modern Company Law for a Competitive Economy: Final Report* (London, DTI, 2001) ('Final Report'). It raised issues and made provisional recommendations in three wide ranging interim reports: *Modern Company Law for a Competitive Economy: The Strategic Framework* (London, DTI, February 1999) ('The Strategic Framework'); *Modern Company Law for a Competitive Economy: Developing the Framework* (London, DTI, March 2000) ('Developing the Framework'); and *Modern Company Law for a Competitive Economy: Completing the Structure* (London, DTI, November 2000) ('Completing the Structure'). It also published some more focused reports, including one on *Company Formation and Capital Maintenance* (London, DTI, October 1999) ('Company Formation'). The Government welcomed the Final Report and indicated that it would first examine the various recommendations in detail and then consult on draft legislation to modernise company law. In July 2002, it published a White Paper entitled 'Modernising Company Law' ('the 2002 White Paper') as its first response to the Company Law Review and began the consultation process. The 2002 White Paper did not, however, deal with the whole range of the Company Law Review, but was merely the first step in the response and consultation process. Given the enormity of the task facing it and the need to get this reform right, the Government decided to carry out this process in stages rather than to produce one complete set of proposals. It defended this staggered approach on the grounds that it should increase the overall amount of time that could be made available for consultation on the various proposals and in particular should facilitate consultation on those matters which had not been raised for discussion in this way during the course of the Company Law Review. See generally on the Company Law Review J Rickford, 'A History of the Company Law Review' and J Parkinson, 'Inclusive Company Law' in J de Lacy (ed), *The Reform of United Kingdom Company Law* (London, Cavendish, 2002) and M Arden, 'Reforming the Companies Acts—The Way Ahead' [2002] *Journal of Business Law* 579.
[61] Final Report at 1.12.
[62] Final Report at 1.13.

The Company Law Review has made specific proposals that will affect the law governing contracting with companies.[63] It did not, however, address this body of law as a whole and did not recommend that it be fundamentally restructured. Instead, it looked at the various pieces of statutory reform and suggested some overhauling of these. It did not, for example, look at the law governing contracts made by corporate agents other than the board of directors, which has been largely untouched by statutory reform. Chapter 6 will argue that there is a case for reforming this area of the relevant law as well.

2.3 Competitiveness, Economic Analysis and Company Law

The Company Law Review identified the improvement of the 'competitiveness' of British companies as a key goal of company law. This acknowledges that the role of companies is an economic one and that company law can be viewed and judged on the basis of its contribution to that role. Chapter 2 of this book will therefore explore the economic role of the company as a legal structure for business firms and the organisation of production. It will also show how economic concepts can be used to analyse rules of company law, including those governing the attribution of contracts to companies. Chapter 2 will develop the idea that these rules of law can be viewed as apportioning risks between companies and third parties and that they can be judged according to the overall balance of risk that they strike.

However, the ideas that will be explored in chapter 2 of this book merit a more detailed introduction and will therefore be addressed in the next section of this chapter.

3   ATTRIBUTION AS ASSIGNMENT OF RISK

For third parties contracting with a company, the possibility that the law might not attribute the contract to the company amounts to a risk of losing the benefit of the contract. Parties to all contracts face some degree of risk that the contract might prove invalid and unenforceable under the general law of contract, but this book is concerned with the additional level of risk that arises from the fact that a contract is made with a company rather than with a natural person.

There are a number of individual risks faced by third parties contracting with a company and these can be related to the various legal issues that will be examined in this book. Thus, there is a risk that the company does

---

[63] See chapters 3, 5 and 7.

not legally exist at the time of contracting or that it has been incorrectly identified. There is a risk that the agent purporting to act for the company has not been duly authorised to enter into the contract in question. If the contract purports to have been approved by the company's board of directors, there is a risk that the board has not acted in accordance with the company's constitution or that the constitution does not empower the board to make the contract in question. And there is also a risk that the contract might involve self-dealing by a director of the company.

The various rules of law examined in this book define the burden that each of these risks places on third parties contracting with a company. A third party may be able to take action to reduce or eliminate the risk, but that merely alters the nature of the burden: in effect, the risk of loss due to the possibility of the contract proving unenforceable is wholly or partially replaced by the cost of avoiding that possibility. The overall burden that these risks place on third parties in accordance with the relevant rules of law can be viewed as an additional cost that has to be incurred when dealing with a company rather than with a natural person. However, third parties are likely to seek some kind of compensation for this additional cost through the terms of their dealings with companies. In this way, the burden that the law places on third parties represents a burden on companies (and their members) as well.

Rules of law therefore define the burden placed on third parties contracting with companies. It should be possible, therefore, to specify these rules so as to minimise the burden on third parties and perhaps even to eliminate it altogether. However, the rules of law do not simply impose a burden on third parties. Instead, they apportion the risks associated with various events or situations between third parties and companies. For each of the risks faced by third parties, there is a correlative risk faced by companies (or, in the case of the risk that the company might not exist, by agents purporting to act for companies). Specifying the rules of law so as to reduce or eliminate the burden on third parties would therefore merely increase the burden of the correlative risks on companies. From an economic perspective, this would only be beneficial if the reduction in the burden on third parties were to be greater than the increase in the burden on companies.

The rules of law governing contracting with companies can therefore be analysed according to how they apportion risks between companies and third parties and evaluated according to the likely burden of these risks. In considering this burden, it is important to note the scope that each party has for avoiding or reducing the risk of loss and the cost of such avoidance action. The rules of law can then be judged according to how far they minimise the overall burden on both parties. If a particular rule could be revised so as to shift the burden of risk from one party to another, but to do so in such a way that the overall burden would be reduced, then such a reform could be justified on the basis that it would make the law more 'efficient'.

3.1 Improving Economic Efficiency through Rules of Law

A change in the law that is likely to produce a net overall benefit for affected parties or a net reduction in overall costs should increase wealth (or welfare) and lead to a more efficient allocation of economic resources.[64] Rules of law such as those governing the attribution of contracts to companies have an economic significance where one party (the 'least-cost-avoider') can bear the risk assigned by a rule at a lower cost than another party, but it would be costly (and maybe prohibitively so) for the parties to ensure that the risk is borne by the least-cost-avoider through mutual bargaining alone.[65] Where this is the case, then specifying the rule of law so that it assigns the risk to the least-cost-avoider should minimise costs overall and improve efficiency.[66]

Some hypothetical scenarios can be used to illustrate the economic significance of the rules of law governing the attribution of contracts to companies. In one such scenario, the relevant law includes an overriding rule of attribution that attributes to a company all contracts made on its behalf by its managing director regardless of his or her actual authority to do this. In this scenario, companies would have to bear the risk of being burdened by unauthorised contracts made by their managing directors. This burden could be reduced through avoidance action. A company's board of directors or members could, for example, establish systems for monitoring and reviewing the activities of its managing director. They could also ensure, so far as possible, that they do not appoint a managing director who is likely to burden the company with unauthorised contracts, or at least not with unauthorised contracts that prove onerous.

The burden on companies in this scenario would be mitigated by the fact that managing directors have good reasons for not exceeding their actual authority, in particular personal liability to their company for breach of their terms of employment. And the burden of the risk on companies

---

[64] The terms 'wealth' and 'welfare' in this context are used to refer in broad terms to that which economic actors attach value and seek to maximise. These terms are broader than the concept of 'utility', which is appropriate for consumers but not for firms. See generally R Cooter and T Ulen, *Law & Economics* (London, Pearson Addison Wesley, 2004) 4th ed ('Cooter & Ulen') at 15–17.

[65] This is one of the normative implications of the so-called 'Coase theorem', which highlights the problem posed by transaction costs in achieving a more efficient allocation of resources: see generally Cooter & Ulen at 85–91.

[66] The concept of 'efficiency' and the idea of the 'least-cost-avoider' will be explored in more detail in chapter 2.

would be offset by any ancillary benefit that they might derive from taking avoidance action, such as enjoying a higher standard of managerial performance. Further, the costs for companies of avoidance action should be spread out over all the activities of its managing director and the costs relating to any one contract in particular would be reduced accordingly.

This scenario can be compared to another one, in which the relevant law includes no overriding rule of attribution at all for contracts made by a company's managing directors. However, companies would still be free to determine the precise level of the actual authority of their managing directors to suit their particular circumstances. In the second scenario, third parties would have to bear the risk that managing directors might exceed their actual authority and that any contract made with a company through its managing director might prove to be unauthorised and unenforceable against the company. Again, this burden could be reduced through taking avoidance action. In particular, third parties could take whatever steps are necessary to ensure that a managing director does have actual authority to make a particular contract. Or they could ensure that the contract is approved on behalf of the company by the company's board or by an agent whom they know to have the necessary actual authority. Both courses of avoidance action would entail additional costs for third parties.

As in the first scenario, the burden on third parties would be mitigated by the fact that managing directors have good reasons not to exceed their authority, including a potential personal liability to third parties for breach of warranty of authority.[67] However, from the point of view of third parties, these reasons would be largely indirect and beyond their control. They would give much less reassurance to third parties in this scenario than they would to companies in the first scenario and thus provide much less mitigation of the additional burden on third parties. Further, third parties would have to take avoidance action in relation to every contract with a company and would have much less scope for spreading the costs of such action compared to companies in the first scenario.

3.2 Improving Economic Efficiency through the Detail of Rules of Law

Comparing the above two scenarios, it is likely that the burden of the risk assigned third parties in the second one would greatly exceed the burden of the risk assigned to companies in the first. In economic terms, an unqualified overriding rule of attribution would achieve greater efficiency than not having one at all, despite the burden placed on companies. The same kind of analysis can be applied to the details or nuances of

---

[67] On this liability, see Bowstead & Reynolds, Art 107 and at 9–060–9–073.

a rule of law to see how far qualifying and fine-tuning it might reduce overall costs and improve economic efficiency.

Thus, in a third scenario, there is an overriding rule of attribution governing contracting with companies through their managing directors, but it is qualified so that it does not apply to unauthorised contracts which are unusual for a managing director to make without further authorisation or where there are suspicious circumstances. Circumstances would be suspicious for this purpose if, for example, the managing director were to have a conflicting personal interest in the contract, such as where a company guarantees or provides security for the personal liability or indebtedness of its managing director. Qualifying the overriding rule in this way exposes third parties to an additional risk of invalidity, but it is confined to a limited range of contracts. The burden of this increased risk on third parties depends on the clarity of the qualification and the ease with which third parties can tell for certain whether or not a particular contract is caught by it. Assuming that third parties can readily identify contracts caught by the qualification, they only have to take avoiding action in relation to such contracts and this reduces the overall burden on them.

Whilst the qualification in this third scenario assigns an increased risk to third parties, it also reduces the correlative risk faced by companies of being bound by unauthorised contracts. To evaluate the qualification, the reduction in the burden on companies should be compared to the increase in the burden on third parties. It is likely that the reduction in the burden on companies is relatively large because the qualification targets unauthorised contracts in which the risk of loss to the company is significantly higher than the norm. And, as noted already, the qualification can be specified so as to limit the increased burden on third parties.

The rules of law governing contracting with companies can therefore be analysed on the basis of the costs they impose on companies and third parties through the risks they apportion between them. The rules can then be judged according to how far they assign risks to the least-cost-avoider. Minimising the costs of contracting with companies through an efficient apportionment of these risks should improve the effectiveness of the company as a legal structure for business and its competitiveness as advocated by the Company Law Review.

Adopting an economic perspective of this kind may provide only rough guidance in analysing the law governing contracting with companies, but it is likely to provide a fuller understanding of the context in which the various rules have to operate and facilitate a deeper analysis of them. The exercise may assist in exposing and challenging assumptions made in the development of the law, which might underlie any shortcomings and dissatisfaction with its operation in practice. Thus, the doctrine of constructive notice was developed on the basis of an assumption that it was reasonable to expect third parties to examine the constitution of every company with which they dealt. And agency law was applied to corporate agents on the basis that a company, like a natural person, should not be bound by the actions of its agent unless it had somehow consented to be bound.

3.3 Rules of Law and the Economics of Information

Chapter 2 will also show how the rules of law governing the attribution of contracts to companies have an economic significance beyond that relating to their role in apportioning risks between parties and thereby imposing costs on them. Welfare can be improved not only by reducing costs and facilitating a better allocation of economic resources, but also by increasing and improving the overall stock of economic resources through more efficient production and innovation. This is relevant to the analysis of the company and the rules of company law since the company provides a legal structure for firms and for arrangements within or between firms.[68] And a firm is an economic device for organising production.

Chapter 2 will show how the company can be analysed as the legal basis for the complex set of arrangements that may be necessary for the organisation of production whereby various inputs are obtained and transformed to produce output (or various outputs). A key factor in the organisation of production is information and rules of law have economic significance through reducing information costs and stimulating flows of information. In this way they can improve the value of the company as a basis for organising production and promoting innovation and thus for improving competitiveness in the sense indicated in the Company Law Review.

The rules governing contracting with companies have economic significance in terms of information in a number of ways. Thus, an overriding rule of attribution, which attributes unauthorised contracts to companies subject to certain qualifications, reduces the information costs faced by third parties by reducing their need to acquire information about the actual authority of the corporate agents with whom they deal. An overriding rule would also create the need for companies to acquire more information about their agents and their activities, thereby increasing companies' information costs. However, the additional information that the overriding rule is likely to stimulate companies into acquiring is likely to be more versatile and thus have greater potential value to companies compared to the information that the rule would save third parties from

---

[68] A large firm, for example, may be structured as a complex network of subsidiaries and two firms may co-operate through forming a joint venture company: see generally D Milman (ed), *Regulating Enterprise: Law and Business Organisation in the UK* (Oxford, Hart Publishing, 1999).

having to acquire. In other words, the information acquired by companies may provide them with additional benefits beyond the reduction in the risk of being bound by unauthorised contracts. An overriding rule of attribution should therefore stimulate flows of information within a company and give a competitive advantage to companies with higher quality agents, greater cohesiveness and better internal communication. In this way, it should improve the competitiveness of companies in general by rewarding these qualities.

Focusing on information and on how rules of law can impose costs in terms of having to acquire information highlights one feature of company law which, it will be argued, is a significant deficiency. This is the lack of prescribed standards on such matters as the terms of a company's constitution, the level of authority vested in a company's board and the level of actual authority vested in key corporate agents such as individual directors and managing directors. This lack of prescription is beneficial inasmuch as it enables the promoters or management of a company to settle on terms and levels of authority that suit the needs of their particular company. It was noted earlier how this freedom reflected the earlier status of companies as unincorporated associations that were clearly in the private sphere and governed by the law of partnership. However, the obverse of this benefit is that the terms and levels of authority in any particular instance cannot be predicted and may prove difficult, and costly, to ascertain.

As chapter 3 will show, the constitution of a company may impose limits on the contractual power of a company's board that even its own directors fail to notice and, in any event, the action necessary to override certain limits can be far from clear. Whilst an ordinary resolution of the members is sufficient to override some limits, others may require a resolution of a distinct class of members.

In the absence of overriding rules of attribution, both third parties and agents acting for companies would have to incur costs in ascertaining the agents' actual authority or face the risk of loss through a contract proving unauthorised and unenforceable. Overriding rules of attribution reduce the costs for third parties, but their effectiveness at doing so depends on the clarity of their specification and on the certainty that they provide to third parties. Such rules do not reduce information costs for corporate agents. The law could reduce both sets of information costs by limiting freedom of choice, by prescribing minimum levels of authority for boards and individual directors and by providing a standard procedure for overriding limits on the board's contractual power.

The Company Law Review has made many proposals for improving company law. It recommended simplifying the form of corporate constitutions, as will be seen in chapter 3. However, it made no recommendations about simplifying the internal structures of companies or limiting the scope for variation. It will be suggested in chapter 2 that one advantage of imposing some minimum standards would be to give a competitive advantage to companies with higher quality (but probably more expensive) agents, who would be less likely to harm their company. This could further contribute to improving the overall competitiveness of companies.

2

Assigning Risk: An Economic Perspective on the Law Governing Contracting with Companies

1 THE AIMS OF THIS CHAPTER

T
HIS CHAPTER WILL explore in more detail how economics can provide a basis for analysing rules of company law. Chapter 1 showed how the rules governing contracting with companies assign certain risks of loss to (on the one hand) companies or those who make contracts on behalf of companies and (on the other) those parties contracting with companies (or 'third parties'). This chapter will examine further the economic significance of these rules of law in terms of the costs and benefits that they assign and how this can help in identifying ways of improving the law.

The next section of this chapter will survey the use that has been made of economics in the analysis of law. It will also note how the Company Law Review has acknowledged the economic significance of company law and indicated that improving economic efficiency and the competitiveness of companies is a valid goal of company law reform.[1]

The third section will examine the meaning of economic efficiency and show that there are differing approaches in economic analysis as regards both the meaning of efficiency and how efficiency can be improved. Much economic analysis of law has been based on 'neo-classical' analysis and this has tended to focus on the allocation of resources and how rules of law can be analysed and judged according to how well they facilitate or inhibit greater 'allocative efficiency', in particular through minimising transaction costs. The third section will review the standards used to identify potential improvements in allocative efficiency. It will also present the alternatives to neo-classical analysis and other conceptions of economic efficiency. It will show how these other approaches can provide a useful basis for

---

[1] See chapter 1 at n 60 for further details of the DTI's Company Law Review, which delivered its Final Report in 2001, and of its various reports and the 2002 White Paper.

understanding and analysing legal institutions such as the company that are designed to operate over time. A key point of difference between the different approaches concerns the nature of uncertainty about the future and how the law can best facilitate the organisation of long-term economic activity.

The fourth section of this chapter will examine the economic analysis of the company and in particular the distinctive 'contractarian' model of the company, which presents it as a focus or 'nexus' for organising the complex arrangements necessary for production as a set of bilateral contractual relationships.[2] In this economic model, the members of a company (who will be referred to as 'shareholders') are viewed as being in an essentially contractual relationship with the company rather than as being its owners.[3] This provides a different perspective on the nature of the risk that shareholders (and others interested in the affairs of a company) face from the company's management. This, in turn, provides a framework for analysing the law governing a company's management structure and its powers, including the power to make contracts on behalf of a company.

The fifth section of this chapter will develop this economic perspective of corporate management and agency. The sixth section will then present an economic framework for analysing the rules of law governing contracting with companies, focusing on the costs that these rules impose on companies and third parties through the assignment of risks. It will argue that the artificial nature of corporate personality and corporate agency should be taken into account in assessing the costs resulting from these risks. This framework can be used to consider how far the various rules of law apportion these costs between companies and third parties so as to improve economic efficiency in its various conceptions.

2 AN ECONOMIC VIEW OF RULES OF LAW

2.1 The Use of Economics in the Analysis of Law

There are three possible objectives in making use of economic concepts in the analysis of legal rules.[4] The first is to provide a better understanding of the law. Here, economics can be used to provide an explanation for the evolution of certain features of the law and to provide a rationale for those

---

[2] For a survey of this and other visions or models of the company, see J Hill, 'Changes in the Role of the Shareholder' in R Grantham and C Rickett (eds), *Corporate Personality in the 20th Century* (Oxford, Hart Publishing, 1998) ('Grantham & Rickett (eds)').

[3] The term 'shareholder' is used to refer to a member of a company limited by shares as opposed to one limited by guarantee. On the different kinds of company and other legal structures available for firms, see P Davies, *Gower and Davies' Principles of Modern Company Law* , 7th edn (London, Sweet & Maxwell, 2003) ('Gower & Davies') at 3–10.

[4] See S Deakin and A Hughes, 'Economic Efficiency and the Proceduralisation of Company Law' [1999] *Company Financial and Insolvency Law Review* 169 ('Deakin & Hughes') and A

rules and principles which the law defines in vague or flexible terms and which tend to be applied intuitively. The second possible objective is to predict the effect of proposed changes in the law. The first two objectives therefore involve positive analysis, but the third involves normative analysis. It aims to provide a rationale or justification for legal rules and to suggest how they might be improved so as to promote greater economic efficiency.

This book will make some use of positive economic analysis in examining the various legal rules governing the attribution of contracts to companies. It will consider the economic significance of these rules in terms of the costs and benefits they impose or confer on affected parties and the balance they strike in this respect. This chapter will draw upon some of the extensive literature on the economic analysis of the company to examine the relationship between a company and an agent purporting to make a contract on its behalf and the relationship between such a corporate agent and a party wishing to make a contract with the company (or 'third party').[5] It will consider how these relationships may be linked to others focused on the company, in particular that with the company's shareholders.

This book will consider how the various rules of law governing contracting with companies might be improved, although it will not treat economic efficiency as the only relevant criterion in this respect.[6] It will, however, argue that an evaluation of each rule of law should take account of its economic context and its economic significance and that this should form the basis of any reform of the relevant law.

2.2 The Economic Significance of Company Law

The Company Law Review has acknowledged the economic significance of company law, but the two Law Commissions in the United Kingdom had already made use of economic analysis as a source of guidance in their joint consultation paper and report on directors' conflicts of interest and the directors' duty of care, published in 1998 and 1999 respectively.[7]

Ogus, 'Economics and Law Reform: Thirty Years of Law Commission Endeavour' (1995) 111 *Law Quarterly Review* 407. See generally R Cooter & T Ulen, *Law and Economics* (London, Pearson Addison Wesley, 2004) (4th ed) ('Cooter & Ulen') and R Posner, *Economic Analysis of Law* (New York, Aspen Publishing, 2002) (6th edn) ('Posner').

[5] On this extensive literature, see generally the section on 'Corporate Law' in B Bouckaert and G De Geest (eds), *Encyclopaedia of Law and Economics*, (Cheltenham, Edward Elgar, 2000) ('Encyclopaedia of Law & Economics'), Volume V, *Regulation of Contracts*.
[6] For a survey of other notions of the public interest that law and other regulation might be viewed as promoting, see A Ogus, *Regulation: Legal Form and Economic Theory* (Oxford, Clarendon Press, 1994) ('Ogus') at 46–54.
[7] See Law Commission, *Company Directors: Regulating Conflicts of Interests and Formulating a Statement of Duties* (Law Commission Consultation Paper No 153, Scottish Law Commission Consultation Paper No 105, The Stationery Office, London, 1998 and Law Commission Report No 261, Scottish Law Commission Report No 173, The Stationery Office, London, 1999).

In its Final Report, published in 2001, the Company Law Review presented the main goals of company law in economic terms, starting with its formulation of a general guiding principle:[8]

> We start with the general principle that company law should be *primarily enabling or facilitative*—ie it should provide the means for those engaged in business and other corporate activity to arrange and manage their affairs in the way which they believe is most likely to lead to mutual success and effective productive activity.

The Company Law Review suggested four reasons why legal and other regulatory intervention might nonetheless be needed and thus why deviation from this general guiding principle might be justified, these reasons including 'substantial risk of market failure'.[9]

The Company Law Review also stated that the 'main driver' in designing conditions attached to the availability of legal facilities, or rules preventing the abuse of such facilities, or rules to protect legitimate public interests in the relevant activities, must in each case be:[10]

> to provide the means for effective collaborative business activity and in particular effective generation of wealth, in the broadest sense. This demands that British companies be competitive, in the sense that they exploit resources in the most efficient way possible to generate such wealth, and that they contribute to an internationally competitive economy. Company law has a significant role to play here, and it needs to be assessed and justified according to its effectiveness in meeting this objective.

The Company Law Review went on to state that company law is also a factor in wider international competitiveness:[11]

> Our company law needs to be internationally competitive, to ensure that we retain our existing companies and attract new ones … we need attractive conditions not only for company management and operation, but also for investment. Companies are both direct users of company law and affected as trading bodies by its application to others.

The Company Law Review's references to 'effective productive activity' and the need to be 'competitive' suggest an economic basis for analysing and evaluating company law, which can be applied to the various rules

---

[8] The Final Report at 1.10 (emphasis in the original).
[9] The Final Report at 1.11. The other three reasons given here are (1) where 'legal provision' is necessary to 'define' a 'desired legal result' and 'make it effective'; (2) where a desired legal result 'is so predictable that it makes sense for the law to provide a ready made, but optional ("default") solution'; and (3) where there is 'a public interest in the activity in question which requires that those involved respond to wider demands'.
[10] The Final Report at 1.12.
[11] The Final Report at 1.13.

governing the attribution of contracts to companies. However, some elaboration of these terms is necessary to establish a useful framework for this exercise.

2.3 'Competitive' Companies: Competition as a Dynamic Process

The notion of competition is complex and has been used to indicate different processes in an economy.[12] This makes the term 'competitive' an ambiguous one. In traditional economics, competition is the essentially reactive and passive process through which the forces of supply and demand achieve or restore price equilibrium and an optimal allocation of economic resources.[13] It also implies a relatively static economy, namely one in which there is a fixed or given stock of resources available for allocation, with the key economic problem being the allocation of these resources. This provides a basis for analysing law in terms of its contribution to 'allocative efficiency', which refers to the idea that wealth or social welfare is maximised when economic resources are allocated to those who value them most.[14] The focus of such analysis, however, is on a given stock of economic resources and not on how that stock might be increased or improved.

There is, however, a dynamic conception of the nature of competition and economic activity, which focuses on increasing and improving the stock of economic resources rather than on how to achieve a better allocation of a given stock of economic resources.[15] The Company Law Review's emphasis on productive activity and the need for companies to be competitive 'in the sense that they exploit resources in the most efficient way possible to generate such wealth' suggests a more dynamic role than merely restoring an equilibrium or achieving a better allocation of a given stock of economic resources.[16] It also connects with the idea that firms can contribute to the welfare and improvement of society through achieving change in the form of entirely new kinds of goods and services or of significantly improved versions of existing products.[17]

---

[12] See generally M Best, *The New Competition: Institutions of Industrial Restructuring* (Cambridge, Polity Press, 1990) ('Best').

[13] See Cooter & Ulen at 33–8.

[14] See Deakin & Hughes at 170–6 for an introduction to different conceptions of economic efficiency and their role in the analysis of law. See also Ogus at 23–28 and N Mercuro and S Medema, *Economics and the Law: From Posner to Postmodernism* (Princeton, Princeton UP, 1997) ('Mercuro & Medema').

[15] See generally Best, R Langlois (ed), *Economics as a Process: Essays in the New Institutional Economics* (Cambridge, Cambridge University Press, 1986) ('Langlois (ed)') and J Krafft (ed) *The Process of Competition* (Cheltenham, Edward Elgar, 2000) ('Krafft (ed)'). See also J Clifton, 'Competition and the Evolution of the Capitalist Mode of Production' (1977) 1 *Cambridge Journal of Economics* 137.

[16] Deakin & Hughes at 174.

[17] This dynamic view of the nature of competition has been associated in particular with Schumpeter: see, for example, Langlois (ed) and Krafft (ed).

From this alternative perspective, improvement in public welfare is achieved through innovation, with competition being the dynamic process through which firms try to establish an advantage over their 'competitors'. Joseph Schumpeter in *Capitalism, Socialism & Democracy* portrayed this dynamic version of competition as follows:[18]

> But in capitalist reality as distinguished from its textbook picture, it is not that [static] kind of competition which counts but the competition from the new commodity, the new technology, the new source of supply, the new type of organization (the largest-scale unit of control for instance) – competition which commands a decisive cost or quality advantage and which strikes not at the margins of the profits and the outputs of the existing firms but at their foundations and their very lives. This kind of competition is as much more effective than the other as a bombardment is in comparison with forcing a door, and so much more important that it becomes a matter of comparative indifference whether competition in the ordinary sense functions more or less promptly; the powerful lever that in the long run expands output and brings down prices is in any case made of other stuff.

Improvements in production and innovation cannot be measured in terms allocative efficiency, but require alternative conceptions of efficiency such as 'productive efficiency' and 'dynamic efficiency'.[19]

2.4 Differing Approaches to Economic Analysis and to the Future

The difference of emphasis reflected in the dichotomy between traditional competition and allocative efficiency (on the one hand) and dynamic competition, productive efficiency and innovation (on the other) can be related to a difference of emphasis between two broad schools of economic analysis, which can for convenience and simplicity of analysis be referred to as 'neo-classical' and 'neo-institutional'.[20] A key point of difference between the respective approaches of these schools concerns the economic role of institutions such as the company in the organisation of economic activity and the economic role of company law in facilitating such organisation.[21]

---

[18] J Schumpeter, *Capitalism, Socialism & Democracy* (with introduction by R Swedberg) (London, Routledge, 1994) ('Schumpeter') at 84–5. See generally Best at 118–125 above n 12.
[19] See Deakin & Hughes at 173–75.
[20] See generally R Langlois, 'The New Institutional Economics: An Introductory Essay' in Langlois (ed) ('Langlois (intro)') and T Eggertsson, *Economic Behaviour and Institutions* (Cambridge, Cambidge University Press, 1990) ('Eggertsson'). This dichotomy is in fact a simplification of a number of differing approaches: see generally Mercuro & Medema.
[21] See also W Bratton, 'The New Economic Theory of the Firm: Critical Perspectives from History' (1989) 41 *Stanford Law Review* 1471 and W Bratton, 'The Nexus of Contracts Corporation: A Critical Appraisal' (1989) 74 *Cornell Law Review* 407.

Economic analysis of law has tended to make use of neo-classical economic analysis and to focus on the implications of rules of law in terms of minimising costs and achieving a more efficient allocation of resources.[22] Its appeal stems in part from its relative simplicity, although this is achieved by making a number of questionable assumptions about the world and human behaviour. However, economic analysis of law need not be based on the neo-classical approach (or at least not exclusively so) and there are other approaches, which do not accept the assumptions underlying neo-classical analysis or which make different assumptions.

These alternatives can be of particular value in analysing company law because of the company's economic role as a structure for organising production. It is the principal legal structure for the firm and the firm is not merely a consumer of economic resources (and as such a party to transactions concerning economic resources), but also a producer and transformer of economic resources. The company is thus an instrument for innovation and improving competitiveness in its dynamic sense, as the Company Law Review acknowledged. There is greater emphasis on change and innovation in the various alternatives to neo-classical economic analysis that are grouped in the 'neo-institutional' school.

One key feature of the neo-classical approach is its conception of the future, which underlies its attitude towards rules of law and other legal institutions that facilitate long-term planning. Stephen Littlechild noted this feature of neo-classical analysis in an essay surveying the different forms of market process.[23] He identified three archetypal forms of market process, the 'neo-classical' being the first of these. Littlechild noted that, in the neo-classical approach, the future is unknown, but predictable in the sense that 'the form that the future can take is known in advance'.[24] In other words, whilst the precise form of the future cannot be known at a particular point of time, what can be known is that it will take one of a number of predictable forms determined by variables that are known and can be measured in advance.[25]

In the neo-classical approach, uncertainty about the future can be presented in terms of quantifiable risk, with the risk of any particular outcome occurring (or proving to be the case) being capable of measurement

---

[22] Thus, Cooter & Ulen and Posner make use of neo-classical economic analysis. For a discussion of the limitations of this approach, see generally Deakin & Hughes.

[23] See S Littlechild, 'Three Types of Market Process' in Langlois (ed) ('Littlechild'). See also K Foss and N Foss, 'Economic Organization in a Process Perspective' in Krafft (ed) ('Foss & Foss').

[24] Littlechild at 28. Littlechild identified this approach with the kind of model used by B Stigum in 'Competitive, Equilibrium under Uncertainty' (1969) 83 *Quarterly Journal of Economics* 533, M Rothschild in 'Models of Market Organization with Imperfect Information' (1973) 81 *Journal of Political Economy* 1283 and R Frydman in 'Towards an Understanding of Market Processes: Individual Expectations, Learning, and Convergence to Rational Expectations Equlibrium' (1982) 72 *American Economic Review* 652.

[25] Littlechild at 28.

and pricing in advance and assignable between parties accordingly. To prosper in such circumstances, firms have to estimate the likelihood of various possible versions of the future and to plan (and revise plans) accordingly.[26]

Littlechild contrasted the neo-classical view of the future with that of the 'Austrian' approach.[27] This term indicates the so-called 'Austrian' school of economic theorists, which derives from the work of the Viennese economist Carl Menger and encompasses the work of such economists as Ludwig von Mises and FA Hayek.[28] In the Austrian approach, the future is unknown and its possible forms cannot be predicted in advance because some of the variables may change or may not be known and therefore cannot be measured in advance.[29] Uncertainty is therefore a much more profound concept than that embodied in the notion of 'risk' and is better characterised in terms of 'ignorance'.[30] Firms that wish to prosper in such circumstances have to 'discover what is worth searching for' and develop qualities of 'alertness' and 'entrepreneurship'.[31] Legal rules and other mechanisms can assist firms in this task by, for example, stimulating flows of information and prompting them to acquire the kind of knowledge that is likely to be useful in this respect.

Littlechild identified a third archetypal form of market process, which he termed the 'radical-subjectivist' approach,[32] although this is arguably a refinement of the 'Austrian' approach.[33] The radical-subjectivist approach emphasises the role of firms and other economic actors in creating the

---

[26] Littlechild at 30.

[27] Littlechild identified this approach with the work of I Kirzner in *Competition and Entrepreneurship* (Chicago, University of Chicago Press, 1973) and in *Perception, Opportunity and Profit* (Chicago, University of Chicago Press, 1979), which 'in turn reflects the ideas of Mises and Hayek (and, to a lesser extent, Schumpeter)': Littlechild at 29. See also I Kirzner, 'Competition and the Market Process: Some Doctrinal Milestones' in Krafft (ed).

[28] See generally N Foss and P Klein, 'Introduction' in N Foss and P Klein (ed), *Entrepreneurship and the Firm: Austrian Perspectives on Economic Organization* (Cheltenham, Edward Elgar, 2002) ('Foss & Klein (ed)').

[29] Littlechild at 28–29.

[30] Littlechild at 30.

[31] *Ibid*. See generally Foss & Klein (eds).

[32] Littlechild used this term to cover 'the distinctive approach' taken by G Shackle in *Decision, Order, and Time in Human Affairs* (Cambridge, Cambridge University Press, 1969) and *Imagination and the Nature of Choice* (Edinburgh, Edinburgh University Press, 1979), L Lachmann in 'From Mises to Shackle: An Essay on Austrian Economics and the Kaleidic Society' (1976) 14 *Journal of Economic Literature* 54 and *Capital, Expectations and the Market Process* (Kansas City, Sheed, Andrews and McMeel, 1977) and J Wiseman in 'Beyond Positive Economics—Dream and Reality' in J Wiseman (ed), *Beyond Positive Economics?* (London, Macmillan, 1983): see Littlechild at 29. The term 'radical subjectivism' is also associated with James Buchanan: see, for example, S Littlechild, 'Buchanan and Shackle on Cost, Choice and Subjective Economics' (1999) in Section 3 of a 'Buchanan Festschrift' available on-line at www.gmu.edu/jbc/fest; and J Buchanan and V Vanberg, 'Constitutional Implications of Radical Subjectivism' (2002) 15 *Review of Austrian Economics* 121.

[33] J O'Neill, 'Radical Subjectivism: Not Radical, Not Subjectivist' (2000) 3 *Quarterly Journal of Austrian Economics* 21.

future through the decisions that they make. In effect, when they make a decision, the future is not merely uncertain or unknown, but 'non-existent or indeterminate'.[34] The challenge for firms that wish to prosper in such circumstances is therefore 'not to estimate or discover, but to create' and to 'exercise imagination'.[35] Further, the creative efforts of economic actors may be driven by their 'personal knowledge and beliefs'.[36] A corollary of this approach is that, from the perspective of one particular economic actor, the future will be the product not only of its own creative imagination, but also of that of other economic actors. Effective planning for the future should therefore include involvement in the decision-making of other economic actors likely to have an impact or reducing dependence on such actors.[37]

3 STANDARDS OF ECONOMIC EFFICIENCY

3.1 Neo-Classical Economic Analysis

3.1.1 Wealth Maximisation and Allocative Efficiency

Neo-classical economic analysis rests on a particular set of assumptions about the behaviour of economic actors (or 'parties'). It assumes that parties (whether firms or individuals) behave as if they are rational and consistent 'maximisers' in the sense of aiming to maximise their own benefit from their actions.[38] This benefit is 'utility' in the case of individuals and profits in the case of firms and can be referred to generally as 'wealth' or 'welfare'.[39] Further, parties are treated as the best assessors of their own costs and benefits for this purpose and their valuation of economic resources is respected accordingly.[40]

In neo-classical economics, the public good is identified with the principle of wealth maximisation. This holds that overall wealth is increased when resources move to a party which values them more than the party which held them previously. On this basis, the best possible allocation of a given set of economic resources is achieved when they are allocated to those parties who value them most. This provides a basis for analysing legal rules in economic terms, but raises the difficult issue of how consequential costs

---

[34] See Littlechild at 29.
[35] *Ibid.*
[36] *Ibid.*
[37] See Littlechild at 31.
[38] See Cooter & Ulen at 15–17. For a general discussion of this behavioural assumption and its implications for the analysis of law, see N Duxbury, *Patterns of American Jurisprudence* (Oxford, Clarendon Press, 1997) (paperback edition) ('Duxbury') at 364–381.
[39] See Duxbury at 398–406 for a discussion of 'utility' and the refinement of this concept into the principle of 'wealth-maximisation' in the economic analysis of law.
[40] See Cooter & Ulen at 15–17.

and losses should be factored into the assessment when deciding how a particular allocation of resources might be improved.

Welfare economics has made use of two standards for the task of identifying improvements in the allocation of economic resources, namely 'Pareto efficiency' and 'Kaldor-Hicks efficiency'. Both have featured in the economic analysis of law and they merit some further explanation.[41]

3.1.2 *Pareto Efficiency*

This holds that a particular allocation of economic resources can only be improved by a reallocation that makes at least one party better off (in terms of having more resources or resources which they value more highly) and makes no party worse off as a result.[42] Accordingly, a proposed reallocation that would benefit one party at the expense of another could not be viewed as an improvement (or as efficient in terms of allocative efficiency) unless the benefiting party were to persuade the other party to accept the reallocation, presumably by paying sufficient compensation to offset the losing party's loss and in effect making the 'losing' party a net gainer as well.

In effect, the Pareto standard of efficiency reflects and reinforces a principle of consent.[43] A legal rule could therefore be viewed as facilitating improvements in accordance with the Pareto standard if it were to facilitate the voluntary exchange of resources between parties who would judge themselves to be better off as a result of the exchange and provided that there were no adverse effects on any other party. It could do this by reducing the transaction costs incurred by parties in settling and executing a voluntary exchange of resources (or 'bargain').

Transaction costs are the various incidental costs incurred by parties in making a bargain and include 'search costs', 'bargain costs' and 'enforcement costs'.[44] A significant form of transaction cost is the cost of obtaining relevant information that may affect the ability or willingness of either party to exchange on a particular set of terms and the lack of which might preclude some efficient bargains from taking place at all. A legal rule could therefore reduce transaction costs by improving the accessibility or reliability of relevant information.

However, Pareto efficiency is not a useful basis for examining many rules of law, including the rules governing contracting with companies, because of its insistence that improvement means that no party can be required to accept a loss. This gives every party affected by a proposed

---

[41] See generally Ogus.

[42] See A Ogus and C Veljanovski, *Readings in the Economics of Law and Regulation* (Oxford, Clarendon Press, 1984), 19–23, Ogus at 24–5 and Cooter & Ulen at 16–17.

[43] See Ogus at 24.

[44] See Cooter & Ulen at 91–5 and Ogus at 17.

reallocation of resources an effective right of veto as to whether it can be considered an improvement.[45] In practice, a proposed reallocation might be likely to produce substantial net gains, but an adversely affected party might be unable or unwilling to consent to its loss because of insuperable transaction costs or other obstacles to bargaining.[46] In such cases 'Kaldor-Hicks efficiency' has come to be preferred as a basis for identifying an improved reallocation.

3.1.3 Kaldor-Hicks Efficiency

This standard holds that a particular allocation of resources can be improved by a reallocation in which the aggregate net benefits for those better off exceed the aggregate net costs for those worse off.[47] The net surplus of benefit over cost means that those who are better off could compensate those who are worse off and still be better off so that Pareto efficiency could be achieved in theory. However, such compensation is left as a theoretical possibility.

The standard of Kaldor-Hicks efficiency does, of course, raise the problematic issue of how to measure and compare potential costs and benefits in the absence of voluntary transactions, but otherwise provides a more realistic basis for analysing legal rules that may have to operate in the absence of consent. It also reflects the neo-classical view of the future inasmuch as the impact of future contingencies on the parties to a bargain is treated as something that can be measured and priced at the time when the bargain is struck so that the risk of their occurrence is something that can be assigned as part of the overall terms of the bargain.

A legal rule might appear to facilitate a Kaldor-Hicks improvement by assigning the risk of a certain contingency occurring (or of a certain fact proving to exist or not to exist, as the case may be) to the party who can bear the risk or avoid its occurrence at least cost ('the least-cost-avoider'), thereby minimising costs overall.[48] Such a view, however, depends on acceptance of the fact that all such risks can be quantified in advance and the least-cost-avoider identified. If this is accepted, then the efficiency of such a rule is clear. On this basis, if a legal rule assigns a particular risk to a party who is not its least-cost-avoider, then by definition this party suffers a cost that is greater than the corresponding benefit to the least-cost-avoider. If these parties wished to override the effect of the rule and reassign the risk to the least-cost-avoider, they would have to incur the

---

[45] See Ogus at 24.

[46] See Cooter & Ulen at 92–3.

[47] See Cooter & Ulen at 48 and Ogus at 24–5.

[48] See E Rasmussen, 'Agency Law and Contract Formation' (2001) Harvard John M Olin Discussion Paper No 323 for an economic analysis of the general law of agency based on the 'least-cost-avoider principle'.

additional transaction costs of doing (or attempting to do) so. The combined effect of the rule's assignment of the risk to a higher-cost-avoider and the transaction costs required to reassign the risk would probably prevent many efficient bargains from taking place at all. Such a rule would not therefore be conducive to an optimal allocation of resources.

3.1.4 Contracting in Neo-Classical Economic Analysis

Neo-classical economic analysis emphasises the importance of markets and voluntary transactions between parties as the best means of achieving an optimal allocation of resources. In effect, the 'invisible hand' of the market is viewed as the best mechanism for settling the terms of bargains and the allocation of resources.

Contracts between parties are viewed as analogous to market transactions inasmuch as they result from voluntary bargaining and settle a particular set of terms at a particular point in time. Contracts are also viewed as complete in the sense that they make adequate provision for all possible contingencies.[49] Contracts, from this perspective, make provision for the future by assigning the risks represented by all such contingencies between the parties.

As regards information, this has a relatively passive and restorative function in neo-classical analysis. The absence of relevant information or the cost of obtaining it adds to transaction costs and this may inhibit or prevent the efficient reallocation of resources through voluntary bargaining. Thus, lack of relevant information may affect a party's ability to assess the potential gains or losses from a proposed transaction. This, in turn, increases the element of risk in entering into the transaction and the minimum return necessary for the transaction to be one worth making. The availability of relevant information would reduce these transaction costs and thereby facilitate efficiency-enhancing transactions. However, information ultimately stands apart from such transactions.

3.1.5 The Role of Legal Rules in Neo-Classical Analysis

The neo-classical approach therefore views bargaining between parties and market transactions as the best means of achieving a better allocation of economic resources and thereby improving public welfare. Rules of law and other legal institutions can facilitate this process by making it less costly and, in terms of normative analysis, can be judged according to how well they do so. Beyond this, however, there is no economic case for interfering with the freedom of parties to make bargains: rules that inhibit

---

[49] On complete and incomplete contracting, see Deakin & Hughes at 177 and Foss & Foss at 35–6.

this freedom are likely to inhibit or prevent potential improvements in allocative efficiency.

Legal rules can reduce transaction costs and facilitate bargaining by dealing with matters and providing solutions to potential problems that reflect so far as possible the solutions that the parties would be likely to agree among themselves if they were able to bargain without facing any costs or other forms of constraint on their ability to reach a solution.[50] On this basis, legal rules should, so far as possible, apportion risks between contracting parties in the way that the parties would most probably settle for themselves under ideal bargaining conditions, which means assigning risk to the least-cost-avoider.

Neo-classical analysis of the rules of company law has, for example, presented them as a set of 'off-the-rack' terms available to parties to complete otherwise 'open-ended contracts'.[51] Viewing them in this way, however, means that parties should be free to vary these rules through bargaining unless such bargaining is likely to be distorted by significant market failure or there are other good policy reasons for preventing them from doing so.

The law can reduce transaction costs both through legal rules that assign risks to the least-cost-avoider and through institutions such as the company, the legal features of which provide a basis for structuring transactions concerning the inputs and outputs of production. In the neo-classical approach, contracting through a legal device such as the company, so that the legal features of the device underpin the terms of the contract, can be viewed as an elaborate form of bargaining between the parties. The parties are free to make use of the features of the device in constructing the terms of their bargain, but these features should ultimately be subordinate to their bargaining. The company can then be presented as an 'instance' of market-like contracting between parties.[52]

3.2 Alternatives to Neo-Classical Analysis

3.2.1 The 'Neo-Institutional' Schools

Certain alternatives to the neo-classical approach are here, for convenience and simplicity of analysis, grouped together and treated collectively as the 'neo-institutional' approach. However, they include a number of differing schools of thought that diverge from the strictures of the neo-classical

---

[50] This is the basis of analysing law in economic terms through applying a 'hypothetical bargaining model:' see generally B Cheffins, *Company Law: Theory, Structure and Operation* (Oxford, OUP, 1997) ('Cheffins'). See also F Easterbrook and D Fischel, *The Economic Structure of Corporate Law* (Cambridge, Mass Harvard University Press, 1996) ('Easterbrook & Fischel') at 34–5. For a critique of this approach, see Deakin & Hughes at 176–180.

[51] See Easterbrook & Fischel at 34–5.

[52] See Langlois (intro) at 16.

approach.[53] Their common characteristic is that they attach much greater significance to the role of institutions in the organisation of economic activity, in effect viewing them as 'alternatives to' rather than as 'instances of' market-like contracting.[54]

As well as those writings which have expressly identified themselves or been identified as 'neo-institutional',[55] this approach encompasses the 'Austrian' school,[56] the 'evolutionary' school inspired by Schumpeter,[57] the 'transaction-cost economics' of Oliver Williamson and Ian MacNeil,[58] and the related theory of 'incomplete contracting'.[59]

3.2.2 *Contracting in the Face of Uncertainty and Opportunism*

The schools within this approach generally view the future as less predictable than in the neo-classical approach. They are also prepared to relax the behavioural assumptions of the neo-classical approach and to attach greater importance to the role of information and to the effect of lack of information on the behaviour of parties.[60] Thus, parties are viewed as having 'bounded rationality' in the sense that their desire to maximise their welfare is limited by a significant veil of ignorance about the future such that their behaviour is '*intendedly* rational, but only *limitedly* so'.[61]

Further, parties are viewed as likely to exploit for their own benefit any advantage that they might enjoy in terms of information even though their private gain from doing so might be exceeded by the costs suffered

---

[53] On the alternatives to the neo-classical approach in the economic analysis of law, also referred to as 'post-Chicago' or 'non-Posnerian' schools of 'Law and Economics', see Duxbury at 406–407. See also the section on 'Schools and Approaches' in *Encyclopaedia of Law & Economics*, Volume I, *The History and Methodology of Law and Economics* (Cheltenham, Edward Elgar, 2000) at 402.

[54] *Ibid.*

[55] See generally, Eggertsson. See also the chapter on 'Neo-institutional Law and Economics' in Mercuro & Medema at 130–56 and the discussion of 'the new institutional economics' in Langlois (intro).

[56] See Langlois (intro) at 1. See generally Foss & Klein (eds) and I Kirzner in Krafft (ed).

[57] See generally R Nelson and S Winter, *An Evolutionary Theory of Economic Change* (Cambridge, Mass The Belknap Press of Harvard University Press, 1982). See also E Penrose, 'Biological Analogies in the Theory of the Firm' (1952) 42 *American Economic Review* at 804 and E Penrose, *The Theory of the Growth of the Firm* (Oxford, Basil Blackwell, 1959) ('Penrose'). On the so-called 'Schumpeterian' and 'Penrosean' theories of the firm, see Best at 118–34, B Loasby, 'Explaining Firms' in Foss & Klein (eds) and W Gick, 'Schumpeter's and Kirzner's Entrepreneur Reconsidered' in Foss & Klein (eds).

[58] See I MacNeil, 'Contracts: Adjustments of Long-Term Economic Relations Under Classical, Neoclassical and Relational Contract Law' (1978) 72 *Northwestern University Law Review* at 854 and O Williamson, *The Economic Institutions of Capitalism* (New York, The Free Press, 1985) ('Williamson (1985)').

[59] See Deakin & Hughes at 178–9.

[60] See generally R Langlois, 'Rationality, Institutions and Explanation' in Langlois (ed).

[61] H Simon, *Administrative Behaviour* (New York, Macmillan, 1961), cited in Mercuro & Medema at 130 (emphasis in the original). On Herbert Simon's theory of bounded rationality, see also Duxbury at 370–71.

by other parties as a result of their action.[62] This propensity has been termed 'strategic action' or 'opportunism' and has been viewed as 'especially important for economic activity that involves transaction-specific investments in human and physical capital'.[63]

The combination of lack of information, the danger of opportunism and an unpredictable future places a formidable barrier in the way of real-locating resources through bargaining and contracting. In the neo-institutional approach, it is generally regarded as an over-simplification to treat this barrier simply as adding to the transaction costs of the bargaining process. Lack of information takes on a much deeper significance if parties are viewed as ignorant rather than uncertain about the impact of the future. It is then misleading to present all future contingencies as quantifiable risks, which parties can be viewed as pricing and assigning through the terms of their contractual arrangements. It is more accurate to view them as including unplanned or unpredictable events and discoveries, which can inflict uncompensated losses or confer windfall gains on a contracting party.

In other words, contracting about the future is not and cannot be complete.[64] Accordingly, some contracts should be viewed not as attempts to achieve a complete assignment of potential risks, but as attempts to establish a mutually acceptable basis for co-ordinating subsequent dealings between the parties once they are confronting unpredictable events.[65] In the neo-institutional approach, this provides an alternative perspective for analysing the economic role of institutions such as the firm.[66]

3.2.3 *Incomplete Contracting*

The neo-institutional approach does not therefore accept that bargaining and contracting at a particular moment in time can be adequate mechanisms for establishing arrangements that have to persist over time. It acknowledges that, one way or another, contracting is incomplete.[67] Parties may simply fail to make adequate provision and in effect make themselves vulnerable to unexpected developments. It is not, however, accurate or useful to regard a party that suffers loss as a consequence of such vulnerability as having accepted the risk that this might happen.

---

[62] See Deakin & Hughes at 176–7.
[63] O Williamson, 'Transaction-Cost Economics: The Governance of Contractual Relations' in O Williamson, *Economic Organization: Firms, Markets and Policy Control* (Hemel Hempstead, Harvester Wheatsheaf, 1986) ('Williamson (1986)') at 101. See generally Williamson (1985).
[64] See Deakin & Hughes at 178–9.
[65] See generally, Mercuro & Medema at 148–156.
[66] Douglass North has defined institutions as 'the rules of the game in a society or, more formally ... the humanly devised constraints that shape human interaction': see D North, *Institutions, Institutional Change, and Economic Performance* (Cambridge: Cambridge University Press, 1990) at 3, cited in Mercuro & Medema at 131.
[67] See Deakin & Hughes at 178–9; Foss & Foss at 35–6.

Parties making contracts that are likely to persist over time are instead viewed as aiming to establish a satisfactory co-ordination mechanism or 'governance structure' for dealing with problems and contingencies as and when they arise. Their bargaining is concerned with settling the features, rules and parameters of the governance structure rather than with attempting to anticipate the solutions it might reach.[68] Such contracts are likely to include terms that are best viewed as safeguards against the abuse of the flexibility in such arrangements. They might, for example, include 'hostages',[69] the main purpose of which is to deter a party from behaving opportunistically by presenting it with a potential burden that is likely to offset any benefit.

The economic role of the law in relation to such contracting is not to assist parties in the *ex ante* completion of their contracts, but rather to assist them in establishing satisfactory *ex post* co-ordination. It does this by providing structures such as the company and legal rules, which parties can draw upon in settling a satisfactory governance structure.[70] In terms of normative analysis, the law can be judged according to the effectiveness of these devices in this respect.

3.3 Other Notions of Economic Efficiency

3.3.1 *Productive Efficiency*

The concept of 'productive efficiency' is a measure of a firm's effectiveness as a producer of goods or services and thus as a transformer of economic resources. A process for producing a given output is efficient by this standard if either it is not possible to produce the same output with a lower-cost combination of inputs or it is not possible to produce more output with the same combination of inputs.[71] If there is scope for improvement in either of these respects, then there is scope for increasing productive efficiency. Innovation is one means for creating such scope and thus for achieving greater productive efficiency.

3.3.2 *Dynamic Efficiency*

'Dynamic efficiency' refers to the potential for improving public welfare through increasing the size or improving the quality of the overall stock of economic resources. It therefore refers to the introduction of new products

---

[68] *Ibid.*
[69] See Mercuro & Medema at 149–150.
[70] See Williamson (1985) at 73–4 and Williamson (1986) at 104–5.
[71] See Cooter & Ulen at 16. Productive efficiency is similar to the concept of 'technical efficiency', which refers to the scope for making better use of a given allocation of resources as opposed to improving the allocation: see Deakin & Hughes at 173.

or the improvement of existing products through innovation and entre-preneurship.[72] It also indicates the 'alertness' of firms to opportunities for innovation and to changes that might reduce their productive efficiency and undermine their competitiveness or otherwise threaten their viability. It therefore relates to the ability of firms to remain competitive in this sense and to survive and prosper over time despite uncertainty and changing circumstances.[73]

Dynamic efficiency has been referred to as increasing the 'ecological diversity and complexity of the economy'.[74] It reflects Schumpeter's obser-vation that capitalism is an evolutionary process and never stationary:[75]

> The fundamental impulse that sets and keeps the capitalist engine in motion comes from the new consumers' goods, the new methods of production or transportation, the new markets, the new forms of industrial organization that capitalist enterprise creates.

A firm that is an effective instrument for achieving the most efficient allo-cation of a given set of resources might prove quite unsatisfactory for engaging in the kind of activity necessary for innovation and improving dynamic efficiency.[76]

3.3.3 Legal Incentives for Innovation

The law can facilitate improvements in dynamic efficiency by providing governance structures that support or encourage the evolution and devel-opment of firms with a capacity to adapt, to change, to respond to oppor-tunities, to survive and to prosper over time. The law can also promote dynamic efficiency through rules which encourage innovation and entre-preneurship or which reduce the risk and uncertainty associated with innovation and entrepreneurship, even when this has to be at the expense of allocative efficiency. It would be hard, for example, to justify the award and protection of intellectual property rights in terms of allocative effi-ciency alone,[77] but they provide an incentive for innovation.[78] And the

---

[72] See Cooter & Ulen at 286–7 and Deakin & Hughes at 173–4.
[73] *Ibid.*
[74] See Langlois (intro) at 15.
[75] See Schumpeter at 82–3.
[76] See Schumpeter at 106 and Best at 121.
[77] See Cooter & Ulen at 122–137.
[78] For a survey of how the economic analysis of intellectual property rights has developed, see C Primo Braga, 'Guidance From Economic Theory' and 'The Developing Country Case For and Against Intellectual Property Protection' in W Siebeck (ed), *Strengthening Protection of Intellectual Property in Developing Countries* (World Bank Discussion Paper No 112, 1990). See generally F Scherer and D Ross, *Industrial Market Structure and Economic Performance* (Boston, Houghton-Mifflin, 1990) and P Menell, 'Intellectual Property: General Theories' in *Encyclopaedia of Law and Economics*, Volume II, *Civil Law and Economics* at 129.

'state of the art' defence against product liability under the Consumer Protection Act 1987 shields firms from some of the unexpected and arguably unpredictable costs of innovation.[79]

The limited liability afforded to the shareholders of a company has been justified as necessary to stimulate innovation.[80] This feature of a company has been justified as promoting allocative efficiency on the basis that it transfers part of the risk of a company's failure from its shareholders to its creditors.[81] The justification is based on the view that the creditors are the least-cost-avoider and that assigning an increased level of risk to them through a rule of law therefore reduces the transaction costs of obtaining equity capital.[82] Creditors can then take account of this increased risk in the terms of their own contractual arrangements with the company.[83] However, justifying limited liability in terms of allocative efficiency alone is much more convincing in the case of public companies. Limiting the risk of loss faced by shareholders in private companies (including the parents of subsidiary companies) is better justified as a necessary incentive for entrepreneurship, innovation and diversification.[84]

---

[79] On product liability, see Cooter & Ulen at 379–383 and M Geistfeld, 'Products Liability' in *Encyclopaedia of Law and Economics*, Volume III, *The Regulation of Contracts* at 347.

[80] The separate legal personality of a company shields its shareholders from liability for the company's debts and liabilities: one person cannot be held responsible for the debts and liabilities of another unless there is a distinct basis of liability: see the judgments of the Court of Appeal and House of Lords in *Rayner v DTI* [1989] Ch 77 and [1990] 2 AC 418. However, shareholders had a potentially unlimited liability to their company until the Limited Liability Act 1855 set a limit on this liability: see chapter 1.

[81] See Cheffins at 499–508, Easterbrook & Fischel at 40–62 and W Carney, 'Limited Liability' in *Encyclopaedia of Law & Economics*, Volume III at 659. See also R Booth, 'Limited Liability and the Efficient Allocation of Resources' (1994) 89 *Northwestern University Law Review* 140, D Goddard, 'Corporate Personality—Limited Recourse and its Limits' in Grantham & Rickett (eds) and P Halpern, M Trebilcock and S Turnbull, 'An Economic Analysis of Limited Liability in Corporation Law' (1980) 30 *University of Toronto Law Journal* 117.

[82] This view is supported by the general practice adopted by unincorporated companies prior to the reforms of 1844 and 1855 of attempting to contract around unlimited liability through standard notices to potential creditors: see chapter 1.

[83] This observation, however, does not apply in the case of 'involuntary' creditors such as tort victims, and it is arguable that many smaller creditors lack the bargaining power or economic incentive to ensure that the terms of the credit extended to a company reflect the risk of limited liability: see J Landers, 'A Unified Approach to Parent, Subsidiary and Affiliate Questions in Bankruptcy' (1975) 42 *University of Chicago Law Review* 589 and 'Another Word ...' (1976) 43 *University of Chicago Law Review* 527 and D Prentice, 'Groups of Companies: The English Experience' in K Hopt (ed), *Groups of Companies in European Laws* (Berlin, de Gruyter, 1982).

[84] See, for example, R Posner, 'The Rights of Creditors of Affiliated Corporations' (1976) 43 *University of Chicago Law Review* 499 and L Ribstein, 'The Deregulation of Limited Liability and the Death of Partnership' (1992) 70 *Washington University Law Quarterly* 417 at 447–8.

3.4 Economic Efficiency and Information

3.4.1 *Information and Transaction Costs*

In ideal bargaining conditions, the parties to a potential transaction would have complete information on its subject matter and would be able to compute its costs and benefits accordingly. In the real world, information is costly and it can be hard or impossible to obtain complete information even if the future is regarded as capable of prediction. A party may therefore have to face a degree of risk when entering into a transaction, but relevant information can enable it to reduce this risk and to calculate it more accurately.

However, the parties to a potential transaction also have to take account of any likely imbalance (or asymmetry) of relevant information between them. A party with superior information has an advantage that it could use opportunistically and the other party's awareness of its vulnerability may block an otherwise beneficial transaction. Further, where one party is operating through an agent, there is another point on which the parties should ideally have complete information, namely the precise scope of the agent's legal authority to bind the company. Subject to any overriding rule of attribution, the possibility that an agent may not have authority to make the transaction increases information costs and thus overall transaction costs.

Rules of law can help to reduce information costs and help to overcome the problem of asymmetric information. The rules governing the attribution of contracts to companies can be analysed in terms of performing this function. This is the main economic significance of the rules of attribution. Thus, an overriding rule of attribution should reduce the information costs of third parties and any qualifications to such a rule should reduce the extent to which companies have to acquire information about the activities of their agents and exert control over them. Moreover, legal rules that reduce information costs, such as an overriding rule of attribution, may also improve dynamic efficiency through the incentives that they create and through shaping business structures and the organisation of economic activity.

One illustration of the problems stemming from information asymmetry and of how rules of law can help to mitigate such problems is the so-called 'market for lemons'.[85] This problem arises where one party is seeking to buy a product of certain quality or with certain features (the 'desired product'), but is unable to discern through inspection or from readily available or low-cost information whether a particular product offered for sale is the desired product or an inferior one (or 'lemon'). The

---

[85] See G Akerlof, 'The Market for "Lemons": Quality Uncertainty and the Market Mechanism' (1970) 84 *Quarterly Journal of Economics* 488.

problem becomes significant where the additional cost of producing and supplying the desired product rather than a lemon is high. A genuine seller of the desired product would have to charge a high enough price to reflect the additional cost, but this would create an opportunity for an unscrupulous seller to make a windfall profit by selling a lemon.

Subject to any legal devices that enable buyers to distinguish the desired product from a lemon at the time of purchase or which reduce their information costs on this point, buyers would have to seek compensation for the risk of buying a lemon (and for the additional information costs associated with this risk) through the price that they pay for the desired product. This would mean a lower market price. Many potential buyers would not in fact be prepared to take the risk at all or to incur the associated costs. And the consequent reduction in the market price would deter many potential sellers from producing the desired product. The effect of this could be to undermine the market in the desired product completely and leave consumers with a market in lemons.

The lemons problem clearly has an adverse effect in terms of dynamic efficiency and innovation since it weakens the incentives for producing new products or better quality products where these could be undermined by lemons. However, focusing on allocative efficiency can mask the nature of the problem since the desired product simply disappears from the given stock of resources and the surviving market in lemons would achieve an efficient allocation of lemons.

The law can provide devices for overcoming this problem. It can, for example, provide signalling devices, such as trade marks and advertising, and ensure their reliability. However, signalling devices still entail information costs and these might still be significant. Thus, a market in which buyers were to be confronted with an array of competing products with varying mixes of desired and lemon-like qualities could prove costly to negotiate and therefore prove unstable. An alternative approach would be to remove the lemons from the market by imposing compulsory minimum standards of quality. This would be hard to justify in terms of allocative efficiency since consumers would lose the opportunity of buying lower priced lemons. However, this device could prove more effective in ensuring the confidence of high quality producers and of buyers interested in the desired product and thereby ensure greater stability in the relevant market.[86] This would provide a greater incentive for innovation and be justifiable in terms of dynamic efficiency.

This observation has relevance for analysing rules of company law if the economic role of these rules is viewed as including the promotion of better quality companies (that are arguably more 'competitive') as well as the reduction of transaction costs.

[86] See Deakin & Hughes at 183.

3.4.2 *Information and the Stimulation of Economic Activity*

In terms of allocative efficiency, therefore, information performs the relatively static function of reducing transaction costs and making risk assessment and allocation more accurate. However, it can also have a dynamic quality and contribute to improvements in productive and dynamic efficiency. It can improve the alertness of firms and aid the discovery or creation of valuable opportunities.[87]

A firm is not merely a unit of production, but an institution for acquiring, conserving and exploiting specialised knowledge and information.[88] The law can therefore be viewed as performing an economic role insofar as it provides incentives that encourage the acquisition and deployment of valuable information. The law can also reinforce systems and procedures that stimulate the flow and use of such information.[89] From this perspective, the firm itself becomes a key economic resource in relation to production and innovation and information becomes a key factor of its effectiveness. This can provide a further basis for analysing the company and the rules of company law.

4 AN ECONOMIC VIEW OF THE COMPANY

4.1 The Legal Institution

In law, a company exists as a person in its own right, separate from its members and managers. This is due to its legal nature as a corporation. It means that a company can act as the focus for a distinct set of legal rights and obligations, which the law treats as the company's own, and that there is no automatic right of recourse to the assets of its members and managers.[90] Enabling companies to become corporations through the relatively straightforward and inexpensive mechanism of registration was a

---

[87] See Langlois (intro) at 20.

[88] On the economic role of the 'learning firm' as a device for handling information, see generally Best and Penrose. See also M Aoki, *The Co-operative Game Theory of the Firm* (Oxford, Clarendon Press, 1984) and H Demsetz, 'The Theory of the Firm Revisited' in H Demsetz, *Ownership, Control and the Firm* (Oxford, Basil Blackwell, 1988) at 144–165.

[89] See Deakin & Hughes at 181–2.

[90] *Salomon v A Salomon & Co Ltd* [1897] AC 22 (HL); *Lee v Lee's Air Farming* [1961] AC 12 (PC); *Multinational Gas v Multinational Services* [1983] Ch 258 (CA); *Rayner v DTI* [1989] Ch 77 (CA) and [1990] 2 AC 418 (HL); *Adams v Cape Industries* [1990] Ch 433 (CA); *Carlton Communications and Granada Media v the Football League* [2002] EWHC 1650. However, there are various legal devices that can enable a company's creditors to reach the assets of those involved in the management of a company's affairs such the personal liability of directors (and shadow directors) for breach of duty and for 'wrongful trading' under s 214 of the Insolvency Act 1986. See generally D Goddard, 'Corporate Personality—Limited Recourse and its Limits' in Grantham & Rickett (eds).

major step forward in the achievement of limited liability.[91] However, until the Limited Liability Act 1855, the potential liability of its members to the company itself to provide it with funds was not limited and, as a legal person, a company had unlimited liability for its own debts and liabilities. After the 1855 reform, the liability of the members of a company limited by shares was limited to any outstanding amount due on their shares.[92] The House of Lords reinforced this limited liability at the end of the nineteenth century by holding that a company and its creditors had no right of recourse to the assets of the company's members even when one member was in effective control of the company's affairs.[93]

A firm is an economic device for obtaining inputs of various kinds and producing output in the form of goods or services.[94] The emergence of the registered company limited by shares as the preferred legal structure for firms has been attributed to four characteristics.[95] These are its separate legal personality, the limited liability enjoyed by its members, the formal separation of its management from its membership (or ownership) with the delegation of management to a hierarchical structure under a board of directors, and the free transferability of its members' interests in the form of shares.

By the end of the nineteenth century, legal structures possessing these characteristics had emerged worldwide and such structures are still viewed as essential for firms today.[96] From an economic perspective, these characteristics have been viewed as making the company the most efficient legal structure for organising production. The emergence of the incorporated company and its displacement of the unincorporated company have been explained as reflecting this economic logic. [97]

The economic value of the company as a structuring device thus rests on more than its separate legal personality. The formal separation of the

---

[91] See chapter 1.

[92] *Ibid.*

[93] *Salomon v A Salomon & Co Ltd* [1897] AC 22 (HL). See generally Grantham & Rickett (eds).

[94] Some commentators have argued that firms produce knowledge in addition to their other output and that recognising the production of knowledge is crucial to a full understanding of the firm: see Best at 128, discussing Penrose at 48 and 56.

[95] See R Harris, *Industrializing English Law* (Cambridge, Cambridge University Press, 2000) ('Harris') at 22–4. See also J Baskin and P Miranti, *A History of Corporate Finance* (Cambridge, Cambridge University Press, 1997) ('Baskin & Miranti').

[96] In their Millennial paper 'The End of History for Corporate Law', Henry Hansmann and Reiner Kraakman expanded these four characteristics into five core functional features: (1) full legal personality, including well-defined authority to bind the firm to contracts and to bond those contracts with assets that are the property of the firm as distinct from the firm's owners; (2) limited liability for owners and managers; (3) shared ownership by investors of capital; (4) delegated management under a board structure; and (5) transferable shares: New York University Center for Law & Business Working Paper (CLB–99–013) (January 2000) and (2001) 89 *Georgetown Law Journal* 439.

[97] See, for example, Easterbrook & Fischel at 10–12. On the historical evolution of the incorporated company in the 125 years prior to the Joint Stock Companies Act 1844, see generally Harris.

management of a company's assets and activities from the 'ownership' rights to profit from those assets and activities means that each of these functions can be vested in a specialist body, namely the board of directors and the body of shareholders. This internal separation is important for analysing the process of contracting by companies since making contracts, and thereby altering a company's rights and liabilities, is part of the management function, but has an impact on the company's financial well being and thus on its shareholders.

Whilst the formal separation of the two functions is a feature of every company, its relevance in practice depends on the particular use to which a company is put. Thus, it is crucial in the case of the public company or its equivalent in other jurisdictions, since it facilitates the free transferability of shares in the company.[98] This, in turn, has enabled the development of secondary markets in shares.[99] The shares of a public company can be offered for sale to the general public and traded on a market such as a stock exchange.[100] Issuing shares in such a company is therefore a means of obtaining or refinancing equity capital and the attractiveness of shares as an investment is enhanced by the availability of a secondary market. The public company has become the principal legal structure for large firms requiring substantial capital assets in order to conduct their business.[101]

In the case of the public company, the company itself functions as the legal basis for structuring the arrangements concerning the raising of equity capital and the payment of the return on this capital. From an economic perspective, it can be viewed as a device for facilitating the raising of equity capital and judged on its effectiveness in this role. Thus, outside investors would be much less willing to supply equity capital to a firm without the protection of limited liability or if they had to play an active role in the management of a company's affairs. The public company provides these advantages and avoids the transaction costs that would otherwise have to be incurred in securing them.

A private company cannot offer its shares for sale to the public and therefore has much less value as a device for raising equity capital. However, a private company still offers the advantages of separate legal personality and limited liability and provides an attractive legal structure

---

[98] On the distinction between a public company and a private company, see Gower & Davies at 12–14.

[99] In the United Kingdom, the 'Bubble Act' of 1720 inhibited the use of unincorporated companies with freely transferable shares prior to its repeal in 1825: see P Davies, *Gower's Principles of Modern Company Law* (London, Sweet & Maxwell, 1997) 6th ed at 27–34 and Harris at 126–7.

[100] A private company is prohibited from offering its shares and other securities to the public: Companies Act 1985, s 81.

[101] On the economics of corporate finance and equity capital, see H Hansmann, 'Ownership of the Firm' (1988) 4 *Journal of Law, Economics & Organisation* 267. For an economic perspective on the public company, see Easterbrook & Fischel. For an historical perspective on the evolution of the public company, see Baskin & Miranti and Harris.

for many firms. It can also be used as a means of internal organisation within a firm and a public company may consist of an elaborate network of subsidiary private companies. In addition a private company can be used as a structure for joint ventures and other inter-firm arrangements.

4.2 The Economic Role of the Company

4.2.1 *The 'Nexus of Contracts' Model*

Economic analysis of company law has presented the company as a 'nexus of contracts' because its separate legal personality provides an efficient basis for structuring the complex set of transactions and relationships that may be necessary for organising the production of goods or services, many of which may have to take place over a long period of time.[102] The cost, complexity and practical difficulty (if not impossibility) of organising these transactions and relationships without the convenient pivot of a separate legal personality provides an economic rationale for the availability of the company as a legal structure for a firm.[103]

A company provides a convenient and flexible legal basis for organising complex, inter-related and long-term transactions by enabling them to be structured as bilateral arrangements with the company itself. Further, for some of these arrangements, the company's management provides a flexible decision-making and problem-solving mechanism or 'governance

---

[102] See Cheffins and Easterbrook & Fischel. The term 'nexus of contracts' is associated in particular with M Jensen and W Meckling, 'Theory of the Firm: Managerial Behaviour, Agency Costs and Capital Structure' (1976) 3 *Journal of Financial Economics* 305. The reference to 'contracts' does not mean the strict legal sense of the word, but rather indicates the broad relationships between a company and each of its major groups of stakeholders, including that with its shareholders. These relationships may include contracts in the strict legal sense, but may also have other components such as the legal features of the company itself, rules of company law, various pieces of legislation, collective arrangements involving the relevant group (such as that effected through the UK Listing Authority's *Listing Rules*) and any regulation applicable to the particular relationship in question. These relationships are referred to as 'contracts' because they are generally voluntary. To emphasise the distinction from contracts in the strict legal sense, this economic presentation of the company has also been termed a 'nexus of treaties', but this expression is not widely used: see M Aoki, B Gustafsson and O Williamson (eds), *The Firm as a Nexus of Treaties* (London, Sage, 1990).

[103] See, for example, R Coase, 'The Nature of the Firm' (1937) 4 *Economica NS* 386; A Alchian and H Demsetz, 'Production, Information Costs and Economic Organization' (1972) 62 *American Economic Review* 777; E Fama and M Jensen, 'Separation of Ownership and Control' (1983) 26 *Journal of Law & Economics* 301; and E Fama and M Jensen, 'Agency Problems and Residual Claims' (1983) 26 *Journal of Law & Economics* 327. The economic analysis of the company is largely based on neo-classical analysis, although there are neo-institutional variants: see W Bratton, (1989) 41 *Stanford Law Review* 1471 and W Bratton, (1989) 74 *Cornell Law Review* 407. For a critique of the neo-classical view of the company from a British perspective, see P Ireland, 'Property and Contract in Contemporary Corporate Theory' (2003) 23 *Legal Studies* 453.

structure' for a wide range of matters. Providing that this governance structure is acceptable to the parties involved, this reduces and can even remove the need to deal with these matters in advance and thus reduces or avoids the transaction costs of attempting to do so (these costs including the risk faced by each party of a matter arising for which they have failed to make adequate provision to protect their interests).

A company does more than provide a convenient legal nexus for organising the activities of a firm. It also provides the legal basis for two crucial sets of arrangements, namely that concerning the company's shareholders and that concerning its management. In economic terms, these can be viewed as arrangements for the supply of two essential inputs to the firm's activities.

In the economic analysis of the company, its relationship with its shareholders has been presented as a 'contract' concerned with the provision of equity capital and the payment of a return on this capital.[104] The return on this input is left unspecified, as is the managerial endeavour necessary to secure the return and maximise it, thereby saving the transaction costs of attempting such specification. However, the risk entailed by this lack of specification is counter-balanced by the shareholders' collective 'ownership' rights over the company and its management body (these being dispersed throughout the body of shareholders in the form of voting rights attached to their shares) and by other features of the shareholders' relationship with the company. This gives a sharply different perspective on the role of shareholders in a company than viewing them simply as its owners.[105] Thus, the limited liability enjoyed by shareholders becomes a crucial feature of the shareholders' 'contract', a necessary precondition of their willingness to contract and one reflected in the overall package of terms, rather than a state-conferred privilege.

4.2.2 The Economic Role of Corporate Management

The significance of the relationship between a company and its shareholders varies according to whether the company is a public company or

---

[104] A key feature of the economic analysis of the company in relation to public companies is that the relationship between a company and its shareholders is construed as a complex and open-ended contractual arrangement concerning the provision of equity capital to the company and the securing of a return on that input of capital. See, for example, Easterbrook & Fischel and H Manne, 'Our Two Corporation Systems: Law and Economics' (1967) 53 *Virginia Law Review* 259.

[105] The shareholders of a company are often referred to as its 'owners': see, for example, *The Report of the Committee on the Financial Aspects of Corporate Governance* ('the Cadbury Report') (Chairman: Sir Adrian Cadbury) (London, Gee, 1992). However, there are significant differences between shareholders and owners in the usual sense, not least their limited liability for the company's activities. On the different visions of the nature of the shareholders' role in their company, see J Hill, 'Changes in the Role of the Shareholder' in Grantham & Rickett (eds).

a private company. In both cases, however, the legal structure of a company means that it is premised on the formal separation of management from shareholding. In effect, it is a term of the shareholders' contract with the company that responsibility for management is vested in a specialist body that is given discretionary power in this respect.

Management's discretionary power to make decisions, including the power to make contracts that are binding on the company, can be viewed as a component in a governance structure through which various transactions that involve the shareholders or are relevant to their interests can be determined. These include the declaration and payment of dividends, decisions on whether to retain or distribute the profits of the company's activities (these profits in effect stemming from the company's dealings with other parties) and the actual conduct of the company's activities so as to make a profit or, as the case may be, incur a loss.

The contractual relationship between a company and its shareholders is also founded upon (and therefore reflects) the company's separate legal personality and the consequential limited liability enjoyed by the shareholders since these limit their responsibility for and thus their need to be concerned with the activities of the company's management.

4.2.3 The Separation of Management from Ownership

In the economic analysis of the company, the formal separation of management from shareholding and the limited liability of shareholders have both been presented as improving allocative efficiency by reducing the transaction costs of providing equity capital to firms inasmuch as they reflect the optimal terms that parties would be likely to settle for themselves under ideal bargaining conditions.[106]

An economic advantage of the separation of management from shareholding is that specialists can perform the function of management, although the value of this depends on the type of company. It is greatest in the case of the public company, where the 'ownership' function of the company's shareholders is in fact used as a device for raising equity capital, which is a major input required by many larger firms. In effect, the company has to engage in transactions whereby equity capital is raised in return for an unspecified claim on the company's subsequent profits. It is the difficulty, if not impossibility, of determining the latter set of transactions *ex ante* which explains why the management of a company and the limits on management's discretion can be analysed as an *ex post* governance structure. The power of a company's board and other agents to make contracts on its behalf can be analysed as a feature of this governance structure.

The formal separation of management from shareholding in the company's legal structure also contributes to its value as a basis for equity

---

[106] See, for example, Easterbrook & Fischel.

investment. It reflects the fact that dividing these functions enables each one to be performed more efficiently. The total number of shareholders does not have to be limited to what is suitable for a managerial body and can expand to a size that is conducive to efficient and diversified risk bearing and thus most effective for the raising of equity capital. For most public companies, this means that their ownership is fragmented among a large number of relatively small shareholders, whose maximum potential loss is fixed by limited liability and who can their maintain a limited investment in any one company and protect themselves through diversification.

The limited liability enjoyed by a company's shareholders contributes to this efficiency in a number of ways.[107] It limits the shareholders' risk of loss and thus the potential costs facing equity investors. Limited liability also reduces the need for shareholders to be involved in or pay close attention to the management of the company since their maximum potential loss is already established. They no longer face the risk of losing all their personal assets. Limited liability thereby reinforces the separation of the functions of management and shareholding so that specialists can perform each one more efficiently.

A further contribution of limited liability is that it improves the quality of shares in a company as an investment by making the attached risk an objective one, related to the performance and prospects of the company and independent of the relative personal wealth of the shareholders. This objectifying of the attached risk also enables shares to be traded more easily, since their value will not be affected by the relative personal wealth of their holders and has thereby facilitated the development of secondary markets in shares such as the London Stock Exchange. This in turn has enabled the risk associated with equity investment to be spread out and countered in diversified portfolios.[108]

4.2.4 Voting Rights as a Contractual Safeguard for Shareholders

In the economic analysis of the company, the shareholders' collective power to control the composition of its board and the other collective powers that give them ultimate control of its destiny have been presented as essentially contractual.[109] The vesting of these powers and their dispersal throughout the body of shareholders in the form of voting rights attached to each share have been presented as terms that are essential for countering the danger of opportunism by the company's management that

---

[107] See Cheffins at 499–508, Easterbrook & Fischel at 40–62 and W Carney, 'Limited Liability' in *Encyclopaedia of Law & Economics*, Volume III at 659. See also R Booth, (1994) 89 *Northwestern University Law Review* 140 and P Halpern, M Trebilcock and S Turnbull, (1980) 30 *University of Toronto Law Journal* 117.

[108] On 'portfolio theory' and its underlying assumptions, see Baskin & Miranti at 11–15.

[109] See Easterbrook & Fischel at 63–72. See chapter 3 for further discussion of the shareholders' collective powers.

could otherwise present an insuperable barrier to the provision of equity capital on acceptable terms.[110] Although the shareholders' rights are dispersed, management face the risk that they can be aggregated and used to cut down their discretion or even to remove them from office altogether.[111]

The potential power comprised in the shareholders' voting rights is the basis of the so-called 'market in corporate control', which has been presented as an important counterweight to the discretionary power of the management of a public company.[112] According to this theory, shareholders can exert influence over their company's directors and management through their ability to sell their shares, which can affect the company's share price. If directors do not ensure that shareholders receive the maximum possible financial return from the company, they risk provoking a sub-optimal share price, with the consequent adverse publicity that would entail, and an increased vulnerability to a takeover bid. After a takeover, the shareholders' voting rights and powers are concentrated in the hands of an effective controller and can be used decisively. However, the precise impact of takeovers on the conduct of directors and management is a matter of speculation and debate.[113]

The shareholders' ownership rights are also protected by other safeguards such as the detailed regulation provided by companies legislation and, if a company's shares are listed on the London Stock Exchange, by the rules governing their listing.[114] Such additional safeguards, for example, require a company's board to disclose detailed information to shareholders through statutory reports and accounts and thereby account for their stewardship of the company.

4.2.5 Managerial Discretion and the Danger of Opportunism

The economic model of the company therefore provides a context for analysing corporate management and the rules of company law relating to corporate management, including those rules that govern the attribution

---

[110] This analysis applies to ordinary shares rather than those with unusual or inferior voting rights: on ordinary shares, see Gower & Davies at 624–5.

[111] For this reason, shareholders' voting rights have been portrayed as equivalent to a set of unspecified promises by management to the company's shareholders: see Easterbrook & Fischel at 6 and 33.

[112] See H Manne, 'Mergers and the Market for Corporate Control' (1965) 73 *Journal of Political Economy* 110 and H Manne, 'Our Two Corporation Systems' (1967) 53 *Virginia Law Review* 259.

[113] See, for example, C Bradley, 'Corporate Control: Markets and Rules' (1990) 53 *Modern Law Review* 170 and S Deakin and G Slinger, 'Hostile Takeovers, Corporate Law and the Theory of the Firm' in S Deakin and A Hughes (eds), *Enterprise and Community: New Directions in Corporate Governance* (Oxford, Basil Blackwell, 1997).

[114] See the UK Listing Authority, *Listing Rules* (London, FSA, 2003) ('the Listing Rules'). The Listing Rules are now made by the Financial Services Authority pursuant to the Official Listing of Securities (Change of Competent Authority) Regulations 2000: SI 2000/968. See also the *City Code on Take-overs and Mergers* (7th edn, 2002).

of contracts to companies. This model presents the discretionary powers conceded to a company's management body by its shareholders as forming part of an overall contractual relationship concerned with their financial return from the company's activities.

The discretionary power vested in a company's management enables them to make use of their specialist knowledge and expertise in their conduct of its affairs by, for example, responding to changes and opportunities and initiating new plans of action. This applies both to a company's management body as a whole and to the individual agents within the body. The benefit to shareholders of conceding discretion to management (in terms of reduced transaction costs) could, however, be undermined by the danger of abuse or managerial 'opportunism'. From an economic perspective, it is therefore not surprising to find features in the law regulating corporate management that can be presented as safeguards for limiting or countering the danger of abuse so as to maximise the shareholders' gain from the relationship overall.

The general powers of management vested by a company's constitution in its board of directors are the basis of the power of its management body (and of individual agents within the body) to make contracts for the company. The limits that the constitution sets on this power, subject to the effect of any overriding rule of attribution, can therefore be viewed as a safeguard against abuse. Whilst company law provides a framework for settling the terms of the constitution and imposes some constraints, there is relatively little prescription and the founders or promoters of a company are largely free to settle the terms of management's contractual power as they think fit.

The role of the constitution of a company as the legal source of the powers of its management body will be examined in chapter 3. It is generally assumed that, in striking the balance of power between a company's management body and its shareholders, its founders are likely to aim at maximising the yield of equity capital and thus to present potential shareholders with the most attractive package of terms overall. However, if the founders were to include a term that favours management at the expense of the shareholders, any resulting reduction in the equity capital yielded by the company's shares could be viewed as a payment for the resulting benefit to company's management.[115] In principle, it should be accepted that the founders of a company might establish a contractual relationship whereby they forgo maximising equity capital in order to increase the freedom of action of the company's management body.[116]

---

[115] See Easterbrook & Fischel at 17.

[116] For a general critique of the 'contractarian' model of the company and its operation in practice, see J Parkinson, *Corporate Power and Responsibility* (Oxford, Clarendon Press, 1993) at 178–190 ('Parkinson').

4.3 Differing Economic Approaches to the Company

The neo-classical and neo-institutional approaches differ on the extent to which the various 'contracts' focused on a company should be treated as complete.[117] The neo-classical approach tends to view a company's contract with its shareholders, which governs and limits the discretionary powers of its management, as complete at the point of contracting, albeit with some flexibility to enable revision from time to time.[118] Further, this particular contract provides the basis for structuring the company's relationships with other parties, which also tend to be viewed as complete.

A key feature of the nexus of contracts model of the company is that its management body is expected to exercise their discretionary powers for the benefit of the company's shareholders and to aim at maximising their financial return from the company's activities.[119] This applies not only to the discretionary powers that the company's constitution vests in them, but also to the discretion and flexibility conceded to the company in the terms of its dealings or relationships with other parties such as creditors and employees. In other words, management is expected to subordinate the interests of other parties to those of the shareholders, even where this might involve behaving opportunistically.[120] In this respect, the terms of the company's relationships with other parties should be viewed as including any relevant regulation or collective arrangements that set limits on management's freedom of action.[121]

The neo-institutional approach, however, views the discretionary powers of corporate management and the accompanying safeguards as a governance structure for settling dealings between a company and its

---

[117] See Deakin & Hughes at 178–9.

[118] See Easterbrook & Fischel above n 50 at 32–4 on the power of revision and 'latecomer' terms.

[119] See Hansmann.

[120] In English law, this is reflected in the nature of the directors' fiduciary duty to exercise their powers *bona fide* in the best interests of their company: see *Multinational Gas v Multinational Services* [1983] Ch 258 (CA). The interests of the company are identified with the interests of the company's shareholders unless and until the company is insolvent, at which point they are to be identified with the interests of its creditors: *West Mercia Safetywear v Dodd* [1988] BCLC 250 (CA); *Re Pantone 485* [2002] 1 BCLC 266; *Colin Gwyer v London Wharf* [2003] 2 BCLC 153. See also the proposed codification of directors' duties set out in the 2002 White Paper (Schedule 2 to the Draft Clauses) following the recommendation of the Company Law Review. The 2002 White Paper endorsed the Company Law Review's conclusion that the basic goal for directors 'should be the success of the company in the collective best interests of the shareholders', but that directors should also recognise the importance of their companies' relationships with other stakeholders.

[121] See *Fulham FC v Cabra Estates* [1992] BCC 863, in which the Court of Appeal confirmed that directors could limit their company's freedom of action and thus their own discretion to act on their company's behalf through giving contractual undertakings provided that they had the contractual power to give such undertakings and believed that giving them would be in the company's best interests. The court at first instance had called into question the effectiveness of this constraint on corporate management's scope to behave opportunistically if they believed that this would benefit their company's shareholders.

shareholders on an ongoing basis so as to achieve an efficient co-ordination of resources.[122] The crucial difference is one of emphasis inasmuch as the focus is on the management structure of a company (including the basis on which it can become party to new contracts) as a co-ordinating mechanism rather than as the outcome of a bargaining process.[123]

One implication of the neo-institutional shift in emphasis is that corporate management as a governance structure may have a co-ordinating role in some of the other relationships focused on a company. These may also not be complete, giving rise to the need for a satisfactory co-ordinating mechanism to fill in the gaps in their terms. From this perspective, requiring (or even permitting) corporate management to exploit any such gaps for the benefit of the company's shareholders could destabilise and produce inefficiency in these other relationships. It may not be enough to rely upon external constraints and the ability of contracting parties (individually or collectively) to devise and impose satisfactory constraints on corporate management's scope for behaving opportunistically.[124]

Further, improving the suitability of the company as a nexus of all the relationships focused upon it should ensure greater stability over time and better serve the goals of productive and dynamic efficiency. Those theories of the firm that attach importance to its role as a means of acquiring, storing and exploiting information over time, also attach importance to the role of a company's employees in this respect and to the value of protecting them from managerial opportunism.[125]

5 AN ECONOMIC VIEW OF CORPORATE MANAGEMENT

5.1 The Management Structure of a Company

The formal separation in a company's legal structure of management from shareholding means that the provision of equity capital to a firm (and the associated risk-bearing function) is detached from the management of the firm's activities. This means that specialists can perform each of these functions, despite their inter-dependence, which should improve the firm's productive efficiency. The managers of a company do not need to have capital and its shareholders do not need managerial expertise. And the performance of each function can be organised in the way that is most effective. For shareholding, this can mean dispersing the risk associated

---

[122] See Deakin & Hughes at 178–9.
[123] See Langlois (intro) at 16–17.
[124] See, for example, J Armour and S Deakin, 'Norms in Private Insolvency: The "London Approach" to the Resolution of Financial Distress' (2001) 1 *Journal of Corporate Law Studies* 21 on how informal regulation has played a role in ensuring the efficient protection of the collective interests of creditors.
[125] See, for example, Best.

with equity capital among a large number of relatively small investors who are then able to protect themselves through diversification.[126] For management, it is likely to mean a hierarchical command and control structure of some kind headed by a relatively small and cohesive body that is effective at active decision-making.[127]

In the English unitary board system of corporate governance, the company's board of directors (or 'board') heads its management structure. Below the board, there may be a network of subordinate agents, the size and organisation of this network depending on the nature and extent of the company's activities. The company's constitution vests powers of management in its board.[128] The board can exercise all of these powers itself as a collective body, but it may be able to delegate some of them down into the company's management structure provided that its constitution permits this.[129] This includes delegation to individual directors or to committees of the board. It is common, for example, for constitutions to permit the board to delegate extensive powers over the day-to-day management of a company's affairs to a managing director or chief executive.[130]

The management structure of a company can be analysed both as a collective unit for providing the input of management to the company (the external perspective) and as an organisation of discrete, disparate and dispersed agents who have to work collectively as a team in order to provide the input of management (the internal perspective). As a collective unit, management has to co-ordinate the various inputs to the firm's activities and organise the production of its output.[131] Some of the inputs (in particular labour) may be located within the boundary of the firm and there may be an extensive overlap between the inputs of labour and management.[132] However, the collective role of management can go beyond that of simply organising an established mode of production and include the dynamic and entrepreneurial functions of being alert to change and innovation.

5.2 The Internal Organisation of Corporate Management

Corporate management should be organised so that it can perform its collective function of running the company's affairs effectively and thereby

---

[126] See Easterbrook & Fischel at 28–30.

[127] See R Coase, (1937) 4 *Economica* NS 386.

[128] See generally chapter 3.

[129] As fiduciaries, the directors of a company are not entitled to delegate their powers unless the company's constitution expressly authorises them to do so. However, constitutions usually include a general power of delegation: see, for example, Companies (Tables A to F) Regulations 1985 SI/1985/805, Table A ('Table A'), reg 72.

[130] See Table A, reg 72.

[131] See A Alchian and H Demsetz, (1972) 62 *American Economic Review* 777.

[132] On the boundaries of the firm, see R Coase, (1937) 4 *Economica* NS 386.

ensure its productive efficiency. At one level, this means managing the input providers to ensure that inputs are provided on the best possible terms. The scope for management to improve productive efficiency in this respect depends on the degree of discretion conceded to the company in the terms of the relevant 'contracts'.

Thus, the company is likely to have a relatively high degree of discretion in relation to many employees, especially when the employees provide their input collectively as members of a team.[133] In such circumstances, the company faces the danger (and associated costs) of a particular form of opportunism known as 'shirking'. This danger arises where a person's return from providing labour or a service of some kind is not directly correlated to what they in fact provide, as when a person works as part of a team and receives a reward based on the performance of a team as a whole. Where an input is provided collectively by a team, each member of the team does not have to bear the full cost of any slacking or shortfall in their personal contribution and equally does not receive the full benefit of any excelling on their part. Team members' private incentives may thus not be perfectly aligned to the team's performance, giving rise to a risk of sub-optimal performance.[134] This can reduce and even undermine the benefits achieved from using a team.

Management has been identified as means of countering the danger of shirking and reducing its cost (this being a reduction in the benefit of making use of a team).[135] In effect, the use of managers to monitor team members and make adjustments on the basis of their observations can be used to replicate some of the incentive effects that team members would face if they had to sell their input individually on the market. Further, since individual managers are themselves susceptible to the danger of shirking, this response requires a hierarchical structure in which superior managers monitor the performance of junior ones and so on up to the top. The management structure of a company is therefore likely to include systems for the supervision and control of the individual agents within it.

5.3 Corporate Agency

Whether the management structure of a company is examined externally as a collective unit or internally as a team of individual agents, there are significant differences from an agent acting on behalf of a natural person. These differences stem from the artificial nature of the company's legal personality. Also, those who might appear to stand in the same relation to

---

[133] See A Alchian and H Demsetz, (1972) 62 *American Economic Review* 777.
[134] *Ibid.*
[135] *Ibid.*

the management structure as a human principal to an agent, namely the company's shareholders, face only limited liability for the actions of the management structure.[136] This means that the management structure of a company, when considered as a unit, does not face the same kind of supervision and control that a human principal, facing the risk of unlimited personal liability, would exercise over an agent's activities.[137]

The absence of constraint from a principal facing unlimited liability should be taken into account when analysing the law governing the attribution to companies of contracts made or approved by those in charge of a company's management structure. However, it is arguable that limited liability also differentiates the position of subordinate agents within a company's management structure from that of agents acting for a natural person. Although a company's board of directors is in overall charge of all its subordinate agents, the board does not face unlimited personal liability for the activities of these agents and cannot therefore be treated as equivalent to a human principal.[138]

6 AN ECONOMIC FRAMEWORK FOR ANALYSING THE RULES GOVERNING CONTRACTING WITH COMPANIES

6.1 Limiting the Authority of Corporate Agents

6.1.1 *The Economic Rationale of Limits on Actual Authority*

The discretionary power to make contracts for a company is an aspect of the company's management. As with other discretionary powers, it may be exercised by the company's board or delegated to subordinate agents

---

[136] *Salomon v A Salomon & Co Ltd* [1897] AC 22 (HL); *Multinational Gas v Multinational Services* [1983] Ch 258 (CA); *Rayner v DTI* [1989] Ch 77 (CA) and [1990] 2 AC 418 (HL).

[137] This is a key factor in the so-called 'separation of ownership and control' of public companies: see A Berle and G Means, *The Modern Corporation and Private Property* (New York, Macmillan, 1932). This separation was believed to give corporate management a discretion for which they were unaccountable and was widely perceived to be an economic problem justifying the regulation of public companies. Neo-classical analysis of the public company, with its emphasis on the contractual nature of shareholding was in part aimed at refuting this perception. See generally the symposium on 'Corporations and Private Property' (1983) 26 *Journal of Law & Economics* 235–496. See also Duxbury at 328–330.

[138] There are, however, some significant qualifications to the limited liability of directors. They may face unlimited personal liability to the company for breach of their duties, including their common law duty of care. Further, if their company goes into insolvent liquidation, they face potential liability for wrongful trading under s 214 of the Insolvency Act 1986. However, the impact of these may be mitigated by the fact that companies are permitted to pay for insurance to indemnify their directors against personal liability for breach of their duty of care: see Companies Act 1985, s 310(3) (as amended by the Companies Act 1989). However, the impact of their duties is reinforced by the danger for directors of insolvent companies of disqualification for 'unfitness' under the Company Directors' Disqualification Act 1986 (as amended by the Insolvency Act 2000): see generally Gower & Davies at 211–224.

within the management structure, thereby conferring actual authority on subordinate agents.[139] The contractual power vested in a company's board does not have to be unlimited and may be limited in various ways, which will be examined further in chapter 3. Limits can be set on the actual authority vested in subordinate agents.

The limits on the authority of corporate agents to make or enter into contracts on behalf of the company can take differing forms. Thus, an agent might be required to seek the approval of a more senior agent or to comply with other procedures. Limiting the actual authority of corporate agents at any level within a company's management structure (leaving aside for now the precise legal effect of such limits) is an aspect of the internal organisation of its management structure.

Limiting the actual authority of corporate agents might improve the overall effectiveness of a company's management structure for two reasons. First, such limits can reinforce its internal organisation, which may include mechanisms for the supervision and control of individual agents or connected groups of agents. The management structure of a company ideally should be organised in a way that exploits the strengths and skills of the company's agents and minimises the impact of their shortcomings. It should also be designed to reflect the company's overall attitude to the assumption of risk, which is relevant to the making of contracts.[140] Limiting the power of agents to make contracts for a company can therefore be viewed as a matter of risk management.

The second reason for limiting the actual authority of corporate agents is to combat a specific economic problem arising from the use of agents known as 'the agency problem'.[141] In economic analysis, the term 'agency' has a looser meaning than its legal definition and refers broadly to the situation where one party is dependent on discretion exercisable by another. The agency problem is a form of opportunism that encompasses shirking, but also takes into account the fact that agents have an enhanced scope for acting contrary to the best interests of their principal if they have discretionary power vested in them. The internal organisation of a company's management structure has to contend with the fact that the interests of the

---

[139] Actual authority refers to an agent's power to bind a principal by virtue of due authorisation by the principal. An agent's power to bind the principal may, however, be expanded by rules of law that enable the agent to bind the principal without being duly authorised to do so such as under the doctrine of ostensible authority. See F Reynolds, *Bowstead & Reynolds on Agency* (London, Sweet & Maxwell, 2001) 17th ed ('Bowstead & Reynolds') at Art 1 and the discussion of the 'concepts of power and authority' in B Markesinis and R Munday, *An Outline of the Law of Agency* (London, Butterworths, 1998) 4th ed ('Markesinis & Munday') at 1–11.

[140] On attitudes towards risk, see generally Cooter & Ulen at 50–3.

[141] See generally M Jensen and W Meckling, 'Theory of the Firm: Managerial Behaviour, Agency Costs and Capital Structure' (1976) 3 *Journal of Financial Economics* 305 and E Fama and M Jensen, 'Agency Problems and Residual Claims' (1983) 26 *Journal of Law & Economics* 327.

company (and through the company, its shareholders), its board and the agents within its management structure are not aligned, and may in fact diverge sharply. The costs attributable to the agency problem, including the costs of devices used for reducing or combating its effects, have been termed 'agency costs'.[142]

Whilst the size and diversity (in terms of knowledge and expertise) of a company's management body may generate economic benefits by enabling it to be party to more contracts or by enabling it to make contracts on better terms, these benefits are liable to be reduced or even undermined by a concomitant increase in agency costs.[143] The specialist knowledge and expertise possessed by an individual agent within a company's management structure might in fact give him or her significant scope for diverging from the pursuit of the company's best interests and for pursuing his or her own interests (or some other agenda) without suffering any adverse consequences or at least without suffering consequences that reflect the cost to the company of the divergence.

The kind of divergence from ideal behaviour that can impose agency costs on a company ranges across a spectrum from shirking, through carelessness and negligence to (at the extreme) self-aggrandisement through fraud or theft. It also includes behaviour that, whilst not necessarily contrary to the company's best interests, diverges from the scheme for managing risk in the company's activities established by those in overall charge of its affairs in this respect. Here, the two reasons for limiting the contractual power of corporate agents overlap and they can in fact be viewed as performing the single composite function of reducing agency costs.

Limiting the actual authority of corporate agents can therefore be viewed as a device for reducing agency costs within a company's management structure and for improving its overall efficiency and effectiveness as a collective unit. The company's constitution may impose some such limits on the management structure, but the board and subordinate management may devise others as part of their management function.

6.1.2 The Economic Implications of the Remedy of Invalidity

The goal of reducing agency costs within a company's management structure therefore provides an economic explanation for setting limits on the actual authority of the corporate agents within it. However, such limits can only be effective as a device for reducing such agency costs if and insofar as corporate agents do not exceed them. Corporate agents have a

---

[142] *Ibid.*

[143] See R Coase, (1937) 4 *Economica NS* 386, who recognised that firms have an optimal size for this reason.

number of incentives to observe the limits on their actual authority, some of these arising from legal rules. Thus, compliance with a company's internal rules, including those setting limits on their actual authority, is likely to affect the remuneration and prospects of corporate agents. And corporate agents face personal liability to their company for any loss that it suffers from any unauthorised contracts that they make.

One way of ensuring the effectiveness of limits on the actual authority of corporate agents as a device reducing agency costs would be for invalidity to be a general remedy for unauthorised contracts. In general agency law, an unauthorised contract is invalid, but this is qualified by the principal's power of ratification and by the ability of the third party to rely upon an overriding rule of attribution such as the doctrine of ostensible authority.[144] If invalidity were to be available as an unqualified general remedy, then companies would not be bound by unauthorised contracts and this would enable them to reduce or avoid the adverse effects of these. In particular, this remedy could provide companies with a more effective means of mitigating or obtaining compensation for any loss than a remedy against the relevant agent personally.

However, the remedy of invalidity affects third parties rather than corporate agents and its incentive effects should be analysed accordingly. Subject to qualification by overriding rules of attribution, it gives third parties a good reason to identify and observe the limits on the actual authority of corporate agents by threatening them with the loss of the benefit of unauthorised contracts. This adverse impact on third parties, including the costs that third parties incur in order to reduce the danger of a contract proving unauthorised and therefore invalid, represents the economic cost of the remedy. In order to assess the overall economic impact of the remedy, this cost should be weighed against the benefit to companies. This means considering the additional benefit of this remedy beyond that resulting from the other incentives that corporate agents have to observe the limits on their actual authority.

From an economic perspective, the remedy of invalidity only improves allocative efficiency insofar as the benefit to companies exceeds the costs to third parties. In practice, the remedy is qualified by the overriding rules of attribution. Also, as will be seen in chapter 7, there are rules of law that may invalidate a contract where a director has a conflict of interest even though the contract has otherwise been duly authorised. The above observations about the costs and benefits of the remedy provide an economic basis for analysing all the rules of law governing contracting with companies. Such a rule has an economic logic insofar as it assigns risk to the 'least-cost-avoider' as between companies and third

---

[144] See generally Bowstead & Reynolds and Markesinis & Munday. The power of ratification is discussed further below and in chapter 3. The concept of ostensible authority (also known as 'apparent authority') is examined further in chapter 6.

parties.[145] However, it may also be useful to consider whether a particular rule of law might also be justifiable in terms of productive or dynamic efficiency or whether this might provide an economic rationale for a rule that seems hard to justify in terms of allocative efficiency alone.

6.2 The Economic Cost for Companies of Overriding Rules of Attribution

6.2.1 *The Risk of Loss from Unauthorised Contracts*

The attribution of unauthorised contracts (and certain authorised contracts involving conflict of interest) exposes companies to a risk of loss from such contracts, but this risk is mitigated insofar as there are other means of combating the danger of a company's agents making unauthorised contracts or reducing the burden that such contracts place on a company. These include the personal incentives that corporate agents have not to exceed the limits on their actual authority or at least not to do so to the detriment of the company.

The risk of being bound by unauthorised contracts imposes a cost on companies insofar as companies face an increased risk of loss from such contracts compared to those made with actual authority. This burden could result from a deficiency in the terms of the contract for the company or from a divergence from the company's policy as regards the management of risk.[146] Thus, a company might be 'risk-seeking' in the sense that it would be willing to run a significant risk of loss in order to pursue the prospect of a substantial gain. Or it might be 'risk-averse' in the sense that it would be prepared to forgo the prospect of a substantial gain in order to avoid a significant risk of loss. A risk-seeking company could view a proposed contract as beneficial whilst a risk-averse one could view a proposed contract on exactly the same set of terms as burdensome.

The increased risk of loss to a company from an unauthorised contract is a feature of the contract at the time of contracting. It should not be confused with the fact that a contract subsequently causes loss to the company (or is otherwise burdensome), although such an outcome might provide evidence that the terms were deficient. A risk-seeking company might be willing to enter into a particular contract even though it entails a significant risk of loss. A risk-seeking company does not therefore suffer a loss if it is bound by such a contract made without actual authority. Being bound by an unauthorised contract only places an increased risk of

---

[145] See the earlier discussion of allocative efficiency and the idea of reducing transaction costs by assigning risk to the 'least-cost-avoider'. See generally E Rasmussen, 'Agency Law and Contract Formation' (2001) Harvard John M Olin Discussion Paper No 323.
[146] See Cooter & Ulen at 50–3.

loss on a company (and thus an economic cost) insofar as it would not have been made on the same terms (or at all) if there had been due compliance with the company's internal rules limiting authority, including any designed to reinforce the company's attitude towards risk.

6.2.2 An Increased Risk of Loss and Limited Liability

The difference between a corporate principal and a human principal in assessing the risk of loss from being bound by unauthorised contracts has already been noted, but needs to be stressed in this context. The shareholders of a company are the ultimate beneficiaries from its activities and therefore suffer from any increased risk of loss to which the company is exposed. However, shareholders enjoy limited liability and this reduces the potential impact of an increased risk of loss from an agent as compared to a human principal. This observation applies both to contracts made or approved by a company's board and to contracts made by subordinate agents. It suggests that there is an economic case for strong overriding rules of attribution and that modelling overriding rules of attribution on those devised for human principals may not be efficient.

The difference between corporate agents and agents of human principals is particularly striking at the level of a company's board. The directors of a company, and thus its board,[147] are agents of the company. However, the idea of the 'company' in this respect, and thus of the board's principal, is very strained. The company is not the same as the company's shareholders, as will be shown in chapter 3, since the power of the shareholders to act collectively on behalf of the company is governed by its constitution. The company as a principal is an abstract construct, in effect represented by the company's constitution. This has implications for those features of agency law that depend on having a separate and identifiable principal such as the power to ratify unauthorised contracts or to make representations conferring ostensible authority.[148]

Agency law has developed on the model of a human principal who can be regarded as having consented to the risk of being bound by unauthorised contracts under the doctrine of ostensible authority. This approach is not appropriate to corporate agency where the idea of a company giving or manifesting 'its' consent is highly artificial. The principle of consent has influenced the development of the overriding rules of attribution nonetheless.[149] The irony here is that, whereas from an economic perspective

---

[147] The terms 'board' or 'board of directors' of a company refer to the directors acting collectively in accordance with its constitution and in effect as the company's main organ of management: see generally chapter 3. The Companies Act 1985 generally uses the term 'the directors' to refer to this organ.
[148] See generally chapter 6.
[149] See generally chapters 5 and 6.

there is a case for having strong overriding rules of attribution in the case of corporate agency, the law's attachment to concepts modelled on agents acting for human principals has made them relatively weak.

As will be shown in chapter 5, however, statutory reform of the relevant law has largely established a general overriding rule of attribution whereby companies are bound by contracts made or approved by their board of directors, regardless of whether or not they have actual authority to do so under their company's constitution.[150] But chapter 6 will show that common law rules, based on the human principal model, still govern the validity of contracts made by other corporate agents.

6.2.3 Factors that Mitigate the Risk of Loss from Unauthorised Contracts

When assessing the economic cost of a legal rule, account should be taken of factors that offset or reduce its adverse impact. In the case of an overriding rule of attribution, this means taking account of any factors that reduce the likelihood of unauthorised contracts being made or of their being made on terms that prove more harmful to the company than if there had been compliance with the company's internal rules. It also means taking account of any factors that reduce the cost of taking avoiding action to reduce the direct risk of loss arising from the rule.

One such mitigating factor is the fact that a corporate agent faces sanctions for acting without authority. Thus, corporate agents are personally liable to their company for exceeding their actual authority.[151] However, the threat actually posed by this potential liability varies according to the overall circumstances of a particular case. These include the nature of a particular agent's deviant behaviour in making an unauthorised contract and the subsequent availability of the agent for redress. It would not, for example, be much of a deterrent to an agent with the opportunity and willingness to commit a large-scale fraud and able to disappear afterwards. It would also not be effective against an agent who had already incurred significant personal liability.

Also, whilst the potential personal liability of corporate agents may reduce the likelihood of their making unauthorised contracts, it is likely to be less satisfactory at reducing any resulting loss to the company than the remedy of invalidity. Further, the threat value of personal liability can be reduced through the insurance of corporate agents against personal liability so far as this is possible.[152] However, whilst this might increase

---

[150] See Companies Act 1985, ss 35–35B and 322A (as amended by the Companies Act 1989).
[151] In the case of directors, this is reinforced by a specific duty to obey their company's constitution: see Companies Act 1985, s 35(3) and 35A(5). This duty is included in the proposed statutory statement of directors' duties: see 2002 White Paper, Draft Clauses, Schedule 2.
[152] See Companies Act 1985, s 310(3).

the likelihood of unauthorised contracts, it would also improve personal liability as a source of compensation to the company.

Corporate agents in any event face internal sanctions for exceeding their actual authority, such as reduced prospects of promotion, loss of benefits or even dismissal. It is also arguable that corporate agents are motivated by a desire to maximise their earning potential in the market for the particular services that they provide and are therefore deterred from engaging in any activity that would reduce their market value.[153] The significance of this factor on an agent's propensity to act without authority is likely to depend on how such unauthorised activity may be viewed by other potential employers. The deterrent effect might, for example, be diminished where the agent is working in a risk-seeking environment.

6.2.4 Taking Avoiding Action to Minimise the Risk of Loss

Overriding rules of attribution mean that companies face a risk of loss from unauthorised contracts. However, companies can take action to avoid the incidence of such contracts and thus reduce the burden of the risk. The economic cost of the risk assigned to companies is the cost of taking such avoiding action plus the burden of the remaining risk, but taking account of the mitigating factors noted in the previous sections. As was noted in chapter 1, a company has much greater scope for reducing the risk assigned by overriding rules of attribution through avoiding action compared to a third party because it can spread the cost of such action over all the contracts made by its agents.

Management is a means of minimising the risk of loss from unauthorised contracts. As noted earlier, management has been presented as a device for combating the agency problem in general. Account should therefore be taken of the other benefits it can yield when considering the extent to which it represents part of the economic cost of overriding rules of attribution. Those in charge of a company's management structure can curb the danger of its agents acting without authority by setting up and operating internal governance systems to suit the size and complexity of the company's management structure.

In any event, the directors' duty of care requires the boards of companies to exercise effective supervision and control over the company's agents.[154] This has been interpreted as requiring them to make sure that adequate systems of control are in place to minimise the company's exposure to liability and loss from the activities of its agents.[155] The fact that directors have an independent reason for ensuring that there are effective

---

[153] On the 'market for managers', see E Fama, 'Agency Problems and the Theory of the Firm' (1980) 88 *Journal of Political Economy* 288.
[154] See, for example, *Re Barings* [1999] 1 BCLC 433 and [2000] 1 BCLC 523 (CA).
[155] *Ibid.*

governance systems in place means that the cost of these systems is not (or at least is not entirely) due to the need to reduce the company's risk of loss from unauthorised contracts. The presence of an independent reason or incentive for taking avoiding action in effect reduces the economic cost of the risk for the company. The directors of companies, especially public companies, also have market incentives to demonstrate that the management of their company complies with recognised standards of good governance, including having good governance systems.

The cost of a company's governance systems can also be offset against any additional benefits that such systems may generate. It is arguable that having good governance systems should improve a company's productive and dynamic efficiency. They stimulate flows of information within a company's management structure and this in turn could make the company, as an organisation, more alert to change and opportunities and thereby improve its capacity for innovation. This in turn should improve the company's ability to adapt and survive over time.

A company might be able to take other forms of avoiding action in response to overriding rules of attribution. It could simply employ fewer agents in the conduct its affairs or at least in situations where there is a substantial risk of agents making unauthorised contracts that could prove harmful. A company might also be able to use warnings or other means of conveying information to third parties to deter them from dealing with certain subordinate agents (at least not without seeking confirmation from superior agents), at least in situations where there is a significant risk of loss to the company. Or a company might be able to take action to ensure that any unauthorised contract would be within the scope of an exception to an overriding rule of attribution, for example by giving clear general warnings to third parties about the actual authority of its agents.

6.2.5 The Quality of Corporate Agents

Having better quality agents within a company's management structure should also help to reduce agency costs and to generate benefits in terms of productive and dynamic efficiency. Whilst this is likely to be costly, inasmuch as better quality agents are likely to be more expensive than lower quality ones, this should be offset against any additional benefits beyond reducing the risk of loss from unauthorised contracts.

This observation reveals a significant benefit that strong overriding rules of attribution can generate (that is, rules that render all unauthorised contracts binding on a company subject to limited exceptions where third parties are clearly the least-cost-avoider). Strong rules of attribution give companies with better quality agents and better quality governance systems a competitive advantage over other companies. They limit the scope for companies with lower quality agents and lower quality governance systems to protect themselves against the likely increase in economic agency costs (in the sense of an increased risk of loss from opportunism, incompetence or divergence from the company's attitude towards risk) by limiting the actual authority of their agents and relying on the remedy of invalidity. In effect, strong rules of attribution limit the extent to which companies can rely on third parties to enforce their internal rules.

Strong rules of attribution should reduce overall transaction costs and thus improve allocative efficiency as long as they do not operate where third parties are clearly the least-cost-avoider. However, they should have an even greater economic value in terms of dynamic efficiency by giving companies the incentive to acquire better quality agents and to adopt better quality governance systems. They should therefore stimulate the development of companies with these attributes.[156] It is arguable that such companies are more likely to be 'competitive' in accordance with the goals of the Company Law Review.

6.2.6 The One-Sided Nature of the Remedy of Invalidity

It is worth noting at this point a further economic reason for having strong overriding rules of attribution. This is to combat the one-sided nature of the remedy of invalidity, which is otherwise available for all unauthorised contracts. As a general rule, the remedy is available to companies, but not to third parties. This means that, all other things being equal, companies have an incentive to seek this remedy to gain an advantage that they might be able to exploit opportunistically. Overriding rules of attribution are necessary to counter this incentive and ensure that unscrupulous companies cannot gain an advantage by setting the actual authority of their agents at an excessively low level. Having the scope for gaining such an advantage increases transaction costs overall and reduces allocative efficiency. It also tends to favour low quality companies and is therefore harmful in terms of dynamic efficiency as well.

The problem stems from the legal nature of an unauthorised contract in agency law. An unauthorised contract is not a legal nullity, but instead has potential validity. A principal has the power to ratify an unauthorised contract made on its behalf whether the agent exceeded his or her actual authority or acted without any authority at all.[157] If a principal ratifies an unauthorised contract, it takes effect as if the agent did have the necessary authority at the time of contracting.[158] Whilst there are some limited

---

[156] This is analogous to the kind of 'procedural' regulation that achieves a beneficial effect indirectly through the action that it encourages regulated parties to adopt in order to mitigate or avoid its primary impact: see Deakin & Hughes at 175–6.

[157] On a principal's power to ratify an unauthorised contract, see Bowstead & Reynolds, Arts 13–20.

[158] *Koenigsblatt v Sweet* [1923] 2 Ch 314 (CA) at 325, per Lord Sterndale MR. See Bowstead & Reynolds, Art 13.

circumstances in which a principal may lose the power to ratify,[159] the invalidity of an unauthorised contract does not give the third party any general right to escape from the contract. If the law did not provide any overriding rules of attribution, then principals would have the ability to pick and choose among unauthorised contracts. And awareness of this ability could influence the level of actual authority that principals choose to vest in their agents.

In the context of corporate agency, if there were no overriding rules of attribution, companies would have an incentive to minimise the contractual power of their agents in order to maximise their scope for escaping from contracts that prove to be burdensome. Third parties would in turn face an excessive risk of contracts made with corporate agents proving to be unauthorised and enforceable and would seek compensation through the terms on which they would be prepared to make contracts with companies in general. Companies would end up bearing a heavier cost than if the overriding rule had imposed the risk on them in the first place.

Challenging the validity of an unauthorised contract is not necessarily a costless course of action for a particular company, even where the contract is burdensome. Such action is likely to have an adverse effect on the company's reputation and this could, among other consequences, have an adverse effect on the terms on which third parties are prepared to deal with the company. This cost of the remedy of invalidity is likely to weigh more heavily on those companies with a longer-term perspective and which attach value to acquiring a good reputation. Those in charge of such a company's management are therefore more likely to make use of other devices to reduce the danger of their agents exceeding their contractual power.

Companies with a longer-term perspective and which attach value to their reputation are also likely to be the kind of high quality companies that are competitive and dynamically efficient. Strong overriding rules of attribution, by negating the alternative advantage that the one-sided nature of the remedy of invalidity would otherwise provide, would therefore give a further incentive for companies to develop these qualities.

6.3 The Cost for Third Parties of a Risk of Invalidity

6.3.1 Transaction Costs

The limits and qualifications of overriding rules of attribution (and the terms of other rules of law governing contracting with companies) mean that third parties face a risk of loss from the invalidity of a contract with

---

[159] See Bowstead & Reynolds, Art 19; *Smith v Henniker-Major* [2002] EWCA Civ 762 at 54–82.

a company. The assignment of such a risk can be viewed as minimising transaction costs and facilitating allocative efficiency insofar as it occurs in circumstances where third parties are likely to be the least-cost-avoider. In assessing the economic cost of the risk of invalidity, it is again necessary to consider the scope that third parties may have for reducing this risk through taking avoiding action.

Third parties can avoid the risk of invalidity by obtaining information about the actual authority of the corporate agents with which they deal, but the efficiency of this course of action depends on its cost. One factor increasing the cost of such information is the absence of any prescribed standard levels of actual authority for corporate agents and this applies even to a company's board of directors. The precise terms of a particular corporate agent's actual authority cannot therefore be discerned from any source of information readily available to third parties such as an objectively defined designation or office title. Instead, the relevant information is specific to each agent and may therefore only be discernible at a relatively high cost.

When dealing with agents in general, third parties should be able to avoid the risk of invalidity by seeking confirmation or reassurance from the agent's principal. However, this is another point where the analogy between a corporate agent and an agent acting for a human principal breaks down. For third parties, a human principal represents a clear point of reference and source of information for third parties. If a human principal confirms that an agent has authority to make a proposed contract or simply approves the contract, then the risk of invalidity for lack of authority is avoided. However, a third party dealing with a corporate agent is likely to find it much harder and more costly to obtain such confirmation or reassurance.

The relatively high cost of seeking reassurance is partly due to the complex nature of some corporate management structures, which may not present third parties with any readily accessible reference point beyond the corporate agent with whom they are dealing. Thus, if the head of a major branch office approves a contract on behalf of a company or confirms that it has been approved in accordance with the company's internal rules,[160] it would be difficult and costly for a third party to seek further reassurance. The costs would include any detrimental effects on the third party's relationship with the agent in question that might follow.

Seeking reassurance on behalf of a company is also difficult because third parties may find it hard to identify a reference point that can reliably speak or act for the company (and in effect *as* the company) in the same way that human principals can speak or act for themselves. Thus, a third party may seek reassurance from a superior agent, but superior agents

---

[160] See, for example, *First Energy v Hungarian International Bank* [1993] BCLC 1409 (CA).

might also lack the actual authority to bind the company to the contract in question, which reduces their value as a source of reassurance.[161] The relatively high information costs of discovering the actual authority of corporate agents because of the scope for variation applies in this context as well. It further increases the cost of seeking reassurance as a means of reducing the risk of invalidity.

6.3.2 Sources of Information for Third Parties

Third parties have a number of potential sources of information about the authority of corporate agents. These include the information implicit in agent's appointment to a particular office, or a particular job title or the fact that an agent is able to perform certain activities on behalf of the company. They also include the circumstances surrounding the making of the contract in question, such as any representations made by the agent and the agent's observable behaviour. The value of such information depends on its reliability. Thus, the lack of prescribed levels of authority reduces the reliability of an agent's title as a source of information.

The cost of information also depends on its accessibility. Information is of relatively high cost if it is difficult or expensive to obtain or if it is embedded in long and complex documentation, as might be the case with information available from a company's public documents.[162] In terms of accessibility, information available from the agent, including his or her behaviour and the circumstances surrounding the contract, is relatively low in cost, although this has to be weighed against its reliability. The inferences that can be drawn from the proposed terms of the transaction (whether, for example, they appear to be against the interests of the company), or from the fact that an agent appears to be acting well beyond the limits of his or her expertise or the traditional functions of his or her office, could therefore be viewed as information available at relatively low cost to third parties.

6.3.3 Agents' Behaviour as a Source of Information

The behaviour of corporate agents in offering or accepting to contract on a particular set of terms on behalf of a company is a source of information to third parties and one that is readily accessible. It might therefore be argued that this should justify qualifying an overriding rule of attribution so that it does not protect third parties against the risk of invalidity where a proposed contract seems not to be in the best interests of the company. This argument would rest on the supposition that the cost of avoiding the increased risk of invalidity would be relatively low because third parties

---

[161] See, for example, *British Bank of the Middle East v Sun Life* [1983] 2 Lloyd's Rep 9 (HL).
[162] The legal significance of information available from a company's public documents has been overridden by statutory reform: see generally chapters 3, 5 and 6.

would have ready access to the necessary information and that third parties would therefore be the least-cost-avoider.

However, other factors can increase the economic cost of taking avoiding action regardless of the accessibility of relevant information. Thus, qualifying an overriding rule of attribution to exclude contracts that do not appear to be beneficial to the company would require third parties to do more than identify the presence of certain objective facts. As the courts have recognised in their interpretation of the directors' duty of good faith,[163] it would involve making a judgment from the terms of the contract. Judging a particular company's interests would require some wider knowledge of the company's affairs including, among other things, its attitude towards risk and this would not be readily accessible to third parties.

The economic cost to third parties of such a qualification of an overriding rule of attribution would also include the fact that they would not be able to pursue their own best interests in their dealing with companies, but would instead have to assume a general responsibility for the behaviour of corporate agents. The increased risk of invalidity would require third parties to take avoiding action when a corporate agent offers or accepts contractual terms that do not appear to be in the company's best interests such as checking that the agent does have actual authority or seeking confirmation from a reliable superior agent.

Faced with such a risk, third parties might find it less burdensome simply to offer or accept terms that are clearly favourable to the company and could not trigger the qualification. This would deprive the third parties of the freedom they usually enjoy to pursue their own best interests in negotiating and settling the terms of a contract as vigorously as possible and otherwise to aim at maximising their own gains from a transaction. It would increase the cost of contracting with companies and would not serve the interests of companies in general. Moreover, it would protect low quality companies with low quality agents from some of the adverse consequences of their poor standards and impose a cost on third parties in general.

However, the fact that a corporate agent offers or is prepared to contract on terms that do not appear to be in the company's interests might simply reflect the fact that an agent is of low quality and lacks the expertise or diligence necessary to protect the company's best interests. It might also reflect the fact that the company does not have good governance systems. It would then be unreasonable simply to assign the risk of having such low quality practices on third parties without further qualification. To put it another way, if a company chooses to save costs by employing low quality agents and operating low quality governance systems, this does not of itself mean

---

[163] *Re Smith & Fawcett* [1942] Ch 304 (CA); *Howard Smith v Ampol Petroleum* [1974] AC 821 (PC); *Colin Gwyer v London Wharf* [2003] BCLC 153.

that the third parties with whom its agents deal should be treated as the least-cost-avoider.[164]

6.3.4 Third Parties as the Least-Cost-Avoider

The balance of cost between companies and third parties does shift where a proposed transaction has a readily discernible feature that brings it within a much narrower class of contracts in which there is a relatively high risk of loss to companies. It also shifts in situations where the cost of requiring the third party to take further action to ensure the contract's validity is relatively small. An overriding rule of law qualified in this way would place a relatively light burden on third parties in general and should be justifiable in terms of a relatively large benefit to companies in terms of a reduced risk of loss.

The kind of features that satisfy these criteria include obvious signs that the agent may be defrauding the company or deliberately harming its interests (as opposed to merely displaying 'low quality' behaviour such as laziness or incompetence) or the fact that the contract is an unusual one or at least it is an unusual one for this particular agent to make.[165] They might also include the fact that the agent is clearly junior or low ranking (in relation to the contract at issue) combined with the fact that it would be relatively easy for the third party to contact the agent's superiors or to check with some other convenient and reliable source of information. However, in determining whether a third party does have the opportunity of taking such relatively low cost avoiding action, it is important to take account of the ease of finding a superior agent who does have the actual authority to give reliable reassurance.[166]

When considering whether a third party is likely to be the least-cost-avoider and thus a better risk bearer than the company, the nature of each party's relationship to the agent is also relevant. In the case of the company, this has the potential to be a relatively long-term one, therefore reducing the costs of avoiding action by enabling them to be spread across many contracts. A third party's dealings with a particular corporate agent, however, may vary from a one-off transaction to a long-term series. The third party's costs should decline as the frequency of transacting rises. However, although third parties can acquire information about a corporate agent through a course of dealing, this information is not necessarily

---

[164] Knox J has acknowledged that expecting third parties to curb their commercial instincts and look out for the interests of the company when dealing with corporate agents would have undesirable consequences: see *Cowan de Groot v Eagle Trust* [1992] 4 All ER 700 at 754–761.

[165] See, for example, the situations in *Underwood v Bank of Liverpool and Martins* [1924] 1 KB 775 (CA) and *Midland Bank v Reckitt* [1933] AC 1 (HL).

[166] See, for example, *British Bank of the Middle East v Sun Life* [1983] 2 Lloyd's Rep 9 (HL).

accurate and might in fact give a quite misleading impression about the agent's actual authority.[167] Such information is not therefore reliable. And third parties could still face relatively high costs in obtaining the further detail that would ensure its precision and accuracy.

7 ANALYSING THE LAW GOVERNING CONTRACTING WITH COMPANIES

The previous section of this chapter has identified a number of potential costs for companies and third parties stemming from the assignment of (respectively) the risk of being bound by unauthorised contracts and a remaining risk of invalidity through the rules of law that govern the attribution of contracts to companies. The imposition of these costs gives the rules of law economic significance and should be taken into account when analysing them and considering the scope for improvement. Adopting this perspective calls into question some of the assumptions made in the development of this law and highlights some fundamental differences between corporate agency and agency for a natural principal.

Economic analysis explains how assigning a risk of invalidity to third parties when companies are in fact the least-cost-avoider is not in the interest of companies in general because it increases overall transaction costs. It also shows how this inefficiency can undermine the competitiveness of companies, contrary to the vision of company law sketched out in the Company Law Review. Improving economic efficiency does not necessarily justify reform of the law, but the imposition of excessive costs does raise the question of whether there are adequate reasons of legal principle or public policy to justify the inefficiency. It has been suggested in this chapter that the goal of improving the competitiveness of companies can be served not only by reducing overall transaction costs, but also by stimulating the development of good quality companies with good systems of governance. At the margin, this could justify tilting the balance of the rules governing contracting with companies in favour of third parties, thereby giving good quality companies a competitive advantage.

The subsequent chapters of this book will analyse the various rules of law that govern contracting with companies. They will also examine the economic implications of these rules and consider how far they have evolved to facilitate efficient contracting and encourage the development of competitive companies. They will take account in particular of the influence of traditional doctrines of contract and agency law that are not necessarily appropriate for artificial contracting parties and artificial principals.

---

[167] See, for example, *Egyptian International Foreign Trade Co v Soplex* [1985] BCLC 404 (CA).

3

The Power to Make Contracts for a Company

1 THE LEGAL SOURCE OF CONTRACTUAL POWER

THE CONSTITUTION OF a company governs the affixing of a company's common seal to any document.[1] It is also the source of the power of anyone to act as an agent on the company's behalf.[2] The constitution is therefore the source of the power of a company's board of directors and of any subordinate agent within its management structure to enter into a contract that the law will attribute to the company and that will therefore be binding on it.[3]

In agency law, an agent's power to act on behalf of a principal so as to affect the principal's relations with third parties is termed 'authority'.[4] An agent's authority to act on a principal's behalf and therefore to make contracts that are binding on the principal arises from the fact that the principal has expressly or impliedly consented to the agent's doing this.[5] Agency law draws a distinction in this respect between 'actual' authority and 'ostensible' (or 'apparent') authority. Actual authority results from a 'manifestation of consent' by the principal to the agent whereas ostensible authority results from a 'manifestation of consent' by the principal to a third party.[6]

A corporate principal, as an artificial legal person, cannot simply manifest 'its' consent that an agent should act on its behalf. The company's consent has to be manifested formally, in a way that company law attributes to the company in question. This can be done by the founders of the company through the terms of the constitution, whereby they express their consent that the company's board should have certain

---

[1] *Ernest v Nicholls* (1857) 6 HLC 401; *TCB v Gray* [1986] Ch 621 at 636.
[2] *Freeman & Lockyer v Buckhurst Park Properties* [1964] 2 QB 480 (CA).
[3] Companies Act 1985, s 36.
[4] See F Reynolds, *Bowstead & Reynolds on Agency* (London, Sweet & Maxwell, 2001) 17th ed ('Bowstead & Reynolds'), Art 1 and the discussion of the 'concepts of power and authority' in B Markesinis and R Munday, *An Outline of the Law of Agency* (London, Butterworths, 1998) 4th edn ('Markesinis & Munday') at 1–11.
[5] Bowstead & Reynolds, Art 1.
[6] *Ibid.*

powers to act on behalf of the company. Otherwise, the company can only manifest its consent through the actions of someone with actual authority to act on its behalf in accordance with the constitution.[7] This usually means through the due delegation of the power to make contracts vested in the company's board.

The role of the constitution in determining who can act so as to affect a company's legal relations with third parties is consistent with its legal nature as a corporation. However, the law governing the constitution reflects the fact that the law of partnership regulated the registered company's unincorporated predecessor.[8] As this chapter will show, this legacy includes the collective power of a company's members (or 'shareholders') to alter the terms of its constitution or to sanction the overriding of these terms.[9] The role of the constitution as the legal source of contractual power is also consistent with the company's economic role as a device for facilitating the organisation of production, as discussed in chapter 2.

The constitution of a company provides the legal foundation of its relationship with its shareholders concerning the provision of equity capital and the organisation of their rights as members. It sets out the terms of the board's discretionary powers of management that enable the company to engage in production over an indefinite period of time. It governs the power of the body of shareholders from time to time to revise these powers of management or to alter their own powers. The power of revision is a necessary element of flexibility in a governance structure that is designed to persist over time and which should therefore have the capacity to respond and adapt to changing circumstances and an uncertain future.

Another legacy of the company's roots in partnership law is that a company is identified with its body of shareholders for many purposes. However, this identification has to be reconciled with the law's treatment of a company as a legal person that exists separately from its shareholders and managers. The body of shareholders is not the principal of the company's agents. If the shareholders act unanimously (or if there is a sole shareholder), they do have unlimited power to revise and override the company's constitution, including those provisions governing the powers of the board. Otherwise, the shareholders have to act collectively through a formal voting procedure and their ability to do this is governed by the company's constitution.

The tension between a company's legal status as a separate legal person and its roots in the law of partnership can lead to complexity, in particular

---

[7] See generally *Freeman & Lockyer v Buckhurst Park Properties* [1964] 2 QB 480 (CA).
[8] See chapter 1.
[9] Since the focus of this book is on the registered company limited by shares, the term 'shareholders' will generally be used to refer to a company's members.

in relation to the procedures for overriding the limits that the constitution of a company may set on the board's actual authority. Thus, the relevant law has drawn a distinction between the powers vested in the company itself and those vested in the company's board.[10] When its constitution does not vest the full range of a company's powers in the board, the shareholders have a complementary power to top up the board's powers, which they can exercise by an ordinary resolution. However, this complementary power does not entitle the shareholders to override the limits on the powers of the company itself.[11]

The shareholders also have various powers that enable them to alter the terms of a company's constitution,[12] although these require at least a special resolution.[13] The shareholders can use these powers to increase both the powers of the company itself and the extent to which these powers are vested in the board. This in effect gives the shareholders a further complementary power to top up the board's powers. In practice, it may be hard to distinguish between the different legal nature of the limits on the actual authority of a company's board and thus to identify which kind of shareholders' resolution may be required to override a particular limit. To add to this complexity, it is possible for certain limits to be entrenched in the constitution or to be classified as class rights, in which case the shareholders can only exceed them in accordance with a special procedure.[14]

The different kinds of limit on the board's actual authority and the different ways in which the shareholders have to act collectively in order to override these limits can be viewed as part of a company's governance structure and thus as part of an overall scheme of protection for its shareholders. However, at first glance, it seems an unnecessarily complex means of doing so. It is likely to add to the potential burden on third parties insofar as they face a risk of invalidity due to the limits on a board's actual authority. Further, the constitution of a company has to work with the unitary board system of governance,[15] which means that there is no

---

[10] *Boschoek Proprietary v Fuke* [1906] Ch 148.

[11] *Ibid.*

[12] The shareholders have mandatory powers to alter the company's objects clause and its articles of association by special resolution: Companies Act 1985, ss 4 and 9. See the further discussion of these powers below.

[13] An ordinary resolution requires a simple majority of votes and is subject to the standard notice requirements for a general meeting (at least 14 days' notice). A special resolution requires a majority in favour of 'not less than three-fourths' of votes and is subject to at least 21 days' notice: Companies Act 1985, s 378(1) and (2). See generally on the various kinds of shareholder resolutions P Davies, *Gower and Davies' Principles of Modern Company Law* 7th ed (London, Sweet & Maxwell, 2003) ('Gower & Davies') at 343–46.

[14] See, for example, *Re Torvale Group* [1999] 2 BCLC 605.

[15] On the management structure of a company and the unitary board system in English company law, see generally Gower & Davies at 38–40 and 316–26. See also *The Report of the Committee on the Financial Aspects of Corporate Governance* ('the Cadbury Report') (Chairman: Sir Adrian Cadbury) (London, Gee, 1992).

special organ that can monitor the board and complement the board's powers on behalf of the shareholders.[16] In effect, the body of shareholders is the only available secondary decision-maker for the company. However, the shareholders may not be well suited for a governance role. This can affect the value of setting limits on the powers of the board as a safeguard in a company's governance structure and has implications for the rules of law discussed in later chapters of this book.

This chapter will explore these issues in more detail. It will start by examining the legal nature of a company's constitution and its role in limiting the actual authority of the company's board. It will then examine the allocation of powers of management—including the power to make contracts—in the unitary board system and the complementary role that shareholders have to play in such a system. This will lead on to a deeper analysis of the various limits that can be placed on the actual authority of a company's board and the significance of these limits for third parties.

2 THE CONSTITUTION OF A COMPANY

2.1 The Legal Role of the Constitution

The constitution of a company, in conjunction with the provisions in the Companies Act 1985 governing its legal effect,[17] is the legal source of the actual authority of a company's board to make contracts on its behalf or to confer actual authority on other corporate agents.[18] It is also the legal source of the authority to affix the company's common seal.

The Companies Act requires the constitution to consist of a separate memorandum and articles of association, but the Company Law Review has recommended a simplified format consisting of one document, with companies no longer required to set out their objects.[19] The Company Law Review has not recommended any change in the legal role of the constitution as the source of the board's contractual power.

---

[16] This can be contrasted with the 'two-tier' or 'supervisory' board systems available in other jurisdictions. English company law currently makes no provision for companies to adopt a two-tier board structure, The SE, which can only be formed by companies already incorporated within the European Union, is designed to facilitate cross-border mergers within the Union. European Companies can be formed in any Member State and they must have the option of adopting a two-tier structure. See V Edwards, 'The European Company—Essential Tool or Eviscerated Dream?' (2003) 40 *Common Market Law Review* 443 and E Werklauff, 'The SE Company—A New Common European Company from 8 October 2004' [2003] *European Business Law Review* 85.

[17] Companies Act 1985, s 14(1).

[18] *Oakbank Oil v Crum* (1882) 8 App Cas 65 at 71, per the Earl of Selborne.

[19] See Company Formation at 2.13–2.29. See also the 2002 White Paper at 2.2–2.5. See chapter 1 at n 60 for further details of the DTI's Company Law Review, its various reports and the 2002 White Paper.

2.2 The Format of a Company's Constitution

A company's memorandum of association must set out its objects.[20] These are usually drafted in the widest possible terms, but nevertheless set an overall limit on the actual authority of a company's board.[21] The typical objects clause also lists in detail various powers that may be exercised on behalf of the company and these form the basis of the board's powers of management, including the power to make contracts. The memorandum sets out the overall limits within which the articles operate. Since the shareholders do not have a mandatory general power to alter the memorandum by special resolution,[22] it can be used to entrench provisions in the constitution.[23] The Company Law Review's proposed reform of the constitution would not preclude the possibility of having entrenched provisions.[24]

A company's articles of association provide detailed rules for organising and managing its affairs in pursuit of the objectives declared in its memorandum. They usually contain the provision that formally vests general powers of management in the board. Thus, the model articles set out in Table A include a regulation in the following terms:[25]

> Subject to the provisions of the Act, the memorandum and the articles and to any directions given by special resolution, the business of the company shall be managed by the directors who may exercise all the powers of the company.

The articles may set further limits on the actual authority of a company's board. They can do this either by limiting the powers of the company itself or by limiting the board's authority to exercise these powers.[26] Both

[20] See Companies Act 1985, s 3(3).
[21] See Companies Act 1985, s 35(3) (as amended by the Companies Act 1989), which ensures that the directors of a company remain under a duty not to exceed its objects clause.
[22] The shareholders have mandatory general powers to alter the objects clause and the articles of association by special resolution: see Companies Act 1985, ss 4(1) and 9(1). These powers are limited so that a member cannot be bound by an alteration imposing an additional burden unless he consents to the alteration in writing: Companies Act 1985, s 16. Dissenting shareholders are also protected against unfair exercise of these powers by a rather nebulous duty of good faith that they should only be exercised *bona fide* in the best interests of the shareholders as a whole and by the remedy against unfair prejudice under s 459 of the Companies Act 1985. On the duty of good faith, see Gower & Davies at 486–94. See also the Company Law Review's discussion of this point: Completing the Structure at 5.94–5.99 and Final Report at 7.52–7.62.
[23] S 17(1) of the Companies Act 1985 provides that any provisions in the memorandum which could lawfully have been set out in the articles may be altered by special resolution, although an application can be made to the court for an alteration to be cancelled. However, s 17(2) provides that this does not apply 'where the memorandum itself provides for or prohibits the alteration of all or any' of the relevant provisions.
[24] See Company Formation at 2.27 and the 2002 White Paper at 2.3.
[25] Companies (Tables A to F) Regulations 1985 SI/1985/805, Table A ('Table A'), reg 70. The Company Law Review has suggested a revised version of Table A for private companies, which includes a clause vesting general powers of management in substantially the same form: see Final Report, Volume II, ch 17.
[26] *Boschoek Proprietary v Fuke* [1906] Ch 148.

the memorandum and the articles of a company can also attach special rights to certain shares, in which case they constitute 'class rights'. Class rights can only be altered or abrogated in accordance with a special procedure.[27] This is a further means of setting entrenched limits on the actual authority of a company's board.[28]

2.3 The Legal Effect of a Company's Constitution

The Companies Act provides:[29]

> Subject to the provisions of this Act, the memorandum and articles, when registered, bind the company and its members to the same extent as if they respectively had been signed and sealed by each member, and contained covenants on the part of each member to observe all the provisions of the memorandum and of the articles.

As a contract, the constitution of a company has some unusual features.[30] Its parties are the company's shareholders from time to time who enter into or exit from the contract through the act of becoming or ceasing to be shareholders. And since the model articles set out in Table A are deemed to be the articles of a company unless any constitution actually registered for the company provides otherwise,[31] shareholders can be deemed to be parties to provisions of which they have no knowledge.

Further, as Steyn LJ noted in *Bratton Seymour Service Co v Oxborough*:[32]

> [T]he contract can be altered by a special resolution without the consent of all the contracting parties. It is also, unlike an ordinary contract, not defeasible on the grounds of misrepresentation, common law mistake, mistake in equity, undue influence or duress. Moreover … it cannot be rectified on the grounds of mistake.

---

[27] Companies Act 1985, s 125. See generally on class rights the judgment of Scott J in *Cumbrian Newspapers Group v Cumberland & Westmorland Herald Newspapers* [1987] Ch 1.

[28] When the shareholders operate collectively, they do so through the voting rights attached to their shares. These too are governed by the company's constitution. Whilst there is a general presumption that all shares should have equal rights and that every share should have one vote, express provisions in the constitution can override this. This provides a further means of altering the practical significance of mandatory powers exercisable through majority voting. A constitution can, for example, give certain shares greater voting rights than others or provide that certain shareholders should have enhanced voting rights in designated circumstances: see, for example, *Pender v Lushington* (1877) 6 Ch D 70 and *Bushell v Faith* [1970] AC 1099 (HL).

[29] Companies Act, s 14(1).

[30] See generally Gower & Davies at 58–65.

[31] Companies Act 1985, s 8(2). Table A only applies to companies limited by shares. There are other models for other kinds of company.

[32] [1992] BCC 471 (CA) at 475. See also *Towcester Racecourse Company v The Racecourse Association* [2002] EWHC 2141 and *Folkes Group plc v Alexander* [2002] EWHC 51.

Steyn LJ summarised the legal nature of the constitution as follows:[33]

> It is ... a statutory contract of a special nature with its own distinctive features. It derives its binding force not from a bargain struck between the parties, but from the terms of the statute. It is binding only in so far as it affects the rights and obligations between the company and the members acting in their capacity as members.

Steyn LJ here touched upon an old debate in company law, namely how far individual shareholders can enforce obligations that the constitution imposes on the company and its management, but which do not relate to the shareholders' position as shareholders in the company.[34] Individual shareholders can enforce provisions in the constitution against the company that relate to their position as shareholders and can on this basis compel the company's management to observe the constitution.[35] A company has a reciprocal right to enforce the terms of the constitution against a shareholder and the shareholders of a company can enforce the terms of its articles directly against each other.[36]

However, case law has suggested that there are limits to a shareholder's right to enforce the terms of a company's constitution, as Steyn LJ noted in the *Bratton Seymour* case:[37]

> If [the constitution] contains provisions conferring rights and obligations on outsiders, then those provisions do not bite as part of the contract between the company and the members, even if the member is coincidentally a member. Similarly, if the provisions are not truly referable to the rights and obligations of members as such, it does not operate as a contract.

It has long been settled that an outsider cannot enforce provisions in a company's constitution that purport to confer some kind of benefit on him or her.[38] The constitution might, for example, provide that the company

---

[33] [1992] BCC 471 at 475.

[34] See Gower & Davies at 62–5 and R Drury, 'The Relative Nature of a Shareholder's Right to Enforce the Company Contract' [1986] *Cambridge Law Journal* 219. See also K Wedderburn, 'Shareholders' Rights and the Rule in *Foss v Harbottle*' [1957] *Cambridge Law Journal* 193 and [1958] *Cambridge Law Journal* 93; G Goldberg, 'The Enforcement of Outsider Rights under s 20(1) of the Companies Act 1948' (1972) 35 *Modern Law Review* 362; G Prentice, 'The Enforcement of "Outsider" Rights' (1980) 1 *Company Lawyer* 179; R Gregory, 'The Section 20 Contract' (1981) 44 *Modern Law Review* 526; and G Goldberg, 'The Controversy on the Section 20 Contract Revisited' (1985) 48 *Modern Law Review* 158. S 20 of the Companies Act 1948 was the predecessor of s 14 of the Companies Act 1985.

[35] *Pender v Lushington* (1877) LR 6 Ch D 70; *Wood v Odessa Waterworks* (1889) LR 42 Ch D 636.

[36] *Hickman v Romney or Kent Sheepbreeders Association* [1915] 1 Ch 881; *Rayfield v Hands* [1960] Ch 1.

[37] [1992] BCC 471 at 475.

[38] *Eley v Positive Government Security Life Assurance Co* (1876) 1 Ex D 88 (CA); *Browne v La Trinidad* (1887) 37 Ch D 1 (CA).

would obtain legal advice from a specified firm or that a specified person should be one of its directors.[39] Outsiders can only make enforceable arrangements for such matters through a separate extrinsic contract with the company that is valid and binding on the company, in accordance with the law governing contracting with companies.[40]

However, in *Hickman v Romney or Kent Sheepbreeders Association*,[41] Astbury J held that shareholders were also unable to enforce such 'outsider' provisions since they did not relate to shareholding, although the point was *obiter* to his decision in that case. On this basis, shareholders would also have to secure enforceable rights on such outsider matters through a separate contract. In *Beattie v Beattie*,[42] the Court of Appeal confirmed Astbury J's view, as did Steyn LJ in the *Bratton Seymour* case. However, this view has attracted academic criticism on the basis that all shareholders should have an enforceable right that the company's affairs be managed in accordance with all the terms of its constitution.[43] The fact that this might enable a shareholder to enforce outsider rights should be irrelevant.

The Company Law Review recommended that individual shareholders should have the right to enforce all provisions in a company's constitution both against the company itself and against other members, unless the constitution expressly provides otherwise.[44] It rejected the view that allowing shareholders to enforce outsider rights in this way would lead to a lengthening of constitutions to include matters normally dealt with outside the constitution, such as in a shareholders' agreement.[45] It recommended, however, that there should be a suitable transitional period before the new rule could apply to existing companies.[46]

---

[39] See *Globalink Telecommunications v Wilmbury* [2002] EWHC 1988 at 30, per Burnton J: 'The Articles are not automatically binding as between a company and its officers as such. In so far as the Articles are applicable to the relationship between a company and its officers, the Articles may be expressly or impliedly incorporated in the contract between the company and a director.' See also *John v Price Waterhouse* [2002] 1 WLR 953 at para 26, per Ferris J.

[40] On how third parties can legitimately impose limits on the discretionary power of a company's board through obtaining contractual undertakings or covenants, see A Griffiths, 'The Best Interests of Fulham FC' [1993] *Journal of Business Law* 576 and T Courtney, 'Fettering Directors' Discretion' (1995) 16 *Company Lawyer* 227.

[41] [1915] 1 Ch 881. The principle was drawn from cases in which outsiders had been unable to enforce provisions in companies' constitutions purporting to confer rights upon them: see *Re Tavarone Mining Co* (1873) LR 8 Ch App 956; *Melhado v Porto Alegre* (1874) LR 9 CP 503; *Eley v Positive Life Assurance Co* (1876) 1 Ex D 503; *Browne v La Trinidad* (1887) 37 Ch D 1.

[42] *Beattie v Beattie* [1938] Ch 708 (CA).

[43] See especially K Wedderburn, 'Shareholders' Rights and the Rule in *Foss v Harbottle*' [1957] CLJ 193 and [1958] CLJ 93.

[44] Completing the Structure at 5.73; Final Report at 7.34–7.40.

[45] Final Report at 7.38.

[46] See Final Report at 7.40.

2.4 The Economic Significance of Shareholders' Rights under the Constitution

It is arguable, however, that there is an economic reason for restricting the right of individual shareholders to enforce the terms of a company's constitution so as to exclude the enforceability of outsider rights and thereby discourage outsider matters from being dealt with in the constitution.[47] Such a restriction maintains a clear separation of the various contractual relationships focused on a company. It limits the constitution to 'ownership' or 'membership' matters. Since outsider rights concern the provision of inputs other than equity capital (or matters unrelated to the provision and rewarding of equity capital), allowing them to intrude into the constitution would undermine the clarity of the separation.

The economic role of the constitution is to provide a basis for the structuring of the contractual relationship concerning the provision of equity capital to the company and the return on that capital. It provides a governance structure for managing this relationship over time and the rights of individual shareholders to enforce the constitution, along with the shareholders' collective powers, form part of that governance structure. Several features of the constitution that are hard to reconcile with the idea of the constitution as a contract among all the shareholders make sense when it is viewed as a governance structure.

The constitution has to establish a governance structure that is flexible, but with adequate safeguards against the abuse of managerial discretion. It has to strike an efficient balance between these competing goals in the sense of maximising the benefits of managerial flexibility, minimising the risk of abuse and minimising the costs of the safeguards employed to reduce the risk of abuse. The collective rights of the shareholders provide a safeguard against abuse and these rights are governed by the constitution.[48]

The efficiency of collective rights as a safeguard is reduced when they are organised in such a way that individuals or relatively small groups have a power of veto since they can exploit this opportunistically, leading to a costly economic problem known as 'holdout'.[49] This provides an economic explanation for enabling shareholders to exercise their collective powers through various forms of majority voting rather than requiring them to do so unanimously. Efficiency is also improved when the holders of collective rights have a broadly similar interest in these rights.[50] This provides an economic reason for preventing outsider rights from intruding into the constitution.

---

[47] See in particular R Drury, [1986] *Cambridge Law Journal* 219 for an analysis of the issue that takes account of its economic significance.
[48] See generally chapter 2.
[49] See R Cooter and T Ulen, *Law & Economics* (London, Pearson Addison Wesley, 2004) 4th ed at 176–8.
[50] See H Hansmann, 'Ownership of the Firm' (1988) 4 *Journal of Law, Economics & Organisation* 267.

The efficiency of collective rights as a safeguard depends on how clearly they are specified and on the avoidance of unnecessary complexity in their structuring. This provides a further reason for excluding outsider rights from the constitution. Outsider rights conflict with the vesting of general powers of management in the board by purporting to pre-empt certain decisions that would otherwise be for the board to take. They may also deal with these matters with less clarity than would be required in a separate contract and may provide inadequate guidance on how the outsider rights are to be reconciled with the board's general discretion over management. Requiring a separate contract for such matters should ensure that they are addressed properly.

3 THE MANAGEMENT STRUCTURE OF A COMPANY

3.1 The Board of Directors

3.1.1 The Board as a Company's Principal Organ of Management

A company has two principal decision-making bodies or 'organs'.[51] These are its board of directors and its body of shareholders.[52] Companies could in theory have additional organs, but company law does not facilitate any significant departure from the unitary board system.[53]

A company's board is its principal organ of management, but company law does not mandate its powers. Company law does not even have a standard term for identifying this body. Although the terms 'the board' and 'the board of directors' are often used in practice, legislation generally refers simply to 'the directors'.[54] The Companies Act 1985 defines a 'director' as 'any person occupying the position of director, by whatever name called' and provides that a company must have a minimum number

[51] The word 'organ' is used here loosely in the sense of a decision-making body that can act on behalf of a company because the company's constitution invests it with the power to act as or for the company for certain matters. In other jurisdictions, the term 'organ' has a different significance because the law may vest certain powers to act for the company directly in such a body. See the judgment of Hoffmann LJ in *El Ajou v Dollar Land Holdings* [1994] BCC 143 at 159 and V Edwards, *EC Company Law* (Oxford, Oxford EC Law Library, 1999) at 33–7.
[52] The term 'shareholders' will be used to refer to the members of a company unless the context requires otherwise. The two expressions tend to be used interchangeably, although strictly speaking the term 'members' is broader since some companies do not have a share capital: see Gower & Davies at 7–10. The shareholders are also referred to collectively as 'the company' or 'the company in general meeting', which reflects the traditional identity of a company with its shareholders as a body: see Gower & Davies at 372.
[53] This may change with the advent of the European Company: see above.
[54] See, for example, Table A. S 35A of the Companies 1985 refers to 'the board of directors' and is a notable exception, reflecting its origins in the European Community's First Company Law Directive: 68/151 [1968] OJ 68 ('the First Directive'). See generally the judgment of Robert Walker LJ in *Smith v Henniker-Major* [2002] EWCA Civ 762 at 19–23. The Company Law Review has proposed that s 35A be replaced with a new provision, which may also refer to 'the board of directors': see the 2002 White Paper, Draft Clauses, clause 17.

of these.[55] However, it is left to the constitution of each company to specify how 'the directors' should operate collectively and exercise the powers of management vested in them.

The management structure of a company includes its board and any subordinate agents, including employees, to whom its board delegates powers of management. A company's constitution usually permits its board to delegate the general powers of management vested in it, but some of the board's powers are non-delegable.[56] Since the law has come to treat directors as fiduciaries,[57] a company's board can only delegate the discretionary powers vested in it if the company's constitution expressly authorises it to do so and in effect vests a power of delegation in the board.[58] A board must, however, exercise any power of delegation in accordance with its duties, in particular its general duty of good faith and its duty of care.[59] Also, the board of a company faces a continuing duty to supervise and control those to whom it has delegated powers of management.[60] This includes ensuring that there are effective control systems in place where this is the appropriate means of exercising supervision and that these systems are working properly.[61]

3.1.2 The Board's Autonomy as an Organ of the Company

The shareholders of a company have a mandatory power to remove directors by ordinary resolution.[62] However, the board has autonomous

---

[55] S 741(1) of the Companies Act 1985 defines a 'director' and s 282 provides that a private company must have at least one director and that every company other than a private company (unless registered before 1 November 1929) must have at least two directors.

[56] The House of Lords has held that a general power of delegation is not sufficient for the board to be able to delegate its power to award remuneration to directors since this power must be expressly vested in the board through an enabling article: *Guinness v Saunders* [1990] 2 AC 663 (HL).

[57] This reflects the use of the trust in unincorporated joint stock companies prior to the Joint Stock Companies Act 1844 to facilitate the holding of property, given that these companies were in fact partnerships of all their members. The members delegated powers of management to directors and vested the company's property in trustees. Trustees were often directors as well. See P Davies, *Gower's Principles of Modern Company Law* (London, Sweet & Maxwell, 1997) 6th ed ('Gower') at 29–30 and see generally R Harris, *Industrializing English Law* (Cambridge, Cambridge University Press, 2000) ('Harris'). However, the law has not always been consistent in its treatment of the directors of incorporated companies as being trustees as well as agents of the company: see, for example, J Hill, 'Changes in the Role of the Shareholder' in R Grantham and C Rickett (eds), *Corporate Personality in the 20th Century* (Oxford, Hart Publishing, 1998) ('Grantham & Rickett') at 179–181. See also L Sealy, 'The Director as Trustee' [1967] *Cambridge Law Journal* 83.

[58] This is included as part of a specific duty relating to 'delegation and independence of judgment' in the proposed codification of directors' duties pursuant to the Company Law Review: see 2002 White Paper, Draft Clauses, Schedule 2, clause 3.

[59] See, for example, *Dorchester Finance Co v Stebbing* [1989] BCLC 498 and *Bishopsgate Management v Maxwell* [1993] BCC 120.

[60] *Re Barings plc (No 5)* [1999] 1 BCLC 433 and *(No 6)* [2000] 1 BCLC 523 (CA).

[61] *Ibid.*

[62] Companies Act 1985, s 303.

discretion to exercise the general powers of management vested in it by the company's constitution within the limits set by the constitution. In other words, the shareholders acting collectively through simple majority voting are not the principal of the board in terms of agency law and therefore have no general power to override or interfere with the board's powers of management.[63]

The shareholders as a body have various powers vested in them by company law and by the constitution of their company, but they must operate collectively in the appropriate manner to exercise these powers. The model articles in Table A, for example, provide that the shareholders can give directions to the board by special resolution.[64] The shareholders also have certain mandatory powers to alter, and thus to override, the terms of the company's constitution by special resolution.[65] By using these powers, the shareholders can extend, tighten or override the limits on the board's powers of management. However, the constitution of a company can be drafted to entrench limits on the board's powers and put them beyond the reach of a special resolution. This is the case where such limits are specified in the company's memorandum, or attached as class rights to certain shares, or where the voting rights attached to certain shares are increased so as to give them a power of veto.[66]

In *Automatic Self-Cleansing Filter Syndicate v Cunninghame*, Collins MR confirmed that the board is an autonomous organ in a company's governance structure set up by the constitution and that the shareholders' collective powers on matters of management are limited accordingly:[67]

> It is by the consensus of all the [shareholders] in the company that these directors become agents and hold their rights as agents. It is not fair to say that a majority at a meeting is for the purposes of this case the principal so as to alter the mandate of the agent. The minority must also be taken into account. There are provisions by which the minority may be over-borne, but that can only be done by special machinery in the shape of special resolutions.[68] Short of that the mandate which must be obeyed is not that of the majority, it is that of the whole entity made up of all the shareholders. If the mandate of the directors is to be altered, it can only be under the machinery of the memorandum and articles themselves.

[63] *Automatic Self-Cleansing Filter Syndicate Co Ltd v Cunninghame* [1906] 2 Ch 34 (CA); *Gramophone & Typewriter v Stanley* [1908] 2 KB 89 (CA); *Quin & Axtens, v Salmon* [1909] AC 442 (HL); *Shaw (John) & Sons (Salford) v Shaw* [1935] 2 KB 113 (CA); *Breckland v London & Suffolk Properties* [1989] BCLC 100.
[64] Table A, reg 70.
[65] See Companies Act 1985, s 4 (objects clause) and s 9 (articles of association).
[66] See above at nn 23–8 on these constitutional devices.
[67] [1906] 2 Ch 34 at 42–3. See also the judgment of Cozens-Hardy LJ at 44–5.
[68] Both Warrington J and the Court of Appeal attached significance to the fact that, at the time of this case, the shareholders' collective power to remove directors was exercisable by special resolution and regarded this as supporting their decision in this case, although in principle it should have made no difference. The power is now exercisable by ordinary resolution: Companies Act 1985, s 303.

Again, in *Shaw v Shaw*, Greer LJ emphasised that the constitution of a company assigns certain powers to its board and certain powers to the shareholders as a collective decision-making body operating through simple majority voting. Each of these organs has autonomy within its own sphere and it would subvert the constitution to allow one organ to usurp powers vested in the other.[69]

However, a company's board only has autonomy within the scope of the general powers of management vested in it. The company must have complementary powers, as the board's principal, to enable it to override these limits and to ratify unauthorised actions. The body of shareholders, as the only other organ of governance, must be able to exercise these complementary powers on behalf of the company. As will be seen, it can exercise some, but not all, of them through simple majority voting.

3.1.3 The Operation of the Board as an Organ of Governance

Table A provides that 'the directors may regulate their proceedings as they think fit';[70] that 'a meeting of directors at which a quorum is present may exercise all powers exercisable by the directors';[71] that the 'quorum for the transaction of the business of the directors may be fixed by the directors and unless so fixed at any other number shall be two';[72] and that a resolution signed in writing by all directors should be as valid and effectual as if it had been passed at a duly-convened meeting.[73] There is therefore little prescription as to how the directors are supposed to act collectively as the board and exercise the powers vested in them in that capacity.

If the directors are not in agreement about the exercise of their powers, then some degree of formality is necessary for them to act as a collective decision-making organ and exercise their powers through majority voting in accordance with the constitution. In *Barron v Potter*,[74] for example, one of a company's two directors attempted to hold a board meeting as his fellow director stepped off a train at Paddington station. He purported to appoint additional directors against the wishes of the other on the basis that he had a casting vote. Warrington J rejected the argument that this amounted to an action of the company's board:[75]

Of course, if directors are willing to hold a meeting they may do so under any circumstances, but one of them cannot be made to attend the board or

---

[69] *John Shaw & Sons (Salford) v Shaw* [1935] 2 KB 113 at 134. See also *Breckland Group Holdings v London and Suffolk Properties Ltd and Others* [1989] BCLC 100.
[70] Table A, reg 88.
[71] Table A, reg 70.
[72] Table A, reg 89.
[73] Table A, reg 93.
[74] [1914] 1 Ch 895.
[75] [1914] 1 Ch 895 at 901.

to convert a casual meeting into a board meeting, and in the present case I do not see how the meeting in question can be treated as a board meeting.

But where the directors of a company are unanimous, or at least concur in a particular course of action, they can exercise the powers vested in them informally as long as the company's constitution does not expressly preclude this.[76] In *Re Bonelli's Telegraph Co*, Sir James Bacon V-C said:[77]

> [T]he 'combined wisdom' [of the directors] is required in this sense, that they must all be of one mind. But I do not know that it is necessary they shall all meet in one place ... If you are satisfied that the persons whose concurrence is necessary to give validity to the act did so concur, with full knowledge of all that they were doing, in my opinion the terms of the law are fully satisfied ...

It has also been held that a director can concur in a decision such that it amounts to a decision of the board without expressing positive approval of the decision.[78]

Nevertheless, collective passive acquiescence may not always be enough and in some situations an active indication of assent may be required from each director.[79] This is likely to depend on the overall circumstances, taking

---

[76] *Re Bonelli's Telegraph Co* (1871) LR 12 Eq 246; *Charterhouse Investment Trust v Tempest Diesels* (1985) 1 BCC 99; *Runciman v Runciman plc* [1993] BCC 223.

[77] (1871) LR 12 Eq 246 at 258.

[78] *Runciman v Runciman plc* [1993] BCC 223. The issue in this case was whether the board of a company had approved an extended term for its former chairman's service contract, given that only the board had the power to do this. The relevant decision had been taken some years before the chairman's dismissal after a takeover, but had never been approved at a board meeting nor discussed by the directors as a body. Simon Brown J held that the board at the time were entitled to act informally because the company's articles did not require otherwise and that they had made a decision because all of the directors of the company, apart from the chairman himself, had concurred in that decision. He held that it did not even matter that some of the directors had not expressly given their positive approval to the extension: '[their] involvement went beyond mere informal acquiescence ... when they were acquainted with the proposals following approval by the non-executive directors they, as directors, had the opportunity to query them. The mere fact that they never apparently did so and that their views were not more explicitly canvassed seems to me nothing to the point: by the time of the implementation of the various salary increases, and more obviously still by the time [the chairman] came to assert his notice term, such terms were indeed "as determined" by the other board members and none of them could possibly have been heard to assert the contrary.' See [1993] BCC 223 at 230.

[79] In *Freeman & Lockyer v Buckhurst Properties*, for example, the Court of Appeal held that the directors of a company had not conferred the actual authority of a managing director on one of their number. All the directors had acquiesced in the situation, but they had not formally met to express their consent. Diplock LJ said, 'I accept that such actual authority could have been conferred by the board without a formal resolution recorded in the minutes, although this would have rendered them liable to a default fine under s 145(4) of the Companies Act 1948. But to confer actual authority would have required not merely the silent acquiescence of the individual members of the board, but the communication by words or conduct of their respective consents to one another and to [the director purporting to act as a managing director]': see [1964] 1 QB 480 at 501. The court did, however, find that the board's conduct amounted to a representation of ostensible authority: see generally chapter 6.

account of the nature of the decision at issue and the extent to which each director has had an opportunity to give the decision consideration and to express a view on it.

The ability of the directors of a company to operate as the board and exercise their collective powers informally bears some resemblance to the unanimous consent rule or so-called '*Duomatic* principle'.[80] This rule permits a company's shareholders to exercise their collective powers informally through unanimous consent or acquiescence.[81] However, the legal basis is different. The unanimous consent rule reflects company law's roots in partnership law and the view of a company's constitution as a contract to which all the shareholders are party.[82] From this perspective, regulations in a constitution prescribing how shareholders must exercise their collective powers can be viewed as contractual entitlements, which the shareholders are free to waive. Informal consent in effect operates as a form of waiver.[83]

The unanimous consent rule can also apply to powers that are vested in the shareholders by statute, but only insofar as these powers are intended merely to benefit the shareholders and do not serve some wider purpose as well.[84] The unanimous consent rule therefore has some flexibility to take account of such factors.[85] In the case of any procedural constraints on the powers of the board, the directors are not the beneficiaries of these constraints and therefore have no power to waive them unless they are also the company's only shareholders.[86] The relevant provisions in a company's constitution should therefore be construed to see whether its directors are required to observe any particular formalities in exercising

---

[80] *Re Duomatic Ltd* [1969] 2 Ch 365; *Cane v Jones* [1980] 1 WLR 1451; *Multinational Gas v Multinational Gas Services* [1983] 1 Ch 258 (CA); *Re New Cedos Engineering* [1994] 1 BCLC 797; *Euro Brokers v Monecor (London)* [2003] EWCA Civ 105.

[81] See Gower & Davies at 305–6 and 334–7. The principle also applies to class rights enjoyed by particular groups of shareholders, in which case it is the relevant group of shareholders that must be unanimous: *Re Torvale Group* [2000] BCC 626; *EIC Services v Phipps* [2003] EWHC 1507.

[82] See above.

[83] See *Re Torvale Group* [2000] BCC 626 at 636; *Euro Brokers v Monecur (London)* [2003] EWCA Civ 105 at 62. Note, however, the comment of Neuberger J in *EIC Services v Phipps*: 'Whether the approval is given in advance or after the event, whether it is characterised as agreement, ratification, waiver or estoppel, and whether members of the group [of shareholders] give their consent in different ways at different times, does not matter': [2003] EWHC 1507 at 122.

[84] *Precision Dippings v Precision Dippings Marketing* [1986] Ch 447 (CA); *Wright v Atlas Wright (Europe)* [1999] 2 BCLC 301 (CA). See J Gray, 'Court of Appeal Applies Duomatic Principle in Dispute over Financing Joint Venture's Regulatory Capital' (2003) 24 *Company Lawyer* 275; R Goddard, 'The Re Duomatic Principle and Sections 320–322 of the Companies Act 1985' [2004] *Journal of Business Law* 121.

[85] Preserving the flexibility of the unanimous consent rule has been put forward as an argument against codifying it in statute: see the 2002 White Paper at 2.31–2.35. The Company Law Review had recommended codifying it: see Developing the Framework at 4.21–4.23, Completing the Structure at 5.13–5.17 and Final Report at 7.17–7.26.

[86] See *Re Express Engineering Works* [1920] 1 Ch 466 (CA). Here, the directors of the company were also its only shareholders.

the powers vested in them collectively.[87] If so, then the directors would have to observe these formalities in order to operate as the board.

The question of whether a contract has been made by the board of a company or by an *ad hoc* grouping of directors (and thus by a subordinate agent) can be crucial to its validity for two reasons. First, certain powers vested in the board may be non-delegable, such as the power to award remuneration to directors.[88] Secondly, as will be seen in chapter 5, there is a statutory rule of attribution that applies to the power of a company's 'board of directors' to make contracts, but not to the power of directors acting in any other capacity.[89]

3.2 The Shareholders

3.2.1 The Role of Shareholders in Corporate Governance

The formal division of function between a company's shareholders and its board distinguishes the company from other legal structures for a business such as the partnership and limited liability partnership. However, the shareholders, who are also referred to as 'the company' or 'the company in general meeting',[90] are often referred to collectively as the 'owners' of their company, as if they were in fact partners.[91] An ownership role is also reflected in the nature of their powers over the company's affairs. Thus, they have ultimate control over management through their mandatory power to remove any of the company's directors from office by ordinary resolution.[92] And the constitutions of companies usually give their shareholders the power to appoint, to reappoint and to confirm the interim appointment of directors.[93] Further, as noted above, the shareholders

---

[87] *Re Bonelli's Telegraph Co* (1871) LR 12 Eq 246.

[88] *Guinness v Saunders* [1990] 2 AC 663 (HL); *Runciman v Runciman plc* [1993] BCC 223. This stems from the rule of equity whereby directors have no inherent entitlement to receive any remuneration from their company: *Hutton v West Cork Railway Co* (1883) 23 Ch D 654 (CA). This rule can be overridden by an enabling provision in the company's constitution such as that in regulation 85 of Table A. However, in *Guinness*, the House of Lords held that the power conferred by an enabling article is non-delegable and must be exercised by the board unless the constitution expressly provides otherwise. A committee of directors had no authority therefore to exercise the power and the House of Lords held that the payment of a bonus authorised by such a committee was void and that the company was entitled to recover it in full: see generally chapter 7.

[89] *Smith v Henniker-Major* [2002] BCC 544 (Ch D); [2002] EWCA Civ 762.

[90] This identification of the shareholders with the company is reflected in the interpretation of the directors' duty of good faith to exercise their powers *bona fide* in the best interests of the company as requiring them to focus on the interests of the shareholders: see generally J Parkinson, *Corporate Power and Responsibility* (Oxford, Clarendon Press, 1993) ('Parkinson') at 74–92.

[91] See, for example, the Cadbury Report.

[92] Companies Act 1985, s 303.

[93] See, for example, Table A, regs 73–80.

have various mandatory powers to alter the company's constitution and thus to reshape or override its governance structure, which are exercisable by special resolution.[94]

A company is supposed to be managed for the benefit of its shareholders,[95] which is consistent with the view that they are the owners of the company. However, their limited liability means that they are not owners in the same way as partners and ownership is only one of a number of ways that the relationship between a company and its shareholders can be portrayed.[96] Also, the vesting of the shareholders' 'ownership' powers in a fragmented body that may consist of a large number of members with relatively small holdings can make it hard in practice for the shareholders collectively to play an active role as owners and exert effective control over the board. This apparent deficiency, which has been termed 'the separation of ownership and control', increases the importance of other devices to ensure that the board of a company does not abuse its control of management and that it does use its powers for the benefit of the shareholders.[97]

In the economic analysis of the company, the shareholders have been presented as the 'residual claimants' on the company,[98] with their open-ended and unspecified claim on the company representing the return on the equity capital originally contributed to the company.[99] From this perspective, the function of the shareholders' collective powers is to give them a safeguard that limits the scope for the company's board to misuse their discretionary powers at the expense of the shareholders.

Since company law does not prescribe the board's role in management or the extent of its powers of management, there is nothing to prevent the shareholders as a body from having a role in management as well.[100] However, the vesting of general discretionary powers of management in

[94] A special resolution would not, however, be sufficient if the alteration would amount to the variation or abrogation of any special 'class rights' enjoyed by a particular class of shareholders: Companies Act 1985, s 125. If the shareholders are unanimous, then the *Duomatic* principle enables them to override any provision in the company's constitution.

[95] *Evans v Brunner Mond & Co* [1921] 1 Ch 359; *Parke v Daily News* [1962] Ch 927; *Multinational Gas and Petrochemical Co v Multinational Gas and Petrochemical Services* [1983] Ch 258 (CA). However, when a company is insolvent or on the verge of insolvency, the interests of its creditors intrude and displace those of the shareholders: *West Mercia Safetywear v Dodd* [1988] BCLC 250 (CA); *Re Pantone 485* [2002] 1 BCLC 266; *Colin Gwyer v London Wharf* [2002] EWHC 2748.

[96] See generally J Hill in Grantham & Rickett.

[97] See A Berle and G Means, *The Modern Corporation and Private Property* (New York, Macmillan, 1932) and the symposium on 'Corporations and Private Property' (1983) 26 *Journal of Law & Economics* 235–496.

[98] See, for example, B Cheffins, *Company Law: Theory, Structure and Operation* (Oxford, OUP, 1997) ('Cheffins') at 54–8.

[99] See generally chapter 2.

[100] The Companies Act 1985 does impose certain responsibilities on the directors of a company, in particular concerning the preparation and filing of the company's annual accounts and complying with other routine administration requirements and the constitution cannot assign these to the shareholders: see Gower & Davies at 295–6.

the board means that initiative on matters of management must lie with the board, unless the constitution expressly provides otherwise.[101] The shareholders' powers in relation to management are therefore largely ancillary to those vested in the board. In particular, they have ancillary powers that arise when the constitution sets limits on the powers vested in the board.

3.2.2 The Operation of the Shareholders as a Decision-Making Body

Subject to certain provisions of the Companies Act, the constitution of a company governs the operation of its shareholders as a collective body. The unanimous consent rule means that the shareholders can usually exercise their powers informally if they are unanimous.[102] Otherwise, they must act formally at duly convened 'general meetings' and by passing resolutions in accordance with the requisite notice periods and majorities prescribed by the Companies Act.[103]

A company's constitution also governs the voting rights of its shareholders and thus the extent of each shareholder's ability to participate in their collective decision-making. Thus, the default position is that every shareholder shall have one vote per share,[104] but the constitution can depart from this.[105] Further, unless the constitution expressly provides otherwise, shareholders vote at general meetings by a show of hands unless a poll is demanded, whereupon shareholders can exercise their full voting rights.[106]

3.2.3 The Shareholders' Powers of Management

Table A provides that the general powers of management vested in the board are subject to 'any directions given by special resolution'.[107] This would appear to vest an overriding power of management in the shareholders. The shareholders of a company could rely on this overriding power to act as its superior organ of management, but would have to be able to operate effectively as a collective body and be able to reach their decisions with the necessary majority. Unless they were unanimous, they would also have to comply with the time limits governing special resolutions and observe all the other formalities governing their ability to act as

---

[101] See, however, Table A, reg 70, which gives the shareholders acting by special resolution an overriding general power of management: see further below.
[102] See above at nn 80–6 on the unanimous consent rule.
[103] Companies Act 1985, s 378(1) and (2). See Gower & Davies at 343–6.
[104] Companies Act 1985, s 370(6).
[105] See, for example, *Pender v Lushington* (1877) 6 Ch D 70 and *Bushell v Faith* [1970] AC 1099 (HL).
[106] Companies Act 1985, ss 373–4. See generally Gower & Davies at 363–5.
[107] Table A, reg 70.

a collective body. This would be very difficult in practice unless the shareholders were a small and cohesive group with a unanimous view on the management of the company, in which case they might as well simply operate as the company's board.[108]

The shareholders also have a default power to act as their company's organ of management if the board is unable or unwilling to act for some reason.[109] This may be because the company has insufficient directors for a quorum or because the board is deadlocked.[110] This power is exercisable by ordinary resolution.[111] The shareholders' others powers relating to management are ancillary to the general powers vested in the board and arise from the limits set on those powers.[112]

3.2.4 *The Ancillary Powers of Ratification and Release*

In agency law, a principal has a complementary power to ratify a contract made by an agent who lacks any or exceeds the limits of his actual authority. [113] The principal can also sanction such a contract in advance. Further, agents are personally liable to their principal for acting without or in excess of their actual authority. A principal has the power to release an agent from this personal liability. These two ancillary powers are legally distinct, although the ratification of a contract usually resolves both issues together.[114]

Where a company is the principal, however, an organ of the company must be found to exercise the ancillary powers on its behalf. This organ is usually the body of shareholders. However, the legal nature of the particular limit at issue determines how the shareholders must act collectively in order to perform this function. This can range from an ordinary resolution (which enables the shareholders to override a simple limit on the board's actual authority to exercise the company's powers) through a special resolution (which is usually sufficient to enable the shareholders to act beyond the limits of the powers of the company) to a unanimous decision (which may be required to override certain limits entrenched in the memorandum). The position, however, is more complex in the case of the

---

[108] See, for example, *Re Express Engineering Works* [1920] 1 Ch 466 (CA).

[109] *Barron v Potter* [1914] 1 Ch 895; *Foster v Foster* [1916] 1 Ch 532.

[110] Assuming that the deadlock does not arise from the exercise of a power of veto or other blocking mechanism forming part of the company's governance structure: *Quin & Axtens, v Salmon* [1909] AC 442 (HL).

[111] See n 109.

[112] As well as the constitution, statute may impose limits on these powers: see, for example, ss 319 and 320 of the Companies Act 1985. These provisions require that the shareholders approve certain transactions to ensure their validity without actually giving the shareholders the power to make such transactions on their own initiative.

[113] See Bowstead & Reynolds, Arts 13–20.

[114] See Bowstead & Reynolds, Art 20 and S Worthington, 'Corporate Governance: Remedying and Ratifying Directors' Breaches' (2000) 116 *Law Quarterly Review* 638.

power to release directors from personal liability since the body of share-holders operating by special resolution or unanimously is not necessarily an appropriate mechanism for this kind of decision-making.[115]

Leaving aside the special difficulty entailed by having to engage in decision-making through special resolution or a more complex procedure, there are difficulties in having to rely on the shareholders to exercise the company's ancillary powers. Performing any role in management entails engaging in active decision-making and the shareholders of a company, as a collective body, are not designed or required to be effective at this func-tion. Instead, as was discussed in chapter 2, this body is likely to evolve in a way that makes it efficient for the risk-bearing function associated with shareholding, especially in the case of a public company.

The shareholders' lack of suitability for managerial decision-making means that sanctioning or ratifying contracts beyond the board's actual authority can be time-consuming and difficult. This means that placing limits on the actual authority of the board may be a costly form of safe-guard for the shareholders. This point merits some further exploration.

3.2.5 Shareholders and Managerial Decision-Making

The shareholders of a company, as a collective body, are not designed to be an effective organ for managerial decision-making, although they may be effective at this function in practice if they are small in number. However, a public company is likely to have a large number of share-holders with little active interest in the company's affairs. It would be prohibitively expensive, if not impossible, for such a body to take deci-sions about the management of the company with any speed or efficiency. It can be difficult in practice for the shareholders of a public company to exercise their mandatory 'ownership' powers. The initiative on matters such as the appointment and removal of directors tends to pass to the board, with the shareholders limited to the passive role of endorsing the decisions or recommendations of the board.[116]

A body of the size and composition of the shareholders of the typical public company is only suitable for passive or responsive decision-making, whereby propositions initiated elsewhere are formally put before the body

---

[115] See generally S Worthington, (2000) 116 *Law Quarterly Review* 638. This point is analogous to the troublesome issue of how to enforce a company's claims against its board or individ-ual directors and the rule in *Foss v Harbottle*: see generally K Wedderburn, 'Shareholders' Rights and the Rule in *Foss v Harbottle*' [1957] *Cambridge Law Journal* 193 and [1958] *Cambridge Law Journal* 93 and Gower & Davies at 443–466.

[116] Shareholders can play an active role in the governance of a company and exercise their powers effectively and decisively if they are relatively small in number. For a public com-pany, this situation can be achieved through a takeover bid, which is one reason why the 'market in corporate control' has been seen as important in the governance of public com-panies: see chapter 2.

and its members are invited to approve or reject the proposition. However, even passive decision-making can be costly and time-consuming to organise. And the shareholders of a public company are unlikely to have the expertise and information necessary to make or review decisions on matters of management. In practice, they are likely to seek and to rely upon guidance from the board.

The smaller the body of the shareholders of a company, the more suitable it is for engaging in active decision-making and exercising managerial powers. However, where the body of shareholders is small, they are also better placed to exercise effective control over the board. In companies with a small number of shareholders, there is also likely to be an extensive overlap between the board and the body of shareholders.[117] Here, the reduction in the cost of setting limits on the board's actual authority as a safeguard against abuse is offset by a reduction in the need for such a safeguard and thus in the benefit that it can yield.

3.2.6 The Governance Implications of the Ancillary Powers

In the unitary board system, there is no additional organ of governance available to exercise the company's ancillary powers.[118] Either the board itself or the body of shareholders has to perform this function. Assigning the function to the board simply means widening the scope of the board's powers and relying on other safeguards to curb the danger of mismanagement. Assigning it to the shareholders can be costly for the reasons noted above. The costs include both the costs in terms of expense and delay of having to obtain a collective decision from the shareholders and the costs in terms of transactions that are foregone (or made on less favourable terms) in order to avoid involving the shareholders.

---

[117] The economic agency problem is unlikely to be significant in such a scenario, but the different danger of a majority shareholder (or a majority grouping of shareholders) abusing their position is much greater. This other danger might lead to the presence of safeguards in the constitution that limit the collective powers of the shareholders as well as the board's actual authority, such as class rights and special voting rights.

[118] One alternative to the unitary board system, which would not require moving to a two-tier system, would be to divide the board into those directors responsible for management and those responsible for monitoring management. The responsibilities of the latter group could then include exercising complementary powers in relation to limits set on the powers of the management structure. Listed public companies are now required to have a minimum number of 'independent' non-executive directors or 'NEDs' and these have come to play an increasingly important role in their governance since the Cadbury Report. However, NEDs still function as part of a unitary board that has overall responsibility for both management and monitoring management. See generally the Cadbury Report; the Hampel Committee, *Final Report of the Committee on Corporate Governance* (London, Gee, 1998) ('the Hampel Report'); D Higgs, *Review of the Role and Effectiveness of Non-Executive Directors* (DTI, January, 2003) ('the Higgs Report'); and *The Combined Code on Corporate Governance* (Financial Reporting Council), which took effect on 1 November 2003 and implemented most, but not all, of the recommendations of the Higgs Report. See Gower & Davies at 321–6.

The practical implication of the above observations is that setting limits on the actual authority of the board of a company is of questionable value as a safeguard for shareholders. The constitutions of many companies, especially public companies, therefore tend to set very wide limits on their board's actual authority. However, since there is no prescription in this respect, those responsible for settling the terms of corporate constitutions are free to adjust and fine-tune the board's authority and can make use of a variety of constitutional devices in this respect. This flexibility, however, raises the costs that third parties must incur when they do have to find out the terms of the board's authority in order to reduce the risk of invalidity. This increases the economic significance of the overriding rules of attribution examined in the later chapters of this book.

The variety of ways in which the actual authority of a company's board can be limited, the variety of ways in which the shareholders may have to operate in order to exercise the company's ancillary powers and the bewildering complexity which some corporate constitutions might achieve all contribute to the scale of the potential transaction costs faced by third parties and will be examined in more detail below. At this point, however, it should be noted that there is an important qualification to the general principle that a company is supposed to be managed for the benefit of its shareholders and that the division of powers between a company's board and its body of shareholders can be analysed on this basis. The general principle only applies whilst a company is solvent. If a company is insolvent, or on the verge of insolvency, it has been established that the interests of the company's creditors intrude and may displace those of the shareholders.

3.2.7 Decision-Making on Behalf of an Insolvent Company

The Court of Appeal in *West Mercia Safetywear v Dodd* held that the nature of the duty of directors to exercise their discretionary powers in good faith in the best interests of the company changes when a company is insolvent.[119] Dillon LJ cited in support of this ruling the following statement by Street CJ in the Australian case of *Kinsela v Russel Kinsela Pty*:[120]

> In a solvent company the proprietary interests of the shareholders entitle them as a general body to be regarded as the company when questions of the duty of directors arise. If, as a general body, they authorise or ratify a particular course of action of the directors, there can be no challenge to the validity

[119] [1988] BCLC 250. See also *Brady v Brady* (1987) 3 BCC 535 (CA); *Re Welfab Engineers* [1990] BCLC 833; *Colin Gwyer v London Wharf (Limehouse)* [2002] EWHC 2748. See Gower & Davies at 372–4; V Finch, 'Directors' Duties Towards Creditors' (1989) 10 *Company Lawyer* 23; and J Lowry, 'The Recognition of Directors Owing Fiduciary Duties to Creditors' (2004) 1 *International Corporate Rescue* 59.
[120] [1988] BCLC 250, citing (1986) 4 NSWLR 722 at 730.

of what the directors have done. But where a company is insolvent the interests of the creditors intrude. They become prospectively entitled through the mechanism of liquidation, to displace the power of the shareholders and directors to deal with the company's assets. It is in a practical sense their assets and not the shareholders' assets that, through the medium of the company, are under the management of the directors pending either liquidation, return to solvency, or the imposition of some alternative administration.

This principle also has implications for the powers of the shareholders of a company, including their ancillary powers that arise from the limits set by the constitution on the actual authority of their company's board.

It has been argued that the shareholders can no longer rely upon the unanimous consent rule to exercise their powers informally if their company is insolvent.[121] The special statutory remedies that are available to the liquidator or administrator of an insolvent company to protect the interests of its creditors can apply to transactions that are approved by the shareholders.[122] It is arguable, therefore, that shareholders should have to take account of the interests of their company's creditors in exercising their ancillary powers and that the company's directors should have to advise them and make recommendations on this basis.[123]

4 THE ACTUAL AUTHORITY OF THE BOARD TO MAKE CONTRACTS

4.1 The Vesting of Contractual Power in the Board

4.1.1 The Vesting Process

The legal process by which the constitution of a company vests contractual power in its board and thereby confers actual authority upon the board can be broken down into stages for analysis. First, the constitution identifies the company's board and specifies how it is to operate as a decision-making organ of the company. Secondly, it formally vests powers of management in the board, including contractual power, setting limits on the power so vested and thus on the board's actual authority.

There are two distinct aspects to the second stage of the vesting process. The constitution determines the powers of the company itself. It may, however, limit the extent to which the powers of the company are

---

[121] See R Goddard [2004] *Journal of Business Law* 121. See *Walker v WA Walker Personnel* [2002] BPIR 621.

[122] For example, 'transactions at an undervalue' and 'preferences': Insolvency Act 1986, ss 238 and 239. See, for example, *Re Conegrade* [2002] EWHC 2411.

[123] See further below on the directors' fiduciary duties to express an honest opinion and not to mislead their company's shareholders when seeking the shareholders' approval to a proposed contract or other transaction.

vested in the board, thereby limiting the board's actual authority to exercise the powers of the company. Distinguishing between the different legal natures of the limits on the board's actual authority is important because the shareholders' complementary power of ratification varies according to the legal nature of the limit. This makes the law complex and the scope for confusion has been increased by the careless use of terminology, in particular by the indiscriminate use of 'ultra vires' as a general term for transactions beyond the limits of the board's contractual power.[124]

At the third stage of the vesting process, the constitution may go on to limit the board's power to delegate contractual power within the company's management structure and thus to confer actual authority on subordinate agents. The constitution may, for example, require the board to approve certain categories of contract.

4.1.2 Identifying the Board

The Companies Act requires companies to have directors and imposes certain duties on the directors of a company as an organ of the company. It does not, however, prescribe how the directors are supposed to act collectively as the board and does not provide any standard template by which a third party could identify the board and thus be certain that a particular decision or other action is in fact that of the board without having to refer to the company's constitution.[125]

The constitution of a particular company might, for example, provide that the quorum for a meeting of its board should be three directors rather than the usual two,[126] in which case a meeting to which only two directors turned up would not count as a meeting of the board.[127] The constitutions of some companies, especially ones with special protection for minority shareholders or ones being used for a joint venture, might contain more elaborate terms governing the operation of the board. Also, a constitution might well exclude any director with a conflicting interest or

---

[124] See the Court of Appeal's discussion of this point in *Rolled Steel v British Steel* [1986] 1 Ch 246, noting the blurring of conceptual distinctions in *Re David Payne & Co* [1904] 2 Ch 608 (CA), *Charterbridge Corporation v Lloyds Bank* [1970] Ch 62 and *Introductions v National Provincial Bank* [1970] Ch 199 (CA). See also Gower & Davies at 130–1.

[125] Regulations 88 to 98 of Table A provide a set of default rules covering the operation of the board, but companies are free to depart from these. A third party would not know whether a particular company had done this without checking its constitution.

[126] Table A, reg 89 provides that the 'quorum for the transaction of the business of the directors may be fixed by the directors and unless so fixed at any other number shall be two.' The quorum would have to be set at one in the case of a sole director and it has been held that a sole director can constitute a 'meeting' of the directors where this is required: see *Neptune (Vehicle Washing Equipment) v Fitzgerald* [1995] BCC 474.

[127] The role of the constitution in identifying the board of a company as well as specifying the board's contractual power was a crucial issue in *Smith v Henniker-Major* [2002] BCC 544 (Ch D) and [2002] EWCA Civ 762. The significance of this case will be discussed in chapter 5.

duty from voting at a board meeting and from counting towards the quorum for the meeting.[128]

It has been argued that the terms of the constitution governing the operation of the board are equivalent to terms setting limits on the contractual power vested in the board.[129] However, the absence of a prescribed template for the board makes this argument hard to sustain. The terms governing the operation of the board determine its identity under English law as the recipient of the contractual power that the constitution vests in the board. These terms are therefore logically prior to those terms that define the power so vested.[130] As will be seen in chapter 5, this presents a problem in applying the statutory overriding rule of attribution relating to contracts made or approved by the board.

4.2 The Specification of the Company's Contractual Power

4.2.1 The Contractual Capacity of a Company

The distinction drawn between the powers of the company and the contractual power of the board (the latter determining the actual authority of the board) is relevant to determining the nature of the shareholders' power to sanction or ratify the overriding of the limits on the board's actual authority. A further source of complication is the distinction drawn between a company's contractual capacity and the powers of the company. The contractual capacity of a company means a company's intrinsic legal ability or competence to be a party to contracts and other transactions and it sets an overall limit on the powers of the company. Again, there is a legal logic in the distinction, but the key practical issue is the nature of the shareholders' power (if any) to sanction the overriding of the limits placed on the board's actual authority.

There are two sources of limitation on the contractual capacity of a company. First, statutory and other rules of company law prohibit companies from entering into certain transactions or from entering into certain transactions in certain circumstances. Natural persons are also limited in this way and it is an aspect of the general issue of 'illegal' contracts.[131] However, company law prevents companies from effecting certain transactions that would not be a problem for natural persons. In particular, companies are subject to detailed regulation concerning the raising and

---

[128] Table A, regs 94 and 95.
[129] See the judgments of Browne-Wilkinson V-C in *International Sales & Agencies v Marcus* [1982] 3 All ER 551 and Robert Walker LJ in *Smith v Henniker-Major* [2002] EWCA Civ 762.
[130] See the judgment of Rimer J in *Smith v Henniker-Major* [2002] BCC 544.
[131] See, for example, *Bowmakers v Barnet Instruments* [1945] 1 KB 65 (CA) and *Shaw v Groom* [1970] 2 QB 504 (CA).

maintenance of share capital and this includes the prohibition of the payment of dividends and the repayment of capital to shareholders except in
accordance with a strict formal procedure and subject to compliance with
strict conditions.[132] Such prohibited contracts are void for illegality and
cannot be enforced by the third party.[133] The courts have indicated that,
when considering whether a particular transaction is in fact one prohibited
by statute, they will look at its substance rather than the form in which it
is presented.[134] Thus, when considering a payment to a shareholder of a
company that is presented as a legitimate transaction, the courts will consider whether the apparent transaction is genuine or whether in reality it
is an illegal dividend or an illegal repayment of capital.

The second source of limitation on a company's contractual capacity is
the objects clause in its memorandum of association.[135] The term 'ultra
vires' tended to be used to indicate the risk of invalidity from this source and
it was long viewed as a major flaw in the law governing contracting with
companies.[136]

4.2.2 Contractual Capacity and the Objects Clause

The general practice of drafting objects clauses in the widest possible
terms reduced the practical significance of this source of limited contractual capacity.[137] Statutory reform has largely overridden its distinctive
legal effect.[138]

The House of Lords in *Ashbury Railway Carriage v Riche* held that a
company has only a limited capacity to be a party to contracts.[139] Their

---

[132] See generally E Ferran, *Company Law & Corporate Finance* (Oxford, OUP, 1999) ('Ferran')
at 355–429.

[133] See, for example, *Heald v O'Connor* [1971] 1 WLR 497; *Aveling Barford v Perion* [1989] BCLC
626; *Bairstow v Queen's Moat Houses* [2001] 2 BCLC 531 (CA).

[134] See *Re Halt Garage* [1982] 3 All ER 1016 and *Aveling Barford* [1989] BCLC 626. The decision
in *Aveling Barford* has been criticised for creating uncertainty about the validity of intra-
group transfers of assets which are based on their book value rather than market value: see
A Mair, 'Ultra Vires and Aveling Barford' [1991] *International Company and Commercial Law
Review* at 37. However, the Company Law Review has proposed amending the definition of
'distribution' in s 263 of the Companies Act 1985 to reduce this uncertainty: Completing the
Structure at 7.20–7.23; Final Report at 10.6.

[135] See *Ashbury Railway Carriage Co v Riche* (1875) LR 7 HL 653.

[136] The Court of Appeal has indicated that the term 'ultra vires' should be limited to this
context: *Rolled Steel v British Steel* [1986] 1 Ch 246.

[137] The House of Lords noted this practice with some consternation in *Cotman v Brougham*
[1918] AC 514. Objects clauses can be given even greater scope by the use of 'sweeper'
clauses, which give the directors power to extend the range of the company's activities at
their discretion: see, for example, *Bell Houses v City Wall Properties* [1966] 2 QB 656 (CA). Note
also the very wide definition given to the expression 'to carry on business as a general commercial company' by s 3A of the Companies Act 1985 (inserted by the Companies Act 1989),
although this does not seem to have led to any reduction in the size of the typical objects
clause in practice. The Company Law Review has proposed that s 3A not be retained: see
Company Formation at 2.17.

[138] Companies Act 1985, s 35(1). This provision will be analysed in chapter 5.

[139] *Ashbury Railway Carriage & Iron Co v Riche* (1875) LR 7 HL 653.

lordships ruled that a company's legal existence is limited to the pursuit of the objects listed in its objects clause and that it has no legal capacity or competence to be a party to a transaction beyond this limit.[140] This view of incapacity is conceptually different from that stemming from a prohibition on what the company can do.[141] But for the statutory mitigation, a contract or transaction beyond this limit would be a legal nullity, unenforceable by either party.[142]

A company cannot enforce a contract that is void for lack of capacity because it has no power to ratify such a contract. The power to ratify operates by conferring actual authority retrospectively on the agent making the contract, but this presupposes that the principal was legally capable of conferring this authority at the relevant time.[143] A company has no more power to authorise a contract for which it lacks contractual capacity than it has to authorise a contract when it does not legally exist.[144]

The Companies Act 1989, which inserted a new section 35 in the Companies Act 1985, has made the effect of the objects clause on a company's contractual capacity largely irrelevant.[145] This provision will be examined further in chapter 5, but it did not address the problem directly so as to give companies an unlimited contractual capacity.[146] The Company Law Review has recommended that this now be done and a proposed clause to this effect was included in the 2002 White Paper.[147]

---

[140] Lord Chelmsford said that a contract made without capacity 'is exactly in the same condition as if no contract at all had been made, and therefore a ratification of it is not possible': (1875) LR 7 HL 653 at 679. The legal effect of a contract made with a non-existent company will be examined in chapter 4.

[141] The House of Lords in *Ashbury* expressly rejected the view that contracts beyond the scope of the objects clause were in effect prohibited by statute and therefore void for illegality. Instead, companies were viewed as having an inherently limited legal existence. In the Court of Exchequer, Blackburn J had taken a different view on this point, in reaching his conclusion that the objects clause merely restricted the contractual power of a company's board: 'I do not entertain any doubt that if, on the true construction of a statute creating a corporation, it appears to be the intention of the legislature, express or implied, that the corporation shall not enter into a particular contract, every Court, whether of law or equity, is bound to treat a contract entered into contrary to the enactment as illegal, and therefore wholly void; and to hold that a contract wholly void (*sic*) cannot be ratified': (1874) LR 9 Ex 224 at 262. As Lord Blackburn, he repeated this view in *AG v Great Eastern Railway*: '[The *Ashbury* case] appears to me to decide at all events this, that where there is an Act of Parliament creating a corporation for a particular purpose, and giving it powers for that particular purpose, what it does not expressly or impliedly authorise is to be taken to be prohibited': (1880) LR 5 HL 473 at 481.

[142] There are no reported cases in which a third party attempted to rely on a company's contractual incapacity to resist enforcement of a contract, although this was acknowledged as a theoretical possibility in *Bell Houses v City Wall*: [1966] 2 QB 656.

[143] See generally Bowstead & Reynolds, Arts 13 and 14.

[144] See generally chapter 4.

[145] The rule is varied for charitable companies: see Companies Act 1985, s 35(4).

[146] This reform followed a report commissioned by the DTI, which had recommended that companies be given unlimited contractual capacity: see generally D Prentice, *Reform of the Ultra Vires Rule: A Consultative Document* (London, DTI, 1986) ('the Prentice Report'). See Gower & Davies at 136–7.

[147] See the 2002 White Paper, Draft Clauses, clause 1(5).

The effect of section 35 is to give a company the power to ratify a contract that is beyond the scope of its objects clause and the shareholders can exercise this power by special resolution.[148]

4.3 The Powers of the Company

4.3.1 The Constitution's Role in Defining the Powers of the Company

Lack of discrimination in the use of the term 'ultra vires' has tended to blur the fact that the objects clause performs two distinct functions. As well as defining the company's contractual capacity, it sets an overall limit on the powers of the company. The distinction is important because section 35 does not address the latter issue beyond establishing that the shareholders can override the objects clause by special resolution.[149] However, the constitution of a company may set other limits on the powers of the company in addition to that resulting from the terms of its objects clause.

The practical significance of the powers of the company is that, insofar as they are not fully vested in the board, they can be exercised by the board acting with the approval of a simple majority of the shareholders. They reflect the idea that the body of shareholders through simple majority voting can also act as an organ of the company, although the vesting of general powers in the board means that it usually has to take a secondary role in management. As in the case of the board, the powers of the body of shareholders that are exercisable through simple majority voting are governed by, and therefore limited by, the terms of a company's constitution. As Lord Selborne LC said in *Oakbank Oil v Crum*:[150]

> It appears to me that directors and general meetings of companies of this sort can have no powers by implication except such as are incident to, or properly to be inferred from, the powers expressed in the memorandum and articles of association. Their powers are entirely created by the law and by the contract founded upon the law which enables such companies to be constituted.

Setting limits on the 'powers of the company' is therefore the means by which a constitution limits the ancillary managerial powers of the body of shareholders that are exercisable through simple majority voting.

---

[148] Companies Act 1985, s 35(3). This provision expressly separates the shareholders' power to validate an 'ultra vires' contract from their power to release the directors from breach of their duty to observe the limits of the board's contractual power. However, individual shareholders also have an express right to restrain the company from entering into an 'ultra vires' contract: Companies Act 1985, s 35(2).
[149] *Ibid.*
[150] (1882) 8 App Cas 65 at 71.

4.3.2 Distinguishing Limits on the Powers of the Company from Limits on the Powers of the Board

The significance of this difference begs the question of how the two kinds of limit are to be distinguished. The relevant case law has made clear that it is a matter of interpreting the relevant terms of the company's constitution, although the distinction can be a fine one in practice. In *Irvine v Union Bank of Australia*,[151] for example, the company's articles provided that

> the directors should have … the power of borrowing and taking up credit … but so, nevertheless, that the total amount to be so taken up should not exceed in aggregate one half of the company's paid up share capital.[152]

The Privy Council construed this as a limit on the powers of the company's board and not as 'a limitation of the general powers of the company or of the whole body of shareholders'. The Privy Council advised that a transaction made by the board beyond this limit could therefore be ratified by the 'company' and made binding,[153] meaning that the shareholders acting by ordinary resolution could exercise the power of ratification. The Privy Council emphasised, however, that the shareholders could not use this power to increase the authority of the directors to make contracts of the kind at issue.[154] That would have required an alteration of the constitution. In effect, the power of the body of shareholders to complement or 'top up' the powers of the board is not one that they can delegate to the board.

The ruling in *Irvine* implied that it is the memorandum of association that settles and limits the powers of the company,[155] but Swinfen Eady J, in *Boschoek Proprietary v Fuke*, held that provisions in a company's articles could be construed to have this effect.[156] Here, the company's articles specified a minimum shareholding qualification for someone to become a director of the company and also stated that the directors' aggregate annual remuneration should not exceed a specified maximum. Swinfen Eady J held that these provisions operated not just as a limit on the board's power to appoint and remunerate directors, but as a limit on the power of the company itself to do so.

Accordingly the body of shareholders did not have any complementary power to approve or ratify appointments made or remuneration awarded by the board in violation of these limits. In effect, as a complementary organ, acting through a simple majority, the shareholders were

---

[151] (1876–77) LR 2 App Cas 366 (PC).
[152] *Ibid* at 372–3.
[153] *Ibid* at 374.
[154] *Ibid* at 375–6.
[155] *Ibid* at 374.
[156] [1906] Ch 148.

bound by the same limits as the board. However, the shareholders did have the power to alter the articles by special resolution and could, in this way, vary or remove the relevant terms of the constitution. On this basis, the shareholders could, by special resolution, have overridden the limits and ratified transactions in excess of them.[157]

4.4 The Powers of the Board

4.4.1 The Limiting Effect of the Objects Clause

The constitution of a company may therefore not vest the full extent of the powers of the company in its board, but the powers of the board (and thus its actual authority) cannot be wider than the powers of the company. The powers of the board are therefore subject to the same limits and, in particular, are restricted by the terms of the objects clause.

The objects clause may in fact limit the board's actual authority more narrowly than the company's contractual capacity. This effect results from the tendency of the typical objects clause to include a list of various powers, in effect the power to enter into various kinds of transaction, and to state that all objects listed in the objects clause, including these powers, are to be treated as independent objects of the company. In *Rolled Steel v British Steel*, the Court of Appeal held that the board's authority to exercise a power derived from the objects clause, whether express or implied, is limited to pursuit of the purposes of the company as set out in that clause.[158] In other words, when determining the scope of the board's actual authority, as opposed to the company's contractual capacity, sub-clauses setting out mere powers must be construed by reference to those sub-clauses that specify the proper business objectives of the company.[159]

The House of Lords had confirmed the independent effect of the objects clause in limiting the board's actual authority in *Ashbury Railway Carriage Co v Riche*,[160] holding that the constitution vests general powers of management in the board only to enable them to pursue the objects set out in the company's memorandum of association.[161] This restrictive effect has persisted despite the statutory reform that has mitigated the

---

[157] *Ibid* at 163.

[158] [1986] 1 Ch 246 at 295. See also *Re David Payne* [1904] 2 Ch 608 (CA).

[159] It is arguable that the same effect is achieved through the directors' distinct fiduciary duty that they must exercise the powers vested in them for a 'proper purpose', this in effect being the management of the company's affairs in pursuit of the business or commercial objectives set out in the objects clause. See, for example, the discussion of this point in *Bamford v Bamford* [1970] Ch 212.

[160] (1875) LR 7 HL 653.

[161] At the time of this decision, a company's objects clause could not be altered. This is now possible by special resolution: see Companies Act 1985, s 4 (as amended by the Companies Act 1989).

legal consequences for third parties if the board of a company exceeds its actual authority.[162] The Company Law Review has suggested that it should still be possible to insert a clause setting out a company's objectives in the proposed new form of constitution and this would presumably have a similar limiting effect on the board's actual authority.[163]

4.4.2 Other Constitutional Limits on the Board's Powers

The terms of the constitution of a company may set other limits on the board's powers. There are no prescribed standards in this respect. The founders of a company (and its shareholders from time to time acting through the appropriate resolutions) are free to limit the board's powers as they think fit. These limits can be structured so that the body of shareholders acting through simple majority voting cannot override them. As well as defining limits as limits on the powers of the company rather than on the powers of the board, the constitution can make express provision as to how particular limits are to be overridden.

The constitution of a company may also set limits on its board's powers by requiring the board to comply with a special procedure or specified formalities in relation to certain kinds of transaction. These include the kind of provision noted above that in effect define the board as an organ of governance. The board itself is likely to have a power of ratification in respect of such limits, but this power would have to be exercised in accordance with the requisite procedure or formalities. If the board could not comply with the limit, then the body of shareholders would have to exercise the power of ratification.

One example of such a procedural limit is the provision in many constitutions, including Table A,[164] which excludes directors from voting on transactions in which they have a conflict of interest and from being counted in the quorum in relation to such a transaction. A board that did not comply with such a provision would not have the actual authority to make or approve the transaction in question on behalf of the company. In effect, a board that did not comply with the limit would not be acting as the board.[165] In *Grant v UK Switchback Railway*,[166] all but one of a company's

---

[162] The severe legal consequences stemming from the restrictive effect of the objects clause on a company's contractual capacity tended to obscure its conceptually distinct role in defining the powers of the company and of the board. The blurring of these issues is reflected in the case law that followed *Ashbury* and explains some of the difficulty associated with that case law. The first attempt at statutory reform compounded this tendency by using one provision to mitigate both problems.

[163] See the 2002 White Paper at 2.2: '[the] constitution would be capable of containing an objects clause but, in the new structure, this would have only internal effect as between directors and the members.'

[164] Table A, regs 94 and 95.

[165] See, for example, *Smith v Henniker-Major* [2002] EWCA Civ 762.

[166] (1889) LR 40 Ch D 135 (CA).

directors had a personal interest in a proposed transaction. The company's articles prohibited any director from voting on a contract in which he had a personal interest and set the board's quorum at two. The Court of Appeal held that the powers of the company included the power to make a contract in which directors were interested, following *Irvine v Union Bank of Australia*.[167] The problem was that the board could only exercise this power of the company if they could comply with the procedural restrictions.

However, it was held that the company's shareholders had a default power in these circumstances to exercise this power of the company and that this default power was exercisable by an ordinary resolution. This meant that the shareholders could ratify the proposed contract by ordinary resolution. The result would have been different if the relevant provisions had been so formulated as to limit the powers of the company so as to exclude making or approving a transaction of the designated kind.

4.4.3 Directors' Duties as Limits on the Board's Powers?

The law places further restrictions on the board's powers of management in the form of the various duties that directors owe to their company as to how they must exercise their powers. These include a duty to obey the terms of their company's constitution, a duty to exercise their powers in good faith in the best interests of the company,[168] a duty to exercise independent judgment (and not to delegate a discretionary power unless the constitution provides for this) and a duty to exercise care and skill.[169] These duties do not necessarily set limits on the scope of the board's actual authority, although they may coincide with these limits and may achieve a similar legal effect.

Their duties expose directors to personal liability to the company for breach, but only some duties expose third parties to remedies as well. The fact that a transaction is made in breach of duty does not therefore mean that it must also be void for lack of actual authority (or lack of contractual

---

[167] (1876–77) LR 2 App Cas 366.

[168] *Re Smith & Fawcett* [1942] Ch 304 (CA); *Charterbridge v Lloyds Bank* [1970] Ch 62; *West Mercia Safetywear v Dodd* [1988] BCLC 250 (CA); *Re Pantone 485* [2002] 1 BCLC 266. This duty applies to the directors' intention or purpose in exercising their powers and not to the objective merits of their decisions or actions: *Howard Smith v Ampol* [1974] AC 821 (PC); *Runciman v Walter Runciman plc* [1993] BCC 223; *Colin Gwyer v London Wharf* [2002] EWHC 2748.

[169] These are the first four duties of the seven listed in the proposed codified statement of directors' duties set out in the 2002 White Paper: Draft Clauses, Schedule 2. On these duties, see generally Gower & Davies at 380–391 and 432–7. See also S Worthington, (2000) 116 *Law Quarterly Review* 638 at 640–1 on the differing legal nature of these duties. Directors owe these duties to the company itself and not to shareholders (or creditors) personally: *Percival v Wright* [1902] 2 Ch 421; *Multinational Gas v Multinational Services* [1983] Ch 258 (CA); *Peskin v Anderson* [2001] 1 BCLC 372 (CA). The shareholders' correlative rights to these duties are therefore collective and depend on their ability to act on behalf of the company in enforcing its rights against a misfeasant director.

capacity). In *Re Halt Garage,* Oliver J stressed the need for conceptual clarity in this respect:[170]

> [There] has been a certain confusion between the requirements for a valid exercise of the fiduciary powers of directors (which have nothing to do with the capacity of the company but everything to do with the propriety of acts done within that capacity), the extent to which powers can be implied or limits be placed, as a matter of construction, on express powers, and the matters which the court will take into consideration at the suit of a minority shareholder in determining the extent to which his interests can be overridden by a majority vote. These three matters, as it seems to me, raise questions which are logically quite distinct but which have sometimes been treated as if they demanded a single universal answer leading to the conclusion that, because a power must not be abused, therefore, beyond the limits of propriety it does not exist.

The duty to obey the constitution by definition coincides with the scope of the actual authority of the board (or individual directors as the case may be). Breach therefore exposes directors to personal liability and the company may also have remedies against the third party to any contract made in breach. However, the latter remedies are subject to the third party's ability to rely upon an overriding rule of attribution.

Breach of the duty of good faith can give a company a remedy against third parties as well as against directors. A third party who is aware that the directors of a company have approved a contract on its behalf in breach of their duty of good faith cannot enforce the contract or rely upon its validity.[171] This reflects a third party's potential liability as an accessory for any breach of fiduciary duty on the basis of 'knowing receipt'.[172] The conditions for establishing a third party's liability for knowing receipt will be examined in chapter 5 since it can apply also to transactions made in breach of the duty to obey the constitution and can therefore negate a third party's ability to rely upon an overriding rule of attribution. A third party who satisfies the conditions of knowing receipt cannot enforce a contract made in breach of duty and is liable to repay or account for anything already received from the company in breach of duty.[173]

Directors are also subject to certain fiduciary duties applying to situations involving a potential conflict of interest and breach of these can affect the validity of a transaction as well as expose directors to personal

---

[170] *Re Halt Garage (1964)* [1982] 3 All ER 1016 at 1029–1030.
[171] *Rolled Steel v British Steel* [1986] Ch 246 (CA) at 295–6; *Colin Gwyer v London Wharf (Limehouse)* [2002] EWHC 2748 at 94.
[172] *BCCI v Akindele* [2001] Ch 437 (CA); *Criterion Properties v Stratford UK Properties* [2002] EWCA Civ 1883.
[173] In *Criterion Properties v Stratford UK Properties,* Hart J treated a third party's liability to account for knowing receipt and its inability to enforce an unperformed contract as 'two sides of the same coin': [2002] EWHC 496 at 29.

liability.[174] These duties are reinforced by various statutory rules, duties and prohibitions, which are currently set out in Part X of the Companies Act 1985. These duties, which will be examined in chapter 7, can invalidate a transaction even when made or approved by an agent with actual authority to bind the company.

4.4.4 *The Proper Purposes Doctrine*

There is one apparent 'duty' of directors that does appear to expose third parties to remedies in the event of breach on the same basis as the constitutional limits on the board's actual authority. It has been suggested that this duty in fact operates simply as a general qualification to the powers vested in the board and thus as an overall limit on the board's actual authority, matching the restrictive effect of the objects clause noted above.[175] This is the requirement that directors must exercise their powers of management for their proper purpose.[176] It has sometimes been presented as an aspect of the duty of good faith,[177] but directors have been found to be in breach of this duty even when they acted in the genuine and honest belief that what they were doing was in the best interests of their company as a firm or of the company's shareholders.[178]

In practice, the 'proper purposes' doctrine has been invoked to prevent the board of a company from using its powers of management to interfere with the 'ownership' powers of the shareholders and thus their ultimate control of the company. It has been portrayed as reinforcing the essential division of function between the board and the shareholders and thus as a counterpart to the limitation on the shareholders' ability to function as a general organ of management established in the *Cunninghame* case.[179] For public companies, the shareholders' ultimate control over the board is crucial for the success of a potential takeover bid.[180]

---

[174] See the other three duties (duties 5, 6 and 7) in the proposed statement of duties in the 2002 White Paper: Draft Clauses, Schedule 2. See generally Gower & Davies at 391–424.

[175] *Re David Payne* [1904] 2 Ch 608 (CA); *Rolled Steel v British Steel* [1986] 1 Ch 246 (CA) at 295.

[176] *Hogg v Cramphorn* [1967] Ch 254; *Bamford v Bamford* [1970] Ch 212 (CA); *Howard Smith v Ampol Petroleum* [1974] AC 821 (PC). See Gower & Davies at 385–7.

[177] *Bamford v Bamford* [1970] Ch 212 (CA).

[178] *Howard Smith v Ampol Petroleum* [1974] AC 821 (PC).

[179] See *Shaw (John) & Sons (Salford) v Shaw* [1935] 2 KB 113 (CA) at 134. See generally the discussion of this doctrine in Parkinson at 137–158.

[180] The neo-classical economic analysis of the company has attached great significance to takeovers as a means by which the comparative weakness of shareholders as an organ of governance is countered and the scale of the potential agency problem faced by shareholders in relation to their company's management is reduced: see generally chapter 2. From this perspective, takeover bids can be viewed as an important feature of the English system of corporate governance and the 'proper purposes doctrine', along with other devices designed to counter the use of defensive tactics by corporate management such as those in the *City Code on Takeovers and Mergers*, can be viewed as a necessary reinforcement of this feature: see generally Parkinson at 137–158.

The managerial power vested in the board that is most likely to be abused in this context is the power to issue shares in the company since this can affect the balance of votes among the shareholders and can therefore be used to discourage or prevent a takeover bid as well as a mechanism for raising equity capital.[181] The power to make contracts can also be used to achieve this effect, for example by binding the company to a 'poison pill' arrangement or any onerous or long-term contract that a prospective bidder is likely to find unappealing.[182] The key factor is that the directors' main purpose in exercising such a power should be to frustrate a potential takeover bid or otherwise frustrate the shareholders' collective ability to exert their ultimate control of the company rather than their proper purpose of managing the affairs of the company.[183]

It has been suggested that the proper purposes doctrine is not a duty, but operates as a general limit on the board's actual authority to exercise the powers of the company and has the same legal effect as such a limit.[184] In practice, the courts have treated a transaction made for an improper purpose as invalid, although they have expressed differing views on its precise legal status.[185] This view of the doctrine is reinforced by its inclusion as an aspect of the directors' duty to obey the constitution in the proposed codified statement of directors' duties further to the Company Law Review.[186]

The Court of Appeal accepted this alternative view of the proper purposes doctrine in *Criterion Properties v Stratford UK Properties*.[187] This concerned the validity of a 'poison pill' arrangement, which was designed to deter a possible takeover bid by giving a joint venture partner an option to be bought out on extremely favourable terms (and thus extremely onerous for the company) in certain specified circumstances. When the third party sought to enforce the contract,[188] the company resisted on the basis

---

[181] *Hogg v Cramphorn* [1967] Ch 254; *Bamford v Bamford* [1970] Ch 212 (CA).

[182] See, for example, *Lee Panavision v Lee Lighting* [1992] BCLC 22 (CA) and *Criterion Properties v Stratford UK Properties* [2002] EWCA Civ 1883. See, however, *Teck Corporation v Millar* (1973) 33 DLR (3d) 288, where the court accepted that the directors had a 'proper' commercial purpose in making the transaction in question.

[183] In *Howard Smith v Ampol Petroleum* [1974] AC 821, the Privy Council ruled that, where the board of a company alleged that it had exercised the power to issue shares for the 'proper purpose' of raising equity capital, the court was entitled to review the evidence, including the company's actual need for equity capital, to ascertain whether or not this was in fact the board's principal purpose. See also *Teck Corporation v Millar* (1973) 33 DLR (3d) 288.

[184] See, for example, P Jaffey, 'Case Comment: *Lee Panavision v Lee Lighting*' (1994) 15 *Company Lawyer* 22.

[185] In *Bamford v Bamford* [1970] Ch 212, which concerned an allotment of shares, the Court of Appeal referred to the allotment as 'voidable'. In *Lee Panavision v Lee Lighting* [1992] BCLC 22, however, which concerned a management agreement whereby control of management was to be delegated to another company, the Court of Appeal referred to the contract in question as 'unconstitutional' and as 'not within the directors' powers at all'.

[186] See 2002 White Paper, Draft Clauses, Schedule 2.

[187] [2002] EWCA Civ 1883.

[188] The takeover had not in fact occurred, but one of the specified events triggering the third party's option was a particular director ceasing to hold office.

that the board had not exercised its power to make contracts for a proper purpose. The Court of Appeal treated the doctrine as setting an overall limit on the board's actual authority. Further, it held that the third party's ability to enforce the contract depended on whether the board had ostensible authority (an overriding rule of attribution) and that this in turn depended on whether or not the third party would have been liable for knowing receipt if the contract had already been performed. The Court of Appeal's judgment on this point will be examined further in chapter 5.

5 CONTRACTING BEYOND THE LIMITS ON THE
BOARD'S AUTHORITY

5.1 The Shareholders' Ancillary Powers

5.1.1 The Need to Override the Limits on the Board

The previous section examined the legal basis on which the board of a company has actual authority to enter into contracts on the company's behalf and the various ways in which the constitution and rules of company law set limits on this authority. In practice, a company's board may wish to exceed these limits and make a contract for which it does not have actual authority. It may take the view that such a contract is in the best interests of the company and its shareholders. The narrower the scope of the board's actual authority, the more likely this is to be the case. It may also be necessary in circumstances where company law has imposed limits on the board's authority or has required the express approval of the shareholders.[189]

The board of a company may seek prior proper approval or ratification of a contract that is beyond the limits of its actual authority for two reasons. First, it may wish to remove the risk of personal liability that the directors or other agents acting on behalf of the company would otherwise face. Secondly, it may wish to reassure the third party that the contract will be valid and binding on the company. Third parties can, of course, rely upon the overriding rules of attribution examined in chapters 5 and 6, which reduce the importance to them of ensuring that a contract is properly authorised. However, the problem may emerge before a contract is made and the third party may have to collaborate with those acting for the company to ensure proper authorisation. As will become clear in chapters 5 and 6, the overriding rules of attribution are not unconditional. In particular, a third party's ability to rely upon an overriding rule can be undermined by knowledge that an agent purporting to act for a

---

[189] See, for example, ss 319 and 320 of the Companies Act 1985.

company lacks the necessary actual authority to do so. A third party can, for example, be exposed to liability for knowing receipt.

The problem then becomes one of identifying who can exercise the company's power as principal to approve or ratify a contract beyond the limits of its agent's actual authority and procuring this approval or ratification. As noted above, the board itself may have this power if the limit in question is a procedural one and the board is able to approve the contract in accordance with the requisite procedure. Otherwise, the board must look for another organ to act on behalf of the company and that means its body of shareholders. However, the shareholders' ability to perform this task depends on how they must act as a collective body and that depends on the nature of the relevant limit. If the shareholders are able to act unanimously, then there should be no difficulty unless company law prohibits the relevant transaction. If they cannot, then there may be difficulty both in identifying the nature of the hurdle and in overcoming it.

5.1.2 The Shareholders' Powers to Override the Limits on the Board

When a constitution does not give the board the authority to exercise the powers of the company to their full extent, then the shareholders acting by ordinary resolution (and in effect as a simple decision-making organ) have a complementary power to make up the deficiency.[190] This power also enables the shareholders to approve or ratify a contract or other action of the board that was made or done for an improper purpose.[191] The power is complementary in the sense that the shareholders acting by ordinary resolution cannot exercise it independently of the board.[192] At this point, the board and the shareholders acting by ordinary resolution have to act as a composite organ and in this way they can exercise the powers of the company to their full extent. As noted above, the shareholders acting by ordinary resolution cannot delegate this complementary power to the board so as to increase the board's actual authority.[193] They must exercise the power themselves. It has also been seen that the shareholders have a complementary power, exercisable by ordinary resolution, to approve or ratify contracts within the scope of the board's actual authority when the board is unable to act for some reason.[194]

These complementary powers of the shareholders are only effective within the limits set by the constitution on the powers of the company. The composite organ consisting of the board and the shareholders acting

---

[190] *Irvine (William) v Union Bank of Australia* (1877) 2 App Cas 366 (PC).
[191] *Bamford v Bamford* [1970] Ch 212 (CA).
[192] *John Shaw & Sons (Salford) v Shaw* [1935] 2 KB 113 (CA).
[193] *Irvine (William) v Union Bank of Australia* (1877) 2 App Cas 366 (PC).
[194] *Grant v United Kingdom Switchback Railway* (1888) 40 Ch D 135 (CA); *Barron v Potter* [1914] 1 Ch 895; *Foster v Foster* [1916] 1 Ch 532.

by ordinary resolution does not have the authority to exceed these limits.[195] The shareholders as a collective body, however, do have the power to alter the constitution and this power enables them to ratify or approve contracts beyond the limits of the company's powers. The shareholders must exercise this power in the same way that would enable them to alter the limit in question. The constitution may in fact specify a procedure by which a limit on the powers of the company can be exceeded. This is the case where the constitution vests a power of veto in a certain person or a particular group of shareholders:[196] in that case, the person or persons with the veto can approve or ratify a contract beyond the limit; or the shareholders can override the limit as long as they act in the way necessary to alter the provision of the constitution setting out the power of veto.[197]

The shareholders acting by special resolution have the power to alter and therefore to override any limits on the powers of the company arising from the objects clause in the memorandum and those provisions of the articles that do not confer class rights.[198] If the limit does reflect a class right,[199] then the shareholders must comply with the special procedure necessary to vary the class rights in question.[200] Thus, if the class rights are set out in the company's articles and there are no special provisions governing their variation, then the relevant class must give their consent by an extraordinary resolution or through the written consent of the holders of at least three quarters (in nominal value) of the relevant shares.[201] Class rights may be even more difficult to override if they are entrenched in the company's memorandum of association.[202] This is in fact the case with any entrenched limits on the company's powers.[203] At the extreme, this may require that the shareholders be unanimous.

5.1.3 The Economic Costs of Setting Limits on the Board's Authority

Identifying how to override a limit on the board's actual authority may be difficult and therefore costly. The board may not be aware of all the limits

---

[195] *Boschoek v Fuke* [1906] Ch 148; *Quin & Axtens v Salmon* [1909] AC 442 (HL).

[196] See, for example, *Quin & Axtens v Salmon* [1909] AC 442 (HL); *Re Torvale Group* [1999] 2 BCLC 605.

[197] *Quin & Axtens v Salmon* [1909] AC 442 (HL).

[198] Companies Act 1985, ss 4, 9 and 125.

[199] These include any special rights attached to designated shares or to a designated shareholder: *Cumbrian Newspapers Group v Cumberland & Westmorland Herald Newspapers* [1987] Ch 1.

[200] Companies Act 1985, ss 125–7. See further on the variation of class rights, Gower & Davies at 495–505.

[201] Companies Act 1985, s 125(2). An extraordinary resolution requires the support of at least three quarters of those voting at a duly convened general meeting of the relevant class.

[202] Companies Act 1985, s 125(3).

[203] Companies Act 1985, s 17.

on its actual authority since not all of these may be readily apparent.[204] It may not be clear whether a particular provision sets limits on the powers of the company or just on the actual authority of the board to exercise those powers and thus whether a special resolution or an ordinary resolution is necessary. The board may therefore seek the support of a special resolution to be certain, but this may be more difficult and add to the cost of the overall exercise.

As well as the costs that may be involved in identifying the limits of the board's actual authority or their legal nature, the procedure for overriding these limits may also be costly. Depending on the nature of the company and its shareholder body, there may be costs in obtaining the consent of the shareholders whether by ordinary resolution or by special resolution. These costs may be even greater if the consent of a particular class of shareholder, or of a veto holder, or the unanimous consent of the entire membership, is required.

5.2 Obtaining the Shareholders' Approval for a Contract

5.2.1 Expense, Delay and Uncertainty

If the shareholders of a company are relatively large in number or not readily accessible to the board, then it is likely that they can only express their consent at a duly convened general meeting. This is costly both in terms of the expense entailed in having to convene such a meeting and by the delay that this must involve. Thus, if it is not possible for the meeting to be held at short notice, then at least 14 days' notice must be given for an ordinary resolution or an extraordinary resolution and at least 21 days' notice for a special resolution.[205] These costs are likely to be substantial for listed public companies.

A further practical issue concerns the capability of the shareholders, as a body, of engaging in the kind of managerial decision-making that consenting to the board exceeding the limits of its actual authority requires. Assuming that the shareholders are not small in number or closely involved in the management of the company, they are unlikely to have the necessary information and expertise that would enable them to judge the

---

[204] See, for example, *Re Torvale Group* [1999] 2 BCLC 605. In *British Racing Drivers' Club v Hextall Erskine* [1997] 1 BCLC 182, neither the board of a company not its legal advisers were aware of a statutory limit on the board's actual authority to enter a particular transaction involving a conflict of interest. See also 'QMH restores £2 billion' in *The Times* of 9 March 1994, which describes a situation in which the board of a company had incurred very substantial debts on its behalf, but did not in fact have the actual authority to do so at the relevant time.

[205] Companies Act 1985, ss 369 and 378. Short notice usually requires the consent of at least 95 per cent of the voting shareholders in terms of nominal value: ss 369(4) and 378(3).

merits of a proposed transaction. In any event, they could face major practical difficulties in reaching a collective view. In practice, therefore, the shareholders are likely to look to the board for guidance and to expect the board to make a recommendation.

The practical effect of setting limits on the board's actual authority (including those set by statute), therefore, is to prompt a process of disclosure and explanation that ensures that the board accounts to shareholders about transactions beyond these limits. This may provide a valuable safeguard for the shareholders and a valuable source of information, but the parties settling the terms of the transaction (the board or other corporate agents and the third party) have to take account of the likely delay and consequent uncertainty in their negotiations.

5.2.2 Mitigating the Uncertainty of Delay

In such circumstances, the negotiating parties are likely to aim at minimising the adverse impact of the delay. In particular, the third party has to combat the risk that simply making a binding contract conditional upon the shareholders' approval would present. The risk would be that the company's board might seek to exploit the delay (and their influence over the shareholders) opportunistically to look for a better deal elsewhere or to renege on the transaction if circumstances were to change. On the other hand, the company's board has to combat the risk that it would face if it were to embark on the process of seeking the shareholders' approval without having a binding commitment from the third party. Accordingly, the company's board has an incentive to convince the third party that they would not exploit the delay opportunistically.

The board can reduce the risk and the cost of delay by giving undertakings to the third party designed to reassure it. The directors could, for example, undertake to use their 'best endeavours' (or some other such recognised formulation) to ensure that the conditions would be satisfied and, in particular, that they would recommend the transaction to the shareholders. However, it has been held that directors owe a distinct fiduciary duty to their shareholders to express an honest opinion and not to mislead them about a proposed transaction at the time of the meeting at which the shareholders have to make their decision and that any undertakings given by the directors to the third party are qualified accordingly.[206] Thus, if, due to a change in circumstances, a proposed contract ceases to be in the best interests of the company at the time of the shareholders' meeting, the board must be free to advise the shareholders to reject the contract. Vinelott J has stated the impact of the directors' overarching duty as follows:[207]

[206] *Rackham v Peek Foods* [1990] BCLC 895 (Templeman J had given this judgment in 1977); *Crowther v Carpets International* [1990] BCLC 460 (Vinelott J had given this judgment in 1985).
[207] [1990] BCLC 460 at 464–5.

The terms of the agreement must clearly be read in the light of the fact known to all parties that directors owe a fiduciary duty to act in the interests of their company and to make full and honest disclosure to shareholders before they vote on such a resolution … It seems to me plain beyond question that directors are under a duty to disclose the facts to the shareholders. Indeed a resolution passed in ignorance of them would be worthless. If directors must disclose the facts, then it seems to me that they must equally express their honest opinion as to what is in the interests of the company.

Directors must therefore give the shareholders honest guidance on how they should exercise their complementary powers of ratification and approval. This duty limits the board's authority to give binding undertakings to third parties to reduce the risk of delay.[208]

The board cannot therefore mitigate the adverse impact of the limits on its actual authority by giving undertakings to third parties where these might involve misleading the shareholders or misrepresenting the board's honest opinion at the relevant time. As in the analogous situation of making recommendations about a proposed takeover bid for their company,[209] the board can presumably still give lesser undertakings such as not to solicit or co-operate with rival offers or not to do anything which might undermine the contract before the shareholders' approval has been obtained. Nevertheless, the restrictive effect of this duty increases the economic cost of setting limits on the board's actual authority.

5.2.3 The Board's Authority to give Undertakings about their Future Conduct

The fiduciary duty noted in the previous section does not limit the board's ability to give other kinds of undertakings that may set limits on their managerial discretion in the future provided that the board has the authority to give such undertakings in the first place. This applies both to undertakings expressed as those of the board or individual directors (in their capacity as directors) and to undertakings expressed as those of the company itself.[210] The board must comply with the various directors' duties when giving such undertakings.

It was argued in *Fulham FC v Cabra Estates,*[211] however, that the directors' general duty of good faith restricts the ability of the board to give any undertakings to third parties that might subsequently require them to

---

[208] See also the discussion of this point by the Court of Session, Outer House in the Scottish case of *Dawson International v Coats Paton* [1989] BCLC 233.

[209] *Gething v Kilner* [1972] 1 All ER 1166; *Heron International v Lord Grade* [1983] BCLC 244 (CA); *Re a Company* (No 008699 of 1985) [1986] BCLC 382; *Dawson v Coats Paton* [1989] BCLC 233 (Outer House) and [1990] BCLC 560 (First Division).

[210] As Lord Prosser remarked in *Dawson International plc v Coats Patons plc* [1991] BCC 276, 'distinctions between the actions of a board and the actions of a company can of course become unreal.'

[211] [1992] BCC 863 (CA).

act in a way that at the time they do not consider to be in the best interests of the company. Such a restriction would severely reduce the board's contractual power and impose an onerous economic cost on companies in general because third parties would be required to obtain the approval of the company's shareholders to ensure the validity any such undertaking.[212]

Contractual undertakings can be divided into those that require the performance of some specified action in the future and those that require the making of a recommendation or the like indicating that a particular belief or opinion is held at some future time and it is debatable how far it is possible, as a matter of logic, to give an undertaking of the latter kind.[213] However, leaving aside the precise meaning of a particular undertaking, the Court of Appeal in the *Fulham FC* case held that the directors' duty to exercise their power in good faith in the best interests of their company applies and is exhausted at the time when an undertaking is given and does not operate to restrict the scope of the undertaking itself:[214]

> It is trite law that directors are under a duty to act bona fide in the interests of their company. However, it does not follow from that proposition that directors can never make a contract by which they bind themselves to the future exercise of their powers in a particular manner, even though the contract taken as a whole is manifestly for the benefit of the company. *Such a rule could well prevent companies from entering into contracts which were commercially beneficial to them.* (emphasis added)

---

[212] This assumes that the company's shareholders would have the power to waive such a duty. The Court of Appeal held that the directors' power to give undertakings was not in fact restricted in the way suggested, but said that, if this had been the case, the company's shareholders would not have had the power to waive the duty: the 'duties owed by the directors are to the company and the company is more than just the sum total of its members. Creditors, both present and potential, are interested, while s 309 of the Companies Act 1985 imposes a specific duty on directors to have regard to the interests of the company's employees in general': [1992] BCC 863 at 876. If the Court of Appeal's reasoning on this were to be correct, it would not be possible for the shareholders alone to sanction an act or transaction that would otherwise be a breach of the directors' duties. Whilst this would be satisfactory in the case of an insolvent company, it could cause great difficulty otherwise both because of the uncertainty as to the precise nature of the rights of employees and creditors in relation to the duties of directors and because of the lack of any institutional device for giving effect to these rights. See generally the discussion of these issues in L Sealy, 'Directors' "Wider" Responsibilities—Problems Conceptual, Practical and Procedural' (1987) 13 *Monash University Law Review* 164.

[213] This point was considered in detail by Lord Prosser in the *Dawson International* case. He expressed the dilemma as follows: '… [a] recommendation entails or implies that the person making the recommendation believes that what he is recommending is good or appropriate. If a future recommendation is contemplated, this belief must also be in the future. To bind oneself to do something which is dependent on one's future beliefs, or even to bind oneself to believe something in the future, is no doubt possible in law. But where it is suggested that someone has done this, I would be inclined to be slow in putting such a construction upon their words and deeds. And more specifically, if someone has thus bound themselves, I think it is clear that any such contract, or the rules regulating its enforcement, would have to allow for the possibility that the person who has bound himself to make the recommendation quite simply cannot do so in good faith, for want of the necessary belief in it': [1991] BCC 276 at 300.

[214] Neill LJ [1992] BCC 863 at 875.

The Court of Appeal drew support on this point from the judgment of Kitto J for the High Court of Australia in *Thorby v Goldberg*:[215]

> [It] seems to me that the proper time for the directors to decide whether their proposed action will be in the interests of the company as a whole is the time when the transaction is being entered into, and not the time when their action under it is required. If at the former time they are bona fide of the opinion that it is in the interests of the company that the transaction should be entered into and carried into effect, I see no reason in law why they should not bind themselves to do whatever under the transaction is to be done by the board.

An undertaking given by company directors that is within the scope of their contractual power and is in accordance with their duty of good faith is not an improper fetter on their future discretion, but merely the consequence of a previous exercise of that discretion.[216]

There is accordingly no good reason in principle why the fact that a contractual party such as a company has to act through agents should relieve it from a risk inherent in all contractual obligations that extend into the future. If the argument put forward in the *Fulham FC* case had been accepted, it would have substantially increased the cost of contracting with companies to the detriment of both third parties and companies themselves.[217]

6 CONCLUSIONS AND REVIEW

6.1 The Rationale of Limiting the Board's Actual Authority

This chapter has examined the legal role of the constitution of a company as the source of its board's actual authority. It has shown how both its constitution and company law can limit the actual authority of a company's board in various ways. These limits in turn define the ability of a company's specialist organ of management to determine and adjust the company's legal relations with other parties.

---

[215] (1964) 112 CLR 597 at 601.

[216] See the judgments of McTiernan J and Windeyer J in *Thorby v Goldberg* (1964) 112 CLR 597 at 617–618: 'it would be impossible to argue that they had, by executing the document, improperly fettered the future exercise of their discretion. In fact they would already have exercised it'.

[217] This outcome would be reinforced in the codified statement of directors' duties proposed by the Company Law Review. See the note qualifying the proposed duty to exercise independent judgment in 2002 White Paper, Draft Clauses, Schedule 2, clause 3: 'Where a director has, in accordance with this Schedule, entered into an agreement which restricts his power to exercise independent judgement later, this paragraph does not prevent him from acting as the agreement requires where (in his independent judgement, and in according to the other provisions of this Schedule) he should do so'.

In chapter 2, it was seen that one reason for seeking to limit the authority of a company's board is to combat the so-called economic 'agency problem', this being the risk to the shareholders that the board might not organise and manage the company's affairs so as to maximise the return on their investment of equity capital. Instead, the board (or individual directors) might take advantage of its discretionary power to pursue the directors' own interests or follow some alternative agenda. As well as providing a safeguard against the agency problem, such limits can reduce the nature of the risk that the shareholders might face from the management of their company, for example by curbing management's scope for being 'risk seeking' rather than 'risk averse'.[218]

These goals can be achieved by setting general boundaries on the board's authority, for example by reference to the amount of consideration or to the value of assets involved either for individual transactions or for aggregate totals. They can also be achieved by limits that are targeted to reduce management's scope for engaging in transactions involving a higher than normal level of risk or at least to ensure disclosure and consultation about such transactions. The UK Listing Authority, for example, imposes a standard set of limits on all listed public companies through its Listing Rules, which focus on the relative value of a transaction.[219] This can be viewed as a form of self-regulation designed to reflect the interests of shareholders in listed public companies as a general class. It should be noted, however, that the Listing Rules only require the boards of affected companies to seek the approval of their shareholders (as opposed to notifying them with prescribed information) for transactions of an exceptionally high relative value, reflecting the high cost of limiting the board's authority.

As for targeted limits, section 320 of the Companies Act 1985 limits the authority of the boards of all companies in respect of transactions involving

---

[218] See chapter 2 on the economic significance of these different attitudes to risk.

[219] UK Listing Authority, *Listing Rules* (London, FSA, 2003) ('the Listing Rules'), chapter 10. These rules specify a series of financial ratios for calculating the 'relative value' of a transaction according to its nature and subject matter (comparison of gross assets, comparison of profits, comparison of turnover, consideration for the transaction compared to the company's market capitalisation, comparison of gross capital) . If the relative value of a transaction by any of these ratios is below five per cent, it is a 'class 3' transaction, which merely requires formal notification. If the relative value is between five per cent and 25 per cent, it is a 'class 2' transaction, which requires formal notification and a circular to the shareholders giving prescribed information. If the relative value is 25 per cent or more, it is a 'class 1' transaction. As well as formal notification and a circular to shareholders, shareholders must give their prior approval by ordinary resolution to a class 1 transaction. Further, chapter 11 of the Listing Rules imposes more stringent requirements for 'related party' transactions. These are transactions involving a shareholder with ten per cent or more of the voting rights in the company or a director of the company or an 'associate' of either of these. If the relative value of a related party transaction is five per cent or more, the shareholders must give their prior approval by ordinary resolution and the related party in question (and any 'associates') must abstain from voting.

'non-cash assets' of a prescribed minimum value and where a director of the company (or of a holding company) has a conflict of interest that falls into a prescribed category.[220] There is likely to be a much higher danger of the agency problem in relation to transactions involving such 'self-dealing'.

6.2 The Balancing Exercise

Limiting the board's actual authority may therefore secure benefits for a company's shareholders and indirectly for other stakeholder groups with an interest in the company's solvency and stability.[221] However, it also entails costs and these may affect both the company's shareholders and third parties, insofar as limits on the board's authority might threaten the validity of contracts or require third parties to take action of some kind to avoid the danger of invalidity. As was discussed in chapter 2, limits on the board's authority cannot be justified as promoting allocative efficiency unless the resulting benefits exceed the aggregate of these costs. As regards the costs for the shareholders, these should be reflected in terms of the limits in a company's constitution, which should strike a balance between the competing goals of ensuring managerial effectiveness and combating the agency problem.

However, the unitary board system of corporate governance affects this balancing exercise because there is no specialist organ that can be used to complement the limited authority of the board. It means that, where the board's authority is limited, then the task of authorising contracts beyond these limits must fall upon the body of shareholders, unless the limits are drafted in such a way as to place a procedural obstacle of some kind in the way of the board, which reduces the agency problem without requiring the shareholders to be involved in the decision-making process.

In the case of private companies, the costs of involving the shareholders in the decision-making process can be reduced by holding meetings at short notice or by obtaining their unanimous consent in writing. However, where this is possible, the benefits of such limits are also likely

---

[220] See chapter 7 on this statutory limit.

[221] These groups can only protect themselves directly against what they might regard as an unacceptable level of risk through the terms of their own dealings with the company (unless it is covered in specific regulation) since the directors of a company owe no general duty of care to these other groups and are not obliged to subordinate the shareholders' interest in profit maximisation, which may entail pursuing a course of action that offers the prospect of high profits with a significant risk of failure, to the interests of other groups, which are likely to be best served by minimising any risk of significant losses or insolvency: see generally *Multinational Gas and Petrochemical Co v Multinational Gas and Petrochemical Services* [1983] Ch 258 (CA). Major creditors may therefore seek to restrict the scope of a company's board to take action that might threaten the company's ability to repay the loan or other credit at issue through undertakings and covenants in the relevant contract. The *Fulham FC* case confirms that a company and its directors can be restricted in this way.

to be much less because the shareholding body should be able to exert much greater control over the board and combat the agency problem at its source. There may, however, be a need to protect minority shareholders from the opportunism of the majority, who can control the composition of the board in the absence of special safeguards. But simple limits on the board's authority would not be enough to combat this danger. It would require more complex restrictions involving, for example, class rights and a shareholders' agreement.

In public companies, the agency problem presents a greater danger because of the shortcomings of the shareholders as a decision-making body. However, setting limits on the board's authority is much more costly as a safeguard for the same reason. In particular, there is no scope for avoiding the need to convene a meeting of the shareholders or for reducing the time that this must involve. And the shareholders of a public company, as a collective body, can only approve or reject a proposal put before them at a general meeting. The proposal has to be formulated elsewhere. In addition, the shareholders are unlikely to have the information and expertise to evaluate any such proposal without guidance from the board. The board therefore has to make a recommendation and its responsibility in this respect is reflected in the distinct fiduciary duty to give the shareholders honest advice and not to mislead them.

6.3 The Scope for Evolving an Efficient Division of Powers

Given the need to balance a complex set of costs and benefits in the setting of limits on the actual authority of the board of a company, corporate constitutions should evolve over time to strike an efficient balance in this respect insofar as the law permits them to do this. There are likely to be variations in this respect, especially in the case of private companies with vulnerable minority shareholders requiring special protection or joint venture companies.

There has been a notable trend towards conferring wide authority in the boards of companies, in particular in the response to the advent of the 'ultra vires doctrine' in the *Ashbury Railway Carriage* case. The law can contribute to the evolution of an efficient balance through removing barriers in its way that are not justified by other policy considerations and by reducing transaction costs in general. From this perspective, the persistence of the ultra vires doctrine has been a hindrance, its continuing cost illustrated by the unnecessarily long and convoluted objects clause of the typical company, both public and private. This is ironic since the doctrine was originally justified as benefiting the shareholders and creditors of a company.[222]

---

[222] See generally the Prentice Report.

There are other features of the relevant law that may hinder the striking of an efficient balance in settling the contractual power of the board of a company. The distinction drawn between the board's authority and the powers of the company does not help in this respect. Neither does the variety of the limits that can be imposed on the powers of the company and their legal complexity. They can be obscure and hard to discern, especially if they are located in the detailed conditions attached to a particular class of shares. Further, it may in practice be hard to identify the precise legal significance of a limit since this may turn on a fine point in the drafting of the relevant provision. This, in turn, can make it hard to decide whether an ordinary resolution or a special resolution or something in addition such as a class resolution is required to override the limit.

From an economic perspective, this kind of legal uncertainty imposes a significant cost. There is even greater uncertainty as to the position when the problem arises after the event. This blurs into the general problem of how to deal with misfeasance by the board in the unitary board system of governance. Thus, it is clear that individual shareholders can prevent the board of their company from acting in breach of the constitution, even when the board is backed by an ordinary resolution, if a special resolution or more is required to override the limit in question. However, it is much less clear what action individual shareholders can take if such a breach has already occurred and a majority of shareholders are disinclined to take any action. This reflects the wider problem of how best to enforce a company's rights and remedies in the unitary board system.

6.4 Problems in Corporate Decision-Making

Decision-making about the enforcement of a company's legal rights is an aspect of the management of a company's affairs. Although the matter is not entirely free from doubt,[223] the power to institute or discontinue legal proceedings in the name of a company is within the general powers of management of the board and therefore is a matter in which the shareholders cannot interfere except by special resolution.[224] This applies even where one or more of the directors has a conflict of interest in the enforcement of their company's legal rights and there is an increased danger of managerial opportunism.

---

[223] See *Marshall's Valve v Manning* [1909] 1 Ch 267 and *Alexander Ward v Samyang* [1975] 1 WLR 673 (HL), noted by K Wedderburn, 'Control of Corporate Litigation' (1976) 39 *Modern Law Review* 327.

[224] *Shaw (John) & Sons (Salford) Ltd v Shaw* [1935] 2 KB 113 (CA); *Breckland Group Holdings Ltd v London & Suffolk Properties Ltd* [1989] BCLC 100, noted by K Wedderburn, 'Control of Corporate Actions' (1989) 52 *Modern Law Review* 401.

The problem is that enforcing a company's legal rights does require managerial decision-making and the shareholders are not necessarily suitable for this task, even where there is a conflict of interest in the board. Decision-making about legal proceedings rarely entails a simple choice between clear alternatives and instead is likely to involve active consideration of a wide range of options and to require detailed knowledge of the company's affairs. However, whilst the board of a company is better suited to this kind of decision-making, its shareholders face the danger that the board may not act in the company's best interests when a director has a conflicting personal interest.

Company law has not resolved this conundrum, but has mitigated it with some limited and rather ambiguous qualifications to the board's power over litigation. As well as leaving room for supposing that the body of shareholders does in some circumstances have an independent power to take action in the name of the company,[225] there is a limited alternative decision-making mechanism in the form of the so-called 'fraud on the minority' exception to the rule in *Foss v Harbottle*.[226] This exception can be rationalised as giving individual shareholders a default power to act as the company's decision-maker in certain circumstances in which there is a conflict of interest that would otherwise prove extremely damaging to the company. In effect, it is a refinement of the company's governance structure to overcome a significant deficiency in the unitary board system. The idea that this exception should be viewed as an attempt to find a reliable alternative decision-maker rather than as conferring a general right on individual shareholders derives some support from the judgment of Knox J in *Smith v Croft (No 2)*,[227] where he took account of the wish expressed by a majority of the non-conflicted shareholders not to pursue the proceedings in question any further.[228]

The problem of decision-making about litigation in circumstances where a director has a conflict of interest applies also to enforcing the limits of the board's actual authority through decisions about ratification and

---

[225] Megarry J noted the 'deep waters' surrounding this point in *Re Argentum Reductions (UK)* [1975] 1 WLR 186 at 189.

[226] See generally K Wedderburn, 'Shareholders' Rights and the Rule in *Foss v Harbottle*' [1957] CLJ 193 and [1958] CLJ 93 and Gower & Davies at 443–466.

[227] [1988] Ch 114, noted by A Boyle, (1990) 11 *Company Lawyer* 3.

[228] See Gower & Davies at 461–3. The rule that shareholders in a company cannot bring actions personally where their loss is 'reflective' of loss suffered by their company (so that they are in effect bound by the collective decision-making achieved through the company's governance structure in relation to the loss in question) and the limited exceptions to the reflective loss rule can also be viewed as a reinforcement and refinement of the governance structure that is focused on a company: see *Prudential Assurance Co v Newman Industries (No 2)* [1982] Ch 204; *Johnson v Gore Wood & Co (No 1)* [2002] 2 AC 1 (HL); *Giles v Rhind* [2002] EWCA Civ 1428; *Shaker v Al-Bedrawi* [2002] 2 WLR 922 (CA); *Gardner v Parker* [2003] EWHC 1463. On the reflective loss rule, see Gower & Davies at 453–8, E Ferran, 'Litigation by Shareholders and Reflective Loss' [2001] *Cambridge Law Journal* 245 and H Hirt, [2003] *Journal of Business Law* 420.

taking action against malfeasant directors. Such intractable problems can be attributed to the inherent limitations of the unitary board system of corporate governance. They can be viewed as part of the price to be paid for the benefits of this system in terms of managerial effectiveness. It represents a further cost of imposing limits on the authority of the board, which is likely to be reflected in the overall balance struck by a company's constitution in this respect.

As regards the delegation of contractual power within the management structure of a company, there is not the same problem in setting limits on the contractual power on subordinate agents since these can be imposed and policed as part of the internal organisation of this structure, with the board in ultimate control. However, a company's constitution may set some limits on this internal organisation and these raise the same kind of conceptual difficulty as those arising from limits on the board's actual authority.

6.5 The Cost for Third Parties

This leaves the question of the cost for third parties of setting limits on the authority of a company's board, which depends on the questions of how far exceeding these limits affects the validity of a transaction and what action a third party must take to avoid the danger of invalidity. This depends on the overriding rules of attribution, which will be examined in chapters 5 and 6.

By way of preliminary observation, however, the lack of prescribed standards in this area, the variety of the legal forms that limits on the authority of the board can take, and the fact that these limits can be complex and obscure, together mean that third parties may face a high level of information costs in identifying the precise scope of the board's authority as well as the practical difficulty of overcoming its limits.

As will be seen in the later chapters, the overriding rules of attribution do not rule out the significance of these limits for third parties completely. In particular, third parties can be prejudiced when they have actual or constructive knowledge of the limits on a corporate agent's authority. Then, like corporate agents, they face the burden of having to overcome the limits in the appropriate way and incur the transaction costs and risks of having to engage in this procedure. Further, whilst there is a strong overriding rule of attribution designed to provide third parties with reassurance about the authority of a company's board, there is none specifically designed to apply when the board is acting in conjunction with a shareholders' resolution.

4

Issues of Identity and Existence

1 INTRODUCTION

A CONTRACT REQUIRES at least two parties to engage in the necessary acts of formation.[1] A company's separate legal personality as a corporation enables it to be a party to a contract. However, for that to occur, the law must recognise the company in question as in existence at the relevant time and as the person to whom the acts of formation are to be attributed. The existence of a company is a matter of legal formality. It must have been duly incorporated and admitted onto the register of companies,[2] but not dissolved and removed from the register.[3] The identity of a company is also a matter of legal formality, but a rather more complex one than its existence. Part XI of the Companies Act 1985 includes a chapter on 'Company Identification'.[4] Among other things, this requires a company's registered name to be displayed at its business premises and on its business stationery and to be used on certain specified documents such as cheques and orders for goods.[5] Further, common law only recognised a corporation by the name with which it was incorporated and would not attribute acts to a corporation if an incorrect name were used.[6] However, from the time of James I, equity has granted relief from this doctrine and it is accepted that companies have other characteristics by which they can be identified.[7]

This chapter will examine the basis on which the courts identify a particular company as the person to whom a contract should be attributed and how they have resolved disputes arising where a company has not been accurately identified by its registered name. It will also examine the legal consequences where the company to which a contract should be

---

[1] See, for example, *Commins v Scott* (1875) LR 20 Eq 11 at 16, per Sir George Jessel MR.
[2] Companies Act 1985, ss 1(1) and 13(3).
[3] This usually follows the winding up of the company, but the registrar also has the power to remove a company from the register if he believes it is defunct: see further below.
[4] Companies Act 1985, ss 348–351.
[5] Companies Act 1985, ss 348(1) and 349(1).
[6] See J Grant, *A Practical Treatise on the Law of Corporations in General As well Aggregate as Sole* (London, 1850) at 145, which Stamp J noted in *F Goldsmith (Sicklesmere) v Baxter* [1970] Ch 85 at 88 and 92.
[7] *Ibid.*

attributed in accordance with the rules of identification proves not in fact to exist at the relevant time. The legal rules governing these issues have economic significance and it will be argued that analysis and evaluation of them should take account of this significance. They can be analysed in terms of the risk and burden that they place on companies and agents purporting to act for companies (on the one hand) and on third parties (on the other). The law can be evaluated in terms of how far it assigns these risks to the least-cost-avoider and thereby minimises overall costs.

A company is formed through the registration of its memorandum of association and other requisite documentation and comes into existence as a body corporate upon the issue of its certificate of incorporation.[8] Its name is the name set out in its memorandum, which must comply with various conditions and restrictions,[9] and this name is set out on its certificate of incorporation. A company can change its registered name if its shareholders pass a special resolution to that effect.[10] The Registrar of Companies then issues a 'certificate of incorporation on change of name' and the new name takes effect from the date on that certificate.[11] A company remains the same legal person when its registered name is changed and continues to have the same legal rights and obligations as under its previous name.[12]

Despite the requirements in the Companies Act as to the display and use of its registered name, a company does not have to use this name for all purposes and can use an abbreviated version or a different name for trading purposes.[13] This possibility, along with the fact that a company can change its registered name, increases the scope for confusion in the use of corporate names as a means of identification. Confusion may arise, for example, when a business is transferred from one company to another and the purchaser wishes to exploit the goodwill associated with the business. The purchaser may change its name to that of the vendor or may use the vendor's name as a trading name.[14] The only permanent feature of a company is its

---

[8] Companies Act 1985, ss 1(1) and 13(3).

[9] See generally P Davies, *Gower and Davies' Principles of Modern Company Law* 7th ed (London, Sweet & Maxwell, 2003) ('Gower & Davies') at 72–7.

[10] Companies Act 1985, s 28.

[11] Companies Act 1985, s 28(6), which re-enacted Companies Act 1981, s 24(1). This gave statutory effect to the decision of the Court of Common Pleas in *Shackleford, Ford & Co v Dangerfield* (1868) LR 3 CP 407, which held that the effect of the previous statutory provisions permitting a company to change its name was that the change did not take place on the passing of the special resolution, but when the certificate of incorporation on change of name was issued. See also the remarks of Nourse LJ in *Oshkosh B'Gosh Inc v Dan Marbel Inc* (1988) 4 BCC 795 (CA) at 796–7.

[12] *Oshkosh B'Gosh Inc v Dan Marbel Inc* (1988) 4 BCC 795 (CA).

[13] See, for example, *F Goldsmith (Sicklesmere) v Baxter* [1970] Ch 85. However, the Business Names Act 1985 requires a company that does not carry on business under its full corporate name to state this on all its business stationery and at all its business premises: Business Names Act 1985, s 4.

[14] See, for example, the scenario in *OTV Birwelco v Technical & General Guarantee Co* [2002] EWHC 2240.

registration number, which is set out on its original certificate of incorporation and on any subsequent certificates of incorporation on change of name. Whilst this must also be displayed on a company's business stationery and order forms,[15] this may not be practical as a ready means of identification and in any event the wrong number might be used.[16]

The courts have established that failure to use the correct registered name of a company in the formation of a contract does not prevent them from being able to identify that company as the party to the contract and thereby able to enforce it and adjudge the company to be bound by its terms. In *Goldsmith (Sicklesmere) v Baxter*, Stamp J said:[17]

> In the absence of authority constraining me to do so—and none has been cited—I would find it impossible to hold that a company incorporated under the Companies Acts has no identity but by reference to its correct name, or that, unless an agent acts on its behalf by that name, or a name so nearly resembling it that it is obviously an error for that name, he acts for nobody. A limited company has, in my judgment, characteristics other than its name by reference to which it can be identified: for example, a particular business, a particular place or places where it carries on business, particular shareholders and particular directors. If there are two limited companies having the same characteristics, then it is hardly to be supposed that each of them was incorporated on the same day and owns the same property.

Until 1990, a company was obliged to have a common seal, which reflected its legal nature as a corporation.[18] A company can still have a common seal and affixing its common seal is still a means by which it can enter into contracts or execute documents.[19] If it does have one, then it is obliged to have 'its name engraved in legible characters on the seal' and is liable to a fine for failing to do so.[20] However, it was held in *OTV Birwelco v Technical & General* that a company can validly execute a document by affixing a seal that is engraved with its trading name rather than its registered name even though such a seal does not comply with this obligation.[21] The courts have adopted the same approach in determining the identity of a corporate contracting party (when this is a matter of dispute) whether the contract is in simple form or a deed and whether it is made through affixing a common seal or by an agent purporting to act on behalf of a company.[22]

---

[15] Companies Act 1985, s 351(1).
[16] See, for example, *OTV Birwelco v Technical & General Guarantee Co* [2002] EWHC 2240.
[17] [1970] Ch 85.
[18] See chapter 1. The Companies Act 1989 retrospectively amended the Companies Act 1985 to this effect, inserting new ss 36 and 36A.
[19] Companies Act 1985, ss 36(a) and 36A(2).
[20] Companies Act 1985, s 350(1).
[21] *OTV Birwelco v Technical & General Guarantee Co* [2002] EWHC 2240.
[22] See chapter 1 on these distinctions.

In contracting with companies, any doubt about the precise identity of a corporate contractual party is likely to become crucial in two situations. The first situation is where one company that is a candidate for being the contractual party is insolvent or is for some other reason less attractive to the third party as a contracting party than another candidate.[23] The third party may, for example, have better legal remedies against another company.[24] The second situation is where the third party wishes to establish that it has contracted with a non-existent company.[25] It may do this to avoid liability under the contract or to secure a remedy against the agent personally. As will be seen later in this chapter, statute now provides that most, though not all, contracts that prove to be made with non-existent companies are to take effect as contracts with the agent purporting to act for the non-existent company.

2 THE IDENTIFICATION OF CORPORATE CONTRACTING PARTIES

2.1 Seeking the 'Presumed Common Intention' of the Parties

From an economic perspective, the law governing identification can promote allocative efficiency by minimising the burden on third parties to ensure that corporate contracting parties are identified accurately. This means ensuring that a third party's reasonable expectations at the time of contracting are not frustrated by any lack of precision in the identification of a company. It does not necessarily mean penalising companies or those purporting to act on behalf of companies for inaccuracies in their identification such that third parties are provided with a means of escaping from a contract that they would rather not have made (or the bonus of an unexpected remedy against another company) simply because of some inaccuracy in the identification of the contracting party. Such an approach would in fact increase the overall costs of contracting with companies. Insofar as there is a wider public interest in ensuring the accurate use of a company's registered name, this should be addressed separately and penalised through legal sanctions that are targeted accordingly.[26]

For third parties in general, the risk of invalidity and the risk of contracting with a company that is not connected to the subject matter of a contract are likely to conflict with their expectations at the time of contracting and are likely to be burdensome. For this reason, one particular third party that wishes to escape from a contract or pursue a remedy against another company is not a good representative of the interests of

---

[23] See, for example, *Porteous v Element Books* [1996] CLY 1029 (CA).

[24] See, for example, *Rhodian River v Halla Maritime* [1984] 1 Lloyd's Rep 373.

[25] See, for example, *Oshkosh B'Gosh Inc v Dan Marbel Inc* (1988) 4 BCC 795 (CA) and *Badgerhill Properties v Cottrell* [1991] BCC 463 (CA).

[26] Such as the criminal sanctions and personal liability under section 349 of the Companies Act 1985: see further below.

third parties in general. In the case law, the courts have generally reached decisions that are consistent with a third party's reasonable expectations at the time of contracting, thereby minimising the overall burden of contracting, but have done so through inferring from the evidence available the 'presumed common intention' of the parties actually involved in the formation of the contract.

The *Goldsmith* case arose from a lack of precision in the identification of a corporate contracting party and illustrates the general approach of the courts.[27] The company had the registered name 'F Goldsmith (Sicklesmere) Limited', but traded under the name 'Goldsmith Coaches'. It purchased a piece of land, which by mistake was conveyed to 'Goldsmith Coaches (Sicklesmere) Limited'. It then agreed to sell this land to the third party, again using the incorrect name. The third party refused to complete the purchase, arguing that the vendor did not exist and that there was therefore no contract.[28] Stamp J rejected this argument and held that the company was entitled to enforce the contract, despite being named in it inaccurately. He said that a company had characteristics other than its name and that these should be used to identify a corporate contracting party in the event of a dispute.[29] Not allowing a company to enforce a contract in such circumstances would 'introduce a source of great confusion and uncertainty in respect of business transactions'.[30] He drew support from a nineteenth century case, *Commins v Scott*,[31] which showed that it was 'not essential for the validity of a contract made on behalf of a limited company that the company should be described with precision'.[32]

In the *Goldsmith* case, the third party was seeking to use the inaccurate naming of a company to escape from liability under the contract. At the time of contracting, the third party presumably expected that he would have to purchase the land from the company that owned it. The precise name of this company was not therefore a material factor. Allowing the third party to avoid liability because of the mistake would therefore have given him a gratuitous benefit. Further, if such a mistake were to invalidate a contract (as opposed to preventing only the company from being able to enforce it), then third parties in general would face a risk of invalidity and suffer the burden of having to ensure the accurate naming of corporate contracting parties in order to avoid this risk. It is hard to see that any public interest in ensuring the precise identification of companies would justify this burden.

---

[27] [1970] Ch 85.
[28] On discovering the mistake, the company's solicitors had arranged for a supplemental conveyance from the original vendor, using the company's correct registered name.
[29] See above.
[30] [1970] Ch 85 at 92.
[31] (1875) LR 20 Eq 11.
[32] [1970] Ch 85 at 92–3. In *Commins v Scott*, Sir George Jessel MR held that an agreement for the sale of land by a company was valid and binding even though the name of the company was not disclosed in the contract. The court was able to infer the identity of the company from the contract.

The *Goldsmith* case concerned a contract that an agent acting for a company entered into on its behalf. In *OTV Birwelco v Technical & General Guarantee Co*[33] the court took the same approach to a contract made through the affixing of a company's common seal, despite the requirement in the Companies Act that a company having a common seal 'shall have its name engraved in legible characters on the seal'.[34] In the *OTV Birwelco* case, a company had executed a performance bond using a seal engraved with its trading name rather than its registered name. Its trading name had been the name of the company from which it had acquired its business.[35] Under the performance bond, the third party guaranteed to pay a specified sum to the main contractor for a project on which the company was working as a sub-contractor in the event of a default by the company. The main contractor was not a party to the bond, but was still entitled to enforce it provided that it had taken effect as a deed.[36] However, when the company did default, the third party claimed that the mistake in the naming of the company meant that it had not guaranteed the performance of this particular company and that, in any event, the bond was not enforceable against it.

The court rejected the third party's claim, applying the approach to identifying a corporate contracting party taken in the *Goldsmith* case. It held that the company that had executed the bond and whose default therefore triggered the third party's liability could be identified from the circumstances surrounding the bond.[37] It also held that the provisions in the Companies Act that indicate how a company can become party to a contract and specify how it should execute a document so that it takes effect as a deed do not require that a company must use its registered name or that it must not use a trading name.[38] In effect, although the Companies Act makes a company and its officers liable to a fine for breach of the requirement that its seal is engraved with its registered name,[39] the penalties do not go beyond this.

2.2 Confusing the Identity of Connected Companies

A mistake in the identification of a company in a contract can prove more troublesome where its effect is to suggest that one company rather than another is the true contracting party and where the agent is in fact the

---

[33] [2002] EWHC 2240.

[34] Companies Act 1985, s 350(1).

[35] The vendor company had changed its name after the sale. However, to add to the scope for confusion, the purchaser company had on occasion used stationery bearing the registered number of the vendor company.

[36] Under the principle in *Beswick v Beswick* [1968] AC 58 (HL): [2002] EWHC 2240 at 12–13.

[37] [2002] EWHC 2240 at 22–7.

[38] [2002] EWHC 2240 at 33, referring to ss 36 and 36A of the Companies Act 1985.

[39] Companies Act, ss 350(1) and (2).

agent of both companies. In such a case, rather than seeking to escape from the contract, the third party may wish to establish the liability of the other company because this provides it with a better remedy, even though this other company may have no direct connection with the subject matter of the contract. Such claims can seem more persuasive, but their success could undermine the integrity of the corporate veil as well as contradicting the actual expectations of third parties at the time of contracting.

Rhodian River v Halla Maritime concerned a group of 'one-ship companies' with common shareholders and directors.[40] The point of this structure was to keep the group's ships legally separate from each other so that, if one ship became the subject of a legal dispute, the others could not be arrested or otherwise involved in any proceedings resulting from that dispute.[41] However, this case arose because an agent with authority to act generally for the companies in the group inserted the name of the wrong company into a charter-party. The chartered ship later sank and the third party took action against the company that had been mistakenly named in the charter-party, arresting this company's ship and the freights payable to it. Bingham J held that the charter-party had not reflected the parties' true contractual intention and should be rectified accordingly, which would prevent the third party from taking action against the other company. Any other conclusion would have been 'inconsistent with the well-understood intentions of those who own and manage one-ship companies'.[42] He found that the third party had intended to contract with the company that owned the chartered ship, drawing this inference in part from 'the belief that, all other things being equal, a charterer would prefer to contract with a party who had the power as well as the duty to perform'.[43]

Bingham J acknowledged that his judgment deprived the third party of a significant advantage in terms of the remedies available to it in response to the sinking of the chartered ship, but also noted that the third party's position was exactly as it would have been if the charter-party had reflected the terms of their actual agreement. The third party had merely been deprived of 'an adventitious benefit for which they never covenanted and which must have come to them as a very pleasant surprise'.[44]

---

[40] *Rhodian River Shipping Co SA & Rhodian Sailor Shipping Co SA v Halla Maritime Corporation* [1984] 1 Lloyd's Rep 373.
[41] Allowing groups of companies to organise themselves so as to minimise their vulnerability to legal proceedings is controversial and morally questionable, but is an accepted use of corporate personality and the Court of Appeal has confirmed its legitimacy in *Adams v Cape Industries*: [1990] Ch 433. In his judgment in that case, Slade LJ cited with approval the observations of Robert Goff LJ in *Bank of Tokyo v Karoon* [1987] AC 45 at 64: 'Counsel suggested beguilingly that it would be technical for us to distinguish between parent and subsidiary company in this context; economically, he said, they were one. But we are concerned not with economics but with law. The distinction between the two is, in law, fundamental and cannot here be bridged'.
[42] [1984] 1 Lloyd's Rep 373 at 376.
[43] *Ibid*.
[44] [1984] 1 Lloyd's Rep 373 at 378.

Bingham J suggested that the third party would have been quick to seek rectification if events had transpired differently and if having the alternative company as the contractual party rather than the actual owner of the chartered ship were to have put them in a worse position than otherwise.

The *Rhodian River* decision can be justified as reinforcing the integrity of the corporate veil. A company's value as an internal partitioning device would be reduced if the internal barriers could be overridden simply as a result of mistakes or misspellings made by corporate agents.[45] This detrimental effect would not be justified by any compensating benefit, given that third parties are not deprived of their reasonable expectations at the time of contracting. If a third party does regard the precise identity of a corporate contracting party as important, then it must make this clear in the contracting process. The decision also does not deprive a third party of the additional remedies that the Companies Act expressly provides as sanctions for the failure to display or use a company's registered name on certain documentation. These additional remedies will be examined below.

The Court of Appeal reached a similar conclusion in *Porteous v Element Books*.[46] Here, a 'new age' publishing company had acquired a subsidiary and the third party had agreed to provide his services to the subsidiary. The contract named the subsidiary as the contracting party, but a director of both companies then purported to sign it on behalf of the parent company. The third party later sued the parent company for breach of contract since the subsidiary was by then in financial difficulties. The Court of Appeal rejected his claim, holding that the subsidiary was the only party to his contract and that the mistake in the signature did not alter this fact. The third party claimed to have believed that the subsidiary was merely a division of the parent company, but Peter Gibson LJ held that the test was objective and depended on the inferences that a reasonable man in the position of the third party would have made at the time of contracting. A third party's subjective and 'irrational' view on this point did not therefore determine the question of identity.

2.3 Ensuring the Accurate Use of a Company's Registered Name

The Companies Act does expose a company, its officers and agents acting on its behalf to various sanctions for failing to display or use the company's registered name as required. These sanctions include the possibility of

---

[45] There may, however, be a breach of the corporate veil in accordance with s 349(4) of the Companies Act 1989, which provides that anyone who 'signs or authorises to be signed on behalf of the company' any document within a specified class comprising 'bills of exchange, promissory notes, endorsements, cheques and orders for money or goods' and where the name of the company has not been accurately mentioned on the document is personally liable on the document unless it is paid by the company.
[46] [1996] CLY 1029.

personal liability to a third party. In particular, section 349(4) provides that if an officer or anyone else acting on behalf of a company:

> signs or authorises to be signed on behalf of the company any bill of exchange, promissory note, endorsement, cheque or order for money or goods in which the company's name is not mentioned as required ...

then this person is liable to a fine and is also personally liable to the holder of the document for the amount of it unless it is duly paid by the company.[47] Section 349(3) provides that an officer or other agent of a company is also liable to a fine if he or she:[48]

> issues or authorises the issue of any business letter of the company, or any notice or other official publication of the company, in which the company's name is not mentioned as required ... or issues or authorises the issue of any bill of parcels, invoice, receipt or letter of credit of the company in which its name is not so mentioned.

The courts have, however, resisted attempts to extend the consequences of breach of the various identification requirements beyond those expressly set out in the Companies Act. They have, for example, rejected arguments that a contract in which a breach occurs should be treated as void for illegality and that a third party should be able to avoid liability accordingly.[49]

The courts have also resisted attempts to extend the personal liability of a company's agent for not using its registered name on the basis that a third party contracting with a misnamed company should be viewed as contracting with a non-existent company. This point came before the Court of Appeal in *Oshkosh B'Gosh Inc v Dan Marbel Inc*,[50] in which a company entered into contracts under a name that it did not yet possess due to 'inefficiency on the part of its then professional advisers'.[51] It had passed a special resolution to change its name to the one used, but this was not filed until much later.[52] The company's agent was not liable under the predecessor of section 349(4) because he had not actually signed the relevant purchase orders.[53]

---

[47] Companies Act 1985, s 349(4).

[48] Companies Act 1985, s 349(3). The company itself is also liable to a fine under s 349(2).

[49] See, for example, *Cotronic (UK) v Dezonie* [1991] BCC 200 (CA) and *OTV Birwelco v Technical & General Guarantee Co* [2002] EWHC 2240.

[50] (1988) 4 BCC 795 (CA).

[51] *Ibid* at 796. The company had been incorporated as a 'ready-made' company and then acquired from its founders by the agent.

[52] Under s 28(6) Companies Act 1985, a new name only becomes effective on the date on which the certificate of incorporation on change of name is issued by the Registrar of Companies.

[53] This claim was also brought under s 108(4) of the Companies Act 1948, which was the predecessor of s 349(4) of the Companies Act 1985.

At first instance, Sir Neil Lawson accepted the third party's argument that it had contracted with a company that had not been 'formed' at the time of contracting and was only formed when the change of name took effect.[54] He therefore found that the agent was personally liable under the statutory provision governing the effect of pre-incorporation contracts. The Court of Appeal, however, rejected this view and held that the third party had contracted with an existing though misnamed company, whose identity could be inferred from the surrounding circumstances.[55]

The Court of Appeal adopted a similar approach in *Badgerhill Properties v Cottrell*.[56] Here, a company used two trading names for different aspects of its business. It displayed its registered name on its business stationery, but did not do so accurately.[57] The third party argued that she had either contracted with the company's agent personally or that she had contracted with a non-existent company with the name actually stated on the notepaper, rendering the agent personally liable in any event. The Court of Appeal rejected both of these arguments on the basis that the intended contractual party was the person or entity using the trading names and that the evidence revealed this to be the company. Woolf LJ, who gave the main judgment, noted that there was evidence to suggest that the third party was not really concerned about the specific identity of the other party at the time of contracting.[58] She was aware that the agent was involved in the contracting process somehow, but did not express any specific intention as to the identity or characteristics of the other party beyond this connection with the agent.

3 THE NON-EXISTENCE OF A CORPORATE CONTRACTUAL PARTY: PRE-INCORPORATION CONTRACTS AND OTHER SCENARIOS

3.1 The Risk of Non-Existence

Unless a third party checks the register of companies to see that a company has been duly incorporated and that it has not been dissolved or struck off the register, it faces a risk of contracting with a non-existent company. An agent acting for a company may also be unaware of its non-existence because, for example, of carelessness on the part of those responsible for forming the company (similar to that which occurred in the *Oshkosh* case) or because he does not know the precise point in the incorporation process at which a company comes into existence. Or the

---

[54] (1988) 4 BCC 442 at 445.
[55] (1988) 4 BCC 795 at 797 and 799.
[56] [1991] BCC 463.
[57] It said 'Badgerhill Property Ltd' rather than 'Badgerhill Properties Ltd'.
[58] [1991] BCC 463 at 466.

agent may not realise that the company has been struck off the register and ceased to exist.[59] Another possibility is that the agent is aware that the company does not yet exist, but may wish to make arrangements on its behalf in advance of its incorporation. In this scenario, it is possible that the third party may also be aware of the company's non-existence, but is willing to be party to arrangements made in advance of incorporation.

The common law rules governing contracting with companies can produce harsh results in the above scenarios and, in particular, do not facilitate the making of arrangements in advance of incorporation. Under these rules, a company is incapable of being party to a contract made at a time when it did not exist and cannot therefore be bound by or enforce any such contract in its own right. These rules were much criticised, one commentator remarking that it was 'rare to hear such a widespread and common opposition against any aspect of English company law',[60] but persisted until section 9(2) of the European Communities Act 1972 mitigated their effect.[61] However, there was only a partial reform of the relevant law and there has been significant doubt about its precise impact on the common law rules.[62] The law is therefore still in a far from satisfactory state, and the Company Law Review and the 2002 White Paper have not made any proposals for further reform.[63] For this reason, it is necessary to start with an analysis of the common law rules since these still underpin the relevant law and still apply in some circumstances.

3.2 The Common Law Rules

A company cannot be a party to a contract unless it exists as a legal person at the time when the contract is made.[64] The fact that a company identified as the party to a contract does subsequently come into existence makes no difference because the effect of the company's non-existence at the time of contracting is to render the contract void *ab initio* and thus a legal nullity.[65] This lack of legal effect is due to the fact that a contract can only be formed if at least two parties, in existence at the relevant time,

---

[59] See, for example, *Cotronic (UK) v Dezonie* [1991] BCC 200 (CA).

[60] J Gross, 'Pre-Incorporation Contracts' (1971) 87 *Law Quarterly Review* 367.

[61] See now s 36C of the Companies Act 1985.

[62] See, in particular, the issues addressed by the Court of Appeal in *Phonogram v Lane* [1982] QB 938; *Cotronic (UK) v Dezonie* [1991] BCC 200; and *Braymist v Wise Finance* [2002] Ch 273.

[63] The Report of the Company Law Committee ('the Jenkins Committee') (1962) (Cmnd 1749) had recommended a comprehensive reform of the common law rules. See chapter 1 at n 60 for further details of the DTI's Company Law Review, which delivered its Final Report in 2001, and of its various reports and the 2002 White Paper.

[64] *Kelner v Baxter* (1866) LR 2 CP 174; *Newborne v Sensolid* [1954] 1 QB 45 (CA); *Black v Smallwood* (1966) 117 CLR 52; *Hawke's Bay Milk Corporation v Watson* [1974] 1 NZLR 236; *Marblestone Industries v Fairchild* [1975] 1 NZLR 543; *Cotronic (UK) v Dezonie* [1991] BCC 200 (CA).

[65] *Ibid.*

engage in corresponding acts of offer and acceptance and comply with the other prerequisites for making a valid and binding contract.[66]

Moreover, whilst agency law permits a person to ratify a contract made on its behalf by an agent acting without the necessary authority (even where the principal was unaware that the agent was purporting to act on its behalf), a company cannot ratify a contract if it did not exist at the relevant time.[67] Ratification is retrospective in its effect and supplies the necessary authority *as at the time of contracting*.[68] Lord Sterndale MR stated the doctrine as follows:[69]

> ... I think it is settled law now, that when once you get a ratification it relates back; it is equivalent to an antecedent authority: *mandato priori aequiparatur*; and when there has been ratification the act that is done is put in the same position as if it had been antecedently authorised.

Accordingly, the purported principal must have been capable and competent to make the contract at the time when it was in fact made, otherwise it cannot ratify.[70] On this basis, a company cannot ratify a contract made before it was duly incorporated even if the contract had been expressly made on its behalf.[71]

Subject to statutory reform, a contract made by an agent purporting to act on behalf of a company that proves not to have existed at the relevant time is therefore a legal nullity unless the court discovers that the true intention of the persons actually making the contract was that the agent was in fact to be party to the contract.[72] If this were found to be the case, there would be a valid and binding contract between the third party and the agent. The agent would therefore be entitled to enforce the contract against the third party, but would also have personal liability.[73] It would still not be possible for the company to ratify this contract since the obstacle of

---

[66] *Kelner v Baxter* (1866) LR 2 CP 174 at 183.

[67] *Ibid.*

[68] *Koenigsblatt v Sweet* [1923] 2 Ch 314 (CA).

[69] [1923] 2 Ch 314 at 325.

[70] Therefore, a company must not only have been in existence at the relevant time, but must also have had the necessary contractual capacity, although s 35 of the Companies Act 1985 (as amended) has removed the practical significance of this: see generally on the requirements of ratification F Reynolds, *Bowstead & Reynolds on Agency* (London, Sweet & Maxwell, 2001) 17th ed ('Bowstead & Reynolds'), Arts 13–20 and B Markesinis and R Munday, *An Outline of the Law of Agency* (London, Butterworths, 1998) 4th ed ('Markesinis & Munday') at 67–74.

[71] *Kelner v Baxter* (1866) LR 2 CP 174; *Re Empress Engineering* (1880) 16 Ch D 125 (CA); *Natal Land v Pauline Colliery Syndicate* [1904] AC 120 (PC); *Re English & Colonial Produce Co* [1906] 2 Ch 435 (CA).

[72] See Bowstead & Reynolds, Art 109.

[73] It is arguable that in any event the third party is entitled to bring an action against the agent for breach of warranty of authority, which would mitigate the effect of a contract proving to be a nullity. See Bowstead & Reynolds, Arts 107–8 and J Gross, (1971) 87 *Law Quarterly Review* 367 at 385–8.

the company's non-existence at the relevant time would remain. The company could only take over the contract and relieve the agent of personal liability through a novation of the contract, which would be equivalent to making a fresh contract at the later time. This would also be necessary to overcome the effect of a contract proving to be a nullity because of the company's non-existence at the relevant time.[74]

For a third party, establishing that the contract should take effect as one made with the agent personally and thereby having a right of action against the agent is, in most circumstances, likely to be preferable to a legal nullity, unless the third party later comes to view the contract as unduly onerous and one from which it is worth escaping. The agent might also prefer to have an enforceable contract, although he might also prefer not to face personal liability. Again, the agent's attitude is likely to be influenced by how he comes to view the contract later. This mixture of attitudes, and the scope for their changing to reflect factors arising later, is unlikely to provide satisfactory evidence from which to infer a presumed common intention on the matter, but this is the only basis on which at common law a contract could have legal effect as one made with the agent personally.[75] The basis on which the courts determined whether there was in fact a contract made with the agent personally or a legal nullity was viewed as highly unsatisfactory since it gave significance to arbitrary matters such as the precise form of the agent's signature.[76]

In the nineteenth century case of *Kelner v Baxter*,[77] the Court of Common Pleas found that there was a contract between the third party and the agent personally on the ground that this was the only basis for giving it any legal effect and the parties could be presumed to have intended to give it some legal effect.[78] However, the judges in that case appear to have stated the principle too widely inasmuch as they suggested that an agent should be personally liable if no one else would be liable as principal.[79] The *Kelner* case concerned a contract which the third party had performed and where both the agent and the third party had known that the company had not yet been incorporated at the time when

---

[74] A novation may be inferred from the subsequent acts of the company: *Howard v Patent Ivory* (1888) 38 Ch D 156. However, such a conclusion was rejected by the Court of Appeal in *Re Northumberland Avenue Hotel Co* (1886) 33 Ch D 16, where a company, acting on an agreement made before its incorporation, entered into possession of land and expended money in building on it. The court concluded that the company could not have intended to make a new contract because it had acted in the mistaken belief that it was bound by the agreement that had been made.

[75] *Cotronic (UK) v Dezonie* [1991] BCC 200 (CA).

[76] See the criticisms of the common law's approach by the Court of Appeal in *Phonogram v Lane* [1982] QB 938.

[77] (1866) LR 2 CP 174.

[78] (1866) LR 2 CP 174 at 185.

[79] See especially the judgment of Byles J at 185.

the contract was made, which provided a good basis for inferring that the agent had accepted personal liability.[80]

It is difficult to justify making such an inference, however, where both parties were unaware of the company's non-existence at the time of contracting and the courts have proved less willing to make such an inference where the contract is executory and it is the third party who disputes the agent's right to enforce the contract. Such a scenario occurred in *Newborne v Sensolid (Great Britain)*,[81] where the Court of Appeal confirmed that a contract with (and thus enforceable by) the agent personally could not be inferred from the mere fact that it would not otherwise have any legal effect at all. However, the court attached significance to the form of the agent's signature and the fact that he had signed as the company rather than in his own name on behalf of the company.[82] The idea that corporate agents can be categorised according to whether or not they are acting 'as the company' has been criticised.[83] Since a company can only act through agents, it is arguable that this is a meaningless distinction and that any agent with the necessary authority to act on behalf of a company acts 'as the company' in this respect.

The High Court of Australia analysed the point in more detail in *Black v Smallwood*.[84] They interpreted the decisions in *Kelner v Baxter* and *Newborne v Sensolid* as establishing that any personal liability of an agent on a pre-incorporation contract had to be based on the express or presumed intention of the parties making the contract that the agent should be a party to the contract. This inference could not be made, without more, from the non-existence of the purported principal. In the case before them, the fact that the agents did not sign in their own names on behalf of the company, but instead signed such that 'their signatures appeared as part of the company's signature', meant that they were not parties to the contract and that it was not possible to impute to them an intention to be bound personally.[85] Although this shifts the emphasis onto

---

[80] The third party had sold a stock of wines to a projected hotel company. The company was later formed and the wines consumed in the business, but the company collapsed before payment was made.

[81] [1954] 1 QB 45 (CA). The putative contract was for the sale of a consignment of tinned meat by a company, which later proved not to have been registered at the relevant time. The market for this meat fell and the buyers refused to take delivery.

[82] See the judgment of Lord Goddard CJ at 51, approving the more detailed judgment of Parker J at 49. The agent was called 'Leopold Newborne and he was forming a company to be called Leopold Newborne (London) Ltd'. He had signed the document 'Yours faithfully, Leopold Newborne (London) Ltd' and underneath this signature was the name Leopold Newborne: [1954] 2 QB 45 at 46.

[83] F Reynolds, 'Personal Liability of an Agent' (1969) 85 *Law Quarterly Review* 92 at 102–3.

[84] (1966) 117 CLR 52. This approach was approved by the Supreme Court of New Zealand in *Hawke's BayMilk Corporation v Watson* [1974] 1 NZLR 236 and *Marblestone Industries v Fairchild* [1975] 1 NZLR 543 and by Oliver LJ in the Court of Appeal in *Phonogram v Lane* [1982] QB 938 at 945.

[85] (1966) 117 CLR 52 at 60, per Barwick CJ, Kitto, Taylor and Owen JJ.

the apparent intention of the agent at the time of contracting, it still attaches significance to the precise form of a signature, which in reality may be accidental rather than deliberate.[86]

The point is analogous to the principle in agency law that an agent can be personally liable on a contract made for a principal who did exist at the time of contracting provided that an intention on the part of the agent to accept such liability (alongside the liability of the principal) can be inferred from the contract.[87] Here, the precise form of an agent's signature and whether it can be viewed as 'descriptive' (thereby showing that the agent was contracting as a party, albeit on behalf of the principal) or 'representative' (thereby showing that the agent was acting merely as the representative of the principal) has been treated as a relevant factor in ascertaining a presumed intention to be bound personally.[88]

In situations where a company's non-existence is unknown to the contracting parties, the precise form of the agent's signature is unlikely to provide reliable evidence of a genuine 'intention' and this approach, though sound in principle, is likely to appear arbitrary in practice.[89] In reality, at the time of making a (purported) contract with a company that proves to be non-existent at the relevant time, the agent is likely to assume that he will be able to enforce the contract, but not to have personal liability. The third party is likely to have a vague conception of the identity of the other contracting party, as in the *Badgerhill* case,[90] but is likely to expect to be able to enforce the contract against someone. This mixture of incompatible assumptions and expectations is likely to provide rather ambiguous evidence that could be invoked to support a presumed intention either way.

For third parties, having to check the precise form of the agent's signature to see whether it is sufficient to support an inference of personal liability would represent a significant burden when contracting with companies, although it is debatable how it would compare with the burden of having to check that the company does in fact exist. Whilst it is relatively easy to check how the agent has in fact signed, the greater burden would arise from the need to respond to an unsatisfactory signature. In any event, the common law rules mean that third parties contracting with companies have to face a risk of invalidity and one that is not easy to combat. This risk in turn represents an additional economic cost in contracting with companies in general. The common law rules only benefit those

---

[86] See also the comments of Windeyer J on the 'ambiguities and limitations' of language in this context: (1966) 117 CLR 52 at 61.

[87] *Bridges and Salmon v The Swan (Owner)* ('*The Swan*') [1968] 1 Lloyd's Rep 5. See Bowstead & Reynolds, Arts 100–1 and F Reynolds, (1969) 85 *Law Quarterly Review* 92.

[88] *Universal Steam Navigation Co v McKelvie* [1923] AC 492 (HL). See Bowstead & Reynolds, Art 101 and Markesinis & Munday at 190–5.

[89] See, for example, the comments of Lord Denning MR in *Phonogram v Lane* [1982] QB 938 at 945.

[90] See above n 56.

third parties seeking an opportunity to escape from a contract that proves to be onerous. Providing such an escape route cannot be justified in terms of either fairness or of economic efficiency. Further, any benefit to certain third parties needing an escape route would be offset by the fact that the escape route would be open to agents as well, given that invalidity prevents both parties from being able to rely on a contract.

3.3 Planning Ahead of Incorporation

The legal nature of the doctrine of ratification underlies the other major deficiency of the common law rules relating to pre-incorporation contracts. There is no simple procedure for enabling a company to take over and become liable for a contract made on its behalf in advance of its incorporation. This affects the nature of the risk faced by third parties in general since, whether they are faced with a nullity or a contract enforceable against the agent personally, they do not acquire a remedy against the company if it does come into existence and a remedy against the agent alone might well prove inferior.

This deficiency of the common law also limits the scope for making arrangements in advance for a new company. It is possible to work around the problem in practice by using a company that has already been incorporated at the relevant time (for example, by acquiring a ready made or 'shelf' company from a formation agent or professional adviser) or by introducing terms into the arrangements which expressly provide for the novation of the relevant obligations and the release of the agent from personal liability once the company has been incorporated.[91] However, such techniques are costly and their cost is increased by any doubt about their efficacy in a given case.

It would be much less costly for there to be a straightforward mechanism akin to ratification whereby a new company could take over a pre-incorporation contract made on its behalf and relieve an agent from liability and also for enabling the third party to enforce a pre-incorporation contract against the company.[92] By reducing the costs of making arrangements for

---

[91] As Wilson J remarked in *Rita Joan Dairies v Thomson* [1974] 1 NZLR 285 at 288, 'careful conveyances take steps to avoid the uncertainty which may result from the lack of express provisions in contracts made by persons on behalf of companies which are not in existence at the time of contracting.' In this case, the agent had tried to escape from personal liability by contracting as a trustee for the non-existent company, and argued that the company had become liable on the contract by taking a benefit derived from the contract. The court rejected the argument because it did not overcome the initial problem that the contract could only take effect as one made with the agent personally and therefore enforceable against the agent personally unless the agent evinced a clear intention not to be bound, in which case it would be a nullity.

[92] In India, the Specific Relief Act 1963 provides that where the promoters of a company have made a contract before its incorporation for the purposes of the company, and if the contract

new companies, such a mechanism could be justified in terms of allocative efficiency and by improving the versatility of the company as a structuring device it could be justified in terms of dynamic efficiency as well.[93]

4 STATUTORY REFORM

4.1 The First European Directive

The European Community's 'First Directive' on the harmonisation of company law required some reform of the law governing the validity of pre-incorporation contracts.[94] This aimed at standardising the protection of third parties and at achieving greater 'security of transaction' for third parties where necessary.[95] Article 7 states:

> If, before a company being formed has acquired legal personality, action has been carried out in its name and the company does not assume the obligations arising from such action, the persons who acted shall, without limit, be jointly and severally liable therefore, unless otherwise agreed.

This identifies pre-incorporation contracts as a specific problem and arguably implies that a company should be able to take over pre-incorporation contracts made on its behalf once it has been formed. However, the statements in the preamble to the First Directive that provide the setting for this provision identify the broader problem of apparently valid contracts proving to be invalid due to the technicalities of company law.[96] This problem can arise in relation to what can be termed 'post-dissolution' contracts as well as pre-incorporation contracts.

Section 9(2) of the European Communities Act 1972 amended the common law rules applying to pre-incorporation contracts pursuant to the First Directive. This provision was consolidated in the Companies Act 1985 as section 36(4), which the Companies Act 1989 later revised and

---

is warranted by the terms of incorporation, the company may enforce it: see A Singh, *Company Law* 14th ed (Lucknow, Eastern Book Company, 2004). And the third party can enforce the contract against the company if the company adopts it after incorporation. See also the examples discussed in J Gross (1971) 87 *Law Quarterly Review* 367 at 395 and R Pennington, 'The Validity of Pre-incorporation Contracts' (2002) 23 *Company Lawyer* 284.

[93] See chapter 2 on these two kinds of efficiency.
[94] 68/151/EEC. See OJ S Edn 1968(1) at 41.
[95] See generally N Green, 'Security of Transaction after Phonogram' (1984) 47 *Modern Law Review* 671 on the philosophy underlying the First Directive.
[96] 'Whereas the protection of third parties must be ensured by provisions which restrict to the greatest possible extent the grounds on which obligations entered into in the name of the company are not valid' and 'Whereas it is necessary, in order to ensure certainty in the law as regards relations between the company and third parties, and also between members, to limit the cases in which nullity can arise and the retroactive effect of a declaration of nullity...'

redesignated as section 36C.[97] The Foreign Companies (Execution of Documents) Regulations 1994 ensured that section 36C would apply to pre-incorporation contracts with companies subsequently incorporated outside Great Britain.[98]

4.2 Section 36C of the Companies Act 1985

4.2.1 *The Terms of the Provision*

Section 36C provides:[99]

> (1) A contract which purports to be made by or on behalf of a company at a time when the company has not been formed has effect, subject to any agreement to the contrary, as one made with the person purporting to act for the company or as agent for it, and he is personally liable on the contract accordingly.
>
> (2) Subsection (1) applies —
>
>> (a) to the making of a deed under the law of England and Wales, and
>> (b) to the undertaking of an obligation under the law of Scotland,
>
> as it applies to the making of a contract.

This wording diverges from that used in the First Directive in a number of respects and the courts have had to consider how this divergence should affect its interpretation.

In the first case on the statutory provision, *Phonogram v Lane*,[100] the Court of Appeal rejected an argument that it should be construed strictly by reference to the First Directive. However, the approach of the courts to the interpretation of statutes designed to comply with obligations under European directives has evolved since that time.[101] In a later case on section 36C, *Braymist v Wise Finance*,[102] the Court of Appeal indicated that the courts must look at the meaning of the relevant directive (as interpreted by the European Court of Justice where applicable) and then construe the statute in conformity with this meaning, even though this might involve some departure from the strict and literal application of its wording.[103] However, the Court of Appeal also noted that this approach does not rule

---

[97] Companies Act 1989, s 130(4). This inserted the revised version with effect from 31 July 1990.

[98] SI 1994/950, as amended by the Foreign Companies (Execution of Documents) (Amendments) Regulations: SI 1995/1729.

[99] The only significant change from the original wording in s 9(2) of the European Communities Act 1972 is that 'by or on behalf of a company' previously read 'by a company or by a person as agent for a company'.

[100] [1982] QB 938.

[101] *Litster v Forth Dry Dock & Engineering Co* [1990] 1 AC 546 (HL).

[102] [2002] EWCA Civ 127.

[103] [2002] EWCA Civ 127 at 48–55.

out the possibility that a statute might go further than the relevant directive actually requires, in which case the directive would not necessarily provide any guidance on a point at issue.[104]

4.2.2 *Legal Issues Arising from the Wording of the Provision*

Section 36C has some vague and ambiguous wording, which does not make it clear how far it has overridden the common law rules. Subsequent case law has clarified some of the main points of uncertainty, but has also revealed the limited ambition of the reform. Its wording does not provide clear guidance on the following issues. First, what must the agent prove in order to be able to invoke the proviso and avoid personal liability? Secondly, can the agent enforce the contract against the third party? Thirdly, who is 'the person purporting to act for the company or as agent for it' and thus personally liable under section 36C? Fourthly, does the provision apply to any contract made on behalf of a company that proves not to exist at the relevant time and, if not, how is its ambit defined?

5 THE MEANING AND EFFECT OF SECTION 36C

5.1 The Proviso to Section 36C

The effect prescribed by section 36C, and thus the personal liability of the agent, is 'subject to any agreement to the contrary'. This raises the question of what the agent must prove in order to establish such an agreement and avoid personal liability under the section. When applying the common law rules, the courts sometimes used the manner of the agent's signature as evidence of an intention not to be bound personally (or of one to accept personal liability) and were prepared to impute a common intention to the parties on the basis of such evidence. For this reason, it was suggested that the courts might be prepared to infer an 'agreement to the contrary' from such evidence of the agent's intention not to be bound and perhaps even from the mere fact that the agent was not contracting as a principal.[105] This would have denied the provision much practical effect and would have maintained the uncertainty and arbitrariness associated with the common law position.

However, the Court of Appeal allayed such fears in *Phonogram v Lane* and held that the agent must show an express agreement to the contrary to avoid liability.[106] This conclusion is not surprising in view of the court's

---

[104] *Ibid.*
[105] See for example D Prentice (1973) 89 *Law Quarterly Review* 518 at 530–3.
[106] [1982] QB 938 at 944 and 946. See further on the proviso N Green, (1984) 47 *Modern Law Review* 671 at 677–682.

criticism in that case of the arbitrary distinctions that the common law approach required to be drawn.

5.2 The Legal Nature of the Contract Given Effect by Section 36C

5.2.1 *Can the Agent Enforce the Contract against the Third Party?*

Section 36C states that the contract 'has effect … as one made with' the agent, but then goes on to state in its 'tailpiece' that the agent 'is personally liable on the contract accordingly'.[107] It does not, however, state that the third party is also to be liable accordingly. This raises the question of whether the contract deemed to take effect by section 36C is a normal mutually enforceable contract and thus enforceable by the agent against the third party as well as by the third party against the agent. If it were not in fact to be enforceable against the third party, this raises the further question of what the legal nature of the contract given effect by section 36C would actually be.

The arguments for not allowing agents to rely upon section 36C are that the First Directive is aimed at protecting third parties and does not require them to be made liable as well and that the tailpiece wording would otherwise appear redundant. The provision itself though does not provide any further guidance. If the agent could not enforce the contract against the third party, the third party would in effect have an option to validate the contract. The agent would, however, still be able to rely on the common law rules to establish a personal right to enforce. The effect of denying the agent a right to enforce under section 36C would therefore be to revive the significance of the common law approach and the fine distinctions on which it was based.

5.2.2 *The Braymist Case: Enforcement against the Third Party*

The point had to be addressed in *Braymist v The Wise Finance Company*,[108] which concerned a third party's refusal to complete a contract for the purchase of land.[109] A company ('the parent company') owned the land, but its controlling shareholder wished to sell the land through a specially formed subsidiary. Accordingly, the vendor was named in the contract as

---

[107] Arden LJ referred to this wording as the 'tailpiece' in *Braymist v Wise Finance* [2002] EWCA Civ 127 at 2.

[108] [2001] 11 EGCS 174; [2001] WL 172108 (Etherton J); [2002] EWCA Civ 127.

[109] Third parties also resisted enforcement of contracts made with companies that proved not to exist at the time of contracting in *Rover International v Cannon Film Sales* (1987) 3 BCC 369 and *Cotronic v Dezonie* [1991] BCC 200 (CA). In these cases, the courts held that the agent could not rely on the statutory provision for other reasons and did not address the issue of mutual enforceability.

'Braymist Ltd', although there was no company with this name in existence at the time of contracting. The parent company later acquired a subsidiary ('the new company') and changed its name to 'Braymist Ltd', but the new company had not been incorporated until after the date on which the contract had been made. The contract was signed by the parent company's firm of solicitors 'as Solicitors and Agents' for the vendor and this firm was therefore the agent acting for the non-existent company in the making of the putative contract with the third party. The third party did not complete the purchase of the land and the agent forfeited the deposit paid by the third party, rescinded the contract and sought to recover damages for breach of contract.[110] The third party argued that the contract was void and that section 36C did not entitle anyone to enforce the contract against it.

At first instance, Etherton J held that section 36C did give an agent as well as a third party the right to enforce a pre-incorporation contract. He found several reasons to support this interpretation. He held that the First Directive did not preclude the imposition of reciprocal obligations on third parties as well as the conferring of rights, which would produce a result 'which is neither unworkable nor unfair'.[111] This interpretation would ensure mutuality, which he said was particularly appropriate because the agent's liability under the provision appeared not to be limited to damages, but to embrace specific performance as well. He explained the presence of the tailpiece wording as emphasising the abolition of the fine distinctions drawn in the common law approach.

5.2.3 *The Court of Appeal's Judgment*

The Court of Appeal upheld Etherton J's decision in the *Braymist* case, but there is a difference of emphasis in their judgments. Latham LJ endorsed Etherton J's reasoning. He said that enabling the agent to enforce the contract against the third party would afford protection both to the nascent company and 'to others who might have relied on the existence of an apparent contract in their dealings with the company; if it were otherwise the fortuitous date of the company's incorporation might affect a series of significant and important transactions'.[112] He found support in the judgments in *Newborne v Sensolid* (a Court of Appeal decision based on the common law rules) for the view that where an agent contracts in circumstances in which he is fixed with personal liability, he is also entitled to

---

[110] The parent company, the new company, the parent company's controlling shareholder and the firm of solicitors were all claimants in this action since the identity of 'the agent' was in dispute. Etherton J held that the agent able to enforce the contract was in fact the firm of solicitors.

[111] [2001] WL 172108 at 25.

[112] [2002] EWCA Civ 127 at 75. He also noted that the Jenkins Committee had recommended that pre-incorporation contracts be mutually enforceable.

enforce the contract.[113] Latham LJ also remarked upon the opportunistic nature of the third party's claim:[114]

> In my judgment, this produces a just result in that there is no good reason why the defendants should be entitled to resile from their obligations under the contract as a result of a pure technicality when in truth they wish to do so because it proved a bad bargain.

Judge LJ said that the presence of the tailpiece wording made it difficult for him to reach the same conclusion, although he reached it nonetheless. He acknowledged that the third party would be bound by the contract if he chose to proceed with it and that he could not, for example, 'cherry-pick the parts which are convenient or favourable to him'.[115]

Judge LJ saw the problem as arising where the third party had done nothing to affirm the contract and did not wish to proceed with it. However, whilst he found that the tailpiece wording clearly indicates that the highlight of section 36C is the protection third parties, he held that:[116]

> The insurmountable difficulty with [limiting the protection to third parties] is that its requires section 36C(1) to be read as if it created a complete option for someone in [the third party's] position, but never for someone in [the agent's] position, either to adopt or reject the contract, a choice to be made unilaterally by him, for good, bad, or no reason.

He acknowledged that permitting the agent to enforce the contract would mean that the third party would be liable to a party with whom he had not expected to make the contract and that the identity of the contracting party could in some circumstances be important to the third party. However, he said that the 'effect' created by section 36C would not override the normal principles of contract law for dealing with such situations in terms of the relief to which the agent would be entitled and that this concern did not mean that the agent should have no right to any relief at all.[117]

Arden LJ also had difficulty in reconciling the view that section 36C gives an agent the right to enforce a pre-incorporation contract with its tailpiece wording. She rejected the idea that it should be dismissed as non-operative or clarificatory and held that its function is to establish the liability of the agent (as required by the First Directive), but 'to leave the question whether the agent can enforce the contract to the general law'.[118] She found guidance

---

[113] [1954] 1 QB 45 (CA). In this case, an agent sought to enforce a pre-incorporation contract against the third party, but was unable to prove that he was in fact the 'intended' party to the contract as the common law rules required.
[114] [2002] EWCA Civ 127 at 76.
[115] [2002] EWCA Civ 127 at 78.
[116] [2002] EWCA Civ 127 at 84.
[117] [2002] EWCA Civ 127 at 83.
[118] [2002] EWCA Civ 127 at 59.

on this general law in *Newborne v Sensolid*,[119] which had referred to a body of case law dealing with the position where an agent makes a contract purporting to act on behalf of another party and then reveals himself to be the true principal.[120] This case law makes it clear that the agent cannot enforce the contract in all circumstances, although it does not specify precisely the circumstances in which he can.[121] In the *Braymist* case itself, however, Arden LJ held that it was clearly of no significance to the third party whether it had contracted with the agent or with the new company.[122]

5.2.4 Review of the Court of Appeal's Judgment in Braymist

Whilst Arden LJ's approach, with its reliance on some of the reasoning in the *Newborne* case and the case law cited there, might seem to complicate matters and perhaps even to suggest that common law distinctions might still have significance, it in fact focuses attention on the expectations of the third party at the time of contracting as opposed to what might be discerned from the form of signature used by the agent. This should give the law a degree of flexibility to ensure that section 36C does not undermine those expectations.

This is both fair and economically sound since the overall terms of the relevant contract can be presumed to reflect a third party's expectations at the point of contracting. This is a different proposition from facilitating a third party's subsequent desire to escape from a contract and thereby gain a gratuitous benefit that would not have been anticipated in the contracting process.[123] This approach is also consistent with the case law on the identification of corporate contracting parties and with the policy reasons supporting the decisions in those cases.

---

[119] [1954] 1 QB 45 (CA).

[120] In particular, *Schmaltz v Avery* (1851) 16 QB 655. This case law overlaps with the case law discussed earlier in this chapter on the circumstances at common law in which an agent can be found to be personally liable under a contract: see n 87.

[121] [2002] EWCA Civ 127 at 62. As Arden LJ put it, 'the circumstances in which he can do so have yet to be fully defined and winnowed out by the courts'. In this respect, it is worth noting Megaw LJ's warning in *Tudor Marine v Tradax Export* ('*The Virgo*') (a case concerning a claim by ship charterers that they were merely agents and did not have any liability of their own under the contract in question). 'We were referred to many other cases. With great respect to Counsel's diligence, I do not think that much help is to be obtained from them, beyond the broad principle that you must look at the contract as a whole in relation to the particular provisions of the particular contract that may be relevant. Contracts are infinitely various in subject-matter, content, word and form — and, indeed, in surrounding circumstances': [1976] 2 Lloyd's Rep 135 (CA) at 145.

[122] [2002] EWCA Civ 127 at 64.

[123] In those cases on pre-incorporation contracts in which it has been the third party who has resisted enforcement by the agent, such as *Newborne v Sensolid* [1954] 1 QB 45 (CA), *Rover International v Cannon Films* (1987) 3 BCC 369 and *Cotronic v Dezonie* [1991] BCC 200 (CA), the third party in each case appears to have had unrelated commercial reasons for wishing to escape from the contract rather than a particular wish at the time of contracting to deal with the company and not with the agent personally.

5.3 Who is 'the person purporting to act for the company or as agent for it' in section 36C?

5.3.1 *Distinguishing Decision-Making from Decision-Implementing Agents*

The deemed party to the contract is defined by the wording 'the person purporting to act for the company or as agent for it'. This raises the question of whether section 36C applies only to the person who actually signs or otherwise makes the contract on behalf of the apparent company or whether it might also include others involved in the overall contracting process. In much of the case law on pre-incorporation contracts, the identity of the agent has not been an issue since the same person was responsible both for taking the decision to enter into the contract with the third party and for actually entering into it. But in the *Braymist* case, the parent company's firm of solicitors ('the firm') had signed the contract, but had been acting on instructions from the controlling shareholder of the parent company ('the controller').

The new company, the parent company, the controller and the firm were all claimants in the proceedings brought against the third party. However, they argued that the agent for the purposes of section 36C (and thus the person entitled to enforce the contract as the vendor) was either (1) the controller alone or (2) the controller jointly with the parent company and the firm on the basis that the agent should be the person 'with the controlling mind in relation to instructions given on behalf of the non-existent company'.[124] The claimants' proposals on this point involved drawing a distinction between the person who makes the decision to contract with the third party on the relevant terms (who can for convenience be termed the 'decision-making agent') and, where this task is not performed by the same person, the person who implements that decision and forms the contract with the third party (who can for convenience be termed the 'decision-implementing agent'). This would entail an examination not simply of the moment of formation or signing of the contract, but of the contracting process as a whole.

5.3.2 *The Braymist Case: Limiting Section 36C to Decision-Implementing Agents*

In the *Braymist* case, Etherton J addressed this point, but it did not go to the Court of Appeal. He rejected both of the claimants' proposals and held that section 36C applied only to the decision-implementing agent and not to the decision-making agent. Accordingly, the firm alone was the deemed party to the contract under section 36C, albeit that its rights and liabilities

---

[124] [2001] WL 172108 at 26.

in this respect would be subject to its relationship with the parent company and the new company.[125]

Etherton J gave four reasons in support of his decision. First, the literal meaning of section 36C is clear on this point and the statutory party to the contract is 'the person who has purported to make the contract', looking to the point of time at which the contract is made. Secondly, the claimants' proposals, which would entail looking for the controlling mind, would defeat the supposed purpose of section 36C of abolishing the common law distinction between those agents who make a pre-incorporation contract and incur personal liability and those who do not. Thirdly, Etherton J said that if he were to accept the claimants' proposals then, if a decision-implementing agent were to exceed his instructions, he would escape personal liability to the third party despite the apparent intention of section 36C to impose such liability. Further, if a decision-implementing agent acting for a principal in existence were to exceed his instructions, he would be liable to the third party for breach of warranty of authority. Fourthly, if the claimants' proposals were to be accepted, there might be considerable difficulty and uncertainty in identifying the decision-making agent (who would be the deemed contractual party) and this might lead to 'a considerable number of people' qualifying for this role.

5.3.3 Review of Etherton J's Judgment in Braymist

For the above reasons, Etherton J rejected the claimant's proposals and held that the contract took effect as if made with the firm alone. Whilst this can be viewed as a practical solution to the case before him, deeming a decision-implementing agent to be the party to a pre-incorporation contract could seem unfair and unjust in other circumstances, especially where the agent's personal liability on the contract rather than his right to enforce it is at issue.

The common law rules did not in fact attempt to differentiate decision-making agents from decision-implementing agents. In cases such as *Newborne v Sensolid*,[126] significance was attached to whether an agent was purporting to act as an agent on behalf of the company or *as* the company (as an apparent executant of *its* will) and this distinction was inferred from such evidence as the precise form of his signature. In this sense, both decision-making and decision-implementing agents might purport to be executants of the company's will when signing a contract.

If a contract is alleged to be made by a decision-implementing agent, then it is true that identifying the decision-making agent responsible for the decision could be difficult and may not be assisted by terming such an

---

[125] [2001] WL 172108 at 27.
[126] [1954] 1 QB 45 (CA). See also *Black v Smallwood* (1966) 117 CLR 52.

agent a 'controlling mind', but there is likely to be an identifiable point at which a decision to proceed on the particular set of terms is reached. Moreover, it is arguable that if a decision-implementing agent were to exceed his instructions, then he would no longer merely be implementing a decision taken elsewhere and would cease to be a mere decision-implementing agent.

The *Braymist* approach to identifying the 'person purporting to act for the company or as agent for it' might prove harder to accept if, for example, the agent signing the contract were to be a relatively junior agent and were merely to be implementing instructions given by a superior agent and the third party were to be seeking enforcement of the contract.

5.4 Contracting with a Company that 'has not been Formed'

5.4.1 Pre-Incorporation Contracts as Part of a Broader Category

Section 36C gives effect to a contract 'which purports to be made by or on behalf of a company at a time when the company has not been formed'. This wording indicates that the provision is directed at pre-incorporation contracts and thus to the context in which the non-existence of a company is most likely to threaten a third party's security of transaction.

However, the wording of the provision could have referred directly to the underlying problem, namely that the company proves not to have existed at the time of contracting. The fact that it does not suggests that it may not cover all contracts made with non-existent companies. This would be an unsatisfactory narrowing of its scope if it were to set arbitrary or illogical boundaries on the protection it affords (both to third parties and to others) and, in particular, if the excluded contracts were to undermine the supposed goal of ensuring security of transaction.

5.4.2 Two Sub-Categories of Pre-Incorporation Contract

Pre-incorporation contracts can arise in two ways and can be categorised on this basis. First, there are pre-incorporation contracts which result from deliberate attempts to make arrangements for a new company before it has been incorporated. Here, the agent acting for the would-be company (and perhaps the third party as well) are aware that the putative company has not yet come into existence, although they are presumably unaware of the legal implications of this.

Under the common law rules, pre-incorporation contracts in the first category would have stood a much better chance of taking effect as contracts made with the agent personally. The parties making the contract would be presumed to have intended that their actions should have some legal effect. Accordingly, their knowledge of the apparent company's non-existence would give rise to a presumption that they had intended the agent to be the contracting party.[127] Although pre-incorporation contracts in this category did present a danger of invalidity to third parties under the common law rules, the main shortcoming of the law for this category was the inability of the new company to adopt and take over the contract once incorporated through some simple process such as ratification.

The second category of pre-incorporation contracts are those which occur because the company purporting to make the contract has not in fact been incorporated at the relevant time for some reason such as delay or oversight. In this scenario, both the third party and the agent are likely to believe or at least assume that the company does exist. It would have been much harder to establish that a contract in this category should take effect as one made with the agent personally under the common law rules.

It is arguable that, for pre-incorporation contracts in the second category, the fact that the non-existent company was in the process of incorporation or that the agent intended to form or acquire a company at some stage is not a crucial factor compared to the simple fact of its non-existence. Pre-incorporation contracts in the second category can be treated as part of a wider class, namely contracts made with an apparent company that proves not to exist. For third parties, the danger of invalidity, and thus the threat to their security of transaction, stems from the fact that a company might not exist and is unrelated to the particular reason for this.

5.4.3 Companies that 'have not been Formed'?

Limiting the scope of section 36C to pre-incorporation contracts rather than to the broader category of contracts with non-existent companies does not therefore appear consistent with its supposed objective of ensuring 'security of transaction.' Third parties still face a risk of invalidity even though the section would reduce it substantially by covering most circumstances in which it is likely to occur. In particular, there would seem to be no good reason for excluding contracts with non-existent companies that are not pre-incorporation contracts and thus leaving third parties exposed to a measure of risk.

A much greater potential shortcoming of the statutory provision as formulated is that its reference to the point of contracting as occurring at a time when the non-existent company 'has not been formed' suggests that the company would be 'formed' at some point. The provision could have been interpreted to so as to cover only contracts with non-existent companies that were subsequently formed.

---

[127] *Kelner v Baxter* (1866) LR 2 CP 174.

Section 36C's reference to a non-existent company as a company that 'has not been formed' in fact raises three questions concerning the ambit of section 36C, all of which have been addressed in the subsequent case law and one of which has been the subject of specific statutory amendment. First, is it necessary that the putative company must have been in the process of incorporation at the time of contracting or, at least, must subsequently come into existence? Secondly, if a company is subsequently formed, is the place of incorporation of this company of any significance? Thirdly, does it exclude contracts with non-existent companies which are not pre-incorporation contracts, in particular 'post-dissolution' contracts, and, if so, how are such contracts to be distinguished?

5.4.4 Must the Non-Existent Company have been Formed Later?

The Court of Appeal addressed this point in *Phonogram v Lane*,[128] which concerned a loan made to an apparent company. This company did not exist at the time of contracting and was in fact never incorporated at all. The third party therefore sought to recover the loan from the agent. The agent argued that the statute could only apply where the apparent company was already in the process of formation at the time of contracting and did come into existence. Where, as here, the company was never formed, there never could have been a time before it was formed. The Court of Appeal rejected the agent's argument, which was justified by reference to the French text of the First Directive.[129] It also rejected an argument that, for a contract to 'purport' to be made by an apparent company, there must be a representation that the company is already in existence.

The Court of Appeal's refusal to confine the statutory provision to whatever might be strictly required to comply with the First Directive is consistent with the approach later endorsed in the *Braymist* case. However, in *Braymist*, the Court of Appeal acknowledged that it must where necessary interpret legislation designed to comply with European directives so as to ensure that it did give effect to the obligations imposed by the relevant directive.

5.4.5 The Place of Incorporation of a Company Subsequently Formed

In *Rover International Ltd v Cannon Film Sales Ltd*,[130] Harman J revealed a serious shortcoming in the wording of the statutory provision. He held that it could only apply to a contract purporting to be made by or on

---

[128] [1982] QB 938 (CA). At the time, the relevant provision was s 9(2) of the European Communities Act 1972.
[129] [1982] QB 938 at 939.
[130] [1987] BCLC 540; (1987) 3 BCC 369.

behalf of a 'company' as defined in the Companies Act 1985.[131] The apparent company therefore must be 'a company formed and registered under [the Companies Act]', thus excluding foreign companies and companies incorporated in the Channel Islands. The Foreign Companies (Execution of Documents) Regulations 1994 ('the 1994 Regulations') reversed this finding,[132] although it is arguable that this interpretation was not correct in any event.[133] Harman J held that the statutory provision did not apply because the apparent company had been subsequently incorporated in Guernsey. As in *Braymist*, it was the third party who subsequently wished to escape from the contract and the agent who sought to rely upon the statutory provision, although in this case the agent's right to do so was not disputed.

What is interesting about the *Rover* case, and has wider significance for the interpretation of section 36C, is how Harman J inferred the identity of the apparent corporate contractual party, and its particular characteristics, from the apparent intentions of the agent and the third party. Thus, he attached significance to the fact that the parties had intended that there should be a non-Italian resident vehicle between them for their venture and that the apparent company was supposed to perform this function. Since the agent was an Italian resident, then if the statutory provision were to have given effect to the contract, it would have undermined this objective.[134]

If the parties' expectations about the contracting party's residential status had amounted to an explicit agreement that the contract should not take effect as one made personally with the agent, the proviso to the statutory provision would have ensured that it would not do so.[135] Otherwise, there is no requirement that the contract deemed by the provision to take effect should be one that would have been acceptable to the parties at the time of contracting. Such expectations might, though, provide a basis for limiting the agent's ability to enforce the contract against the third party, as the Court of Appeal later indicated in the *Braymist* case. Otherwise, the statutory provision deems the contract to take effect as one made with the

---

[131] S 735(4) of the Companies Act 1985 requires the definition set out in s 735(1) to apply 'unless the contrary intention appears'. Harman J held that there was nothing in the terms of the provision 'requiring one to construe the word differently': see (1987) 3 BCC 369 at 372. S 735(1) in fact defines 'a company' as 'a company formed and registered under this Act, or an existing company', 'existing company' being defined as a company formed and registered under certain former Companies Acts. Harman J said that this meant 'a UK Company', but since the Companies Act does not apply to Northern Ireland, the definition must be limited to companies formed and registered in Great Britain.

[132] As amended by the Foreign Companies (Execution of Documents) (Amendment) Regulations 1995: see above.

[133] See A Griffiths, 'Agents Without Principals' (1993) 13 *Legal Studies* 241 at 250–2.

[134] (1987) 3 BCC 369 at 372.

[135] After the decision in *Phonogram v Lane* [1982] QB 938, there must be an express agreement to exclude the effect of the provision. See above on this.

agent once its requirements are satisfied. Harman J did not base his decision on the proviso or on a qualification of the agent's right to enforce, but on the fact that the parties had apparently intended that a company formed in Guernsey should make the contract. If they had intended that a company incorporated in Great Britain should make the contract, then presumably they would have undermined their objective in any event.

The 1994 Regulations now provide that, with effect from 16 May 1994, section 36C (along with other sections in section 36) 'shall apply to companies incorporated outside Great Britain' and that references 'to a company shall be construed as references to a company incorporated outside Great Britain'.[136] Despite the statutory reversal of the judgment in the *Rover* case, that judgment is disturbing because Harman J used the apparent intention of the agent on certain peripheral matters in order to impute a common intention to the parties that the intended contractual party should have specific characteristics. Such an imputation of a presumed common intention, which is modelled on the common law approach, was made after the third party had challenged the validity of the contract in question for ulterior commercial reasons that appear to have arisen after contracting.

The statutory provision was designed in part to remove the need for courts to look for evidence of a common intention to deal with a contingency that the parties are in fact unlikely to have anticipated. It would therefore be better to limit any investigation into the parties' assumptions and expectations at the time of contracting to one that makes sure that the statutory provision does not undermine the third party's likely expectations at the time, since contradicting these would undermine the third party's 'security of transaction'. This is consistent with the approach of the Court of Appeal in the *Braymist* case.

5.4.6 *The Exclusion of Post-Dissolution Contracts*

The question of whether or not section 36C should give effect to post-dissolution contracts as well as pre-incorporation contracts raises two issues. First, it is arguable that the potential invalidity of both of these threatens a third party's 'security of transaction'. Excluding post-dissolution contracts would therefore undermine the furtherance of that goal. Secondly, if post-dissolution contracts are to be excluded, then the courts would have to find a way of distinguishing them from pre-incorporation contracts.

A company is most likely to be dissolved following its winding up, but under section 652 of the Companies Act, the Registrar of Companies has the power to institute a procedure that may result in the company being

[136] Regs 2 and 3.

struck off the register if he has reasonable cause to believe that a company is not carrying on business or is not in operation.[137] If a company is struck off following such a procedure, it is thereby dissolved and ceases to exist. The most likely cause of the Registrar believing a company to be inactive (assuming that the company does not formally invite dissolution in this way) is the fact it has failed to file its annual return and accounts as required. This may be due to the inadequate management of the company, but it may also reflect failings on the part of the company's professional advisers. This would make it more likely that those actively involved in the company's affairs would be unaware that the procedure for striking it off the register has been invoked. It is open to those interested in a company to apply to the court to have the company restored to the register under section 653 of the Companies Act.[138] If the company is restored then, subject to compliance with relevant procedural requirements, the company is 'deemed to have continued in existence as if its name had not been struck off'.[139]

Whilst third parties probably face a relatively low risk of contracting with a company that has been struck off the register, there is still a risk. If the company is restored, then it is likely that any contract made during the period of non-existence would be revived.[140] However, third parties could not assume that the company would be revived in this way. From the perspective of third parties, there is no good reason for limiting section 36C to exclude post-dissolution contracts. It is also arguable that, from the perspective of third parties, there is no satisfactory means of differentiating contracts made with companies that prove not to exist according to the particular reason for that non-existence without having to rely on arbitrary factors and inquiring into the assumptions and expectations of the agent at the time of contracting. In other words, excluding post-dissolution contracts could require the courts to engage in the kind of practice that led to the criticism of the common law rules.

The decision of the Court of Appeal in *Cotronic (UK) Ltd v Dezonie* revealed some of the dangers in this respect.[141] As with *Braymist* and *Rover*, it was the agent who wished to rely upon the statutory provision to avoid invalidity whereas the third party wished to escape from the contract. The third party had employed a company called 'Wendaland Builders Ltd' to do some building work. The agent with whom she was dealing had controlled a company with that name, but was unaware of the fact that this company had already been struck off the Register and

---

[137] See generally Gower & Davies at 866–870.
[138] *Ibid.*
[139] Companies Act 1985, s 653(3).
[140] See *Top Creative v St Albans DC* [2000] 2 BCLC 379 (CA), although this dealt with the institution of legal proceedings.
[141] [1991] BCC 200.

dissolved at the time of contracting. When the agent discovered this error later, he formed a new company with the same name.

In subsequent legal proceedings, the validity of the contract with the third party became an issue.[142] The agent claimed that it had taken effect under the statutory provision and that he could enforce it, but the third party disputed his right to do so. If the third party had sought to enforce the contract under the statutory provision and had been held to be unable to do so, this case would have highlighted the provision's failure to ensure 'security of transaction'. The agent's ability to rely upon the statutory provision was not raised as an issue in this case. In any event, the agent would probably have satisfied the criteria laid down later in the *Braymist* case: the third party did not appear to have attached any significance to the precise identity of the contracting party at the time of contracting. Therefore, in this scenario, if the agent could not rely upon the statutory provision, then the third party could not have done so either.

The Court of Appeal in the *Cotronic* case rejected an initial argument that all contracts with non-existent companies should be void for illegality pursuant to section 34 of the Companies Act 1985.[143] However, in applying the statutory provision, the Court of Appeal took the view that the contract could only 'purport' to have been made by either the old company or the new company. The court thus rejected the idea that the party purporting to make the contract could merely be an indeterminate company for which the agent was entitled to act and which could be treated as not having been formed at the time of contracting simply because there was no such company in existence at this time.

In order to ascertain the identity of the company purporting to have made the contract, the Court of Appeal looked for the common intention of the parties making the contract on this point. In effect, the court had to impute such an intention from the evidence available. Dillon LJ held that the party purporting to make the contract could not have been the new company because no one had thought of it. In particular, the agent had not thought of it because he 'thought that the original company was still in being'.[144] In effect, he inferred a common intention on the identity of the company purporting to make the contract by attaching significance to

---

[142] These proceedings resulted from a claim against the new company and the agent by another company. The defendants instituted third party proceedings against the third party claiming an indemnity under the contract and payment for the work done.

[143] 'If any person trades or carries on business under a name or title of which "limited" or [the Welsh equivalent] "cyfyngedig", or any contraction or imitation of either of those words, is the last word, that person, unless duly incorporated with limited liability, is liable to a fine and, for continued contravention, to a daily default fine.' The Court of Appeal, applying the approach towards 'illegal' contracts adopted in such cases as *Bowmakers v Barnet Instruments* [1945] 1 KB 65 (CA) and *Shaw v Groom* [1970] 2 QB 504 (CA) held that this section does not expressly forbid the making of contracts on behalf of non-existent companies and that a fine is therefore the sole penalty for breach of this provision.

[144] [1991] BCC 200 at 204.

the agent's mistaken belief that a specific company had not been dissolved. He did not therefore focus on the agent's mistaken belief (shared with the third party) that a suitable company was already in existence.

Having established that the contract purported to have been made by the old company, the Court of Appeal held that statutory provision did not apply because the old company had already been formed at the time of contracting. The fact that the old company had also been dissolved did not contradict the fact that it had already been formed. Dillon LJ said that the contract in the *Cotronic* case was therefore not one to which the statutory provision had been directed.

5.4.7 *Review of the Cotronic Decision*

The Court of Appeal's decision in the *Cotronic* case means that third parties cannot enforce a contract made with a company that is non-existent if there is evidence to suggest that the agent intended to bind a particular company that had been formed in the past. The court did not take account of the third party's expectations at the time of contracting. There was in fact nothing to suggest that this particular third party had attached any significance to having the old company as a contracting party or that she had assumed anything other than that she was contracting with a company which the agent was using as a vehicle for his business.

For third parties in general, the distinction drawn in the *Cotronic* case between pre-incorporation contracts and post-dissolution is as arbitrary and unpredictable as the fine distinction drawn between different kinds of agent by the common law. It means that there is a continuing risk of invalidity due to a company proving not to exist, which can only be removed by ensuring that the company has not been struck off the register and ceased to exist as a legal person. This risk is a much lower one than the risk of invalidity under the common law rules, but it would be better to eliminate it.

5.5 Claims for a *Quantum Meruit* for Work Done

In the *Cotronic* case, the Court of Appeal held that, whilst the agent could not enforce the purported contract since it was in fact a legal nullity, there might be other actions available to him such as a claim for a *quantum meruit* for the work already done.[145]

In relation to *quantum meruit* claims, it has been established that section 36C entitles a third party to recover a reasonable sum on this basis from an agent acting for a company that proves not to exist. In *Hellmuth Obata*

---

[145] [1991] BCC 200 at 205–6.

v King,[146] the judge had to consider a case concerning a company that did not exist (and was never formed) with the added complication that no contract was formed. There was evidence that the negotiating parties had a serious intention to enter into a contract, but this was not sufficient to establish that the essential requirements of forming a contract had been satisfied. The third party had performed services in the mistaken belief that there was a contract. The judge held that this third party did have a claim 'sounding in restitution' (based upon a 'quasi contract' as he put it) for a *quantum meruit* for the work already done. Further, this claim was based upon the fact that, in the circumstances, it would be 'right to infer a contract with an implied term that a reasonable remuneration would be paid'.[147] The judge held that the third party should be able to bring this claim against the agent acting for the proposed company on the basis that section 36C should apply to this situation since it was within the 'mischief' at which the section was aimed.[148]

This is an interesting application of section 36C, but may have to be revisited since it is not generally accepted that claims for a *quantum meruit* are based upon an implied contract or 'quasi contract'.[149]

6 THE CONTRACTS (RIGHTS OF THIRD PARTIES) ACT 1999

6.1 Novation and Ratification at Common Law

The statutory provision aimed at pre-incorporation contracts, now set out in section 36C, did not deal with the inability of a new company to ratify and take over pre-incorporation contracts made on its behalf. However, the Contracts (Rights of Third Parties) Act 1999 ('the 1999 Act') has mitigated this inability as part of its general reform of the common law doctrine of privity of contract.

Some care is needed with terminology in this context. This book uses the term 'third party' (and thus 'third parties' as well) in its traditional agency law sense to refer to the party that makes or attempts to make a contract with a principal through an agent.[150] However, the 1999 Act uses the term 'third parties' to indicate those who may benefit under the terms of a contract, but are not actually party to it. In relation to the 1999 Act, an unformed company may be the 'third party' to a contract made

---

[146] *Hellmuth, Obata & Kassabaum (t/a Hok Sport) v King and Frauenstein* [2000] WL 1480187 (QBD, Technology & Construction Court) before Colin Reese QC.
[147] [2000] WL 1480187 at 82.
[148] *Ibid.*
[149] See, for example, the discussion of 'quasi contract' in P Birks, *An Introduction to the Law of Restitution* (Oxford, Clarendon Press, 1989) at 29–39.
[150] See, for example, Bowstead & Reynolds, Art 1.

for its benefit. This section will continue to use the term 'third party' to refer to the party contracting with the agent and refer to the company simply as 'the company' or as 'the beneficiary', unless the context requires otherwise.

The conditions attached to the agency law doctrine of ratification mean that a company can only take over a contract made prior to its incorporation (whatever the legal effect of that contract) through a novation of the contract.[151] If the contract takes effect as one binding on the agent personally, then novation is necessary to release the agent from personal liability to the third party. Therefore, if those setting up a company (with the co-operation of relevant third parties) wish to make binding contracts for the company in advance of its incorporation and also to ensure that the company once formed does take them over and release those agents actually party to the contracts from personal liability, then they must include complex undertakings in the contracts providing for this to happen. However, these complex undertakings would not be binding on the company and the novation would not take effect until the parties actually bound had complied with them.

6.2 A Company's Right to Enforce Pre-Incorporation Contracts

The 1999 Act enables a company to enforce a contract made for its benefit, but to which it is not party, provided that the contract expressly identifies it by name, class or description, and it does not matter if the company was not in existence at the time when the contract was made.[152] The fact that a company can be identified by description gives some flexibility if the precise name of the company is not known when the contract is made. The 1999 Act, however, maintains the doctrine of privity as regards the imposition of burdens and liabilities and therefore does not enable third parties to enforce pre-incorporation contracts directly against a company once formed even though the company can now acquire rights enforceable directly against third parties.

The 1999 Act does, however, give some assistance to third parties who wish to ensure that they can enforce a pre-incorporation contract directly against a company. It is possible to link a company's right under the 1999 Act to enforce certain terms in a pre-incorporation contract against a third party to the company's performance of those terms that benefit the third party.[153] If the company fails to perform these terms, then although the

---

[151] See Bowstead & Reynolds, Art 15.
[152] Contracts (Rights of Third Parties) Act 1999, s 1(3). It is open to the contracting parties to override the 1999 Act and provide that the company should not be entitled to enforce the terms of the contract.
[153] *Ibid*, s 1(4).

third party would still not be able to take action directly against the company, it would have a defence against any action by the company.[154]

In order to underpin a beneficiary's right to enforce a contract made for its benefit, the 1999 Act restricts the normal right of contracting parties to vary or rescind the terms of their contract and makes this subject to the consent of the beneficiary.[155] However, the beneficiary has to 'crystallise' its rights under the contract before it acquires this right of veto. In the case of a pre-incorporation contract, a company cannot crystallise its rights before it is incorporated since only someone entitled to act for the beneficiary can do this. Once in existence, however, it would be possible for a company to do this. It would have to assent to the terms of the contract and communicate this assent to the third party or, if it had relied upon its rights under the contract without notifying the third party of its assent, either show that the third party was aware of its reliance on the contract or show that the third party ought reasonably to have foreseen its reliance.[156]

7 CONCLUSIONS AND REVIEW

In applying the common law rules governing the identification of contracting parties to contracts made for companies, the courts have struck a balance between the interests of companies and the reasonable expectations of third parties that is generally fair and efficient. Where a company is identified by an incorrect or inaccurate name, there may be a case for penalising the agent acting for the company or others responsible for the mistake such as the company's directors, but this does not mean that third parties should automatically have the bonus of an additional remedy when their expectations at the time of contracting have not been undermined.

The Company Law Review has in fact indicated that corporate agents already face an unduly harsh penalty under section 349(4) of the Companies Act, which makes those signing or authorising the signing of certain documents on which the company's full name is not properly stated personally liable to the third party.[157] The Company Law Review said that this remedy could be disproportionate and could give a remedy to third parties who had not been misled by the mistake and where the real cause of their loss was an extraneous factor such as the company's insolvency.

The Company Law Review therefore recommended that the penalty under section 349(4) be narrowed so as 'to target it more closely on those

---

[154] *Ibid*, s 3(2).
[155] *Ibid*, s 2(1).
[156] See generally C Perkin, 'Corporate Beneficiaries and Privity of Contract' (2000) 21 *Company Lawyer* 277.
[157] Final Report at 11.57.

who are really responsible for the breach, and on cases where there is a genuine causal link between it and any loss suffered by the relevant third party'.[158] This would be consistent with the courts' attitude towards opportunistic attempts by third parties to exploit section 36C so as to gain an additional remedy. However, the Company Law Review has counter-balanced this proposal with recommendations that the range of documents on which it is required to state the full name of a company accurately and thus which can be caught by section 349(4) should be expanded.[159]

The common law rules governing the consequences of a contract being made with a company that does not exist at the time of contracting have proved far less satisfactory. Under these rules, a third party would face a high risk of a contract proving invalid, with the only alternative, namely that of being able to enforce the contract against the agent personally, depending on arbitrary factors such as how clearly the agent had demonstrated his assumption that he was acting for a company in existence. Given the formalistic basis on which a company acquires legal existence and the role usually played by professional advisers in this respect, the common law rules could also be unduly harsh on agents, on new companies and on those interested in them.[160]

The inefficiency of the common law rules stems from the risk of invalidity (or of having a remedy against the agent alone), which represents a cost for third parties or at least entails costs in reducing or avoiding the risk. It also stems from the inability of new companies to ratify pre-incorporation contracts and the obstacle this places before those setting up a new company who wish to make binding arrangements on its behalf in advance of its incorporation. This deficiency may lead to lost opportunities and requires extra transaction costs to be incurred in order to structure arrangements around it. It must therefore reduce the value of a company as a device for structuring business ventures and therefore has an adverse impact on dynamic efficiency as well as on the allocation and use of resources. In the language of the 2002 White Paper, it must impair the ability of the company to contribute towards the promotion of enterprise and improved competitiveness.

Statutory reform has mitigated the deficiencies of the common law rules, but there is still scope for improving the fairness and the efficiency of the relevant law. The 1999 Act has, for example, made it easier for companies to take over the benefit of pre-incorporation contracts, but it is still not possible for a new company to ratify such a contract (or be deemed to have ratified it) in the same way as if the contract had been made just after its incorporation.

---

[158] *Ibid.*
[159] *Ibid* at 11.55–56.
[160] As Latham LJ noted in the *Braymist* case: [2002] EWCA Civ 127 at 75.

Section 36C has done much to ensure greater security of transaction, especially after the purposive application made in the *Phonogram* and *Braymist* cases, but the approach taken in the *Cotronic* case shows that it has not removed the risk (and associated costs) of nullity and that the much-criticised common law distinctions still make the law less efficient than it should be.

5

Contracting with the Board

1 INTRODUCTION

1.1 The Need for a Reliable Reference Point for Third Parties

T HIS CHAPTER WILL examine the power of the board of directors of a company to enter into a contract that will bind the company and the extent to which third parties can rely upon the board
as having unlimited power in this respect. The board's powers of management give it the power to approve the making of contracts in writing
under the company's common seal (if it has one),[1] to authorise the execution of documents by the company either through the affixing of its common seal or through the alternative procedure available since the reforms
of 1989,[2] to act as an agent on the company's behalf in making or approving a contract,[3] and to delegate to other 'subordinate' agents the power to
act as an agent on the company's behalf in making a contract. Chapter three
showed how the constitution of a company can subject the board's powers
in this respect to conditions and limits, thereby restricting the board's actual
authority to bind the company to contracts in these various ways.[4]

However, third parties need not be concerned about the terms or scope
of a board's actual authority if they can rely upon 'overriding rules of
attribution' that remove or reduce the resulting risk of invalidity. This
chapter will examine the overriding rules of attribution that apply when
a contract is entered into or approved by the board of a company, including
contracts that are executed as deeds and contracts made under a company's
common seal. Chapter six will then examine the overriding rules of attribution that apply when a subordinate agent of some kind enters into a
contract on behalf of a company.

---

[1] Companies Act 1985, s 36(a).
[2] Companies Act 1985, s 36A(2) and (4). These provisions were inserted in their current
form retrospectively pursuant to the Companies Act 1989 with effect from 31st July 1990:
SI 1990/ 1392.
[3] Companies Act 1985, s 36(b).
[4] On the concepts of 'power' and 'authority', see F Reynolds, *Bowstead & Reynolds on Agency*
(London, Sweet & Maxwell, 2001) (17th ed) ('Bowstead & Reynolds'), Art 1 and B Markesinis
and R Munday, *An Outline of the Law of Agency* (London, Butterworths, 1998) (4th ed)
('Markesinis & Munday') at 1–11.

Insofar as third parties do face a risk of invalidity because the board of a company exceeds its actual authority, then third parties are in effect responsible for policing the company's constitution and its internal governance. As was seen in chapter two, however, imposing such a responsibility can conflict with the usual process of bargaining between potential contracting parties (in which each party strives to maximise its own benefit) and thereby increase the costs of contracting with companies. This interference would be particularly costly if third parties were to have an open-ended responsibility to ensure that those who are supposed to be striving to maximise a company's gains from a proposed transaction are in fact doing so. To ensure the efficiency of bargaining and contracting with companies, there should be a body that third parties can use as an ultimate reference point (if necessary) to speak on behalf of a company and confirm that it is willing to enter into a particular contract. Such a reference point would in effect be equivalent to the company being able to speak for itself. Being able to refer to such a body would enable third parties to eliminate the risk of invalidity. Further, such a body would have ultimate responsibility for the internal governance of the company. Third parties would have no need to question this body's business judgment or distract themselves from striving to maximise their own gains from the transaction with the company.

This chapter will therefore review the overriding rules of attribution governing contracts made or approved by a company's board and consider how far they do in fact enable third parties to look to the board as a reliable reference point. The economic significance of these rules can be gauged in terms of the burden that third parties face in order to comply with them and of any remaining risk of invalidity that third parties still face. They can then be judged according to whether or not they leave third parties exposed to a risk of invalidity only where it is reasonable to expect third parties to assume some responsibility for a company's internal governance or where third parties are in effect the 'least-cost-avoider'. The burden of complying with an overriding rule of attribution includes the impact of any conditions that limit the ability of third parties to rely upon the rule and the action that a third party must take to remove the risk of invalidity if such a condition is not met. For example, if an overriding rule is limited, so that a third party cannot rely upon it once he knows that the board does lack the actual authority to make a particular contract, then the cost of this condition would depend on how easy it would be for such a third party to seek confirmation from a superior reference point and the degree of certainty that this superior reference point would provide.

Chapter three revealed some deficiencies of the law governing corporate constitutions in this respect. The only available superior reference point is the company's body of shareholders. For some companies, having to consult this body and obtain its approval can be costly in terms of expense and delay. Further, whilst the body of shareholders has various ancillary powers that enable it to act as a superior reference point, the precise legal nature of a limit on the board's actual authority determines how the body of shareholders must act as a collective body to authorise a contract that involves exceeding the limit. The shareholders acting by ordinary resolution (that is, through simple majority voting) cannot function as a reliable superior reference point.

One feature of the relevant law analysed in this chapter is that there is a special statutory overriding rule of attribution applicable to contracts made or approved by a company's board, but none applicable to contracts that are referred to the company's shareholders for approval. This limits the reliability of the company acting by ordinary resolution (or even by special resolution) as a superior reference point and should be taken into account in analysing the main statutory rule and assessing how far the law gives third parties security of transaction.

1.2 The Obligation to Ensure that Third Parties Enjoy 'Security of Transaction'

At the level of a company's board (as opposed to subordinate agents), statute is now the main source of the overriding rules of attribution. Compliance with the European Community's First Directive on company law harmonisation ('the First Directive') required that third parties be given 'security of transaction' when dealing with a company's 'organs' and that they should be protected from any risk of invalidity resulting from the terms of the company's constitution.[5] The Companies Act 1985 now includes some provisions that are supposed to give third parties this security of transaction by mitigating the various ways in which the terms of a company's constitution can limit the actual authority of its board. However, common law rules still underlie these provisions and prevail beyond their limits and therefore determine the nature of the risk to which third parties dealing with a company's board are still exposed.

Sections 35, 35A, 35B and 322A of the Companies Act 1985, which the Companies Act 1989 inserted in this form with effect from 1991,[6] set out the overriding rules of attribution that apply to contracts in general, whether made in writing under a company's common seal or by an agent acting on behalf of a company. Section 36A(6) and section 74(1) of the Law of Property Act 1925, which took effect in their current form in 1990,[7] contain

---

[5] EEC/68/151. See generally N Green, 'Security of Transaction after Phonogram' (1984) 47 *Modern Law Review* 671 on this aim of the First Directive.
[6] The Companies Act 1989, s 108 substituted these provisions with effect from 4th February 1991, subject to transitional and saving provisions: SI 1990/2569.
[7] See above.

additional overriding rules that apply to documents that are executed as deeds.[8] The Company Law Review has recommended some changes to these provisions and the 2002 White Paper included draft clauses based on these recommendations.[9] The Law Commission has also recommended that some improvements be made to the provisions governing the execution of deeds and these are likely to be implemented by way of a Regulatory Reform Order.[10]

The statutory provisions have taken account of the fact that at common law the terms of a company's constitution limited both a company's contractual capacity as a legal person and the board's actual authority to act on the company's behalf. The statutory rules have to override both of these effects to give third parties security of transaction and to enable them to look to a company's board of directors as a reliable reference point.

2 OVERRIDING A COMPANY'S LIMITED CONTRACTUAL CAPACITY

2.1 The Current Position

Section 35(1) of the Companies Act 1985 provides as follows:

> The validity of an act done by a company shall not be called into question on the ground of lack of capacity by reason of anything in the company's memorandum.

The Companies Act 1989 substituted this provision following a report commissioned by the DTI ('The Prentice Report').[11]

---

[8] S 36A(6) is expressed to apply to documents executed by the alternative method, leaving s 74(1) to cover documents executed under seal. However, it has been held that section 36A(6) applies to documents executed by a company under its common seal: *Johnsey Estates (1990) v Newport Marketworld* (10th May 1996, unreported but noted and discussed in the Law Commission's Consultation Paper). Discrepancies in the wording between the two sections have left the relevant law ambiguous and the Law Commission has recommended that it be clarified: see Execution of Deeds (CP) n 10 below at 11.30–11.35.

[9] See chapter one at n 60 for further details of the DTI's Company Law Review, which delivered its Final Report in 2001, and of its various reports and the 2002 White Paper.

[10] The Law Commission, *The Execution of Deeds and Documents by or on behalf of Bodies Corporate* (Law Commission Consultation Paper No. 143, The Stationery Office, London, 1996 ('Execution of Deeds (CP)'); The Law Commission, *The Execution of Deeds and Documents by or on behalf of Bodies Corporate* (Law Commission Report No. 253, The Stationery Office, London, 1998) ('Execution of Deeds (Rep)'); Lord Chancellor's Department, *The Execution of Deeds and Documents: A Consultation Paper on the Implementation of the Law Commission's Report 'The Execution of Deeds and Documents by or on behalf of Bodies Corporate' by way of a Regulatory Reform Order* (September 2002) and Department of Constitutional Affairs, *Response to the Consultation Paper* (January 2004) ('Execution of Deeds (Response)').

[11] D Prentice, *Reform of the Ultra Vires Rule: A Consultative Document* (London, DTI, 1986). The Prentice Report followed an earlier reform of the law by s 9(1) of the European Communities Act 1972, later consolidated as the original version of s 35(1) of the Companies Act 1985.

The Prentice Report had recommended that companies be given the contractual capacity of a natural person, but section 35 does not do that. It instead seeks to negate the impact of a company's limited contractual capacity on the validity of the resulting contract whilst preserving its internal effect.[12] The statutory provision was designed to mitigate, and effectively abolish, the common law doctrine of ultra vires, which the House of Lords had first invoked in *Ashbury Railway Carriage Co v Riche*.[13]

2.2 The Common Law Doctrine of Ultra Vires

2.2.1 *The Nature of the Doctrine*

The doctrine of ultra vires was drawn from public law and reflected the fact that, until the mid nineteenth century, companies could only be formed as corporations (and thus with a separate legal personality) by a grant of royal charter or by a private act of parliament.[14] In the *Ashbury* case, the House of Lords held that the doctrine applied to companies formed through registration as well. It held that such companies did not have an unlimited contractual capacity, but one that was limited to the pursuit of the objects for which they had been incorporated. These were set out in the objects clause of a company's memorandum of association.

There is a need for caution with the term 'ultra vires'.[15] It has been used to refer not only to transactions beyond the limits of a company's contractual capacity, but also to illegal transactions and transactions beyond the actual authority of a company's board. Thus, the courts have had to reject arguments that section 35 should apply to contracts or other transactions prohibited by the Companies Act such as paying an illegal dividend or an illegal repayment of capital.[16] Such contracts are void for illegality and subject to the general law governing the validity of illegal contracts. The fact that section 35 does not validate such contracts might seem obvious, but the scope for confusion on this point arises from a tendency to refer to such illegal contracts as 'ultra vires'.[17] Where this tendency to blur legal distinctions has been noted, the courts have recommended that the term be used only to refer to contracts that

---

[12] Companies Act 1985, s 35(2). There is also special provision for companies which are charities: s 35(4). See generally P Davies, *Gower and Davies' Principles of Modern Company Law* (7th ed) (London, Sweet & Maxwell, 2003) ('Gower & Davies') at 136–41 on the reform made by the Companies Act 1989.

[13] *Ashbury Railway Carriage v Riche* (1875) LR 7 HL 653.

[14] See Gower & Davies at 130–34.

[15] *Ibid.*

[16] See, for example, *Re Halt Garage (1964)* [1982] 3 All ER 1016; *Aveling Barford v Perion* [1989] BCLC 626; and *Bairstow v Queen's Moat Houses* [2001] 2 BCLC 531 (CA).

[17] *Ibid.*

a company has no contractual capacity to make because of the terms of its objects clause.[18]

2.2.2 The Legal Effect of the Doctrine

If a contract was beyond the contractual capacity of a company, its legal effect was the same as if the company had not been in existence at the time of contracting.[19] A contract made by a company that lacked the capacity to make it was therefore void *ab initio* and treated as a legal nullity. The legal problem stemmed from an inherent disability of the company itself and it did not matter therefore who attempted to make or approve the contract on behalf of the company. In particular, the legal effect was not confined to contracts made or approved by the board alone. A company's shareholders had no complementary power to enable the board to exceed the limits of its contractual capacity, not even when acting unanimously.

At the time of the *Ashbury Railway* case, companies could not alter their objects clause, but it later became possible to do this by special resolution.[20] Once this did become possible, shareholders could act in advance to enable a company to become party to a contract beyond its contractual capacity by passing a special resolution to increase this capacity as required. However, it was not possible for the shareholders to validate an ultra vires contract retrospectively through the agency law doctrine of ratification.[21] This doctrine only entitles a principal to give retrospective validity to a contract made by an agent lacking the necessary authority.[22] The principal must have been legally capable of making the contract at the relevant time and this includes having the necessary contractual capacity.[23] If the shareholders wished to validate an ultra

---

[18] The Court of Appeal in *Rolled Steel v British Steel* [1986] 1 Ch 246 noted the tendency to use the term indiscriminately to refer both to limited contractual capacity and to limited contractual power (or authority) when reviewing the decisions in *Re David Payne & Co* [1904] 2 Ch 608 (CA), *Charterbridge Corporation v Lloyds Bank* [1970] Ch 62 and *Introductions v National Provincial Bank* [1970] Ch 199 (CA).

[19] *Ashbury Railway Carriage v Riche* (1875) LR 7 HL 653.

[20] See now s 4 of the Companies Act 1985 (as amended by the Companies Act 1989). Shareholders now have an unrestricted right to alter the objects clause by special resolution, but dissenting shareholders have a limited right to apply to the court for an alteration to be cancelled under s 5 of the Companies Act 1985.

[21] The possibility of ratification was the main point at issue in the *Ashbury Railway* case. Before this case, it had been assumed that the objects clause merely limited the actual authority of a company's board and that the shareholders therefore did have the power to ratify an 'ultra vires' transaction. The Court of Appeal had held that the objects clause operated as a limit on the board's power to bind the company and could therefore be overridden by the shareholders: *Riche v Ashbury Railway Carriage Co* (1874) LR 9 Ex 224. The House of Lords held that this was not possible, Lord Chelmsford holding that a contract made without capacity 'is exactly in the same condition as if no contract at all had been made, and therefore a ratification of it is not possible': (1875) LR 7 HL 653 at 679.

[22] *Koenigsblatt v Sweet* [1923] 2 Ch 314 (CA).

[23] See Bowstead & Reynolds, Art 14.

vires contract retrospectively, they would have to increase the company's contractual capacity as necessary and then novate the contract.

The inability of a company to ratify an ultra vires contract meant that, as with a contract with a non-existent company, neither the company nor the third party could enforce it or rely upon its validity. The doctrine of ultra vires therefore presented a risk of invalidity both to third parties and to companies. However, unlike the case law on pre-incorporation contracts, there have been no reported cases involving third parties seeking to exploit the doctrine to escape from a contract. The Court of Appeal did nevertheless acknowledge that it must be possible for third parties to invoke the doctrine and not just companies.[24]

2.2.3 The Rationale of the Doctrine

The House of Lords in the *Ashbury Railway* case justified the ultra vires doctrine as protecting a company's shareholders and creditors by ensuring that the company's assets could only be used for the purposes set out in its objects clause.[25] However, the response to the doctrine in practice was that the typical objects clause evolved from a relatively concise and pertinent declaration of a company's proposed activities, such as the one at issue in the *Ashbury Railway* case, to a prolix and comprehensive list of every conceivable business activity and every ancillary power that a company might need to exercise, such as the one at issue some forty years later in *Cotman v Brougham*.[26] This evolution contradicted any economic logic in the House of Lords' judgment in *Ashbury* since it showed that in practice shareholders attached greater importance to their companies having the widest possible contractual capacity and that any resistance to this development from creditors was not sufficient to prevent it. It meant that the typical objects clause would provide little useful guidance to shareholders and creditors as to the nature of the risk they might be running.

Despite this erosion of any benefit that the doctrine might have provided, it presented a significant and costly risk of invalidity to third parties dealing

---

[24] *Bell Houses v City Wall Properties* [1966] 2 QB 656 (CA).

[25] See, for example, the comments of Lord Chelmsford that it 'was necessary, not only for the protection of those who might join such companies, but also of persons who might enter into contracts with them' and of Lord Hatherley that 'I think the Legislature had in view distinctly the object of protecting outside dealers and contractors with this limited company': (1875) LR 7 HL 653 at 678 and 687. The tone of the judgments is consistent with the so-called 'concession' theory of the company, which held that incorporation, with its concomitant benefits of separate legal personality and limited liability, was a privilege granted by the State subject to certain conditions imposed for the public benefit: see, for example, the comments of Lord O'Hagan at 690–91. This theory is now regarded as of historic interest only. See further on this theory M Stokes, 'Company Law and Legal Theory' in W Twining (ed), *Legal Theory and the Common Law* (Oxford, Basil Blackwell, 1986) and J Parkinson, *Corporate Power and Corporate Responsibility* (Oxford, Clarendon Press, 1993) at 25–32.

[26] [1918] AC 514 (HL). See also chapter three on this transformation of the objects clause.

with companies. However, the common law did not evolve in response to these economic factors to remove the risk of invalidity and thereby reduce the consequential burden on both third parties and on companies in general. This failure to evolve may have been due to the fact that the ultra vires doctrine came to provide a basis on which liquidators of insolvent companies could challenge dubious transactions by which assets were removed from the company prior to insolvency. Liquidators now have specific remedies for challenging such transactions under the Insolvency Act 1986.[27]

2.3 The Need for Reform

At common law, third parties faced a significant risk that a contract with a company might prove to be invalid for lack of capacity and this risk was not one that it could easily remove. A third party would either have to run this risk or incur the costs of checking the company's objects clause to ensure that it did not exist. If a company lacked the necessary contractual capacity (or it appeared arguable that it might do so), then the company's shareholders would have to be persuaded to increase its capacity accordingly by special resolution.

The First Directive requires that this particular threat to the security of transaction of third parties be removed.[28] Article 9.1 provides:

> Acts done by the organs of the company shall be binding upon it even if those acts are not within the objects of the company, unless such acts exceed the powers that the law confers or allows to be conferred on those organs.
>
> However, Member States may provide that the company shall not be bound where such acts are outside the objects of the company, if it proves that the third party knew that the act was outside those objects or could not in view of the circumstances have been unaware of it; disclosure of the [constitution] shall not of itself be sufficient proof thereof.

The original statutory reform of the doctrine of ultra vires addressed this problem, but dealt with it together with the conceptually distinct problem of the limits set by a company's constitution on its board's actual authority.[29]

The original reform was criticised as an inadequate and unsatisfactory implementation of the First Directive. In part, this was due to its failure to deal separately with the distinct issues of a company's contractual capacity

---

[27] See especially Insolvency Act 1986, s 238 (transactions at an undervalue) and s 239 (preferences).

[28] EEC/68/151.

[29] See s 9(1) of the European Communities Act 1972. This was later consolidated as s 35(1) of the Companies Act 1985. The Companies Act 1989 removed this version with effect from 4th February 1991 and substituted the current statutory provisions.

and its board's actual authority. Following the Prentice Report, the Companies Act 1989 substituted the current version of section 35 that addresses the specific issue of lack of contractual capacity.

2.4 Section 35 of the Companies Act 1985

2.4.1 A Presumption of Unlimited Contractual Capacity?

Section 35 was designed to remove the specific danger of invalidity due to the fact that a company's objects clause limits its contractual capacity. There has been nothing to suggest that it has not had that effect, although there has not been any case law directly on the point. However, its convoluted wording is not entirely satisfactory and does not put the point entirely beyond doubt. Thus, it is possible that 'an act done by a company' might be interpreted so to exclude an act done by its board in breach of duty or beyond the scope of its contractual power, meaning that such an act could still be a legal nullity despite section 35.[30] Whilst there has been no indication that the courts would be prepared to undermine section 35 in this way, the Company Law Review has recommended that the matter be put beyond doubt by expressly giving companies an unlimited contractual capacity and amending the Companies Act to include a provision to that effect.[31] A draft clause is set out in the 2002 White Paper.[32] Such a reform would remove any lingering doubts and ensure that invalidity due to lack of contractual capacity is no longer a risk for third parties.

Section 35, like the other statutory provisions implementing the First Directive, refers to a company. This suggests that it is limited to companies registered under the Companies Act and therefore does not include any company incorporated in Northern Ireland, the Isle of Man and the Channel Islands, nor any foreign company.[33]

---

[30] In *Rolled Steel v BSC*, Browne-Wilkinson LJ commented that 'directors like any other agents can only bind the company by acts done in accordance with the formal requirements of their agency … Acts done otherwise than in accordance with these formal requirements will not be the acts of the company': [1986] 1 Ch 246 at 304. See also E Ferran *Company Law and Corporate Finance* (Oxford, OUP, 1999) at 89–97.

[31] See The Final Report at 9.10.

[32] Draft clause 1(5) set out in the 2002 White Paper provides that 'a company formed under this Act has unlimited capacity'. The 'Table of Correspondence between the Draft Bill and the Companies Act 1985' set out in Annex C to the 2002 White Paper suggests that clause 1(5) will replace s 35. The Company Law Review has also recommended that private companies be no longer required to state their objects in their constitution: see generally chapter three of this book.

[33] See, for example, *Janred Properties v Ente Nazionale Italiane per Il Turismo* (14 July 1983, unreported) concerning s 9(1) of the European Communities Act 1972. The Foreign Companies (Execution of Documents) Regulations 1994, as amended by the Foreign Companies (Execution of Documents) (Amendments) Regulations 1995, have extended the provisions of ss 36–36C of the Companies Act 1985 to foreign companies.

2.4.2 *Distinguishing a Company's Limited Contractual Capacity from the Limited Actual Authority of its Board*

Section 35 applies to the effect of a company's objects clause on its contractual capacity, but does not deal with the other legal effects of that clause. The objects clause continues to set an overall boundary on the powers of the company and on the actual authority of the board to exercise those powers, albeit a boundary that is usually drawn very wide.[34] By limiting the powers of the company, it means that the company's shareholders can only authorise or ratify the overriding of these limits by special resolution. Section 35 does not provide third parties with any reassurance about the danger of invalidity due to these other legal effects of the objects clause. It expressly confirms that the objects clause still has internal significance. It gives individual shareholders the right to take action to restrain an act that would otherwise be beyond the scope of a company's contractual capacity, although not if the company has already become obliged to perform such an act.[35]

Section 35 gives the shareholders of a company the power to override the objects clause and to ratify a contract beyond its limits, but this power is only exercisable by special resolution.[36] Section 35 also states that the company's board of directors remain under a duty to observe the limitations on their contractual power flowing from its memorandum of association and that they can only be relieved from personal liability for breaching this duty by a special resolution, which must be passed separately from any special resolution ratifying the transaction in question.[37] Hence, section 35 has probably removed the risk of invalidity due to a company's limited contractual capacity, but does not of itself remove the other risks of invalidity stemming from the terms of a company's objects clause unless the relevant contract is approved by a special resolution.

3 THE BOARD'S ACTUAL AUTHORITY

3.1 The Limits on a Board's Actual Authority

Chapter three showed how the constitution of a company is the source of the actual authority of the board and reviewed the various kinds of limit that the constitution might place on this power. In effect, the founders of a company (and the body of shareholders from time to time insofar as they have the power to revise the terms of the company's constitution) act

---

[34] See generally chapter three on these effects of the objects clause.
[35] Companies Act 1985, s 35(2).
[36] *Ibid.*
[37] *Ibid.*

as the company in conferring actual authority on the company's board as the company's agent. The Companies Act 1985 states that a company can become a party to a contract in one of two ways. The first is by writing under the company's common seal if it has one.[38] The second is through an agent acting on the company's behalf and under its authority.[39] Prior to 1990, a company could only execute a document and therefore make a contract that would take effect as a deed through the affixing of its common seal in accordance with its constitution. The Companies Act 1985 now however, provides that a company need not have a common seal,[40] and that, whether or not it does:[41]

> A document signed by a director and the secretary of a company, or by two directors of a company, and expressed (in whatever form of words) to be executed by the company has the same effect as if executed under the common seal of the company.

It has been held that a document can be treated as being duly executed as a deed by this alternative method if two directors sign it and there is the requisite expression of intention even if the two directors were in fact purporting to countersign the affixing of the company's common seal.[42]

Although the Companies Act requires that a company's common seal be engraved with its registered name,[43] subjecting a company and its officers to a fine in the event of default,[44] this is not specified as condition of the valid execution of a document through the affixing of its seal and has not been viewed as such.[45] Thus, it has been held that a company can execute a contract as a deed through affixing its common seal engraved with its trading name.[46] However, whatever the method of execution, a contract that is executed as a deed must be executed in accordance with any relevant terms of the company's constitution,[47] although the effect of any breach is subject to the various overriding rules of attribution. The constitution of a company therefore sets limits on the actual authority of its

---

[38] Companies Act 1985, s 36(a).

[39] *Ibid* s 36(b).

[40] *Ibid* s 36A(3).

[41] *Ibid* s 36A(4). See generally Execution of Deeds (CP), Execution of Deeds (Report) and Execution of Deeds (Response). The Regulatory Reform Order is likely to make it clear that a contract made under a company's common seal, but not expressed to be executed as a deed, should not take effect as a deed.

[42] *OTV Birwelco v Technical & General Guarantee Co* [2002] EWHC 2240 at 70. The point was *obiter* since the judge found that the company had in any event validly executed the contract in question through affixing its common seal.

[43] Companies Act 1985, s 350(1).

[44] *Ibid* s 350(2).

[45] *OTV Birwelco v Technical & General Guarantee Co* [2002] EWHC 2240 at 56–59. See also Execution of Deeds (CP) at 4.13–4.14.

[46] *OTV Birwelco v Technical & General Guarantee Co* [2002] EWHC 2240 at 56–59.

[47] See, for example, *TCB v Gray* [1986] Ch 621 at 636. See Execution of Deeds (CP) at 4.3.

board that apply to all the various ways in which the board might make a contract on behalf of the company.

The objects clause of a company sets an overall limit on the actual authority of its board. As well as limiting a company's contractual capacity in accordance with the ultra vires doctrine, a company's objects clause defines the powers of the company and in this way sets an overall boundary round the board's actual authority. Where an objects clause sets out a list of ancillary powers (in the sense of the power to engage in various kinds of transaction) as well as a list of businesses and commercial activities and declares them to be independent objects of the company, then the courts have been prepared to find that this sets a tighter limit on the board's actual authority than on the company's contractual capacity. In *Rolled Steel v British Steel*,[48] the Court of Appeal held that the actual authority of a company's board to exercise an ancillary power included the company's objects clause was limited by reference to the purposes of the company as set out in that clause.[49] In other words, when determining the scope of the board's actual authority, the court construed the sub-clauses setting out mere ancillary powers with reference to those sub-clauses that specify proper business objectives for the company.

The directors of a company owe their company a distinct fiduciary duty not to exceed the limits of their actual authority. Their position is analogous to that of trustees and their duty in this respect is analogous to the trustees' duty not to breach the terms of their trust. If the board of a company exceeds the limits set by the constitution on its actual authority, this is treated as equivalent to a breach of trust.[50] The 2002 White Paper has made this particular duty the first in its proposed codification of directors' duties:[51]

Obeying the constitution and other lawful decisions
A director of a company must act in accordance with —

    (a) the company's constitution, and
    (b) decisions taken under the constitution (or by the company, or any class of members, under any enactment or rule of law as to means of taking company or class decisions),

and must exercise his powers for their proper purpose.

The fact that the directors of a company owe this fiduciary duty has implications for third parties who know that the board is acting beyond the

---

[48] [1986] 1 Ch 246.
[49] [1986] 1 Ch 246 at 295. See also *Re David Payne* [1904] 2 Ch 608 (CA). This is also the effect of the directors' duty to exercise their powers for a proper purpose, which has been treated as limiting their authority under the constitution: see further on this in chapter three.
[50] *Re Oxford Benefit Building and Investment Society* (1886) 35 Ch D 502; *Leeds Estate Building and Investment Company v Shepherd* (1887) 36 Ch D 787; *Lands Allotment Co* [1894] 1 Ch 616 (CA); *Belmont Finance Corp v Williams Furniture (No 2)* [1980] 1 All ER 393 (CA).
[51] See Schedule 2, 'General Principles by which Directors are Bound', to the Draft Clauses included in the 2002 White Paper.

scope of its actual authority. As well as (perhaps) undermining their ability to rely upon an overriding rule of attribution, such third parties may face liability as accessories to a breach of fiduciary duty. This potential liability for 'knowing receipt' will be examined later in this chapter.

3.2 The Legal Effect of a Contract Made Without Actual Authority

At common law, if a company's board makes or approves a contract beyond the scope of its actual authority, the contract is void and unenforceable by the third party, subject to the effect of any applicable overriding rule of attribution. It is not 'an act of the company' and has no legal effect at all unless ratified by the company.[52] The third party would not be able to enforce the contract against the company and the company could recover any consideration that had already passed to the third party (on the basis that it still belonged to the company),[53] again subject to the possibility of ratification. The contract is void *ab initio* and its invalidity is not contingent on its being rescinded by the company or by the court,[54] as would be the case if the contract were merely 'voidable'.[55]

A voidable contract is one that is valid and effective until it is rescinded and a third party acquires rights under it, albeit rights that are provisional. Also, with a voidable contract, rescission can be barred and the third party's rights under the contract ensured if, for example, there has been unreasonable delay or the company cannot make restitution of any benefits received by it under the contract.[56] A contract that is void for lack of authority is not voidable and does not have to be rescinded. It does not bind the company. Emphasising this distinction is made difficult by a lack of precise terminology to differentiate contracts that are void according to

---

[52] *Rolled Steel v British Steel* [1986] 1 Ch 246 at 304.

[53] *Guinness v Saunders* [1990] 2 AC 663 (HL); *Jyske Bank v Spjeldnaes* [1999] WL 819062 (CA), reported in *The Times* 28th September, 1999.

[54] In *Rolled Steel v British Steel*, Browne-Wilkinson LJ held that a contract within the contractual capacity of a company, but beyond the contractual power of its board is 'not absolutely void' and would 'be set aside at the instance of the shareholders': [1986] 1 Ch 246 at 306. However, he was contrasting the fact that such a contract could be ratified with the fact that a contract void for lack of capacity could not be and went on to hold that a third party unable to rely upon an overriding rule of attribution 'cannot enforce such transaction against the company and will be accountable as constructive trustee for any money or property of the company received by the third party': [1986] 1 Ch 246 at 307. Any implication that such a contract is valid unless and until rescinded has been contradicted by the judgments of the House of Lords in *Guinness v Saunders* [1990] 2 AC 663 and of the Court of Appeal in *Jyske Bank v Spjeldnaes* [1999] WL 819062.

[55] For example, where the validity of a contract is governed by s 322 and 322A of the Companies Act 1985.

[56] *Guinness v Saunders* [1990] 2 AC 663 (HL); *Runciman v Runciman* [1992] BCLC 1084. If voidability is prescribed by statute, as in s 322 and 322A of the Companies Act 1985, then rescission is subject to any conditions specified in the relevant statute.

whether or not they can be ratified and given retrospective validity, as Nourse LJ recognised in *Spjeldnaes v Jyske Bank* when considering the precise legal status of a contract that was void for lack of authority:[57]

> Where an agent is known by the other party to a purported contract to have no authority to bind his principal, no contract comes into existence. The agent does not purport to contract on his own behalf and the knowledge of the other party unclothes him of [the overriding rule of attribution referred to as having] ostensible authority to contract on behalf of the principal. Whether or not such a transaction is accurately described as a void contract, it is plainly not voidable. If no contract comes into existence, there is nothing to avoid or rescind, nor can any property pass under it.

In agency law, the doctrine of ratification enables a principal to confer retrospective validity on an unauthorised contract.[58] The principal in effect cures the absence or excess of actual authority *ab initio* and the contract has the same legal effect as if the agent had had the necessary actual authority at the time of contracting.[59] Whereas this doctrine cannot enable a company to ratify a contract made at a time when it did not exist or for which it lacked contractual capacity, it does enable a company to validate a contract made by an agent acting without actual authority.

When the principal is a company rather than a natural person, however, it cannot ratify the contract itself, but has to exercise this power through an agent. As was seen in chapter three, it is not always easy to discover who has the power to ratify a contract for which a company's board lacks the necessary actual authority. The shareholders have this power as a collective body, but how they must act collectively in order to exercise this power depends on the form and nature of the relevant limit in the company's constitution. This may depend on fine points of construction.[60]

3.3 The Overriding Rules of Attribution Applicable to Contracts Made or Approved by a Company's Board

3.3.1 The Common Law Approach

Overriding rules reduce the significance of the limits on the actual authority of the board of a company for third parties and thereby reduce the risk of invalidity due to such limits. They diminish third parties'

---

[57] [1999] WL 819062, reported in *The Times* of 28th September, 1999. See also the emphasis on the lack of legal effect of such a contract in *Guinness v Saunders* [1990] 2 AC 663.
[58] See Bowstead & Reynolds, Art 13.
[59] *Grant v UK Switchback Railway* (1889) LR 40 Ch D 135 (CA); *Koenigsblatt v Sweet* [1923] 2 Ch 314 (CA).
[60] See, for example, *Boschoek Proprietary v Fuke* [1906] Ch 148.

transaction costs accordingly. They do not, however, relieve the members of the board from the consequences of exceeding their contractual power. If there were no overriding rules of attribution applicable to contracts made or approved by the board of a company, third parties would face an onerous task in combating the risk of invalidity since they would have to ascertain both the limits of the actual authority of the board of the company in question and whether or not the board had in fact exceeded these limits. This would place an excessive and inefficient burden on third parties and present an unfair threat to their security of transaction. A key factor in this burden is that, as was shown in chapter three, company law does not prescribe any standards as regards the actual authority of a company's board. Further, a constitution may set limits in a complex variety of ways and forms, some of which may not even be apparent to the directors on the board.[61]

Common law provided an overriding rule of attribution, which was analogous to the agency law doctrine of ostensible authority. This rule, known as the 'indoor management rule' (or the 'internal management rule' or the 'rule in *Turquand*'), will be examined in chapter six since it still has relevance to subordinate corporate agents.[62] It enabled a third party to enforce a contract made or approved by a company's board in excess of its actual authority against the company unless the third party knew that the board was exceeding its actual authority or had actual or constructive notice of this lack of actual authority.[63] Constructive notice is a flexible concept that ensures that third parties are judged not only on the basis of what they actually know, but also on the basis of what they might reasonably be expected to know or to have found out. It ensures that the careless, the reckless and those who deliberately close their minds to the obvious do not thereby gain an unfair advantage.[64] However, in the context of contracting with companies, the term 'constructive notice' has come to be associated with the specific doctrine that third parties dealing with a company should be treated as having notice of the terms of its constitution and in effect be deemed to know these terms.[65]

---

[61] See, for example, *Re Torvale Group* [1999] 2 BCLC 605. See also 'QMH restores £2 billion' in *The Times* of 9th March 1994.

[62] This rule emerged in the nineteenth century case of *Royal British Bank v Turquand* (1855) 5 El & Bl 248; (1856) 6 El & Bl 327. See also Execution of Deeds (CP) at 5.11–5.15.

[63] *Russo-Chinese Bank v Li Yay Sam* [1910] AC 174 (PC); *Rolled Steel v BSC* [1986] 1 Ch. 246 (CA). See generally Bowstead & Reynolds, Art 75.

[64] Thus, constructive notice has been described as 'fault of a lesser degree', which 'embraces everything that a recipient acting with reasonable prudence would have discovered and everything that an agent acting for the recipient in the transaction discovered or should reasonably have discovered': Lord Nicholls, 'Knowing Receipt: The Need for a New Landmark' in W Cornish *et al.* (eds), *Restitution: Past, Present & Future* (Oxford, Hart Publishing, 1998). See generally D Fox, 'Constructive Notice and Knowing Receipt: An Economic Analysis' [1998] *Cambridge Law Journal* 391.

[65] See generally The Prentice Report at 21–24 and Execution of Deeds (CP) at 5.10.

The indoor management rule ensured that, in the absence of evidence to the contrary, third parties could assume that the internal affairs of a company were in good order and that, for example, the board of a company was acting in accordance with the company's internal rules in making a contract.[66] It reflected the approach in partnership law that third parties are not affected by any limit on the actual authority of a partner to bind his fellow partners unless they have notice of the limit. However, when the Joint Stock Companies Act 1844 made incorporation possible through registration, companies were obliged to register their constitutions as part of the incorporation process.[67] Jervis CJ said that third parties were bound to read the terms of a company's constitution, but they were not expected to do more than that.[68] However, in *Ernest v Nicholls*,[69] the House of Lords ruled that registration gave third parties notice of any limits set by the constitution on the authority of those entitled to incur liabilities on a company's behalf and emphasised the limitations of the indoor management rule. It held that third parties must take notice of public information about the company, including the terms of its constitution:[70]

> If they do not choose to acquaint themselves with the powers of the directors, it is their own fault and if they give credit to any unauthorised persons they must be content to look to them only and not to the company at large.

Third parties were not therefore entitled to presume that the actual authority of a company's board was unlimited, but only that the board was acting properly within the limits set for it by the constitution.

The doctrine of constructive notice therefore treated the company's constitution as the means by which a company's founders could specify and publicise limits on the actual authority of the company's board. Third parties thus faced a risk of invalidity if the board acted beyond these publicised limits, but only insofar as any excess of authority would be apparent from an inspection of the company's constitution and other public documents.[71] If an inspection would merely reveal the possibility of a lack of authority, then third parties would be entitled to presume that the

---

[66] In *Morris v Kanssen*, the House of Lords expressly approved the statement of the rule in *Halsbury's Laws of England* (2nd ed) vol. V (1932) at 423, namely that 'persons contracting with a company and dealing in good faith may assume that acts within its constitution and powers have been properly and duly performed and are not bound to inquire whether acts of internal management have been regular': [1946] AC 459 at 474, per Lord Simonds. The Court of Appeal applied this statement of the rule in *Rolled Steel v British Steel* [1986] 1 Ch 246.
[67] See chapter one.
[68] (1856) 6 El & Bl 327 at 332.
[69] (1857) 6 HLC 401.
[70] (1857) 6 HLC 401 at 419.
[71] *Mahony v East Holyford Mining* (1875) LR 7 HL 869; *Irvine v Union Bank of Australia* (1876–77) LR 2 App Cas 366 (PC) at 379–80; *Rama v Proved Tin and General Investments* [1952] 2 QB 147.

board was acting properly unless the third party had actual notice of facts that showed that it was not doing so.[72] This increased the significance of the difference between limits set by the constitution on the powers of the company and those on the actual authority of the board to exercise these powers.[73] The shareholders can only override the former by special resolution (at the least) and these, unlike ordinary resolutions, are supposed to be filed.[74] Compliance with simple limits on the board's actual authority to exercise the company's powers could therefore be treated as a matter of indoor management.

3.3.2 The Need for Statutory Reform

The corporate doctrine of constructive notice was therefore a significant limitation on the effectiveness of the common law overriding rule of attribution in ensuring the security of transaction of third parties dealing with the boards of companies and a major focus of the criticism of that law.[75] The protection afforded to third parties against the risk of invalidity due to the limits placed by a company's constitution on its board's actual authority was not sufficient to satisfy the First Directive. Article 9 of the First Directive provides as follows: [76]

> 1 Acts done by the organs of the company shall be binding upon it even if those acts are not within the objects of the company, unless such acts exceed the powers that the law confers or allows to be conferred on those organs.
> However, Member States may provide that the company shall not be bound where such acts are outside the objects of the company, if it proves that the third party knew that the act was outside those objects or could not in view of the circumstances have been unaware of it; disclosure of the [constitution] shall not of itself be sufficient proof thereof.
> 2 The limits on the powers of the organs of the company, arising under [its constitution] or from a decision of the competent organs, may never be relied on as against third parties, even if they have been disclosed.

The European Court of Justice (or 'ECJ') has ruled that the purpose of the First Directive is 'to co-ordinate the safeguards required by Member States … for the purpose of protecting the interests of, inter alia, third parties'.[77]

The ECJ, however, also ruled that this article does not apply to 'the national laws applicable where a member of an organ finds himself in a conflict of interests with the company represented because of his personal

---

[72] *Re Jon Beaufort (London)* [1953] Ch 131.
[73] See generally chapter three.
[74] Companies Act 1985, s 380.
[75] See generally The Prentice Report.
[76] EEC/68/151.
[77] *Cooperatieve Rabobank v Minderhoud* (Case C-104/96) [1998] 2 CMLR 270 at 279.

circumstances'.[78] As will be seen, the statutory provisions enacted to comply with this directive treat certain contracts involving a conflict of interest differently. Such contracts are subject to more stringent rules governing their attribution in any event and these additional rules will be examined in chapter seven.

4 THE STATUTORY RULES OF ATTRIBUTION

4.1 Section 36A(6)

The provisions of the Companies Act designed to implement the First Directive apply to all contracts whether they are in simple form or executed as deeds. However, section 36A(6) sets out an additional overriding rule of attribution for the benefit of third parties to deeds:[79]

> In favour of a purchaser a document shall be deemed to have been duly executed by a company if it purports to be signed by a director and the secretary of the company or by two directors of the company and, where it makes it clear on its face that it is intended by the person or persons making it to be a deed, to have been delivered upon its being executed.

As noted already, this provision has been held to apply to deeds that are executed through the affixing of a company's common seal, although section 74(1) of the Law of Property Act 1925 also applies to these.[80] The Law Commission has recommended improvements to the law governing the execution of deeds by companies to remove some ambiguity and inconsistencies, which are likely to be implemented by a Regulatory Reform Order.[81] It has recommended retaining the presumption of due execution in section 36A(6) and repealing the apparently irrebuttable presumption of delivery.[82]

Section 36A(6) may provide better protection for eligible third parties than section 35A, as will be seen below, because it refers to those acting on behalf of a company by reference to their office and does not require that they collectively be acting as the company's board. In effect, it prescribes a more easily verifiable minimum standard. However, to qualify for this protection, a third party must be a 'purchaser', which section 36A(6)

[78] *Ibid.*
[79] S 36A(5) provides: 'A document executed by a company which makes it clear on its face that it is intended by the person or persons making it to be a deed has effect, upon delivery, as a deed; and it shall be presumed, unless a contrary intention is proved, to be delivered upon its being executed.'
[80] *Johnsey Estates (1990) v Newport Marketworld* (10th May 1996, unreported). See generally Execution of Deeds (CP) at 11.30–11.35.
[81] See generally Execution of Deeds (Report) and Execution of Deeds (Response).
[82] See Execution of Deeds (Report) at 5.13, 5.33 and 6.43. It recommended that the rebuttable presumption of delivery upon execution, as set out in s 36A(5), should be retained: 6.36.

defines as a 'purchaser in good faith for valuable consideration and includes a lessee, mortgagee or other person who for valuable consideration acquires an interest in property'. Unlike section 35A, it does not elaborate on the requirement of good faith or make a presumption of 'good faith'. The meaning of this concept will be examined below.

4.2 Section 35A

4.2.1 The Nature of the Statutory Reform

Section 35A of the Companies Act 1985, which is supplemented by sections 35B and 322A, now supersedes the common law rules. The Companies Act 1989 amended the original version of the statutory reform and inserted these provisions in their current form.[83] Section 35A(1) provides that:

> In favour of a person dealing with a company in good faith, the power of the board of directors to bind the company, or authorise others to do so, shall be deemed to be free of any limitation under the company's constitution.

This provision is subject to the same basic qualifications already noted in relation to section 35.[84] In particular, it does not purport to give the board of a company unlimited actual authority and it does not prescribe a minimum level of authority. It leaves the company's constitution to determine this and does not set any limits on the forms that these limits might take. However, for third parties who are entitled to rely upon section 35A, this provision makes the limits set on a board's actual authority an internal matter and removes the risk of invalidity.

4.2.2 Elaboration of the Terms of Section 35A

There is some elaboration of the terminology used in the provision. Thus, a person 'deals with' a company if 'he is party to any transaction or other act to which the company is a party'.[85] As regards the 'good faith' qualification,

---

[83] Companies Act 1989, s 108. The substitution took effect from 4th February 1991: SI 1990/2569.

[84] The right of shareholders to bring proceedings to restrain an act beyond the powers of the board is unaffected: s 35A(4) (although this right is qualified by the principle of majority rule unlike the right to restrain an ultra vires act preserved in s 35(2)); the personal liability of directors for exceeding their powers is unaffected: s 35A(5); the operation of the section is restricted in relation to companies which are charities: s 35A(6). Also, the limitations on the powers of the board covered by this provision are stated to 'include limitations deriving — (a) from a resolution of the company in general meeting or a meeting of any class of shareholders, or (b) from any agreement between the members of the company of any class of shareholders': s 35A(3).

[85] Companies Act 1985, s 35A(2)(a).

it states that a person 'shall not be regarded as acting in bad faith by reason only of his knowing that an act is beyond the powers of the directors under the company's constitution' and that a person 'shall be presumed to have acted in good faith unless the contrary is proved'.[86]

Section 35B then overrides the doctrine of constructive notice in this context by stating that a third party to a transaction 'is not bound to enquire as to whether it is permitted by the company's memorandum or as to any limitation on the powers of the board of directors to bind the company or authorise others to do so'.

4.2.3 *The Company Law Review's Recommendations*

The Company Law Review has recommended that section 35A be substantially retained, although some different wording was proposed.[87] The 2002 White Paper included a revised version in its draft clauses.[88] This would provide that the board of a company should be deemed to have 'authority' to 'exercise any power of the company' and to 'authorise others to do so' and that 'this applies regardless of any limitations in the company's constitution on the board's authority.'[89]

The revised provision would apply to 'any question whether a transaction fails to bind a company because of lack of authority on the part of the person exercising (or purporting to exercise) the company's powers.'[90] A key difference is the absence of any express reference to 'good faith', although it is arguable that a third party's potential liability for 'knowing receipt' achieves the same effect in substance and this will be considered below. The Company Law Review also recommended that the doctrine of constructive notice should be abolished.[91]

4.2.4 *Qualification by Section 322A*

Section 35A does not appear to place any restriction on the persons who can rely upon it,[92] but section 322A varies the legal consequences for specified categories of third party such as directors and persons connected to directors of the company.[93] Section 322A(2) qualifies the effect of section 35A

---

[86] *Ibid* s 35A(2)(b) and (c).
[87] Company Formation and Capital Maintenance at 2.37 to 2.40.
[88] 2002 White Paper, draft clause 17.
[89] Draft clause 17(2).
[90] Draft clause 17(1).
[91] Company Formation and Capital Maintenance at 2.42. This was in fact supposed to have been achieved by the insertion of a new s 711A into the Companies Act 1985 pursuant to the Companies Act 1989, but the provision was never enacted.
[92] See, however, the judgments of the Court of Appeal in *Smith v Henniker-Major* on this point: [2002] EWCA Civ 762.
[93] This section applies to (a) a director of the company or its holding company; (b) a person connected with such a director or a company with whom such a director is associated, these expressions being defined in s 346 of the Companies Act 1985.

by rendering transactions within its scope voidable at the instance of the company. Since it targets contracts with directors or with persons connected to directors, this qualification can be justified on the basis that directors can reasonably be expected to make a greater effort to ensure that the board has the necessary actual authority to approve a contract with them personally (or with persons connected to them) and to accept a higher risk of invalidity accordingly.[94]

A company's right to rescind contracts that section 322A renders voidable is subject to some specified bars on rescission.[95] Section 322A also contains a provision that applies to unauthorised contracts with more than one party where one party is entitled to rely on section 35A, but another is subject to section 322A. This provides that the third party protected by section 35A or the company may apply to the court and the court may 'make such order affirming, severing or setting aside the transaction, on such terms, as appear to the court to be just.'[96] The draft clause proposed in the 2002 White Paper would remove section 322A and instead simply state that the statutory rule of attribution would not apply in favour of those third parties within the ambit of section 322A.[97]

4.2.5 Analysis of Section 35A

The statutory provision would seem to give a third party the right to enforce a contract against a company regardless of the provisions of the company's constitution (and thus of the limits on the actual authority on the board) provided the third party can establish:

(1) He, she or it is a person dealing with the company; and
(2) The contract has been made or approved by the board of directors of the company.

The company may still be able to prevent the third party from enforcing the contract (or to seek to reverse it) if it can show:

(3) The third party was not dealing with it in good faith; or
(4) The third party is within section 322A; or
(5) Another party to the contract is within section 322A and it makes an application to the court under section 322A(7).

This scheme identifies the main issues raised by section 35A and provides a basis for analysing the current state of the law. Although the significance of some of these issues is likely to disappear or vary if the new provision

---

[94] See, for example, *Morris v Kanssen* [1946] AC 459 (HL).
[95] Companies Act 1985, s 322A(5).
[96] Companies Act 1985, s 322A(7).
[97] Draft clause 17(5).

set out in the 2002 White Paper is implemented, it is far from clear when this might be at the time of writing.

4.3 A Person Dealing with a Company

4.3.1 Any Legal Person Other than the Company

At first glance, section 35A's wording seems clear on this point. Since any legal person, including a company's own members and directors, can be party to a transaction or other legal relationship with the company,[98] then any legal person other than the company itself should be entitled to rely upon section 35A.[99] On this basis, section 35A should be available to a shareholder and to a director and even to a sole director, though section 322A might also apply and limit its effect. The First Directive requires Member States to ensure that any constitutional limits on the powers of a company's organs to bind the company should not prejudice 'third parties',[100] but does not define this term or give any indication that shareholders or directors are to be excluded from its ambit.[101]

However, there has been doubt about the precise meaning of section 35A in this respect and case law has added to this uncertainty. It has centred on two issues, which will be considered in turn: first, whether directors of a company can rely upon section 35A to validate an unauthorised transaction; and secondly, whether shareholders can do so.

---

[98] See, for example, *Salomon v A Salomon & Co Ltd* [1897] AC 22 (HL) and *Lee v Lee's Air Farming* [1961] AC 12 (PC).

[99] See *Cottrell v King* [2004] EWHC 397 at 26–9. The claimant had inherited shares in a company from her late husband, which were transferred into her name. However, the company's articles included pre-emption rights in favour of another shareholder, who was also a director of the company. It was held that, since the claimant was not a *bona fide* purchaser for value, she had received the shares subject to an equitable interest in favour of this other shareholder. The claimant argued that s 35A entitled her to take the shares free of any limitation under the constitution, including pre-emption rights. The judge indicated that the claimant was not 'a person dealing with' the company as required by this section because the company was not party to the transfer of shares: they had been transferred to her from her late husband and the equitable interest arose in favour of the other shareholder. However, the judge based his decision that s 35A did not apply in this case on the fact that the matter at issue was not whether or not the company was bound by any act or transaction, but whether or not the claimant was bound by the other shareholder's equitable interest. He ruled that s 35A said nothing about this issue. Further, the fact that the other shareholder was also a director and in that capacity had had the power to refuse to register the transfer, which in fact he had not used, was not relevant to his rights as a shareholder.

[100] 68/151/EEC, art 9.2.

[101] As will be seen below, Peter Gibson LJ found support for the exclusion of shareholders in the wording of the sixth preamble, which states: 'Whereas it is necessary, in order to ensure certainty in the law as regards relations between the company and third parties, and also between members, to limit the cases in which nullity can arise …': see *EIC Services v Phipps* [2004] EWCA Civ 1069 at 37.

4.3.2 Section 35A and Directors

One cause of uncertainty here has been in the precise relationship between section 35A and section 322A. It is not immediately clear whether section 322A should be construed simply as an alternative provision to section 35A that applies where the party to an unauthorised transaction is a director (or other designated persons) or rather as a supplemental provision that overrides the effect of section 35A. If section 322A were to operate as an alternative, then all unauthorised transactions within its ambit would be voidable rather than void even when the company could prove that the third party had not been dealing with it in good faith. Given that the difference between void and voidable transactions can be significant,[102] this result would be hard to justify since transactions with 'insiders' lacking good faith might be treated differently — and more favourably – than those with 'outsiders' lacking good faith.

However, section 322A(4) states that the provisions of section 322A should not be construed as 'excluding the operation of any other enactment or rule of law by virtue of which the transaction may be called in question or any liability to the company may arise'. This implies that section 322A should not apply where the contract would otherwise be void for lack of actual authority. This in turn implies that section 322A only applies to those unauthorised contracts that section 35A would validate. Further, if the third party were also to be liable to the company as a constructive trustee for knowing receipt, this should also prevail over section 322A.

The Court of Appeal considered the ability of a director to rely upon section 35A in *Smith v Henniker-Major*.[103] The third party ('Smith') was one of only two directors of the company and had acted for the company in effecting the transaction in question. The case was also unusual because the transaction was the assignment of a chose in action, namely the company's right to sue a firm of solicitors ('the firm') for breach of various duties.

Smith, purporting to act as the company's board, assigned its right of action against the firm to himself. He then began proceedings against the firm, but the firm claimed that Smith did not have actual authority to make the assignment and that he therefore did not have the right to bring the action. Smith had been the only director (out of two) present at the relevant board meeting, but he had mistakenly believed that he could still act as the company's board. However, the company's articles, which were based on Table A,[104] set the quorum for a board meeting at two. Smith argued that he, as the third party to the transaction, was entitled to rely on section 35A to overcome his deficiency in actual authority and that the

---

[102] The difference between the concepts was regarded as crucial in *Guinness v Saunders* [1990] 2 AC 663 (HL) and *Jyske Bank v Spjeldnaes* [1999] WL 819062 (CA).
[103] [2002] EWCA Civ 762.
[104] Companies (Tables A to F) Regulations 1985 SI 1985/805, Table A ('Table A').

assignment should be treated as valid. The firm claimed that Smith satisfied neither of the two conditions of section 35A.

The Court of Appeal acknowledged that this was an unfortunate factual background against which to test the precise meaning of section 35A.[105] Moreover, the ability of anyone to bring proceedings against the firm came to depend entirely on the validity of the assignment. Due to the lapse of time, the company could no longer have taken action in its own name and the Court of Appeal held that the company could no longer exercise its power of ratification.[106] Further, the firm's employee whose conduct was at issue in the company's claim against it had died.

4.3.3 Certain Directors cannot be 'a person dealing with a company'

The firm argued that Smith, as a director of the company, should not be treated as 'a person dealing with' the company: he was not the kind of third party whose security of transaction had been envisaged in the First Directive and thus protecting him was not within the legislative purpose of section 35A.[107] The majority of the Court of Appeal agreed with the firm and held that Smith failed at this first hurdle. This was the *ratio* of their decision, but their reasoning on the point is far from clear.[108]

Carnwath LJ acknowledged that the wording of sections 35A and 322A is wide enough to include directors.[109] He declined to express a view on the position of directors generally, but held that Smith could not rely upon section 35A because he had been the chairman of the board:[110]

> As Chairman of the company, it was his duty to ensure that the constitution was properly applied; yet, he was personally responsible for the error, by which he purported to turn himself into a one-man Board … I do not see how he can rely on his own error to turn his own decision, which had no validity of any kind under the company's constitution, into a decision of 'the Board'. I see nothing in section 35A, however purposefully interpreted, to give it that magical effect.

[105] [2002] EWCA Civ 762 at 28, per Robert Walker LJ.
[106] [2002] EWCA Civ 762 at 54–82, per Robert Walker LJ. The company had already attempted to ratify the assignment, but this was held to be ineffective because the limitation period had expired. On this limit to the power of ratification, see also Bowstead & Reynolds, Art 19.
[107] [2002] EWCA Civ 762 at 49. The firm argued that it was the real third party in this scenario and that its interests would in fact be prejudiced by allowing Smith to rely upon s 35A.
[108] See A Walters, 'Section 35A and Quorum Requirements: Confusion Reigns' (2002) 23 *Company Lawyer* 325 and C Howell, 'Companies Act 1985, Sections 35A and 322A: *Smith v Henniker-Major* and the Proposed Reforms' (2003) 24 *Company Lawyer* 264.
[109] [2002] EWCA Civ 762 at 109.
[110] [2002] EWCA Civ 762 at 110. He also justified this view on the House of Lords' judgment in *Morris v Kanssen* [1946] AC 459, which had held that directors could not rely on the common law indoor management rule to overcome procedural irregularities since this would otherwise 'encourage ignorance and condone dereliction from duty'.

Schiemann LJ attached significance to the fact that it was Smith himself who had made an error in believing that he alone could constitute a valid meeting of the board and if he could rely upon section 35A to overcome this error, it would be prejudicial to the firm, which he perceived as a genuine third party:[111]

> By contrast, the solicitor firm in the present case is a third party. This provision was intended to prevent the company, and perhaps others such as the delinquent director, from relying on those limits as against a third party. It was not in my judgment intended to prevent a third party from relying on those limits.

In a dissenting judgment, Robert Walker LJ held that directors such as Smith could rely upon section 35A.[112]

The Court of Appeal's judgment in the *Henniker-Major* case does not provide any clear and satisfactory guidance as to when a director cannot rely upon section 35A. It provides support for the proposition that a sole director acting on both sides of a transaction should not be treated as 'dealing with the company'. However, it not clear whether the exclusion should also apply to a director who is not the only one acting on behalf of the company, but who is nevertheless actively involved in the company's decision-making. Neuberger J has commented on the case as follows:[113]

> The majority view in Smith was that the policy behind section 35A was such that the very director responsible for the mistake should not be able to rely upon section 35A.

It seems unlikely that the exclusion should apply to directors who are not involved in the company's decision-making.

As Robert Walker LJ acknowledged, it is hard to justify interpreting the concept of 'a person dealing with a company' so as to exclude any directors at all.[114] The revision of section 35A proposed in the 2002 White Paper would remove this problem since anyone within the ambit of section 322A would not be entitled to rely on the new statutory provision.

4.3.4 Section 35A and Shareholders

The Court of Appeal has exacerbated the confusion about the ambit of section 35A in its judgment in *EIC Services v Phipps*.[115] This case concerned

---

[111] [2002] EWCA Civ 762 at 116–17.
[112] [2002] EWCA Civ 762 at 50–53. He expressly disagreed with the view of Carnwath LJ that *Morris v Kanseen* provided any guidance on the interpretation of section 35A: [2002] EWCA Civ 762 at 53.
[113] *EIC Services v Phipps* [2003] EWHC 1507 at 203.
[114] See also A Walters, (2002) 23 *Company Lawyer* 325 on this point.
[115] [2004] EWCA Civ 1069, reversing [2003] EWHC 1507.

186 *Contracting with the Board*

the validity of an issue of bonus shares that the board of a company had allotted to its shareholders. It was claimed that the allotment should be declared void because the company's articles did not authorise the issue of bonus shares in respect of shares that were not fully paid and because the issue had not been authorised on behalf of the company by the shareholders by ordinary resolution or the like.

At first instance, Neuberger J held that a shareholder receiving an allotment of shares from a company is a 'person dealing with a company' for the purposes of section 35A and that section 35A was therefore capable, in principle, of validating this particular issue of bonus shares as fully paid.[116] He held that the wording of section 35A did not justify excluding shareholders from its ambit and that this conclusion was consistent with the policy underlying the section as stated in the *Henniker-Major* case.[117] Thus, since a company is party to an issue of shares, a recipient of such shares is a person dealing with the company for the purposes of section 35A.[118]

However, the Court of Appeal disagreed with this interpretation of section 35A. Peter Gibson LJ, who gave the judgment of the court,[119] said that section 35A could not validate this bonus issue and justified his view both on the narrow ground that a shareholder receiving such an issue of shares is not a 'person dealing with a company' and on the wider ground that a shareholder in any event is not such a person because the members of a company are not 'third parties' as envisaged in the First Directive.[120] In relation to the narrow ground, he commented:[121]

> The section contemplates a bilateral transaction between the company and the person dealing with the company or an act to which both are parties ... It would be very surprising if a bonus issue made by a single resolution applicable to all shareholders were to be rendered by the section binding in part but void in part depending on the circumstances of the individual shareholders.

As regards the wider ground, Peter Gibson LJ said that it was 'tolerably clear' from the wording of the First Directive that the term third parties does not include shareholders:[122]

---

[116] [2003] EWHC 1507 at 203–8.

[117] *Ibid.*

[118] A company is not, however, a party to a transfer of shares from a shareholder to another party and a recipient of such a transfer is not therefore a person dealing with the company: see *Cottrell v King* [2004] EWHC 397 at 26–29.

[119] Sedley LJ and Newman J simply endorsed his judgment: [2004] EWCA Civ 1069 at 43 and 44.

[120] [2004] EWCA Civ 1069 at 35–38.

[121] *Ibid* at 35.

[122] *Ibid* at 37, referring to the sixth preamble as supporting this view: see above at n 101.

In the context of a company, the term 'third parties' naturally refers to persons other than the company and its members.

He disagreed with the view of Neuberger J that the First Directive's use of the term 'third parties' did not provide much assistance in interpreting section 35A on this point.[123] Neuberger J had also attached significance to the fact that section 35A did not have to be construed as just implementing the First Directive and could go further,[124] a point which Schiemann LJ had made in the *Henniker-Major* case.[125] Peter Gibson LJ, however, contended that:[126]

> in construing section 35A, given that its purpose was to implement the [First] Directive, it must be relevant to have regard to the extent of the requirement of Art 9(2) in the absence of any other known mischief which the section was designed to counteract.

However, after implying that a shareholder in any event should not be able to rely upon section 35A, Peter Gibson LJ summarised his conclusion on this point rather ambiguously:[127]

> In my judgment, the [First] Directive supports the view that a member receiving a bonus issue is not 'a person dealing with a company'.

He also said that, unlike Neuberger J, he found neither the Court of Appeal's judgment in the *Henniker-Major* case on the ability of directors to rely upon section 35A nor the fact that section 322A makes special provision for directors and connected persons to be of any relevance to the question of whether or not a shareholder is a 'person dealing with a company':[128]

> It does not follow from the fact that the legislature has dealt specifically with transactions between a director and a company that an inference can be drawn about the applicability of section 35A to shareholders who *in that capacity* deal with the company (emphasis added).

This comment, however, suggests that the Court of Appeal's apparent exclusion of shareholders from the ambit of section 35A may be limited to transactions in which they deal with their company *qua* shareholder and not in some other capacity. Nevertheless, this point will require further clarification and, in any event, there would still be a significant limit on the ambit of section 35A.

---

[123] *Ibid.*
[124] [2003] EWHC 1507 at 197.
[125] [2002] EWCA Civ 762 at 119.
[126] [2004] EWCA Civ 1069 at 37.
[127] *Ibid.*
[128] [2004] EWCA Civ 1069 at 38.

4.4 The 'Power of the Board of Directors'

4.4.1 Identifying the 'Board of Directors'

Smith v Henniker-Major highlighted a further deficiency of section 35A and one which the revised provision proposed in the 2002 White Paper would not remedy. Having highlighted the point, it failed to resolve it since the point was *obiter* to the majority's decision in the case.

Section 35A deems the power of 'the board of directors' of a company to be free of any limitation under its constitution, but a company's board is as much an artificial construct as the company itself. A company's board is its directors (or sole director where this is permitted) acting collectively as a decision-making body in accordance with its constitution. In effect, a company's constitution defines its board as well as defining the board's actual authority.[129]

4.4.2 The Relevance of Procedural Regulations such as Quorum Requirements

In the *Henniker-Major* case, a single director purported to act as a company's board in authorising the execution of an assignment, but the constitution did not authorise him to act as the board because a quorum of two directors was required. A third party has no means of knowing whether something that purports to be a decision or action of a company's board has been made or done in compliance with those regulations in the company's constitution that govern the operation of its board as a decision-making body except by checking the constitution. However, requiring third parties to check a company's constitution for this purpose would contradict the underlying purpose of section 35A and expose them to an onerous risk of invalidity.

Terms in the constitution specifying the quorum for meetings of the board pose a particular danger in this respect. In the *Henniker-Major* case, the question arose because the purported board meeting did not have the standard quorum of two directors, but the same issue would have been raised by an unusual procedural restriction. A company's constitution might, for example, specify a quorum of three or more or require certain directors (such as one representing a particular shareholder or class of shareholders) to be included in the quorum. Such special provisions might be included in the constitutions of joint venture companies or used to protect minority shareholders. Also, constitutions based on Table A exclude directors with a conflict of interest in a particular transaction from being included in the quorum of a meeting that approves (or takes some other decision concerning) the transaction.[130] Such provisions increase the

---

[129] See generally chapter 3 on the operation of the board.
[130] *Grant v UK Switchback Railway* (1889) LR 40 Ch D 135 (CA).

danger that an action purporting to be that of the board might prove not to be so under the constitution.

4.4.3 Do Procedural Regulations Define the Board or Merely Limit its Powers?

It was argued in the *Henniker-Major* case that those regulations in a company's constitution prescribing how the board should operate when exercising its powers should be viewed as limitations on the 'power of the board of directors' for the purposes of section 35A. The *Henniker-Major* case was complicated by the fact that the third party was also a director and that a director might reasonably be expected to know the procedural restrictions on the board. However, this fact should not be relevant to this particular condition of section 35A, although it might be relevant to the question of whether the presumption of good faith could be rebutted.[131]

It is difficult to see how this risk to third parties can be removed without having a prescribed objective standard as to what a third party can presume to be an action of the board of a company. Such a standard should also address the question of minimum evidence, for example by providing that a third party could rely upon a minute signed by two directors of a company or by a director and the company's secretary, along the lines of section 36A(6).[132] However, section 35A provides no standard of this kind and no guidance as to what it might be.

The apparent risk of invalidity to third parties stemming from the second condition of section 35A had been identified in relation to section 9(1) of the European Communities Act 1972, the predecessor of section 35A, in *TCB v Gray*.[133] This case concerned the validity of a debenture that had been executed by the attorney of a director rather than by a director as required by the company's constitution. Sir Nicholas Browne-Wilkinson V-C said that the 'manifest purpose' of the First Directive and the statutory provision was to 'enable people to deal with a company in good faith without being adversely affected by … its rules for internal management' and that 'any provision in the articles as to the manner in which the directors can act as agents for the company is a limitation on their power to bind the company and as such falls within … section 9(1)'.[134] However, he also found that all the directors of the company had approved the debenture, albeit not at a meeting,[135] and case law has established that an informal

---

[131] In the *Henniker-Major* case, the question of whether the firm of solicitors could rebut the presumption that Smith had been dealing with the company in good faith would have been a matter for any full trial of the action so the Court of Appeal had to proceed on the basis of the presumption of good faith.
[132] See Section 4.1 above.
[133] [1987] Ch 458.
[134] [1987] Ch 458 at 635–6.
[135] [1987] Ch 458 at 637.

decision in which all the directors of a company acquiesce is as much a decision of the directors (in the sense of the board) as one taken formally at a meeting.[136] This must limit the value of his view that procedural restrictions should also be covered by the statutory provision.[137]

4.4.4 The Approach to the Issue in the Henniker-Major Case

The *Henniker-Major* case raised the problem much more sharply than *TCB v. Gray* had done. Smith could only rely upon section 35A to validate the assignment if the quorum requirement could be treated as a limitation on the actual authority of the company's board so that Smith acting alone as the board could still be treated as the company's 'board of directors' for this purpose. At first instance, Rimer J had followed the logic of the wording of section 35A and held that it could only apply to an action of the board of directors in accordance with the procedure, and thus the procedural restrictions, specified in the company's constitution. On this basis, Smith could not rely on section 35A because the company's board could not operate through an inquorate meeting and the power of 'the board of directors' was not therefore relevant.

Rimer J acknowledged that his decision would have been the same if the constitution had set the quorum at three and a meeting of two directors had purported to act as the board:[138]

> The point of inquiry as to whether section 35A has any application has simply not been reached. It is irrelevant to inquire whether a particular power is free of a particular limitation in a case in which the power has not been exercised at all.

According to Rimer J, therefore, section 35A was irrelevant in the *Henniker-Major* case. Smith had purported to act as the board, but was not the board as defined by the terms of the company's constitution. This definitional problem was not one that section 35A addressed.

A majority of the Court of Appeal disagreed with Rimer J's interpretation of section 35A, although their decision on the point is much less clearly reasoned.[139] Robert Walker LJ expressed the issue in terms of having to find an 'irreducible minimum' at which point section 35A would be 'engaged' and a third party would be able to rely upon a purported action of the board of a company as something that would bind the company

---

[136] *Re Bonelli's Telegraph Co* (1871) LR 12 Eq 246; *Charterhouse Investment Trust v Tempest Diesels* (1985) 1 BCC 99; *Runciman v Walter Runciman plc* [1992] BCLC 1084. See chapter three.

[137] Rimer J, at first instance in *Smith v Henniker-Major* [2002] BCC 544, noted this finding and treated the *TCB* judgment as consistent with his own judgment that section 35A does not apply to procedural restrictions.

[138] [2002] BCC 544 at 549–50.

[139] See generally A Walters, (2002) 23 *Company Lawyer* 325.

regardless of any procedural restrictions in the company's constitution. He suggested a rudimentary definition of this irreducible minimum:[140]

> In my judgment, the irreducible minimum, if section 35A is to be engaged, is a genuine decision taken by a person or persons who can on substantial grounds claim to be the board of directors acting as such (even if the proceedings of the board are marred by procedural irregularities of a more or less serious character). This is not a precise test and it would have to be worked out on a case by case basis. But the essential distinction is between nullity (or non-event) and procedural irregularity.

His reference to the fact that whoever purports to act as the board must have "substantial grounds" for claiming to be so was designed to ensure that section 35A could not expose companies to the danger of being bound by impostors or by an ambitious office boy pretending to be on the board. Presumably, this definition would include defectively appointed directors and *de facto* directors, but not junior officers or impostors.[141]

Robert Walker LJ found support for his approach in the judgment of Sir Nicholas Browne-Wilkinson V-C in *TCB v Gray* and in particular his finding that the debenture was valid because the directors had all approved it informally even though they had not done so formally at a meeting.[142] However, as noted above, there is case law to suggest that the directors of a company can exercise the powers of the board when they act informally but unanimously.[143] In any event, it is arguable that Robert Walker LJ's definition of the 'irreducible minimum' restates the problem rather than solving it, as he appears to have realised. Given his finding that section 35A did apply to Smith's action in the *Henniker-Major* case, the problem could only be solved through an explicit presumption that one director of a company has the authority to make or approve a contract (or other transaction) when he purports to act as the board of a company. Any further question as to the reasonableness of a particular third party relying upon this presumption in a particular set of circumstances would not be relevant at this point, but would be relevant to the good faith qualification.

In the case of a public company, which is required to have at least two directors in most cases,[144] it would be appropriate for the presumption to apply to two directors purporting to act as the board. Only a presumption along these lines would ensure a third party's security of transaction and remove the need for third parties to have to check the constitution. However, it involves stretching the wording of section 35A and it would

---

[140] [2002] EWCA Civ 762 at 41.
[141] See the definition of a 'director' in s 741(1) of the Companies Act 1985 as including 'any person occupying the position of director by whatever name called'.
[142] [1987] Ch 458 at 637.
[143] *Runciman v Walter Runciman plc* [1992] BCLC 1084.
[144] Companies Act 1985, s 282.

be better if it were stated explicitly in the relevant provision rather than having to be inferred by the courts.

Carnwath LJ commented on the need to establish a minimum threshold for section 35A as follows:[145]

> I would be reluctant, however, to treat that reasoning [in *TCB*], which was related to the facts of the case, as laying down a general test. Nor is this the case in which to attempt the task. A purposive test to the section suggests a low threshold. The general policy seems to be that, if a document is put forward as a decision of the Board by someone appearing to act on behalf of the company, in circumstances where there is no reason to doubt its authenticity, a person dealing with the company in good faith should be able to take it at face value.

This comes quite close to the solution suggested above, although it is not categorical enough to provide third parties with the reassurance necessary to ensure security of transaction. Again, there is a blurring of the 'irreducible minimum' with the question of a particular third party's good faith and it is in relation to the latter point that the question of whether or not there is any 'reason to doubt its authenticity' should be considered.

Schiemann LJ did not express a view on the minimum threshold, although he did remark:[146]

> The fact we are dealing with a one man board meeting I agree is irrelevant. My reasoning and conclusions would be the same if the articles required a quorum of three and there had been merely two who attended the board meeting which resolved to part with the company's assets to them.

However, he was presumably referring to his finding that Smith, as an interested director, was unable to rely upon section 35A at all.

4.4.5 *Review of the Second Condition after the Henniker-Major Judgments*

Since Carnwath LJ and Schiemann LJ reached their decision in this case on the basis that Smith did not satisfy the first condition and that he could not therefore rely upon section 35A in any event, the Court of Appeal's judgments on the point at which section 35A is engaged are *obiter*. Thus, although the judges recognised that Rimer J's decision on this point would reduce the reassurance that section 35A is supposed to provide to third parties and give third parties a continuing reason to check the constitutions of companies, the Court of Appeal did not provide a coherent and convincing rebuttal of his interpretation.

---

[145] [2002] EWCA Civ 762 at 108.
[146] [2002] EWCA Civ 762 at 126.

The *Henniker-Major* case has therefore left the law on this point in a state of uncertainty. It is possible to speculate that if another case comes before the courts, in which an 'outsider' third party seeks to rely upon section 35A to overcome a failure to comply with an unusual quorum requirement, they would make a purposive interpretation of the section along the lines of those that Robert Walker LJ and Carnwath LJ attempted. This would give the third party the security of transaction anticipated in the First Directive without having to rely upon the common law rules and consider the possible impact of the doctrine of constructive notice. However, until there is such a case, the scope for speculating along these lines does not remove the greater risk of invalidity that third parties have to face.

The proposed revision of section 35A set out in the 2002 White Paper would not resolve the problem exposed by the *Henniker-Major* case because it still refers to the 'board of directors' and the 'authority' of the board to exercise any power of the company or to authorise others to do so.[147] It would therefore leave it to the courts to decide whether to follow the line taken by Rimer J or to develop the approach suggested in the Court of Appeal and define an 'irreducible minimum' that would trigger the statutory provision regardless of the procedural regulations governing the operation of the board. The proposed abolition of the doctrine of constructive notice would, however, make it much easier for third parties to rely upon the common law rules.[148]

However, as is clear from the provisional definitions suggested by Robert Walker LJ and Carnwath LJ in the *Henniker-Major* case, it may prove difficult for the courts to do this with the clarity necessary to provide useful guidance to third parties in general without explicit guidance in the statute. It would therefore be better if this issue were to be addressed as part of the reform process so that a revised version of section 35A does specify the 'irreducible minimum'.

4.4.6 *The Complementary Powers of the Shareholders*

There is another situation that would not satisfy the second condition of section 35A. This is where the shareholders of a company approve a contract in order to override a limit on the board's actual authority. As was noted in chapter three, the shareholders' power to do this stems from various complementary powers, including their power to alter the provisions in the constitution that impose the relevant limits on the board's actual authority. However, as was also noted in chapter three, the way in which the shareholders must act collectively in order to exercise these

---

[147] 2002 White Paper, Draft Clauses at 17(2).
[148] *Ibid* at 17(8).

complementary powers varies according to the nature and form of the limit. Thus, whereas the shareholders can approve a contract that is within the powers of the company by ordinary resolution, they may have to act unanimously to override a limit that is entrenched in the company's memorandum. One particular source of uncertainty is the possibility that class rights may set limits on the board's authority.[149]

Third parties may therefore lack certainty as to how a company's shareholders should act in order to approve a particular contract in accordance with its constitution. This uncertainty could only be removed if the shareholders are unanimous in their approval, but that may not be practical. In practice, it can prove difficult to identify all the limits on the board's actual authority and the legal nature of these limits.[150] Third parties therefore face a potentially onerous risk of invalidity for this reason. The common law rules provide limited reassurance because of the doctrine of constructive notice.

The principle of security of transaction that underlies section 35A means that third parties should have reassurance in this kind of scenario (in effect, an 'irreducible minimum') that is equivalent to section 35A's reassurance about the power of the board. It should protect third parties against any limits on the actual authority of the board arising from the terms of a company's constitution. For example, it could take the form of a presumption that a contract made or approved by the board of a company and with the approval of an ordinary resolution of the shareholders is sufficient to bind the company. As with section 35A, this would not override the internal consequences of acting in breach of the terms of a company's constitution where something more than an ordinary resolution is in fact required. It could also be subject to the good faith qualification, which will be examined in the next section.

5 THE GOOD FAITH QUALIFICATION

5.1 A Third Condition of Section 35A

A third party who can satisfy the first two conditions of being able to rely upon section 35A to ensure the validity of an unauthorised contract may still be unable to do so if they can be shown not to have been dealing with the company 'in good faith'. The provision includes a presumption that a third party has acted in good faith 'unless the contrary is proved'.[151] At this stage, therefore, the onus shifts to the company (or whoever else might be seeking to establish that the transaction at issue is void for lack

[149] As in *Re Torvale Group* [1999] 2 BCLC 605.
[150] See also *Boschoek Proprietary v Fuke* [1906] Ch 148.
[151] Companies Act 1985, s 35A(2)(c).

of authority) to prove that the third party was not in fact dealing with the company in good faith. There is some guidance in the provision as to what does not amount to bad faith (or lack of good faith), but this guidance is somewhat equivocal. Such elaboration as there is seems designed to remove those features of the common law approach that had attracted most criticism and to remedy perceived weaknesses in the original attempt to implement the First Directive.[152]

Good faith is a flexible concept, developed in equity, which has been rarely defined in statutes.[153] In provisions that are designed to protect third parties from the consequences of an agent's lack of authority or some other legal disability, it generally indicates a combination of lack of knowledge of the relevant disability and probity in not having this knowledge. In this respect, it correlates closely to the concept of 'constructive notice' in its broad sense. Thus, Lord Wilberforce, when reviewing the evolution of the concept of 'good faith' in the context of conveyancing, commented:[154]

> [I]t would generally be true to say that the words 'in good faith' related to the existence of notice. Equity, in other words, required not only absence of notice, but genuine and honest absence of notice. As the law developed, this requirement became crystallised in the doctrine of constructive notice … But … it would be a mistake to suppose that the requirement of good faith extended only to the matter of notice, or that when notice came to be regulated by statute, the requirement of good faith became obsolete. Equity still retained its interest in and power over the purchaser's conscience.

As will be seen, sections 35A and 35B override the specific company law doctrine of constructive notice inasmuch as third parties are no longer deemed to have notice of the contents of a company's public documents. However, as will be seen, the broader concept of constructive notice (or constructive knowledge), and in particular the idea of 'unconcionability', can provide guidance on the circumstances in which a third party might be deemed not to be dealing with a company in good faith for the purposes of section 35A.

5.2 The Common Law Background

5.2.1 *The Indoor Management Rule and Constructive Notice*

The underlying common law may therefore provide some guidance on the meaning of the good faith qualification to section 35A. Before statutory

---

[152] See generally *The Prentice Report*.
[153] See the comments to this effect of Lord Denning MR in *Central Estates (Belgravia) v Woolgar* [1972] 1 QB 48 (CA) at 55.
[154] *Midland Bank Trust Co v Green* [1981] AC 513 (HL) at 528.

reform, the indoor management rule, as qualified by the doctrine of constructive notice, governed a third party's ability to enforce an unauthorised contract made or approved by a company's board. The indoor management rule also applied to contracts made or approved by directors when acting as subordinate agents and it will therefore be examined in more detail in chapter six.

In order to analyse the concept of good faith in relation to section 35A, it is useful to note precisely how the indoor management rule was qualified. This necessitates some clarification of the term 'constructive notice' in this context. This came to be associated with the rigid doctrine that third parties are deemed to have notice of the public documents of a company, but this is perhaps better referred to now as 'deemed notice' to distinguish it from the broader and more flexible use of the term in other contexts.[155] In the guise of 'deemed notice' of a company's constitution, the doctrine of constructive notice came to be applied in a strict and inflexible manner in the corporate context, without any regard to the burden it placed on third parties in general.[156] However, this particular application of constructive notice was part of an otherwise reasonable and flexible limitation of the indoor management rule and was originally based on the view that it was reasonable to expect third parties to study the constitutions of companies with which they dealt and for third parties to use this as a means of protecting themselves.[157]

The general limitation of the indoor management rule reflected the view of the courts that, in certain circumstances, a third party had a duty to find out more about the authority of the agent with whom they were dealing and could not simply rely upon the presumption of regularity established by the indoor management rule. In such circumstances, the presumption was displaced and the third party was 'put on inquiry' and was be deemed to have 'constructive knowledge' of what this inquiry would have revealed.[158]

5.2.2 A Duty to Make Further Inquiry as an Efficient Allocation of Risk

The indoor management rule therefore assigned a risk of invalidity to the third party in certain circumstances in the guise of a duty to acquire more information. Such a limitation of the general rule could be justified as minimising overall transaction costs (and therefore achieving greater

---

[155] S 142 of the Companies Act 1989 used this term in the heading of the new s 711A of the Companies Act 1985, which would have excluded the doctrine, but was never implemented.
[156] For an example of a rigid application of the doctrine of 'constructive notice', see *Re Jon Beaufort (London)* [1953] Ch 131.
[157] *Ernest v Nicholls* (1857) 6 HLC 401.
[158] *Howard v Patent Ivory Manufacturing Co.* (1888) LR 38 Ch D 156; *Morris v Kanssen* [1946] AC 459 (HL); *Rolled Steel v British Steel* [1986] Ch 246 (CA); *Northside Developments Pty v Registrar-General* (1990) 64 ALJR 427.

allocative efficiency) insofar as it targeted situations in which the risk of loss to the company from the board's actions would be relatively high and in which the additional cost to the third party of the risk of invalidity would be relatively low.

In the early formulations of the indoor management rule, the courts held that third parties were subject to certain general duties, which limited their ability to rely upon the presumption of regularity. This included a duty to acquaint themselves with the relevant terms of the company's constitution, which underpinned the rigid doctrine of deemed notice, but also a duty to exercise 'ordinary care and precaution' and to make 'all those ordinary inquiries' which 'mercantile men' would make 'in the course of their business'.[159] However, this general duty was refined into a specific duty to make further inquiry when the transaction was 'unusual' or there were 'suspicious circumstances'.

County of Gloucester Bank v Rudry Merthyr, for example, concerned the validity of a mortgage by a colliery company of its land, mines and premises. Lindley LJ held that the third party had not been put on inquiry since there was nothing unusual about the transaction in question.[160] In other cases, however, it was held that an overt conflict of interest on the part of the agent was sufficient to impose a duty on the third party to make further inquiry. In *Rolled Steel v British Steel*, for example, a company executed a guarantee and security on behalf of an associated company.[161] The third party knew that the guaranteed debt was unlikely to be paid and that a director of the company had already given a personal guarantee of this debt.[162] In such a situation, there is a clear risk not only of the agent acting without authority, but also of the agent benefiting personally at the expense of the company.[163]

Apart from an overt conflict of interest on the part of the agent, the case law suggests a few other sets of circumstances in which a duty to make further inquiry would arise. In *Northside Developments*,[164] a case before the High Court of Australia, Brennan J suggested that a third party would be put on inquiry if the transaction were to involve a company giving a guarantee on behalf of another party where the company's business is not ordinarily the giving of guarantees, although in that case there was in any event an overt

---

[159] *Mahony v East Holyford Mining Co* (1875) LR 7 HL 869 at 895, per Lord Hatherley.
[160] *County of Gloucester Bank v Rudry Merthyr Steam and House Coal Colliery* [1895] 1 Ch 629 (CA) at 636.
[161] [1986] 1 Ch 246.
[162] See also *Underwood v Bank of Liverpool and Martins* [1924] 1 KB 775 (CA); *Midland Bank v Reckitt* [1933] AC 1 (HL); *EBM Co v Dominion Bank* [1937] 3 All ER 555 (PC).
[163] See, for example, the acknowledgement of the enhanced risk to the company in such a scenario as imposing a duty to make further inquiries in the cross examination of the third party's London manager noted by Atkin LJ in his judgment in the *Underwood* case: [1924] 1 KB 775 at 796–98.
[164] *Northside Developments Pty v Registrar-General* (1990) 64 ALJR 427 at 442.

conflict of interest on the part of the agent. In *Morris v Kanssen*,[165] the House of Lords held that a third party who was also a director of the company in question was under a duty to see that the company acts in accordance with its constitution and that its transactions are regular and orderly.[166] In *Re Introductions*,[167] the Court of Appeal held that the third party was put on inquiry, when it knew the intended purpose of a transaction, to make sure that it was within the scope of the company's objects clause, although this reflected the rigid common law doctrine that a third party had a duty to check the constitution and had deemed notice of its contents.[168]

5.3 Rebutting the Statutory Presumption of Good Faith

5.3.1 *The Economic Role of the Good Faith Qualification*

In section 35A, the 'good faith qualification' now provides the principal balancing mechanism for allocating risk between companies and third parties. The balance has clearly been shifted in favour of third parties. To minimise transaction costs, the good faith qualification should only expose third parties to a risk of invalidity in situations where the third party is clearly the least-cost-avoider taking account of the factors discussed in chapter two. It is arguable that the balancing exercise should also take account of how rules that favour good quality companies and prompt companies to adopt good systems of internal governance are likely to promote dynamic efficiency.

In evaluating rules of attribution, such as that in section 35A, it is important to keep in mind that the main costs to companies stemming from the risk of the attribution of unauthorised contracts (to be weighed against the cost to third parties of the risk of invalidity) are the 'avoidance' costs of ensuring that their boards do not make contracts of this kind, or at least of ensuring that any contracts that their boards do make are unlikely to prove onerous. One key cost in this respect is that of having a high quality board as part of a high quality management structure. Thus, the fact that, in a particular scenario, a company with a low quality (and perhaps therefore low cost) board might suffer a major loss from a contract made or approved by that board in excess of its actual authority does not, without more, mean that it would promote efficiency to allow the company to avoid that loss by denying the third party the protection of an overriding

---

[165] [1946] AC 459 at 475–76.
[166] See also *Howard v Patent Ivory Manufacturing Co* (1888) LR 38 Ch D 156 at 170–71.
[167] [1970] Ch 199 at 210–11.
[168] If, however, a third party had no actual notice of the purpose of a transaction such as a loan, it would not be under a duty to check that it was in fact for a purpose within the scope of the objects clause: *Re David Payne* [1904] 2 Ch 608 (CA).

rule of attribution, especially if the board's actual authority were to be set at an unusually low level or subject to unusually tight restrictions.

5.3.2 *The Inefficiency of Knowledge as a Qualifying Factor*

Rules of attribution that are based on the particular terms of a company's constitution as opposed to reflecting external standards are therefore likely to be inefficient. The common law doctrine of deemed notice was therefore inefficient as well as being unfair for penalising third parties on the basis of information which they were unlikely to possess and which it would be burdensome for them to acquire. Apart from the particular problem of deemed notice, overriding rules of attribution can be ineffi-cient if they attach significance to the actual or constructive knowledge of third parties (or at least do so without requiring this knowledge to be weighed against other factors). The statement in section 35A that 'a per-son shall not be regarded as acting in bad faith by reason only of his knowing that an act is beyond the powers of the directors under the com-pany's constitution' implies that something more than knowledge of the board's lack of authority to bind the company is required, even where the third party's knowledge is actual rather than constructive.[169]

The Prentice Report had recommended that a transaction with a third party having actual knowledge of a board's lack of authority should only be binding on the company if the shareholders were to ratify it.[170] The Prentice Report proposed that this should also be the case where the third party had certain kinds of constructive knowledge, arguing that actual knowledge should extend to a situation where a third party 'wilfully shuts his eyes' or 'wilfully and recklessly fails to make such inquiries as an honest and reasonable man would make'.[171] It concluded on this point:[172]

> The concept of actual knowledge in all likelihood embraces this type of knowledge. A third party should be able to trust appearances, but not appearances known to be false. Also, there will at least be a tincture of a want of probity where a third party proceeds with a contract despite a direc-tor's or a board's lack of authority.

The reference to 'want of probity' is significant and may provide a better framework for analysing 'good faith' in this context rather than focusing on whether or not the third party knew (or should have known) about the relevant limits.

---

[169] Companies Act 1985, s 35A(2)(b).
[170] The Prentice Report at 32.
[171] The Prentice Report drew this formulation of constructive notice from *Belmont Finance Corporation v Williams Furniture* [1979] Ch 250 (CA) at 267. It also cited C Harpum (1986) 102 *Law Quarterly Review* at 122–23.
[172] The Prentice Report at 32 (para. 39).

5.3.3 Good Faith and Liability for Knowing Receipt

Directors are in a position analogous to trustees and are treated as such when engaging in transactions involving the transfer of property or assets belonging to the company.[173] If third parties deal with trustees who are acting in breach of trust, they face potential liability as accessories on the basis of a constructive trust which can arise in two sets of circumstances, these being termed 'knowing receipt' and 'knowing assistance'.[174] If therefore third parties deal with directors who are acting in excess or abuse of their powers (including their actual authority), they face potential liability for knowing receipt and this liability has not been affected by the statutory overriding rules of attribution.[175]

The law governing knowing receipt may, therefore, provide some useful guidance on the good faith qualification. The fact that third parties face this potential liability in any event would explain the apparent removal of the good faith qualification in the revised version of section 35A set out in the 2002 White Paper even though the Company Law Review had recommended that the protection afforded to third parties by section 35A should continue on the same basis. This in turn suggests that the good faith qualification in section 35A and the liability of third parties for knowing receipt are co-extensive.[176]

Before examining the law governing knowing receipt, it is worth looking more closely at the position of a third party that is also a company because here rules of attribution are necessary to identify the third party's knowledge and determine its good faith.

5.4 Attributing Knowledge to a Corporate Third Party

5.4.1 The Problem of Attributing or Imputing Knowledge to a Company

When a third party is itself a company (or some other kind of collective organisation), it is necessary to have some means of identifying its knowledge, whether actual or constructive, and of determining its good faith. As with making contracts, this is a matter of attribution. A company may have numerous agents, who may change over time, and they may acquire information in various ways and this information may or may not be

---

[173] *Belmont Finance v Williams Furniture* [1979] Ch 250 (CA). They face personal liability for exceeding or abusing their powers accordingly: *Re Sharpe* [1892] 1 Ch 154; *Selangor United Rubber Estates v Craddock* [1968] 1 WLR 1555. Their liability is strict, but individual directors may be relieved under the Companies Act 1985, s 727.

[174] These two forms of accessory liability were identified by Lord Selborne in *Barnes v Addy* (1874) 9 Ch App 244.

[175] *International Sales & Agencies v Marcus* [1982] 3 All ER 551.

[176] See Gower & Davies at 147–48.

stored such that it is accessible to other agents of the company. Further, they may acquire or possess knowledge and information for reasons other than their role as an agent of the company. There has to be some basis for determining how much of this knowledge and information should be attributed or imputed to the company.

The general approach of agency law is to identify a principal with his agent and to impute to a principal knowledge relating to the subject matter of the agency that the agent acquires while acting within the scope of his authority.[177] However, it is also recognised that there is special difficulty in the case of companies and other principals with multiple agents.[178] An agent engaged on a particular transaction might not know of information acquired or possessed by another agent. Or such an agent may not have ready access to documents and other information already stored in the company.[179]

The Prentice Report recommended that only the knowledge of those agents engaged on a particular transaction should be attributed to a corporate third party in order to determine its state of knowledge and good faith.[180] The wording of section 35A does not explicitly follow this recommendation. However, the qualification that knowledge should not be equated to bad faith provides a basis for taking this consideration into account when judging the good faith of a corporate third party.[181] There is also support for this view in the law governing the attribution of knowledge to a company for the purpose of determining it liability for knowing receipt.

5.4.2 Determining the Knowledge of a Company for the Purposes of Knowing Receipt

The Court of Appeal provided guidance on this issue in *El Ajou v Dollar Land Holdings*.[182] In this case, some fraudsters used the proceeds of their fraudulent transactions to invest in a property development scheme in conjunction with an investment company ('DLH'). Later, DLH bought out the fraudsters' share of the joint venture. The victim of the fraud sued DLH in knowing receipt to recover the money that the fraudsters had invested in the scheme or, alternatively, to recover the value of their investment. The chairman of DLH ('F') was a non-executive director, but was instrumental in setting up the transaction whereby the fraudsters invested in the scheme. However, he had also acted as an agent of the

---

[177] Bowstead & Reynolds, Art 97(1).
[178] Bowstead & Reynolds, Art 97 at 8–214.
[179] The Prentice Report at 34–5.
[180] *Ibid.*
[181] Companies Act 1985, s 35A(2)(b).
[182] [1994] BCC 143. See generally Bowstead & Reynolds, Art 97.

fraudsters and, in this capacity, knew that the investment represented the proceeds of fraud. DLH's liability turned on whether or not F's knowledge could be attributed to it.

The Court of Appeal held that there were two grounds upon which the knowledge of an agent could be attributed to a company. The first was where the agent was 'the directing mind and will' of the company in relation to the transaction in question. The second depended on the general law of agency. As regards the first ground, it has been established that, for the purposes of determining a company's criminal liability, the mind of an agent or of certain agents of a company can be viewed as the company's 'directing mind and will' and treated as the mind of the company itself.[183] The Court of Appeal applied this doctrine in the *El Ajou* case and held that F's knowledge should be treated as that of the company on this basis. It held that F was DLH's directing mind and will because he had negotiated the terms on which the fraudsters made their investment and had control of DLH in this respect. He had discretionary power to act on behalf of DLH, and in effect to act as DLH, on this matter. It did not matter that he had not been involved in the completion of the transaction.

As regards agency law, Hoffmann LJ identified three situations in which an agent's knowledge could be attributed to his principal.[184] First, where an agent is authorised to enter into a transaction and his own knowledge is material, knowledge that he acquires outside his capacity as agent may also be imputed to the principal.[185] Hoffmann LJ cited an insurance contract, in which the broker acts as the agent of the insured, as an example of this situation.[186] Secondly, where the principal is under a duty to investigate or to make disclosure, material facts known to the agent may be attributed to the principal unless the agent is committing a fraud against the principal.[187] Thirdly, where an agent is authorised to receive communications on behalf of his principal, then information communicated to the agent is treated as having been communicated to the principal.[188]

The Court of Appeal held that F was not within any of these situations and that his knowledge of the fraudulent origins of the fraudsters' investment could not therefore be attributed to DLH on this basis. It had been argued that the knowledge of an agent could also be attributed to his principal for this purpose if the agent was under a duty to disclose it to

---

[183] *Lennard's Carrying Co v Asiatic Petroleum Co* [1915] AC 705 (HL); *Tesco Supermarkets v Nattrass* [1972] AC 153 (HL). See, however, Lord Hoffmann's criticism of this approach in *Meridian Global Funds Management Asia v Securities Commission* [1995] 2 AC 500 at 509 (PC).
[184] [1994] BCC 143 at 156–58. See, however, Bowstead & Reynolds at 8-208–8-213 for a critical appraisal of this categorisation.
[185] See also Bowstead & Reynolds, Art 97(2).
[186] But see Bowstead & Reynolds at 8-210.
[187] See also Bowstead & Reynolds, Art 97(3).
[188] See also Bowstead & Reynolds, Art 96.

his principal. The Court of Appeal accepted that F had owed a duty to DLH to reveal what he knew about the origins of the fraudsters' money, but held that this was not sufficient for it to be attributed to DLH. DLH must also have had a duty to investigate the origins of the money it received,[189] in effect bringing it within the second of the above situations. Here, DLH had not been put on inquiry and therefore had no duty to investigate.

The above principles provide some guidance for corporate third parties seeking to rely upon section 35A. The 'directing mind and will' doctrine is controversial since it reflects the recurring tendency of trying to identify a company with a person or persons involved in its affairs and arguably obscures the true nature of attribution and corporate personality.[190]As regards agency law, the second of the three situations identified by Hoffmann LJ is of interest since the idea of being put on inquiry and thereby having a duty to investigate is a feature of the common law indoor management rule, which underlies section 35A. Failure to make further inquiry in such circumstances in effect negates a third party's good faith.

However, in the context of knowing receipt, the law has evolved so that good faith is judged in the round, with a recipient's state of knowledge being one relevant factor. This would also prove a basis for considering the significance of the knowledge of the agents of a corporate third party and for interpreting the declaration in section 35A that a person should not be treated as acting in bad faith 'by reason only of his knowing' that an act is beyond the actual authority of a company's board.

6 A THIRD PARTY'S LIABILITY FOR KNOWING RECEIPT

6.1 The Conditions of Liability

In *El Ajou v Dollar Land Holdings*, Hoffmann LJ held that to establish liability as a constructive trustee for knowing receipt, it was necessary to show first a disposal of assets in breach of fiduciary duty, secondly receipt of assets which are traceable as representing those assets and thirdly knowledge on the part of the recipient that the assets are traceable to a breach of fiduciary duty.[191] For third parties dealing with companies, the first of these requirements should be satisfied where the board of a company (or one or more of its directors) makes or approves a transaction in excess of its actual authority and thus in violation of its 'mandate' under

---

[189] *Re David Payne* [1904] 2 Ch 608 (CA).
[190] Hoffmann LJ noted how it had been derived from German law, which distinguishes a company's organs from its agents: [1994] BCC 143 at 159. As Lord Hoffmann, he criticised the doctrine in the *Meridian Global Funds* case: [1995] 2 AC 500 at 509 (PC).
[191] [1994] BCC 143 at 154.

the constitution. However, liability for knowing receipt has generally been associated with fraud or with breach by the directors of their duty to exercise their powers in good faith in the best interests of the company, although abuse of power can overlap extensively with excess of power.[192]

The first *El Ajou* condition should also be satisfied where the board of a company or any of its directors exercise their powers for an improper purpose. As noted in chapter three, it is not clear whether the 'proper purposes doctrine' should be viewed as reflecting a distinct fiduciary duty governing the exercise of the board's discretionary powers or a general limitation on the scope of the actual authority which the constitution of a company vests in its board. The courts have, for example, treated transactions made for an improper purpose as merely voidable rather than as void, which is consistent with a breach of duty rather than lack of authority.[193] In *Criterion Properties, v Stratford UK Properties*,[194] however, the Court of Appeal treated the proper purposes doctrine as limiting a board's actual authority, although the House of Lords subsequently indicated that whether or not the board had actual or ostensible authority was a logically prior issue.[195] The Court of Appeal in *Criterion* treated a third party's ability to enforce a contract made for an improper purpose as limited by its potential liability for knowing receipt, even where the third party had not yet been a recipient of any money or property from the company.[196] At first instance, Hart J. had presented a third party's ability to enforce an unperformed contract and its potential liability for knowing receipt as 'two sides of the same coin':[197]

> To put the point in another way the contractual rights received by [the third party] under the debenture can be viewed either as flawed by lack of authority in the counterparty (the apparent authority point), or as themselves property transferred to [the third party] in breach of trust.

The House of Lords disputed this linkage and indicated that the limits on a third party's ability to enforce an executory contract and its potential liability for knowing receipt are quite different.[198] Nevertheless, it is

---

[192] See, for example, *International Sales & Agencies v Marcus* [1982] 3 All ER 551 and *Rolled Steel* [1986] 1 Ch 246.

[193] See, for example, *Bamford v Bamford* [1970] Ch 212 (CA).

[194] [2002] EWCA Civ 1883; [2004] UKHL 28.

[195] The House of Lords also ruled that there is insufficient evidence to establish that the company's board had in fact approved the contract in question.

[196] [2002] EWCA Civ 1883 at 32–33. The third party did not seek to rely upon s 35A and the Court of Appeal treated the agency law doctrine of ostensible authority, which will be examined in chapter six, as the basis on which the third party could enforce the contract. The House of Lords, however, indicated that s 35A would be relevant to the issue of authority: [2004] UKHL 28 at 28–29.

[197] [2002] EWHC 496 at 29, referring back to the Court of Appeal's judgment in *Rolled Steel v British Steel* [1986] Ch 246.

[198] [2004] UKHL 28 at 27.

submitted that where a contract has been made in excess or abuse of an agent's actual authority, a third party's potential liability for knowing receipt in respect of any assets received pursuant to the terms of the contract should reflect the limits of the third party's ability to enforce those terms when unperformed, whatever the precise legal basis of these limits.

6.2 The Requirement of Knowledge

The condition in the exposition of knowing receipt in the *El Ajou* case that has proved most problematic and given rise to most debate and discussion is that of the third party's 'knowledge' and whether this should include constructive knowledge as well as actual knowledge.[199]

In *Baden Delvaux and Lecuit v Société Générale*, Peter Gibson J approved a list of five different mental states that could be viewed as giving rise to knowledge.[200] However, in *BCCI v Akindele*,[201] Nourse LJ expressed grave concern about this kind of approach:[202]

> Any categorisation is of little value unless the purpose it is to serve is adequately defined, whether it be fivefold, as in the *Baden* case, or twofold, as in the classical division between actual and constructive knowledge, a division which itself has become blurred in recent authorities.

He indicated that it would be preferable to apply a single test of knowledge along the lines of the test which had been devised for the 'dishonesty' requirement in the action for knowing assistance, the other form of accessory liability.

As well as doubts about the definition of 'constructive knowledge' in this context, there has also been a longstanding wariness of invoking the concept in relation to commercial transactions. One reason for this wariness is that 'constructive knowledge' tends to be equated to 'constructive notice', leading to a fear that a third party could be deemed to have constructive knowledge of all information that he, she or it might have been able to find out rather than just that information which it was reasonable to have expected the third party to find out in the circumstances.[203] Thus,

---

[199] See generally Lord Nicholls, 'Knowing Receipt: The Need for a New Landmark' in W Cornish *et al* (eds), *Restitution: Past, Present & Future* (Oxford, Hart Publishing, 1998).

[200] [1993] 1 WLR 509 at 575–6: (i) actual knowledge; (ii) wilfully shutting one's eyes to the obvious; (iii) wilfully and recklessly failing to make such inquiries as an honest and reasonable man would make; (iv) knowledge of circumstances which would indicate the facts to an honest and reasonable man; (v) knowledge of circumstances which would put an honest and reasonable man on inquiry. See generally G Moffat, *Trusts Law: Texts and Materials* (London, Butterworths, 1999) at 556–561.

[201] [2001] Ch 437 (CA).

[202] [2001] Ch 437 at 455.

[203] See generally D Fox, [1998] *Cambridge Law Journal* 391.

in *Manchester Trust v Furness*,[204] it was argued that a party to a bill of lading should be treated as knowing of certain special conditions set out in a charterparty referred to incidentally in the bill of lading. Lindley LJ rejected this argument and gave a classic warning against importing doctrines evolved in the leisurely world of conveyancing into the busy world of commercial transactions:[205]

> If we were to extend the doctrine of constructive notice to commercial transactions we should be doing infinite mischief and paralysing the trade of the country.

However, as has already been noted in relation to the indoor management rule, a third party should only be treated as having constructive knowledge (as opposed to constructive notice) of something if the third party was under a duty to make an inquiry that would have revealed this information. Thus, an unusual or suspicious transaction might put a third party 'on inquiry', giving rise to such a duty.

Attributing constructive knowledge to a third party should not therefore mean that the third party is, without more, deemed to know everything that he might have been able to find out.[206] Applied carefully, the concept of constructive knowledge should provide the means of striking a fair and efficient balance between the interests of companies and third parties.

6.3 A Third Party's Right to Pursue its Own Commercial Interests

6.3.1 *The Danger of an Inefficient Risk of Liability*

There has also been concern about the idea, implicit in some formulations of constructive knowledge, that a third party's awareness of certain facts that are consistent with a possible breach of duty by the directors of a company should put the third party under a duty to make sure that

---

[204] [1895] 2 QB 539 (CA). See also *Greer v Downs Supply* [1927] 2 KB 28 (CA).
[205] [1895] 2 QB 539 at 545.
[206] In *Wilson v Kelland* [1910] 2 Ch 306, which is the main case cited in support of the view that registration of a charge under what is now s 395 of the Companies Act 1985 gives subsequent chargees notice of the registered charge, Eve J said that the registration of a floating charge 'amounted to constructive notice of a charge affecting the property, but not of any special provisions contained in that charge restricting the company from dealing with their property in the usual manner when the subsisting charge is a floating security': [1910] 2 Ch 306 at 313. This comment was *obiter*, but it confirms the view that having constructive notice of a document does not, without more, mean having constructive knowledge of the entire contents of the document: constructive knowledge should depend on the nature of the duty to make further inquiry that circumstances imposed on the third party. See generally J deLacy 'Reflections on the Ambit and Reform of Part 12 of the Companies Act 1985 and the Doctrine of Constructive Notice' in J deLacy (ed) *The Reform of UK Company Law* (London Cavendish, 2002) at 369–80.

the directors are not acting in breach of duty and thereby fix the third party with constructive knowledge of the breach of duty. In particular, it has been suggested that this should normally be the case where a third party knows or has reason to believe that an agent is entering a contract which is 'contrary to the commercial interests of the agent's principal'. On this basis, if the contract proves to have been made in excess or abuse of the agent's actual authority, the third party would be unable to enforce it.[207] Such an approach would, in effect, subject third parties to a general duty to 'look out' for the interests of the companies with which they deal, and ensure that they are being properly managed where there is evidence to suggest that they might not be. Further, third parties would have to give this duty priority over the pursuit of their own commercial interests.

It is arguable, however, that a duty to make further inquiry should be limited to doing only what is reasonable in the overall circumstances and that this should not require a third party to subordinate its own commercial interests when confronted with a poorly managed company since it would place an unfair and inefficient burden on companies in general. As has been seen in chapter two, companies are likely to be the least-cost-avoider in this kind of situation, unless the circumstances that trigger the duty are narrowed down to highlight situations in which companies face a high risk of loss. Further, subjecting third parties to a broad duty of inquiry would remove a competitive advantage that well managed companies would otherwise enjoy over poorly managed ones.

Knox J recognised the need for caution in defining the kind of circumstances that should trigger a duty of inquiry in *Cowan de Groot Properties v Eagle Trust*.[208] He noted in particular the difficulties that a broad duty of inquiry could create where a third party is itself a company acting through directors or other agents, who are already subject to a fiduciary duty to act in their own company's best interests:[209]

> The duty of directors of a purchasing company is to buy as cheaply as they can in the light of the mode and terms of the proposed sale and it would in my judgment be a slippery slope upon which to embark to impose upon directors of a company a positive duty to make inquiries into the reasons for an offer being made to their company at what appears to be a bargain price. The line should in my judgment be drawn at the point where the figure in question, regard being had not only to the open market value but also to the terms and mode of sale, is indicative of dishonesty on the party of the directors of a vendor company.

---

[207] *Criterion Properties v Stratford UK Properties* [2004] UKHL 28 at 31.
[208] [1992] 4 All ER 700 at 754–61.
[209] [1992] 4 All ER 700 at p 761b–c.

He went on to find that:[210]

> In my judgment it may well be that the underlying broad principle which
> runs through the authorities regarding commercial transactions is that the
> court will impute knowledge, on the basis of what a reasonable person
> would have learned, to a person who is guilty of commercially unacceptable
> conduct in the particular context involved.

In other words, the third party should have to be confronted with circumstances that suggest the likelihood of fraud rather than poor or
incompetent management before a duty of inquiry is triggered.

6.3.2 The Akindele Case

In *BCCI v Akindele*,[211] the Court of Appeal had to consider whether a third
party who was offered very favourable terms to enter into a transaction
was thereby put on inquiry to make sure that there were no underlying
breaches of duty. In this case, an investment company in the BCCI group
('Overseas') had offered to sell to the third party ('Akindele') a block of
shares in a holding company in the BCCI group for $10 million. However,
the proposed terms gave Akindele the option to require Overseas to
repurchase the shares after a period of two years at a price that would
guarantee Akindele a profit equivalent to compound interest at the rate of
15 per cent per annum. Further, the block of shares was not to be transferred to Akindele, but was to remain with nominees, pending this option.

Fraudulent internal arrangements in the BCCI group, which involved
breaches of fiduciary duty by its employees, lay behind the favourable
terms that Overseas offered to Akindele. These arrangements were
designed to present the group as being in a much stronger financial position than was in fact the case. They included paying certain nominees to
buy shares in the holding company. These payments were presented as
being loans, but were in effect 'dummy loans' since there was no intention
to service or repay them. There was a danger, however, that auditors or
regulatory bodies might recognise them as dummy loans and require
them to be written off, thereby undermining their intended effect. The
fraudulent employees therefore needed to procure temporary finance to
help create the impression that the dummy loans were in fact regular and
performing normally. This led to the offer to Akindele, who was in effect
being asked to lend money at a very high rate of interest.

---

[210] [1992] 4 All ER 700 at 761. In *Royal Brunei Airlines v Philip Tan Kok Ming*, a case concerning
'knowing assistance', Lord Nicholls for the Privy Council formulated a single test for 'dishonesty' drawing upon this reference to 'commercially unacceptable conduct': [1995] 2 AC
378 at 389.
[211] [2001] Ch 437.

Akindele exercised his option to call on Overseas to repurchase the shares some three years later and received a payment of over $16 million for them. Employees in the BCCI group had to make further fraudulent internal arrangements to give Overseas the funds to make this payment. The courts held that the contract between Akindele and Overseas was not a sham and that Akindele had no actual knowledge of the fraudulent arrangements that lay behind it. The liquidators of Overseas (and another company in the BCCI group) argued that Akindele held the proceeds of the transaction on a constructive trust on the basis of knowing receipt. They argued that despite his lack of actual knowledge of the frauds, he should have been able to deduce this knowledge from the information that was available to him, namely the fact that the transaction was not a genuine purchase of shares and the unusually high rate of interest.

Carnwath J at first instance held that Akindele was entitled to assume that the terms were being offered to him in good faith and for proper reasons. Further, Akindele owed no duty to the bank that made it dishonest for him to accept these terms or to do anything other than look after his own interests. The Court of Appeal upheld this decision, but took the opportunity to rationalise the required 'knowledge' that would establish liability for knowing receipt.

6.3.3 The Akindele Test of 'Unconscionability'

In the *Akindele* case, the Court of Appeal formulated a single test for the 'knowledge' condition of liability for knowing receipt:[212]

> What then, in the context of knowing receipt, is the purpose to be served by a categorisation of knowledge? It can only be to enable the court to determine whether, in the words of Buckley LJ in *Belmont Finance Corpn v Williams Furniture (No 2)*,[213] the recipient can 'conscientiously retain [the] funds against the company' or, in the words of Sir Robert Megarry V-C in *Re Montagu's Settlement Trusts*,[214] '[the recipient's] conscience is sufficiently affected for it to be right to bind him by the obligations of a constructive trustee'. But, if that is the purpose, there is no need for categorisation. All that is necessary is that the recipient's state of knowledge must be such as to make it unconscionable for him to retain the benefit of the receipt. A test in that form, though it cannot, any more than any other, avoid difficulties of application, ought to avoid those of definition and allocation to which the previous categorisations have led. Moreover, it should better enable the courts to give commonsense decisions in the commercial context in which claims in knowing receipt are now frequently made …

---

[212] [2001] Ch 437 at 455.
[213] [1980] 1 All ER 393 (CA) at 405.
[214] [1987] Ch 264 at 273.

The Court of Appeal thus formulated a test for knowledge in terms of unconscionability. It found that it had not, in the circumstances, been unconscionable for Akindele to proceed with the transaction and receive the agreed payment for the shares. The relevant circumstances included the judge's findings that Akindele had not been aware of the fraudulent nature of the underlying arrangements and that he was entitled to treat the proposed terms as a genuine offer and pursue his own best interests in settling the transaction.

In the *Criterion Properties* case,[215] the Court of Appeal held that this test should determine whether or not a third party could enforce a contract where a company's board had acted for an improper purpose in making it.[216] In this case, the company and the third party were already parties to a joint venture agreement, structured as a limited partnership. They entered into a further contract ('the option contract'), which gave the third party an option to call on the company to buy out the third party's stake in the joint venture on terms that were very favourable to the third party. The option was only exercisable in certain specified circumstances, which included a change in control of the company and the departure from office of certain directors of the company.

The terms of the option contract were therefore very favourable to the third party, but only if the events triggering the option were in fact to occur. The company's board was willing to contract on these terms in order to stave off a potential takeover bid. In effect, the contract was a 'poison pill', designed to make the company unpalatable to a new controller. However, the proper purposes doctrine holds that the board of a company cannot use its powers to interfere with the shareholders' ultimate control over the company and its management body by, for example, seeking to deter or prevent a potential takeover bid.[217] The Court of Appeal held that the board of the company had acted in breach of the proper purposes doctrine and accordingly did not have actual authority to enter into the option contract.[218]

In the event, there was no takeover bid, but one of the directors designated in the option contract did leave office. The third party decided to exercise its right to sell its share in the joint venture to the company. The company sought a declaration that the third party could not enforce the

---

[215] [2002] EWCA Civ 1883.

[216] The House of Lords ruled, however, that there was insufficient evidence to support the conclusion that the company's board of directors had approved the contract. The House of Lords also ruled that the question of whether the board (or signatory directors) had actual or ostensible should have been addressed as a logically prior issue: [2004] UKHL 28.

[217] See generally chapter three.

[218] The House of Lords ruled that the question of the board's authority (or the authority of the signatory directors) should be addressed first and that this would entail consideration of s 35A or of those rules of agency which govern the validity of contracts made by subordinate agents (which will be discussed in chapter six): [2004] UKHL 28 at 2 and 30.

option contract and applied for summary judgment, which meant that the case turned on whether or not the third party had any real prospect of defending the company's claim at a full trial. At first instance, Hart J held that the third party had no defence because it had known of the circumstances that had put the board in breach of its duty to exercise its powers only for a proper purpose. On his interpretation of the *Akindele* test, Hart J held that the third party would be liable as a constructive trustee for knowing receipt and could not therefore enforce the option contract.

The Court of Appeal, however, allowed the third party's appeal, holding that Hart J had applied too narrow an interpretation of the *Akindele* test. The Court of Appeal held that the *Akindele* test entailed moving beyond the narrow question of what facts the third party did or did not know. Instead, the court had to look at the third party's knowledge as one aspect of the overall circumstances of the case. These circumstances also included the behaviour of the company's own directors and the legal advice given to the parties. The House of Lords upheld the Court of Appeal's conclusion that the agreed evidence was insufficient to support a summary judgment, although they also found this evidence wanting on certain issues that they viewed as logically prior to the issues that Hart J and the Court of Appeal had addressed.[219] The House of Lords did not therefore rule on the *Akindele* test.[220]

Carnwath LJ, who gave the main judgment in the Court of Appeal, held that to focus solely on what the third party knew, without having any regard to the behaviour of the company's directors, would be to take 'too narrow and one-sided a view of the matter'.[221] He said that the option contract was 'one element in a continuing commercial relationship between two parties acting at arms-length and should have been judged in that light':[222]

> In particular, I do not see how one can consider the 'conscionability' of the actions of one party to the agreement without considering the position of the other. It is wholly artificial, in the context of this case, to consider the actions and motivations of the directors of [the third party], and to ignore those of the directors of [the company], particularly if it was they ... who were the principal instigators of the [option contract].

Carnwath LJ also said that the legal advice received by the two parties concerning the option agreement might also be relevant in applying the *Akindele* test, holding that there was nothing in its formulation 'which excludes legal advice as a factor, in an appropriate case'.[223]

---

[219] See above.

[220] Lord Nicholls, however, remarked that the Court of Appeal in the *Akindele* case had fallen 'into error': [2004] UKHL 28 at 4.

[221] [2002] EWCA Civ 1883 at 38.

[222] *Ibid.*

[223] [2002] EWCA Civ 1883 at 39.

6.4 The Good Faith Qualification to Section 35A

The *Akindele* test may also provide a suitable test for determining a third party's ability to rely upon section 35A.[224] It meets the concerns about the concept of constructive knowledge raised by Lindley LJ in *Manchester Trust* and by Knox J in *Cowan de Groot* and is consistent with the role of constructive notice in the early formulations of the indoor management rule before that term became associated with the rigid doctrine of deemed notice of a company's constitution.

If the good faith qualification is equated to liability for knowing receipt in accordance with the *Akindele* test, then a third party should be entitled to presume that the board of a company can bind it to any transaction unless there are circumstances that would make it unconscionable for the third party to proceed on this assumption without making further inquiry. A third party who proceeded without making further inquiry could then be viewed as having constructive knowledge of the board's lack of authority, or as behaving unconscionably, or as guilty of commercially unacceptable conduct, or as simply lacking good faith. The key focus, whatever the terminology, should be on the circumstances that would make it unconscionable to proceed without making further inquiry. The mere fact that the terms of the transaction are very beneficial to the third party and appear to be unfavourable to the company would not be sufficient. Instead, there should be clear evidence that the company's board is acting fraudulently or otherwise in breach of their fiduciary duties.

This leaves open the question of whether a third party with actual knowledge of a board's lack of actual authority could still be dealing in good faith, as suggested in the elaboration in section 35A.[225] This would not seem to be possible under the *Akindele* test. However, it is possible to envisage scenarios in which it would not be unconscionable or commercially unacceptable for a third party to proceed with a transaction despite finding out that the board lacks the necessary actual authority.

Such a scenario could arise if the relevant limits on the board's actual authority were obscure or contestable or if the delay that would be needed to overcome the limits would undermine the transaction. In such a scenario, it would seem harsh to penalise a third party for not remaining

---

[224] There is, however, some uncertainty as to whether the *Akindele* test is correct in relation to knowing receipt. In *Twinsectra v Yardley*, there were claims against a defendant both for knowing receipt and for knowing assistance. However, the Court of Appeal treated the claim in knowing receipt as being subject to a condition of 'dishonesty' and applied a single test of dishonesty for both claims: [1999] *Lloyd's Rep* 438. For criticism of this aspect of the judgment, see S Baughen, '"Quistclose Trusts" and Knowing Receipt' [2000] *Conveyancer* 351. The House of Lords reversed the Court of Appeal's decision on the claim for knowing assistance and ruled on the meaning of 'dishonesty' in that context, but did not comment on the correct test for knowing receipt: [2002] UKHL 12. See also Lord Nicholls's *obiter* criticism of the *Akindele* test in *Criterion Properties* [2004] UKHL 28 at 4.

[225] Companies Act, s 35A(2)(b).

ignorant about these limits, although this judgment would depend on the nature of the particular limits at issue. Thus, if they were clearly designed to protect the shareholders in general or a particular class of shareholders, and if there was good reason to doubt that this class would approve the transaction, then it would be unconscionable for a third party to ignore the limits.[226] The factors that the Court of Appeal in the *Criterion* case said should be taken into account, such as the nature of any legal advice and the behaviour of the company's board, should have significance in judging a third party's good faith in this context.

7 CONTRACTS WITH DIRECTORS OR OTHER DESIGNATED PERSONS

7.1 Section 322A

7.1.1 *The Ambit and Effect of Section 322A*

Section 322A applies where a company enters into a contract and the third party is a director of the company, or a director of its holding company,[227] or a person connected with such a director, or a company with whom such a director is associated. The terms 'a person connected with such a director' and 'a company with whom such a director is associated' are used elsewhere in Part X of the Companies Act 1985 and are defined in section 346. They include spouses and business partners of directors and companies in which a director, alone or together with persons connected to him, holds at least one-fifth of the equity share capital or of the voting shares.

Section 322A applies where the board of a company 'exceed any limitation on their powers under the company's constitution' in connection with a transaction with a third party falling into one of the designated categories.[228] It renders the transaction 'voidable at the instance of the company'.[229] Lack of authority could render such a transaction void so it would seem logical to assume that section 322A only applies if the third party would otherwise be able to rely upon an overriding rule of attribution and, in particular, would otherwise satisfy the conditions of section 35A.

However, in *Re Torvale Group*,[230] the only reported case so far on section 322A, it was assumed that section 322A governed the validity of a debenture

---

[226] See, for example, *British Racing Drivers' Club v Hextall Erskine* [1997] 1 BCLC 182. In this case, it was known that the company's shareholders would probably oppose the transaction. The limit in question was imposed by the Companies Act 1985, s 320 and was designed to protect shareholders against major acquisitions or disposals of assets in which a director has a conflicting interest. This provision will be examined in chapter 7.

[227] See s 736(1) of the Companies Act 1985 on the meaning of this term.

[228] Companies Act 1985, s 322A(1).

[229] *Ibid* s 322A(2).

[230] [1999] 2 BCLC 605.

made with the chairman and major shareholder of the company without first checking as a preliminary issue that this person would in fact be entitled to rely on section 35A.[231] This is hard to reconcile with the judgments of Carnwath LJ and Schiemann LJ in the *Henniker-Major* case.

By rendering a transaction voidable, section 322A ensures that its validity is only provisional. However, the company must take action to avoid it. The section lists four sets of circumstances in which the transaction cannot be set aside, including the impossibility of restitution, the indemnification of the company for any loss or damage, the acquisition of rights by another party 'bona fide for value and without actual notice of the directors' exceeding their powers' and the ratification of the transaction in the appropriate way.[232]

Section 322A also provides that, whether or not the company does succeed in avoiding the transaction, the third party, along with any director authorising the transaction, is liable to account to the company for any gain made by the transaction and to indemnify it against any resulting loss or damage.[233] However, it provides that the third party will not be personally liable in this way 'if he shows that at the time the transaction was entered into he did not know that the directors were exceeding their powers', unless he is a director of the company.[234]

7.1.2 The Rationale of Section 322A

The Prentice Report had recognised the case for expecting directors and other officers of a company to know the limits of the board's actual authority and for giving them much less protection than that extended to third parties in general. It therefore proposed that such an 'insider' third party should still be deemed to know the limits on the actual authority of the company's board where such knowledge 'may reasonably be expected of a person carrying out the functions of that director or officer in relation to that company'.[235]

The Prentice Report's proposal would have given the company the common law remedy of invalidity in respect of unauthorised transactions with such third parties and reflected the common law view that such insiders owe a duty to their company to look after its affairs and ensure that its transactions are regular and orderly. Directors and other officers were put on inquiry to ensure that any transaction was properly authorised

---

[231] The point was in fact left open pending further evidence of whether the breach of the relevant limitation in the constitution had in fact been ratified by the unanimous consent of the relevant shareholders in accordance with the principle in *Re Duomatic* [1969] 2 Ch 365.
[232] Companies Act 1985, s 322A(5).
[233] *Ibid* s 322A(3).
[234] *Ibid* s 322A(6).
[235] The Prentice Report at 33.

to discourage ignorance about the limits on the board's powers and deter dereliction from this duty.[236] At common law, directors could not rely upon the indoor management rule or the doctrine of ostensible authority.[237]

In *Re Torvale Group*,[238] Neuberger J considered the policy considerations underlying section 322A and viewed it as a safeguard against conflict of interest:[239]

> [It] seems to me that the purpose of section 322A is to protect a company in cir- cumstances where its directors exceed their powers in connection with trans- actions entered into by the company with one or more of their number (or their associates) to the disadvantage of the company and to the advantage of one or more of the directors (or associates). It is true that the effect of the section is wider than that, and it may well have been intended to ensure that directors are penalised if they fail to behave with particular propriety in connection with transactions between the company and themselves. However, I do not think that detracts from the main mischief at which the section is directed.

Both the Law Commission and the Company Law Review have reviewed section 322A. The Law Commission in their joint report with the Scottish Law Commission on directors' duties did not find any major deficiencies and recommended that it be retained as it stands.[240]

However, the Company Law Review indicated that the elaborate detail of section 322A is unnecessary and that adding an additional layer of reg- ulation to the main statutory provision in section 35A is confusing.[241] It therefore proposed that third parties within section 322A simply be denied the protection of section 35A and this proposal is reflected in the revised version of section 35A set out in the 2002 White Paper.[242]

7.2 Section 322A and Multi-Party Contracts

In *Re Torvale Group*,[243] Neuberger J also had to consider the validity of two debentures granted by the company to the trustees of a retirement bene- fits scheme, including one who was also a director of the company.[244] In

---

[236] *Morris v Kanssen* [1946] AC 459 at 475–76.
[237] See also *Hely-Hutchinson v Brayhead* [1968] 1 QB 549 (CA).
[238] [1999] 2 BCLC 605.
[239] *Ibid* at 622.
[240] See Law Commission, *Company Directors: Regulating Conflicts of Interests and Formulating a Statement of Duties* (Law Commission Report No 261, Scottish Law Commission Report No 173, The Stationery Office, London, 1999) at 10.38.
[241] See Company Formation at 2.41.
[242] 2002 White Paper, Draft Clauses, clauses 17(5) and 17(6).
[243] [1999] 2 BCLC 605.
[244] Again, the question of whether the debentures were in fact valid and binding under the *Duomatic* principle was left open.

relation to these, the trustees invited the court to exercise its discretion under section 322A(7). This applies to transactions involving more than one third party and provides:

> [Where] a transaction is voidable by virtue of [section 322A] and valid by virtue of [section 35A] in favour of [a third party not within section 322A], the court may, on the application of that person or of the company, make such order affirming, severing or setting aside the transaction, on such terms, as appear to the court to be just.

Neuberger J held that this section did apply and that, in the circumstances, he would declare the debentures valid. In reaching this conclusion, Neuberger J took account of various factors, which suggested that there was nothing improper about the transaction and that the failure to obtain the approval of the relevant class of shareholders had been a genuine oversight. These factors included the reasonable terms of the loan secured by the debenture and the moderate rate of interest, the fact that the relevant director had received no personal benefit from the transaction and the fact that there was no suggestion that any of the trustees had lacked good faith.

Despite the approach adopted by Neuberger J, it is arguable that section 322A(7) undermines the goal of 'security of transaction' underlying section 35A by creating a risk of invalidity for third parties in general. It casts doubt on the validity of multi-party transactions within its ambit by giving the court a wide and vague discretion over the legal effect of such contracts. Thus, a third party able to rely upon section 35A faces a risk that the company might apply to the court under this section simply because another party to the same transaction is caught by section 322A. This problem would be removed if section 35A were to be revised as proposed in the 2002 White Paper.

8 CONCLUSIONS AND REVIEW

There is a case, in terms of both economic efficiency and good corporate governance, for enabling third parties to be able to treat the board of a company as having unlimited power to speak on behalf of the company without having any general responsibility to look behind its actions. In particular, third parties should not be required to consider whether the board is in fact acting in the best interests of the company (and those interested in its affairs) and should be free to strive to maximise their own best interests in their dealings with a company's board. In effect, third parties should be free to assume that the board is exercising its business judgment properly in this respect whether or not the merits of its decisions are readily apparent to outsiders.

There is therefore a case for keeping the circumstances in which a third party is exposed to a risk of invalidity because of a board's lack of actual authority to an absolute minimum. In a unitary board system of corporate governance, in which there may be no easily accessible default reference point and where the nature of the power of the body of shareholders to perform this function can be far from certain, there is a good case for enabling third parties to rely upon the board to bind a company even where third parties are aware of the limits on a board's actual authority.

Section 35A of the Companies Act 1985 has done much to ensure that third parties dealing with companies can treat their boards as a reliable reference point. If a contract is made or approved by the board, third parties now face a small risk of invalidity in the event of the board proving to have lacked the necessary actual authority. There are three reasons for the remaining risk of invalidity. First, the board may not in fact have been the board because the director or directors approving the contract in question did not act in accordance with those provisions of the constitution governing their ability to act as the board. Secondly, the third party may be shown not to have been dealing with the company in good faith. Thirdly, the contract may be a multi-party contract caught by section 322A(7) so that its validity may be subject to the court's discretion.

Of these three factors that give rise to the remaining risk of invalidity, there are no good reasons of policy or principle for the first and the third and there is a case for eliminating them in any revision of the statutory provision. The extent of the risk due to each of these factors is a matter of speculation though. Thus, the courts may have the opportunity to remove the uncertainty as regards the first factor after the *Henniker-Major* case,[245] but that does not mean that they can be relied upon to do so. It would be better for the statutory provision to specify an 'irreducible minimum' on which third parties acting in good faith can rely such as two directors purporting to act as their company's board or perhaps even one in the case of a private company.

The risk of invalidity due to the good faith qualification can be justified provided it is limited to circumstances in which a third party is clearly the least-cost-avoider (taking account of the factors discussed in chapter two) or where there is some other good reason for making third parties responsible for the misfeasance of a company's board. However, in judging when it would be appropriate to subject third parties to a risk of invalidity on this basis, full account should be taken of the need for third parties to have a reliable reference point that they can regard as speaking for the company and of the difficulties of finding a default reference point in the unitary board system.

---

[245] [2002] EWCA Civ 762.

The *Akindele* test, which determines a recipient's potential liability for knowing receipt, provides a basis for applying the good faith qualification in a way that strikes a fair and efficient balance of risk between companies and third parties. In particular, it recognises the danger of giving third parties any vague or open-ended responsibility to question and check the terms that a company's board is prepared to offer or accept on the basis that they appear to be unduly favourable to the third party. In effect, there should be clear evidence not only of a potential loss to the company, but also of a personal gain by one or more directors, as in the *Rolled Steel* case.[246] In any event, a third party's good faith should be judged according to the totality of circumstances and weight should be given to how far it would be reasonable to expect a third party to assume some responsibility for the company's governance such that it would be unconscionable for the third party to proceed without further inquiry.

The main problem area concerning the good faith qualification is the significance of a third party's actual knowledge of the board's lack of actual authority. It is arguable that this should not negate good faith, but be a factor in the overall assessment of the third party's conduct. In particular, weight should be given to the fact that the board is a company's supreme organ of management and may provide the most practical means of judging a company's best interests, especially given the absence of an accessible and reliable default reference point.

The other major limitation of section 35A is the fact that it applies only to contracts made or approved by a company's board. There is no equivalent overriding rule applicable to situations where the board does seek the approval of the company's shareholders as well. It was seen in chapter three that the constitutional limits on a board's actual authority may be obscure and complex and that even the board may have difficulty in discerning them. The persistence of the doctrine of deemed notice adds to the risk of invalidity in this situation. The abolition of that doctrine would therefore do much to remove this risk, but it would be preferable for this to be covered by a suitable statutory rule giving third parties complete security of transaction.

---

[246] [1986] 1 Ch 246.

6

Contracting with Other Corporate Agents

1 INTRODUCTION

1.1 The Case for Ensuring Reliability

THIS CHAPTER WILL focus on contracts that are made or approved on behalf of a company by an agent other than its board of directors. The risk of invalidity to the third party raises different issues because third parties dealing with subordinate agents do have a superior reference point. Subject to the limitations noted in chapter five, the board of a company can be viewed as the agent's principal for this purpose. A third party who wishes to avoid the risk of invalidity can require that the company's board approves the contract to ensure its validity or at least obtain confirmation from the board that the agent does have the necessary authority to make the contract.[1]

However, in practice, it may be difficult and costly for third parties to seek and obtain such assurance about corporate agents. Such costs could prevent many transactions taking place at all, although their size and impact would depend on such factors as the value and nature of the particular contract and the size and structure of the particular company's management body. There is an economic case therefore for ensuring that subordinate agents can give reliable assurance on behalf of their company within certain bounds. As discussed in chapter two, the rules of law that underpin such reliability can confer economic benefits by reducing the overall costs of transacting (including the costs of associated risks) and by prompting companies to develop good internal systems of governance that minimise their risk of being bound by unauthorised contracts that might prove burdensome. A key factor in assessing an appropriate degree of reliability for corporate agents is to consider the burden that third parties would face if they could not rely upon a particular agent and had to look for assurance from elsewhere within the company's management body.

---

[1] As noted in chapter five, directors purporting to act as the board, but in violation of the relevant procedural regulations in the company's constitution, may not be treated as the board. Depending on how s 35A of the Companies Act 1985 is interpreted on this point, the validity of their actions may be governed by the rules of law analysed in this chapter.

1.2 The Authority of Subordinate Agents

The size and structure of a company's management body may vary widely in practice and a company may have a wide range of subordinate agents. At the top, such agents include directors of the company when they are not acting as its board, such as executive directors and committees of the board. In the terminology of agency law, an agent who has been duly invested with the power to make a particular contract on behalf of a company in accordance with the company's constitution and other internal rules has 'actual authority' to make the contract.[2] In effect, the company is treated as having given its consent to the agent to act on its behalf in this respect. Whilst the constitution is the original expression of the company's consent and thus the ultimate source of the actual authority of all corporate agents, it is not the only source of limitation on an agent's actual authority.

Whilst it is possible in principle for the constitution of a company to confer actual authority directly upon subordinate agents, this is unusual and any provision purporting to do this would have to be construed carefully to ensure that it would be consistent with the general discretionary powers of management vested in the board.[3] The limits on the actual authority of a company's subordinate agents are set by the terms on which contractual power is delegated from its board and down through its management structure.

The constitution may place limits on the board's authority to delegate contractual power. However, there can be many stages in the process by which a particular agent acquires actual authority to make contracts, depending on the size and organisation of the company's management and the position of the subordinate agent within the overall hierarchy. Limits affecting a subordinate agent's actual authority may be set at any stage in this process.

1.3 Dealing with Subordinate Agents

The overriding rules of attribution that apply to contracts made or approved by subordinate corporate agents are still based on the common law of agency.[4] There has been no statutory intervention beneath the level

---

[2] See F Reynolds, *Bowstead & Reynolds on Agency* (London, Sweet & Maxwell, 2001) 17th edn ('Bowstead & Reynolds'), Art 1 and B Markesinis and R Munday, *An Outline of the Law of Agency* (London, Butterworths, 1998) 4th. edn ('Markesinis & Munday') at 1–11.

[3] The problem here is the same as the one discussed in chapter three concerning provisions in a company's constitution which purport to confer enforceable rights on parties in relation to matters of management such as the provision of legal services: *Eley v Positive Government Security Life Assurance* (1875–76) LR 1 Ex D 88.

[4] This book uses the term 'overriding rule of attribution' to refer to a rule of law that ensures that a company is bound by a contract even though the agent making it lacks actual authority to do so: see chapters one and two.

of the board. However, section 35A has indirect relevance in this context because it deems the power of a company's board to authorise others to bind the company to be free of any limitation under its constitution.[5] It therefore covers the board's power to confer actual authority on subordinate agents. Therefore, if a board purports to confer sufficient authority to enter into a particular contract on a subordinate agent, a third party entitled to rely on section 35A should be able to rely upon the validity of that contract even where the company's constitution expressly precludes the subordinate agent from having this authority.

The practical problem facing third parties is how to ascertain the actual authority of a subordinate corporate agent. In part, this is a problem because the law does not vest actual authority in corporate agents directly by virtue of their status or prescribe any standards in this respect. The actual authority enjoyed by corporate agents can therefore vary widely, even as between agents of comparable standing. There is not even any consistent and reliable terminology enabling companies to indicate to third parties that a corporate agent has a particular level of actual authority. Not even the fact that someone is a director of a company gives any clear idea as to their actual authority.

The difficulty of ascertaining the actual authority of a corporate agent is exacerbated by the potential for complexity and uncertainty in the process by which it may be conferred through delegation within a company's management structure. At the top, the directors may not be aware of all the constitutional limits on the board's actual authority or on the board's power to delegate authority to other agents. Further down, contractual power may be delegated in a way that leaves a subordinate agent's precise level of actual authority unclear. In particular, actual authority may well be conferred implicitly rather than explicitly.[6]

In agency law, appointing someone to a designated office in a company (such as managing director) entails an implicit delegation of the 'usual authority' associated with that office.[7] However, with many office titles or designations, the precise boundaries of the agent's usual authority may not be certain. Delegation of actual authority can also be inferred from the general conduct of those with the power to delegate it. In *Hely-Hutchinson v Brayhead*,[8] for example, the directors of a company acquiesced in one of their number behaving as though he were the managing director of the company, although they had never formally appointed him to this office. The Court of Appeal held that they had implicitly delegated the usual authority of a managing director to this director.

---

[5] Companies Act 1985, s 35A(1).
[6] See generally on implied authority Bowstead & Reynolds at 3–018–3–039 and Markesinis & Munday at 22–29.
[7] See generally on usual authority Bowstead & Reynolds at 3–006 and Markesinis & Munday at 29–36.
[8] [1968] 1 QB 549 (CA).

Thus, corporate agents who start to assume responsibilities beyond those normally associated with their office may, if their superiors do not restrain them, at some point acquire an additional level of actual authority commensurate with these additional responsibilities. The problem for third parties is that it may be hard to discern the precise level of the actual authority conferred in this way and it may be hard to identify the precise point at which the implied delegation takes effect.

1.4 The Economic Role of the Overriding Rules of Attribution Applicable to Subordinate Agents

In economic terms, third parties dealing with corporate agents face difficulty in acquiring reliable information about the actual authority of such agents. They would therefore face substantial costs if this were the only way of avoiding the risk of invalidity for lack of actual authority. Overriding rules of attribution therefore have economic significance by reducing these potential costs.

Also, in terms of the practicalities of litigation, the precise extent of an agent's actual authority derives from the terms of the agent's relationship with the company. This is private and not something that an outsider would find easy to prove. In practice, it is much easier for third parties to rely directly on overriding rules of attribution to establish the validity of a contract made with a company. This enables them to prove the validity of a contract on the basis of the external appearance of the agent's relationship with the company rather than on its internal content. This further increases the economic importance of having overriding rules that provide third parties with clear guidance on how to minimise the risk of invalidity.

From the perspective of third parties therefore, the function of the overriding rules of attribution is to mitigate the risk of invalidity due to an agent's lack of actual authority. However, the risk of invalidity to third parties has to be weighed against the risk to companies (and those interested in companies) of being bound by unauthorised contracts. This risk represents a cost to companies, which includes the costs of reducing or avoiding the risk by ensuring that corporate agents do not act without or in excess of their actual authority. The applicable overriding rules of attribution must take these costs into account if they are to minimise costs overall.

Chapter two reviewed the various factors that are relevant to assessing the respective costs to companies and third parties from the making of unauthorised contracts. Overall costs can be minimised by ensuring, so far as possible, that risk is assigned to the 'least-cost-avoider' as between these two groups. It was also argued, however, that there is an economic case for rules that give a competitive advantage to good quality companies with good governance systems and thus minimise the extent to which third parties have to assume some responsibility for a company's internal governance in order to avoid the risk of invalidity.

Factors that are relevant to understanding the cost implications of how the law apportions the risk associated with unauthorised contracts include the position of a subordinate agent within a company's management structure and the ease with which a third party can obtain assurance from a superior agent. The cost of such assurance depends, among other factors, on its reliability in ensuring that the company is bound and that there is no risk of invalidity.

As with contracts made or approved by the board, it is important to note the cost implications of putting third parties under a general risk of invalidity simply because an agent appears not to be acting in the best interests of a company. At an intuitive level, it might seem reasonable to expect third parties to have to protect the interests of companies in such circumstances. However, such an expectation would undermine the ability of third parties to act in their own best interests and insulate companies from the effects of having poor quality agents or poor systems of governance. Thus, whilst there may well be a case for expecting third parties to seek confirmation or assurance when they are dealing with a relatively junior agent, it would be unreasonable and inefficient to expect this of third parties dealing with a relatively senior agent who might appear to outsiders not to be acting in the company's best interests. The latter situation represents a risk of loss to the company, but the situation is one for which the company is likely to be the least-cost-avoider, unless there are additional factors apparent to the third party.

An agent's failure to pursue the company's best interests may be due to incompetence, lack of motivation or to deficiencies in the company's internal governance systems and these are deficiencies that the company is best placed to rectify. Ensuring that a third party can take advantage of such failings by not (without more) exposing them to the risk of invalidity would give good quality companies with better agents and good systems of governance a competitive advantage and prompt poor quality companies to improve in this respect. To subject third parties to a risk of invalidity would transfer some of the costs of poor governance away from poor quality companies and onto third parties in general.

As a general rule, companies are likely to be the least-cost-avoider of the risk of unauthorised contracts except in those situations where there is information readily available to third parties (in the form of signals that should be readily apparent to the third party) indicating that the agent probably does lack authority or that the company would be facing an unusually high risk of loss if the agent were to be acting without authority. However, to minimise overall costs, the law should also enable third parties to take action in response to these signals and to seek reliable confirmation without undue difficulty and at a relatively low cost.

2 THE FRAMEWORK OF THE LAW

2.1 Ostensible Authority

In agency law, an agent cannot bind his principal to a contract unless the principal has somehow consented that the agent should act on his behalf so as to affect his legal relations with other parties.[9] Actual authority results from a manifestation of consent made by the principal to the agent directly or indirectly. However, a principal can also give the necessary consent by manifesting it to the third party. This is known as 'ostensible' (or 'apparent') authority.[10] Bowstead & Reynolds states the doctrine as follows:[11]

> Where a person, by words or conduct, represents or permits it to be represented that another person has authority to act on his behalf, he is bound by the acts of that other person with respect to anyone dealing with him as agent on the faith of any such representation, to the same extent as if such other person had the authority that he was represented to have, even though he had no actual authority.

Finding that a principal has conferred ostensible authority on an agent and that a third party is entitled to rely upon this ostensible authority is common law's overriding rule of attribution.

With a company as the principal, however, the exercise becomes artificial. A company can only manifest 'its' consent through its constitution or through the actions of someone whose actions can be attributed to the company.[12] As with the process of conferring actual authority on a corporate agent, the actions whereby a company can be deemed to have manifested its consent to a third party may be vague and hard to construe with precision and clarity, embracing inferences drawn from conduct and the concept of usual authority.[13] Further, with ostensible authority, the focus is on the external appearance of a principal's actions rather than their internal content. Where a principal is artificial, then identifying 'its' actions and their external appearance is artificial. This creates scope for the law to become strained and complex, which is not conducive to reducing transaction costs and improving economic efficiency.

---

[9] Bowstead & Reynolds, Art 1.

[10] These terms are synonymous in the English law of agency.

[11] Bowstead & Reynolds, Art 74. See generally on ostensible authority, Bowstead & Reynolds at 8–013–8–050 and Markesinis & Munday at 36–50.

[12] *Freeman & Lockyer v Buckhurst Park Properties* [1964] 2 QB 480.

[13] See generally Bowstead & Reynolds at 3–024–3–041.

2.2 Determining the Ostensible Authority of Corporate Agents

The rules of law to be examined in this chapter are the common law's responses to the problem of how to determine whether a corporate agent has ostensible authority to act on behalf of a company and, if so, whether a third party can rely upon this ostensible authority. Common law in fact developed two responses to this problem. These are the 'indoor management rule' (also referred to as the 'rule in *Turquand*'), which evolved as a specific doctrine applicable to corporate agents, and Diplock LJ's restatement of the doctrine of ostensible authority for application to corporate agents in his judgment in *Freeman & Lockyer v Buckhurst Properties* (which will be referred to in this chapter as the Diplock approach).[14]

The indoor management rule emerged in relation to companies that were incorporated through registration under the Joint Stock Companies Act 1844 and reflects the registered company's background in partnership law.[15] Prior to this legislation, joint stock companies were mainly unincorporated associations with the legal status of partnerships.[16] As partners, their members faced potentially unlimited personal liability for the debts and other liabilities incurred by those managing the company's affairs.[17] Their liability could only be limited through express notification to third parties. After the 1844 reform, a company that was incorporated through registration had its own legal personality and was therefore solely responsible for the debts and liabilities incurred through the conduct of its affairs, although its members still faced a potentially unlimited liability to put the company in funds until the Limited Liability Act 1855.[18]

However, a key aspect of the 1844 reform was that companies were required to register their constitutions as part of the incorporation process. The courts viewed this as a means whereby the members of a registered company could notify third parties of the limits on the authority of those to whom the management of the company's affairs had been entrusted to incur liabilities for which the company (and thus its members) would be responsible.[19] This was the basis of the doctrine of constructive (or deemed) notice of a company's public documents and the indoor management rule was in effect a gloss on this doctrine. The rule indicated that, as in partnership law, the onus was on the members of a

---

[14] [1964] 2 QB 480.
[15] See *Royal British Bank v Turquand* (1855) 5 El & Bl 248 and (1856) 6 El & Bl 327 and *Ernest v Nicholls* (1857) 6 HLC 401.
[16] See chapter one.
[17] The unlimited liability of partners stemming from their mutual agency in the conduct of a firm's business has been codified in s 5 of the Partnership Act 1890. See generally D Milman and T Flanagan, *Modern Partnership Law* (London, Croom Helm, 1983).
[18] See chapter one.
[19] See *Royal British Bank v Turquand* (1856) 6 El & Bl 327 at 332 and *Ernest v Nicholls* (1857) 6 HLC 401 at 419–420.

company rather than third parties to ensure that those entrusted with the management of a company's affairs did so properly and in accordance with the company's internal rules as long as they did not stray beyond those limits that had been formally notified to third parties.[20]

In *Morris v Kanssen*,[21] Lord Simonds said that the indoor management rule and the doctrine of ostensible authority were both applications of the fundamental legal maxim *omnia praesumuntur rite esse acta*.[22] The courts applied the indoor management rule both to contracts made through the affixing of a company's common seal and to contracts made by directors and senior managers acting as agents of a company. Statute, currently in the form of section 35A of the Companies Act 1985, has largely removed any role for the indoor management rule in relation to contracts made or approved by a company's board. And the Diplock approach has effectively eclipsed it in relation to subordinate agents. The ascendancy of this adaptation of the doctrine of ostensible authority, being drawn from the general law of agency, and the decline of the indoor management rule arguably reflect a much stronger perception of a company as a separate entity rather than as essentially a partnership among its shareholders.[23] At the time of its eclipse, the indoor management rule had come to be perceived as unsatisfactory and lacking a clear doctrinal structure, with a rather motley set of limitations and qualifications.[24] However, despite its deficiencies, the indoor management rule treated corporate agency as something fundamentally distinct from acting for a human principal and provided the basis for an approach to unauthorised contracts that acknowledged the significance of this distinction.

The Diplock approach holds that a third party can only enforce an unauthorised contract against a company if the company's agent has ostensible authority to make it. However, this requires a manifestation or 'representation' of consent to the third party that can be attributed to the company as the agent's principal.[25] This means that the representation must have come from the company's constitution or have been made by someone with the actual or ostensible authority to make it on behalf of the company. In the case of relatively junior agents within a large management

---

[20] See also *Smith v The Hull Glass Co* (1852) CP 11 CB 897.

[21] [1946] AC 459.

[22] [1946] AC 459 at 475.

[23] On these conflicting visions of the company and their role in the development of company law, see M Horwitz, '*Santa Clara* Revisited: The Development of Corporate Theory' (1985) 88 *West Virginia Law Review* 173, M Stokes, 'Company Law and Legal Theory' in W Twining (ed), *Legal Theory and Common Law* (Oxford, Basil Blackwell, 1986) and J Hill, Changes in the Role of the Shareholder in R Grantham and C Rickett (eds), *Corporate Personality in the 20th Century* (Oxford, Hart Publishing, 1998).

[24] See, for example, D Milman and A Evans, 'Corporate Officers and the Outsider Protection Regime' (1985) 6 *Company Lawyer* 68.

[25] See Bowstead & Reynolds, Art 1.

body, this may involve having to trace ostensible authority through a whole series of representations right up to the company's board, at which point the third party can rely on the representation being subject to the statutory presumption in section 35A.

The basis of the Diplock approach in classical agency law, with its emphasis on the need to show the principal's consent to a particular agent making a particular contract on its behalf, means that it does not readily accommodate the interests of third parties, not even where achieving fairness and efficiency means ensuring that third parties have certainty on this point. However, the courts have shown some willingness to distort the Diplock approach in order to avoid an unfair and inefficient result and have done so at the expense of doctrinal clarity.

3 THE INDOOR MANAGEMENT RULE

3.1 The Nature of the Rule

3.1.1 A Presumption of Regularity

The indoor management rule evolved from the judgments of the Exchequer Chamber in *Royal British Bank v Turquand*.[26] In *Morris v Kanssen*,[27] the House of Lords approved the following statement of the rule taken from Halsbury's Laws of England:[28]

> [P]ersons contracting with a company and dealing in good faith may assume that acts within its constitution and powers have been properly and duly performed and are not bound to inquire whether acts of internal management have been regular.

Lord Simonds said that the rationale of this rule was that the 'wheels of business will not go smoothly round unless it may be assumed that that is in order which appears to be in order'.[29]

The wheels of business tend to turn more smoothly when transaction costs are minimised, including the cost to third parties of the risk of invalidity due to a corporate agent's lack of actual authority. However, the main condition attached to the indoor management rule, namely that the presumption of regularity would only apply within the limits set by a company's constitution, rested on the unrealistic assumption that third

---

[26] (1855) 5 El & Bl 248 and (1856) 6 El & Bl 327.
[27] [1946] AC 459 at 474, per Lord Simonds.
[28] 2nd edn vol. V (1932) at 423. See also *Rolled Steel v British Steel* [1986] 1 Ch 246 (CA) at 283, per Slade LJ.
[29] [1946] AC 459 at 475.

parties would in the ordinary course be able and willing to examine the constitutions of the companies with which they dealt. The indoor management rule did not therefore enable the wheels of business to turn as smoothly as they might have done.

3.1.2 Constructive Notice of Irregularity

As noted above, the indoor management rule evolved in conjunction with the common law doctrine of constructive notice whereby third parties were deemed to have notice of a company's public documents and thus of the overall limits on the actual authority of the company's agents set by the company's constitution.[30] The problem with the juxtaposition of the indoor management rule with this doctrine was that it obscured the basis of the presumption of regularity, which reflected the company's roots in partnership law. Some statements in the case law implied that the rule operated as a supplement to the actual knowledge of a company's constitution that a third party was assumed to have acquired already. Thus, in *Biggerstaff v Rowatt's Wharf*, Lindley LJ remarked:[31]

> What must persons look to when they deal with directors? They must see whether according to the constitution of the company the directors could have the powers which they are purporting to exercise ... The [third party] must look to the articles, and see that the managing director might have power to do what he purports to do, and that is enough for a person dealing with him bona fide.

In practice, a third party was most unlikely to have inspected a company's constitution and to be acting on a specific belief that the company's affairs were being conducted on the basis prescribed by the constitution. Instead, such third parties were more likely to operate on the assumption that a director or managers acting on behalf of a company in the conduct of its affairs had the necessary authority to do so, in the same way that they would when dealing with a partner in the conduct of a partnership's business.

In other words, it was unrealistic to expect third parties to behave in the way that Lindley LJ imagined. Third parties would be unlikely to perform the duty that the doctrine of constructive notice purported to impose on them. Instead, the doctrine operated negatively as a penalty for their failure to do so. In economic terms, third parties tended to avoid the costs of checking a company's public documents, but the resulting risk of invalidity imposed a cost on them nonetheless.

When the Court of Appeal in the *Freeman & Lockyer* case reviewed the role of the doctrine of constructive notice in the indoor management rule,

---

[30] *Ernest v Nicholls* (1857) 6 HLC 401; *Mahony v Liquidator of the East Holyford Mining Co* (1875) LR 7 HL 869.
[31] [1896] 2 Ch 93 (CA) at 102.

the judges confirmed that it had a purely negative operation and that a third party's deemed notice of the constitution was not the legal foundation of the presumption of regularity.[32] Willmer LJ explained Lindley LJ's mode of expression in the *Biggerstaffe* case as follows:[33]

> I take Lindley LJ to mean, not that persons dealing with the supposed managing director must actually look at the articles, but that, being affected with notice of them, they must have regard thereto. Consequently, if in that case the articles of association had conferred no power to appoint a managing director, the [third party] could not have been heard to say that the [agent] had been held out by the company as its managing director.

3.1.3 Statement of the Indoor Management Rule

The indoor management rule can be summarised as follows:

(1) There is a presumption that an agent acting in the course of a company's business, who appears to have the authority to bind a company and has at least some *de facto* connection with the company, does have this authority. This can be termed the 'presumption of regularity'.

(2) The presumption is limited to the scope of the authority that could have been vested in the agent in accordance with the terms of the company's constitution. The third party is subject to the doctrine of 'constructive notice' in the sense of having deemed notice of the company's public documents.

(3) A third party cannot rely upon the presumption of regularity if he has notice that the agent does not in fact have actual authority to bind the company.[34] This includes actual or constructive notice and an agent without such notice is said to be dealing with the agent 'in good faith'. As well as constructive notice of the company's public documents, a third party has constructive notice of an agent's lack of actual authority if there are circumstances that put him 'on inquiry'.

3.2 An Analysis of the Indoor Management Rule

3.2.1 A Corporate Agent's Appearance of Authority

In the early case law on the indoor management rule, it was sufficient for the agent to have an appearance of authority, regardless of whether the

---

[32] [1964] 2 QB 480 (CA).
[33] [1964] 2 QB 480 at 491–92. See also Diplock LJ at 504.
[34] The agency law doctrine of ostensible authority is subject to this proviso: see Bowstead & Reynolds, Art 75.

agent had been duly appointed as a director (or as the board) or other officer of the company, although the agent always had at least a *de facto* connection with the company and its management. The courts did not attach significance to the precise legal nature or terms of the agent's relationship with the company.

The indoor management rule was thus applied in cases involving the actions of those who had not been formally and properly appointed to their offices in accordance with the company's constitution.[35] In *Duck v Tower*,[36] for example, a sole trader had turned a business into a company, but no formal meetings were ever held and no directors formally appointed. Nevertheless, it was held that those purporting to act as its directors could bind the company to a debenture:[37]

> [It] has always been held that it is not incumbent on the holder of such a document purporting to be issued by a company to inquire whether the persons pretending to sign as directors have been duly appointed ... there has been ample authority to show that no informality will alter the rights possessed by a bona fide holder for value upon a document that purports to be in order.

Again, in *Biggerstaff v Rowatt's Wharf*,[38] a person acting as *de facto* managing director of a company hypothecated certain debts of the company to a third party. Lindley LJ remarked that it would be a very serious matter to mercantile companies if this third party were not to be able to rely upon the indoor management rule.[39]

The presumption of regularity also applied where the board of a company had exceeded the limits on its own authority to exercise the powers of the company under the constitution, whether the limits were substantive,[40] or procedural.[41]

3.2.2 The Doctrine of Constructive Notice

In the early case law, the courts did not explore the basis of the presumption of regularity, but moved straight on to deciding whether or not the presumption would be consistent with the company's external face as revealed by its public documents. They would then consider whether

---

[35] *Re County Life Assurance Co* (1869–70) LR 5 Ch App 288 (CA); *Mahony v Liquidator of the East Holyford Mining Co* (1875) LR 7 HL 869. See now Companies Act 1985, s 285.
[36] [1901] 2 KB 314.
[37] *Ibid* at 318, per Lord Alverstone CJ.
[38] [1896] 2 Ch 93 (CA).
[39] [1896] 2 Ch 93 at 100.
[40] *Royal British Bank v Turquand* (1855) 5 El & Bl 248 and (1856) 6 El & Bl 327.
[41] *County of Gloucester Bank v Rudry Merthyr Steam and House Coal Colliery Co* [1895] 1 Ch 629 (CA).

there was anything in the circumstances of the case to put the third party on inquiry and prevent it from relying upon the presumption. The *Turquand* case itself, for example, concerned the validity of a bond executed by two directors of the company under its common seal. The bond had not been approved by a resolution of the company's shareholders in general meeting as required by the constitution. The court held that this defect was an internal matter between the company's shareholders and its directors and that the bond was binding the company:[42]

> If the [third party] must be presumed to have had notice of the contents of the registered [constitution], there is nothing to show that the directors might not have had authority to execute the bond as they asserted.

However, in confirming the original judgment, Jervis CJ emphasised the third party's duty to take note of the company's external face as defined by its constitution:[43]

> We may now take for granted that … parties dealing with [companies] are bound to read the statute and the [company's constitution]. But they are not bound to do more. And the party here, on reading the [constitution], would find, not a prohibition from borrowing, but a permission to do so on certain conditions. Finding that the authority might be made complete by a resolution, he would have a right to infer the fact of a resolution authorising that which on the face of the document appeared to be legitimately done.

In *Ernest v Nicholls*,[44] the House of Lords confirmed that third parties were obliged to look at a company's public documents 'otherwise the shareholders have not the protection which it was clearly intended to give them'.[45]

In *Mahony v East Holyford Mining*,[46] the House of Lords discussed the significance of a third party's deemed notice of the constitution of a company in a case where they found that the presumption of regularity did apply so as to ensure the validity of a transaction. Lord Hatherley stated that third parties had no right 'to suppose that anything has been done or can be done that is not permitted by' a company's constitution and that, in this respect, the third party 'must be taken to have perfect knowledge' of the terms of the constitution:[47]

> But, after that, when there are persons conducting the affairs of the company in a manner which appears to be perfectly consonant with the articles

---

[42] (1855) 5 El & Bl 248 at 261–62, per Lord Campbell CJ. The Exchequer Chamber heard the case.
[43] (1856) 6 El & Bl 329 at 332. The second judgment of the Exchequer Chamber rejected the defendant's plea of error.
[44] (1857) 6 HLC 401.
[45] *Ibid* at 421.
[46] *Mahony v Liquidator of the East Holyford Mining Co* (1875) LR 7 HL 869.
[47] (1875) LR 7 HL 869 at 894.

of association, then those so dealing with them, externally, are not to be affected by any irregularities which may take place in the internal management of the company.

This linking of an agent's appearance of authority with the third party's duty to inspect the company's constitution and ascertain the maximum scope of the actual authority that could have been vested in the agent anticipated the remarks of Lindley LJ in *Biggerstaff v Rowatt's Wharf* noted above.[48]

The impact of statutory reform on the doctrine of constructive notice and its proposed abolition will be discussed in a later section of this chapter. The doctrine came to be regarded as an excessive and unnecessary burden on third parties and, in relation to the boards of companies at least, did not comply with the First Company Law Directive.[49] The resulting risk of invalidity was increased by the fact that, as has been seen in chapter three, the constitutions of companies can vary widely and the terms governing the authority of corporate agents can be obscure, complex and unclear.

3.3 Circumstances that put a Third Party on Inquiry

3.3.1 A Third Party's Duty to find out more

The indoor management rule enabled a third party to presume that the board or a director or another officer of a company had the power to bind it unless the third party had actual or constructive notice to the contrary. Third parties were treated as knowing that which the court decided they ought to have found out. Knowledge of an agent's lack of authority was sufficient to prevent third parties from relying upon the agent's appearance of authority. As it has also been put, such knowledge negated the third party's 'good faith' and good faith was treated as a condition of a third party's ability to rely upon the indoor management rule.[50]

The concept of good faith and its association with the idea of constructive notice (or constructive knowledge) has already been examined in chapter five. It was also seen that care is needed with this terminology. In particular, the expression 'constructive notice', as well as being used to refer to the company law doctrine of deemed notice of a company's public documents, also has a specific meaning in the context of conveyancing. The term constructive knowledge will therefore be used to refer to the broader concept of that information which the courts decide that third parties should have found out.

---

[48] [1896] 2 Ch 93 at 102.
[49] EEC/68/151. See generally chapter five.
[50] *Royal British Bank v Turquand* (1855) 5 El & Bl 248 at 261–62; *Rolled Steel v British Steel* [1986] 1 Ch 246 (CA).

Constructive knowledge was based on the idea that a third party would sometimes be subject to a duty to find out more about an agent's authority and was in effect a penalty for not performing this duty. Thus, a third party's deemed notice of the terms of a company's constitution was based on a duty to study the company's public documents, which the courts did not originally view as an unreasonable burden. The general qualification to the indoor management rule stemmed from the more flexible duty to make further inquiry if the circumstances of the transaction were such as to put the third party 'on inquiry'.

3.3.2 Circumstances Putting a Third Party on Inquiry

The circumstances of the *Turquand* case itself did not put the third party on inquiry and the court merely hinted at the factors that might have altered their judgment on this point. It held that the transaction was a normal business transaction and that there were no overt signs that the directors were acting against the interests of the company:[51]

> Looking to the business to be carried on by this Company, it might well be presumed that opening such an account and carrying on such dealings with a banking house as are described in the condition would be within the authority of the directors, and would be for the benefit of the shareholders.

This was also consistent with the parameters of a partner's liability under the doctrine of mutual agency.[52]

In *Ernest v Nicholls*,[53] the House of Lords focused on the two qualifications to the indoor management rule indicated in the *Turquand* case and held that they both applied in the case before them. The transaction at issue was the acquisition of the business of the third party and one of the company's directors was also a director of the third party. The statute under which the company had been incorporated provided that a transaction of this kind had to be approved by the company's shareholders because of the conflict of interest. The House of Lords held that the third party could not rely upon the indoor management rule because of its deemed notice of the statutory provision and also because of the unusual nature of the transaction:[54]

> [This] is not a question about goods supplied, or services performed in the way of trade in the ordinary course, but a question as to a special contract to do the very unusual thing of purchasing by one Company the trade of

---

[51] (1855) 5 El & Bl 248 at 261, per Lord Campbell CJ.
[52] Partnership Act 1890, s 5.
[53] (1857) 6 HLC 401.
[54] *Ibid.*

another. Such a contract clearly does not bind, unless it is authorised by the [constitution], and it is made strictly according to its provisions.

The House of Lords elaborated on the general qualification to the indoor management rule in *Mahony v East Holyford Mining*,[55] which concerned the validity of cheques signed by directors (and the company's secretary) who had never been formally appointed to their offices.

In the *Mahony* case, the House of Lords found that the third party had dealt with the company's *de facto* directors in good faith and without having any reason to doubt their authority as directors.[56] Lord Hatherley presented the issue as follows:[57]

> Now, if the question came to be which of two innocent parties (as it is said) was to suffer loss, I apprehend, my lords, that in point of law what must be considered in cases of that kind is this: which of the two parties was bound to do, or to avoid, any act by which the loss has been sustained.

This amounted to an allocation of risk as between the company and the third party based on an assignment of duties. He recognised that a company (meaning the shareholders or superior management as the case may be) has responsibility for the activities of its agents and that the onus on third parties to check up on the authority of corporate agents must be judged in that context.

A third party was entitled to enforce an unauthorised contract unless the company's own responsibility for its agents was outweighed by a duty on the third party to find out more. The qualifications to the indoor management rule reflected such countervailing duties. However, in the *Mahony* case, it was the company's shareholders who should have ensured that those acting as directors of the company were doing so with proper authority and that the affairs of the company were being properly managed.[58] The third party had a duty to make any additional inquiries that adopting a reasonable standard of care and caution would entail,[59] but had no obligation beyond this to ensure that the company's internal affairs were in good order.[60]

3.3.3 Circumstances in which Third Parties are the Least-Cost-Avoider

The idea that the indoor management rule should apply unless the circumstances of a transaction placed the third party under a duty to make

---

[55] *Mahony v Liquidator of the East Holyford Mining Company* (1875) LR 7 HL 869.
[56] (1875) LR 7 HL 869 at 892, per Lord Cairns LC.
[57] *Ibid* at 897.
[58] *Ibid* at 897–98.
[59] *Ibid* at 895, per Lord Hatherley.
[60] *Ibid* at 898–99.

further inquiry could be viewed as a rudimentary mechanism for assigning responsibility and therefore risk to the party that is the least-cost-avoider and thereby as minimising costs overall. In most ordinary business situations, that would mean placing responsibility on the company's management body because of their greater knowledge of the company's agents and of how their unauthorised activities might adversely affect the company. For the third party, the company's agent would be more than just an agent acting for another party: the agent would be the third party's main point of contact with the company and its main source of information about the company. To the third party, the agent would be the external face of the company itself. In such circumstances, it would be inefficient to assign responsibility for the agent's activities to the third party.

To justify shifting responsibility to the third party, the circumstances of the transaction should have some feature that would alter the normal balance of cost and undermine the third party's case for viewing the agent as the external face of the company. They should warn the third party that it must look beyond the agent to find the company. Further, having to look beyond the agent should not be a disproportionate burden for the third party.

In *Morris v Kanssen*, Lord Simonds alluded to the necessary shift in the balance of responsibility as follows:[61]

> [The indoor management rule] is a rule designed for the protection of those who are entitled to assume, just because they cannot know, that the person with whom they deal has the authority which he claims. This is clearly shown by the fact that the rule cannot be invoked if the condition is no longer satisfied, that is, if he who would invoke it is put upon his inquiry. He cannot presume in his own favour that things are rightly done if inquiry that he ought to make would tell him that they were wrongly done.

Putting a third party 'upon his inquiry' to find out more and judging him on the basis of the information that such an inquiry would 'tell him' gives the third party an incentive to acquire this information. Such an incentive would be justifiable as long as the company's management hierarchy should not have been able to find out that 'things were wrongly done' at a lower cost. In chapter five, it was seen how the same kind of approach, in relation to a third party's potential liability for knowing receipt, has led to the courts looking for circumstances which would make it commercially unacceptable or 'unconscionable' for a third party not to make further inquiry and to attribute 'constructive knowledge' accordingly.[62]

---

[61] [1946] AC 459 at 475.
[62] *BCCI v Akindele* [2001] Ch 437 (CA); *Criterion Properties v Stratford UK Properties* [2002] EWCA Civ 1883.

3.3.4 *Factors Putting Third Parties 'on Inquiry'*

In the *Turquand* and *Mahony* cases, the courts did not find that the circumstances put the third parties on inquiry and three factors appear significant in this respect: first, the transactions were ordinary business transactions and thus not unusual in themselves; secondly, it was not unusual for agents of the kind at issue to be authorised to make the transactions at issue; and thirdly, there was nothing to suggest to the third parties that the agents might acting to advance their own interests at the expense of the best interests of the company. These factors also explain cases in which the third party was able to rely upon the presumption of regularity such as *County of Gloucester Bank v Rudry Merthyr*,[63] *Biggerstaff v Rowatt's Wharf*,[64] and *British Thomson-Houston v Federated European Bank*.[65] In the latter case, in which a guarantee had been executed by the chairman of the company's board alone and not by two directors, Greer LJ justified the presumption of regularity as enabling third parties to have a point of contact with a company to whom they could look to bind it.[66]

The development of rules that enable third parties to have certainty in their dealings with companies on ordinary business transactions is important in English company law given the lack of prescribed standards as regards the actual authority of a company's board or of individual directors or of any particular corporate agent whatever their designation. There is a strong intuitive case and an economic one for ensuring that third parties can rely on a corporate agent's appearance of authority to bind the company where having such authority would conform to standard practice or at least not be unusual.

However, there is also a case for shifting the onus onto third parties where it would be unusual for a particular corporate agent to have authority to represent the company or where there is something that should indicate to the third party that the agent should not be viewed as a reliable representative of the company's interests. This would be the case where an agent makes a contract that would normally have to be approved by agents higher up the management hierarchy.[67] Also, the third party's own suspicion as regards the agent's authority can be enough undermine the presumption of regularity.[68]

The main factor that has been held to put third parties on inquiry and prevent them from relying on the presumption of regularity has been the presence of circumstances that should alert the third party to the danger of a conflict of interest on the part of the agent. Such circumstances have

---

[63] [1895] 1 Ch 629 (CA).
[64] [1896] 2 Ch 93 (CA).
[65] [1932] 2 KB 176 (CA).
[66] [1932] 2 KB 176 at 182.
[67] See, for example, *Kreditbank Cassel v Schenkers* [1927] 1 KB 826 (CA).
[68] See, for example, *Houghton v Northard, Lowe & Wills* [1927] 1 KB 246 (CA).

included an overt or obvious conflicting personal interest in a transaction and the fact that a transaction had features that appear to operate against the company's interests and to the benefit of the agent.[69]

There is an economic logic to shifting the risk to third parties in such circumstances provided that the factors triggering the shifting of risk are readily discernible to third parties. The circumstances would demark a distinct sub-group of transactions in which the risk of harm to the company (and thus the cost to the company of having to bear the risk of being bound by the contract) would be significantly enhanced and in which the third party would be better placed to protect the interests of the company (and thus be the least-cost-avoider) by making further inquiry.

In practice, shifting the risk to third parties in such circumstances should help deter agents from acting to the company's detriment. However, this observation only applies where the circumstances call into question the honesty as opposed to the competence of the agent. As was emphasised at the beginning of this chapter, the observation does not apply where the agent merely appears to be making a bad bargain for the company and there is no obvious personal gain to the agent from the company's apparent disadvantage. Such a situation reveals a risk to the company from poor governance and it is one for which the company is likely to be the least-cost-avoider. A third party could be put on inquiry if the transaction were an unusual one for an agent of the particular rank to make, but otherwise the effect of shifting the risk onto third parties at this point would be to inhibit them from the pursuit of their own commercial interests. This would impose a cost on third parties in general in order to protect companies that operate with poor systems of governance or poor quality agents.

In the cases in which the courts have held that the third party was put on inquiry and unable to rely upon the presumption of regularity, there have usually been indications of a likely conflict of interest either alone or in conjunction with other unusual circumstances. In *Underwood v Bank of Liverpool and Martins*,[70] for example, the sole director of a company had endorsed cheques payable to his company in favour of himself and paid them into his own account.[71] The Court of Appeal held that there was an obvious risk that the director was doing this to profit at the expense of the

---

[69] See, for example, *Houghton v Nothard, Lowe & Wills* [1927] 1 KB 246 (CA), *Kreditbank Cassel v Schenkers* [1927] 1 KB 826 (CA), *EBM Co v Dominion Bank* [1937] 3 All ER 555 (PC), *Rolled Steel v British Steel* [1986] 1 Ch 246 (CA).

[70] [1924] 1 KB 775 (CA).

[71] The bank, which had collected the cheques and paid them into the director's personal account, would have been liable for conversion of the cheques unless they could show that the agent had had the necessary authority or could bring themselves within the protection of s 82 of the Bills of Exchange Act 1882, which required them to show that they had acted in good faith and 'without negligence'.

company and that this put the bank on inquiry to make sure that the agent had been properly authorised to do this.[72]

The fact that a third party is also a director of the company has also been held to prevent him from being able to rely upon the presumption of regularity.[73] In *Morris v Kanssen*, for example, the third party was a director, albeit only just appointed, and Lord Simonds held that the countervailing duty, which had put the third party on inquiry, stemmed from this fact:[74]

> It is the duty of directors, and equally of those who purport to act as directors, to look after the affairs of the company, to see that it acts within its powers and that its transactions are regular and orderly. To admit in their favour a presumption that that is rightly done which they have themselves wrongly done is to encourage ignorance and condone dereliction from duty... His duty as director is to know; his interest, when he invokes the [indoor management] rule, is to disclaim knowledge. Such a conflict can be resolved in only one way.

Forgery has also been presented as an exception to the indoor management rule.[75] This proved a source of confusion, in particular when judges treated the affixing of a company's common seal without due authorisation as an instance of forgery.[76] The better view now is that forgery should not be viewed as an additional exception and does not raise any special issues beyond the general question of whether suspicious circumstances should have put the third party on inquiry.[77]

3.4 The Displacement of the Indoor Management Rule

3.4.1 *The Presumption of Regularity as an Instance of Ostensible Authority*

In twentieth century case law, long before the Court of Appeal's judgment in *Freeman & Lockyer*, the indoor management rule had come to be viewed as an application of the general agency law doctrine of ostensible authority

---

[72] See [1924] 1 KB 775 at 787–88, per Bankes LJ, who relied on Lord Hatherley's qualification of the indoor management rule in *Mahony's* case, and at 796–98, per Atkin LJ. The House of Lords approved and followed this decision in *Midland Bank v Reckitt* [1933] AC 1, where a solicitor had used a power of attorney entitling him to draw cheques on a client's bank account for his own benefit.

[73] *Morris v Kanssen* [1946] AC 459 (HL); *Howard v Patent Ivory* (1888) 38 Ch D 156.

[74] [1946] AC 459 at 476.

[75] The House of Lords held that the rule could not be used to validate a 'forgery' in *Ruben v Great Fingall Consolidated* [1906] AC 439.

[76] *Kreditbank Cassel v Schenkers* [1927] 1 KB 826 (CA); *South London Greyhound Racecourses v Wake* [1931] 1 Ch 496.

[77] See The Law Commission, *The Execution of Deeds and Documents by or on behalf of Bodies Corporate* (Law Commission Consultation Paper No. 143, The Stationery Office, London, 1996 ('Execution of Deeds (CP)') at 5.29–5.32.

rather than a distinct company law doctrine, especially when the actions of a single director or officer were at issue.[78] However, ostensible authority could not be based upon the mere appearance of authority, but required an overarching manifestation or representation of consent from the company to the third party. The courts thus became preoccupied with discovering the representations that could explain the operation of the indoor management rule. In *Houghton v Nothard, Lowe & Wills,*[79] for example, the Court of Appeal expressly rejected an argument that the third party's deemed notice of the constitution constituted the necessary representation of authority,[80] although some doubt was expressed as to whether denying that this doctrine could operate to the benefit of third parties could be reconciled with its negative impact on them.[81]

Although the courts came to regard the validity of a contract made by a corporate agent as depending on the agent's ostensible authority, they still attached significance to whether or not the circumstances of the transaction had put the third party on inquiry. Thus, in *British Thomson-Houston Co v Federated European Bank,*[82] the Court of Appeal held that a third party could rely upon a presumption of regularity because this finding was seen as consistent with the cases in which the indoor management rule had been applied, such as the *Mahony* case. In particular, there had been nothing to put the third party on inquiry. Thus, the agent in the *British Thomson-Houston* case, who was in fact the chairman of the company's board, would normally be expected to have authority to enter into a contract of the kind at issue and the transaction had no unusual features.[83]

3.4.2 The Problem of Finding a Representation of Ostensible Authority

In *Rama v Proved Tin,*[84] Slade J found it impossible to reconcile the Court of Appeal's decision in the *British Thomson-Houston* case with cases in which the third party had not been able to rely upon the presumption of regularity. There appeared to be no representation of authority that could support the agent's ostensible authority. In the *Rama* case itself, there were clearly circumstances that would have put the third party on inquiry.[85]

---

[78] *Underwood v Bank of Liverpool and Martins* [1924] 1 KB 775 (CA), *Houghton v Nothard, Lowe & Wills* [1927] 1 KB 246 (CA), *Kreditbank Cassel v Schenkers* [1927] 1 KB 826 (CA), *British Thomson-Houston v Federated European Bank* [1932] 2 KB 176 (CA).
[79] [1927] 1 KB 246.
[80] [1927] 1 KB 246 at 266–67, per Sargant LJ with Atkin LJ concurring.
[81] *Kreditbank Cassel v Schenkers* [1927] 1 KB 826 at 833–34, per Scrutton LJ.
[82] [1932] 2 KB 176 (CA).
[83] [1932] 2 KB 176 at 181.
[84] *Rama Corporation v Proved Tin & General Investments* [1952] 2 QB 147.
[85] The agent was a director of a company, who had agreed that the company would participate in a joint venture with the third party. The third party paid a cheque made out to the agent personally in accordance with the terms of this agreement. The agent misappropriated the money.

However, Slade J held that a third party could only rely upon the indoor management rule if it had actual knowledge of a provision in the company's constitution that would entitle the company's board to delegate the necessary authority to the agent in question (a director in this case) to make the contract at issue. In other words, he saw the constitution as the only means by which the company could have made a representation about the authority of this agent so that the third party's lack of knowledge of the constitution prevented it from being able to rely on the agent as having ostensible authority in any event.

If the indoor management rule were to have been restricted in this way, it would have lost its practical value in providing a platform of presumed information on which third parties dealing with corporate agents could rely. This platform had been undermined from the beginning by third parties' deemed notice of the company's external face, but the *Rama* case placed an even greater onus on third parties to study the terms of a company's constitution and imposed on them an even greater risk for failing to do so. The Court of Appeal resolved the problem in its judgment in *Freeman & Lockyer v Buckhurst Park Properties*.[86] The formulation of the 'Diplock Approach' marked the complete displacement of the indoor management rule by agency law for contracts made by subordinate corporate agents. The Diplock approach provided a set of rules that can be applied to any corporate agent regardless of their position in a company's hierarchy.

Diplock LJ (as he then was) rejected Slade J's view that third parties can only rely upon corporate agents (at least in the case of individual directors and senior officers of the company) as having ostensible authority if they have actual knowledge of the company's constitution. Instead, he held that the necessary representation of authority was made when the agent was appointed to a particular office or was allowed to assume an office *de facto*.

4 THE DIPLOCK APPROACH TO CORPORATE AGENCY

4.1 Adapting Agency Law to Corporate Personality

Agency law is based on a model in which a principal is a natural person who, among other things, can make representations (or manifestations of consent) to third parties.[87] A human principal provides a sharp focus for any inquiry as to whether he (rather than the third party) should have to bear the risk of his agent's actions in making a contract. In the general law

---

[86] [1964] 2 QB 480.
[87] See, for example, Bowstead & Reynolds, Art 1.

of agency, this inquiry evolved into one as to whether the principal has done something to manifest his consent to or acceptance of this risk.[88]

An artificial principal cannot make a representation any more than it can enter into a contract. A human agent can purport to make a representation on a company's behalf, which gives rise to the legal issue of whether that representation can be attributed to the company. This begs the question of whose representations can be attributed to the company for this purpose so that the company can be treated as having accepted the risk of being bound by the actions of a particular agent in making a contract on its behalf.

In corporate agency, there is nothing analogous to a human principal. Those who are entitled to speak for or act on behalf of a company (such as its board and its body of shareholders) do not, unlike a human principal, face unlimited personal liability for the actions of the company's agents. And for a third party contracting with a company, an agent can 'be' the company as much as anyone else. The third party may have no obvious, or at least no convenient, alternative reference point for establishing an independent relationship with the company about the agent.

Despite these conceptual difficulties, the indoor management rule came to be viewed as governing the ostensible authority of corporate agents rather than as an independent rule of company law. In *Freeman & Lockyer v Buckhurst Park Properties*,[89] the Court of Appeal confirmed that this was in fact the case and Diplock LJ restated the law in terms grounded in the concepts of agency law. This restatement has since been endorsed as governing the law regulating the enforceability of contracts made by corporate agents other than the board of a company.[90]

4.2 The Restatement of the Law in the *Freeman & Lockyer* Case

The *Freeman & Lockyer* case concerned the liability of a company for the fees of a firm of architects, which had been engaged by one of its directors to provide certain services in connection with the development and sale of an estate. The company's board had not formally appointed this agent to the office of managing director and had not authorised him to engage the firm of architects. Instead, the agent had acted as a *de facto* managing director and the other directors had acquiesced in this behaviour. The company's articles included a provision under which the board could

---

[88] See I Brown, 'The Agent's Apparent Authority: Paradigm or Paradox?' [1995] *Journal of Business Law* 360.

[89] [1964] 2 QB 480 (CA).

[90] See the judgments of the House of Lords in *British Bank of the Middle East v Sun Life* [1983] 2 Lloyd's Rep 9 and *Armagas v Mundogas* [1986] AC 717 and of the Court of Appeal in *Egyptian International Foreign Trade Co v Soplex* [1985] BCLC 404 and *First Energy v Hungarian International Bank* [1993] BCLC 1409.

have appointed the agent as managing director and given him the actual authority to make the contract in question.

Diplock LJ looked back at the case law on the indoor management rule, which Slade J had reviewed in *Rama v Proved Tin*:[91]

> This branch of the law has developed pragmatically rather than logically owing to the early history of the action of *assumpsit* and the consequent absence of a general *jus quaesitum tertii* in English law. But it is possible (and for the determination of this appeal I think it is desirable) to restate it upon a rational basis.

He did this by restating the law in terms of the common law of agency, but made some adjustments to take account of the peculiarities of having an artificial principal.

The indoor management rule had viewed corporate agents in the specific context of corporate management and attached significance to the company's 'external' position and what took place 'indoors'. The Diplock approach started with the simple triangle of relationships in a standard agency situation involving a human principal. Whereas an agent's actual authority stems from the relationship between the principal and the agent, and to which the third party is a stranger, ostensible authority can only stem from the relationship between the principal and the third party:[92]

> An 'apparent' or 'ostensible' authority, on the other hand, is a legal relationship between the principal and the [third party] created by a representation, made by the principal to the [third party], intended to be and in fact acted upon by the [third party], that the agent has authority to enter on behalf of the principal into a contract of a kind within the scope of the 'apparent' authority, so as to render the principal liable to perform any obligations imposed upon him by such contract. To the relationship so created the agent is a stranger. He need not be (although he generally is) aware of the existence of the representation but he must not purport to make the agreement as principal himself. The representation, when acted upon by the [third party] by entering into a contract with the agent, operates as an estoppel, preventing the principal from asserting that he is not bound by the contract.

Diplock LJ stressed that, whilst the third party might receive information about the agent's authority from both the principal and the agent, it was only the information from the principal that would be relevant to the agent's ostensible authority. Information from the agent might, however, constitute a warranty of authority, but that would merely expose the agent to personal liability.[93]

---

[91] [1964] 2 QB 480 at 502, referring to [1952] 2 QB 147.
[92] [1964] 2 QB 480 at 503.
[93] *Ibid.*

It is arguable that a third party's perception of a corporate principal is fundamentally different from their perception of a human principal. The agent may be the third party's main or only point of contact with the company and the third party may therefore perceive the agent as representing the company or even just *as* the company. In reality, a corporate agent might be the main controller and beneficiary of the company's activities or might be one human face of an extensive bureaucratic management structure, the details of which would be as unlikely to be known by the third party as the details of the agent's actual authority.

In his restatement of the law, Diplock LJ recognised that the artificial nature of corporate personality required certain adjustments to be made to the doctrine of ostensible authority. The two features of a company that he saw as significant in this respect were the company's limited contractual capacity and the fact that a company could only act, and therefore could only make representations, through agents acting on its behalf.[94] He regarded the doctrine of ultra vires and its restrictive effect on a company's contractual capacity as explaining the role played by a third party's deemed notice of a company's constitution under the indoor management rule.[95]

Diplock LJ said that the doctrine of ultra vires limited both a company's ability to be party to a contract and the ability of a company's board to delegate authority to subordinate agents and that an agent's ostensible authority was subject to these overriding limits.[96] He thus agreed with the view expressed by Slade J in the *Rama* case that deemed notice of a company's constitution has a purely negative effect on ostensible authority. He also indicated that a third party would be affected by all provisions of the constitution that define and limit the powers of the company vested in its board and that the negative effect of deemed notice might be even more severe than under the indoor management rule.[97]

As regards the fact that a company can act only though agents, Diplock LJ still presented ostensible authority as triangular in the sense that, in order to make the necessary representation of authority, the company must somehow have communicated with (and manifested its consent to) the third party independently of the agent making the contract. Diplock LJ in fact stated that the representation would have to be made by some person or persons with actual authority from the company to make the representation, either under the constitution or by due delegation of authority in accordance with the constitution.[98]

---

[94] [1964] 2 QB 480 at 504.
[95] See generally chapter five.
[96] [1964] 2 QB 480 at 504.
[97] *Ibid.*
[98] [1964] 2 QB 480 at 504–05.

4.3 The Diplock Approach

4.3.1 The Four Conditions of Ostensible Authority

Diplock LJ restated the law governing the ostensible authority of a corporate agent as four conditions which would have to be fulfilled before a third party could enforce a contract made by a corporate agent without actual authority:[99]

(1) A representation that the agent had authority to make a contract of the kind in question on behalf of the company was made to the third party.
(2) This representation was made by a person or persons who had 'actual' authority to manage the business of the company either generally or in respect of those matters to which the contract relates.
(3) The third party was induced by this representation to enter into the contract, that is, he in fact relied upon it.
(4) The memorandum and articles of association of the company did not deprive the company of the capacity either to enter into a contract of the kind in question or to delegate authority to enter into a contract of that kind to the agent.

4.3.2 The Implications of the Diplock Approach

This restatement of the law is doctrinally tidy, but it places a complex series of obstacles in the way of third parties and does not simplify the law from their perspective. Judged in terms of security of transaction and economic efficiency, the main deficiency of the indoor management rule was the third party's deemed notice of the constitution. This deficiency is preserved in conditions (2) and (4) of the Diplock approach. In fact, it is arguable that condition (2), with its requirement of actual authority in accordance with the company's constitution, increases the negative impact of a company's constitution compared to the indoor management rule. Whilst the statutory reform has mitigated this impact, it would have mitigated the indoor management rule in any event. It is also striking that the general qualification of the indoor management rule, namely that a third party could not rely upon it if put on inquiry, is not present in Diplock LJ's restatement. It is arguable that the qualification is now reflected in both conditions (1) and (3).

Diplock LJ said that the confusion in the law that had become apparent in the *Rama* case stemmed from a failure to distinguish between the four separate conditions.[100] However, an analysis of them will show that they

---

[99] [1964] 2 QB 480 at 505.
[100] [1964] 2 QB 480 at 506.

are inter-connected. Thus, a third party may have to start with condition (3) and attempt to identify the representation or various representations that induced its entry into the contract before considering whether or not they satisfy conditions (1) and (2). Further, it will be seen that a company could be found to have made a bewildering array of representations to a third party. These representations might cover not just the authority of an agent to make the contract in question, but such matters as the authority of an agent to make representations about the authority of the company's agents or to communicate information to third parties on which third parties can rely without having to check its accuracy. This has added to the complexity of the law rather than reducing it.

5 AN ANALYSIS OF THE FOUR CONDITIONS OF OSTENSIBLE AUTHORITY

5.1 A Representation of Authority

5.1.1 Representing the Authority of a Corporate Agent

This is the legal foundation on which the third party has to rely.[101] In practice, more than one representation may have been made to the third party about the agent's authority. However, to support ostensible authority, at least one of these must be sufficient to cover the contract in question.

Diplock LJ said that the commonest form of representation was by conduct, 'namely by permitting the agent to act in the management or conduct of the principal's business'.[102] By permitting an agent to act in this way, the board of a company make a representation to all third parties who deal with the agent that he has authority to make contracts 'of a kind which an agent authorised to do acts of the kind which he is in fact permitted to do usually enters into in the ordinary course of such business'.[103] This is analogous to, though conceptually distinct from, the way in which a company can confer actual authority on its agents through conduct, for example by implicitly conferring the 'usual authority' associated with a particular office or level of responsibility.[104]

In cases such as *Houghton*, *Kreditbank Cassel* and *Rama*, in which the third party had not been able to rely upon the indoor management rule, Diplock LJ saw the real barrier as the fact that the representation of authority had been insufficient to cover the contract in question. In each case, those responsible for appointing the agent to his office with the company had

---

[101] Ostensible authority is often presented as a form of estoppel whereby the principal is estopped from denying that the agent has authority. See Bowstead & Reynolds at 8–029.
[102] [1964] 2 QB 480 at 505
[103] *Ibid.*
[104] See Bowstead & Reynolds at 3–006 and Markesinis & Munday at 36–9.

thereby made a representation about his authority, but it was not sufficient to cover the particular contract at issue. The contract in each case was not one that an agent 'occupying the position in relation to the company's business' which the third party knew that the agent occupied would normally be authorised to enter.[105] Diplock LJ noted how the third parties in these cases had sought to rely upon provisions in the companies' constitutions that permitted their boards to delegate the necessary authority to the agents. However, such provisions were not in themselves sufficient to widen the ostensible authority of an agent beyond the usual authority of his office. A third party would also have to prove that he knew about and relied on the relevant provision and in addition show that

> the conduct of the board in the light of that knowledge would be understood by a reasonable man as a representation that the agent had authority to enter into the contract sought to be enforced.[106]

5.1.2 *The Scope of a Representation of Authority*

The scope of a representation of authority deemed to be made by permitting an agent to act in the management of a company has been explored further. In *Egyptian International Foreign Trade Co v Soplex*,[107] Lawton LJ warned that Diplock LJ's restatement should not be treated as though it were a statute.[108] He noted that, in another judgment in the *Freeman & Lockyer* case, Willmer LJ had said that whether or not a particular contract was within the scope of an agent's usual authority depended on whether or not it was one within 'what would ordinarily be expected to be the scope of the authority of the officer purporting to act on behalf of the company'.[109] In the *Soplex* case, Lawton LJ rejected an argument that the use in the *Freeman & Lockyer* judgments of expressions such as 'ordinarily' and 'usually' meant 'in the great majority of cases' and instead held that they implied that:[110]

> anyone dealing with an office holder of a particular and well-recognised kind could reasonably expect him to have the kind of authority which most, but not necessarily the great majority, of such office holders actually had.

The *Soplex* case concerned the validity of a guarantee that a specified sum would be paid to the third party in specified circumstances.[111] The manager

[105] [1964] 2 QB 480 at 507–08.
[106] *Ibid*. He drew support for this from the judgment of Sargant LJ in the *Houghton* case, in which Atkin LJ had concurred: [1927] 1 KB 246 at 266–67.
[107] [1985] 2 Lloyd's Rep 36; [1985] BCLC 404.
[108] [1985] 2 Lloyd's Rep 36 at 48.
[109] [1964] 2 QB 480 at 494.
[110] [1985] 2 Lloyd's Rep 36 at 48.
[111] The guarantee arose from a contract whereby the third party had bought a consignment of cement from a client of the company, which was a trading bank. The client had undertaken

of the company's documentary credits department had given the guarantee on behalf of the company, a small trading bank. He was not a director, but was answerable directly to the company's board.

Browne-Wilkinson LJ held that in order to ascertain the scope of the representation of authority that the company had made to the third party, it was not enough just to look at the office title. The whole course of the company's conduct in relation to the third party should be taken into account. This meant that the court should not consider only the level of authority that might normally be vested in a holder of the office held by the agent.[112] In effect, by allowing the agent to behave in the same way as an officer who enjoyed a greater level of responsibility and authority than was usually associated with his own office, the company's board had made a further representation to the third party that the agent had the level of authority commensurate with his actual behaviour.

The indoor management rule denied third parties the ability to rely upon the presumption of regularity if the circumstances were found to have put the third party on inquiry. This might be because the transaction was unusual. In terms of the Diplock approach, an unusual transaction would be beyond the scope of a representation of usual authority, which would thus fail to satisfy condition (1). However, under the indoor management rule, an overt conflict of interest could also put a third party on inquiry. Such a conflict of interest might occur in a transaction that is otherwise usual. In terms of the Diplock approach, a representation of usual authority would be sufficient to satisfy condition (1) despite the conflict of interest. However, if this conflict were to be treated as putting the third party on inquiry and thereby giving the third party constructive knowledge of the agent's lack of authority, the third party would not satisfy condition (3).

5.2 Someone with Actual Authority to Manage the Company must make the Representation

5.2.1 The Representation must be Attributable to the Company

Condition (2) in the Diplock approach has created most difficulty. Diplock LJ specified the condition in stringent terms, stating that the person making the representation must have 'actual authority' to manage the business of the company. Lawton LJ's warning about not treating the judgment of Diplock LJ as though it were a statute is pertinent here as well.[113] In

to repay a specified sum to the third party if the cement were late or deficient and the company, acting through the agent, guaranteed this obligation. In the event, the cement had petrified and was unusable.

[112] [1985] 2 Lloyd's Rep 36 at 41.
[113] *Egyptian International Foreign Trade Co v Soplex* [1985] 2 Lloyd's Rep 36 at 48.

248 Contracting with Other Corporate Agents

principle, there is no reason why the necessary representation should not be made by someone with ostensible authority to make it, as long as ultimately there is a foundational representation that is binding on the company. The foundational representation would have to be made by someone with actual authority to make it or be binding on the company under section 35A of the Companies Act 1985. The House of Lords has subsequently applied the Diplock approach on the basis that third parties would satisfy condition (2) if they could show that the representation of authority had been made by someone with ostensible authority to make it.[114]

The subsequent difficulty with condition (2) has concerned the scope of the authority, whether actual or ostensible, that the person making the representation must have. In particular, the question has arisen as to whether it must include the authority to make the contract in question. It has been suggested that it should be sufficient if the person making the representation has authority to make statements of fact about the company's affairs. Such statements of fact could then include the fact that an agent has the necessary authority to make a contract or that a contract has been approved in accordance with the company's internal rules.

In specifying condition (2), Diplock LJ simply stated that the person making the representation must have authority to manage the company's affairs. However, in discussing the *Mahony* and *British Thomson-Houston* cases (in which the third party had been able to rely upon the indoor management rule), he said that those making the relevant representations had 'authority to make the representations on behalf of the company'.[115] This provides some support for the view that an agent who does not have the authority to make a particular contract may nevertheless have the authority to make representations on behalf of the company about the contract.

5.2.2 Authority to be a Reliable Reference Point for Third Parties?

In *First Energy v Hungarian International Bank*,[116] the Court of Appeal accepted and applied the idea that an agent could have the authority to make binding representations about a contract even though he did not have authority to approve the contract. It used the idea to justify the controversial conclusion that an agent had ostensible authority to confirm that a contract had been approved internally and therefore to make a binding offer on behalf of the company to a third party even though the third party knew that the agent lacked the authority to enter the contract. This conclusion meant that it was legally possible for a corporate agent to make a representation about his own authority and to support his own

[114] *British Bank of the Middle East v Sun Life* [1983] 2 Lloyd's Rep 9; *Armagas v Mundogas* [1986] AC 717.
[115] [1964] 2 QB 480 at 506–07.
[116] [1993] BCC 533; [1993] BCLC 1409.

ostensible authority in bilateral dealings with the third party, without any external manifestation of the principal's consent being necessary.

The Court of Appeal's judgment in the *First Energy* case appeared to contradict a fundamental principle of agency law.[117] It opened up the controversial possibility of a 'self-authorising' agent. Also, the idea of agents having authority to make representations of fact, as something distinct from their authority to enter into contracts, had been seen as attaching undue significance to fine distinctions based on the precise form of a representation made to a third party. Thus, in *Armagas v Mundogas*,[118] Staughton J had held that an agent who did not have ostensible authority to enter into the relevant contract nevertheless did have ostensible authority to tell the third party that he had obtained actual authority to do so. In the Court of Appeal, Robert Goff LJ found this 'a most surprising conclusion':[119]

> It results in an extraordinary distinction between (1) a case where an agent, having no ostensible authority to enter into the relevant contract, wrongly asserts that he is invested with actual authority to do so, in which event the principal is not bound; and (2) a case where an agent, having no ostensible authority, wrongly asserts after negotiations that he has gone back to his principal and obtained actual authority, in which event the principal is bound. As a matter of common sense, this is most unlikely to be the law.

However, there are important economic issues underlying these fine legal distinctions.

Chapter two considered the economic case for assigning a risk of invalidity to the third party where he is the least-cost-avoider. There is also an economic case for ensuring that, when risk is assigned to the third party, the burden on the third party is clearly specified and kept to a minimum. This minimises the overall burden of costs and should ensure that the third party can in fact bear the assigned risk at a lower cost than the company. The action that the third party must take to remove the risk of invalidity or shift the risk of the agent's lack of authority back to the company should therefore be as clear and undemanding as possible.

The burden of risk on third parties may be a simple matter of checking with an obvious superior who clearly does have the authority to bind the company and can act as a reliable reference point. In many cases, however, a third party may have no obvious reliable reference point for reassurance to eliminate the risk of invalidity. The agent may be the third party's sole point of contact with the company's management structure and it may be far from clear what further action would lead the third party to a reliable source of reassurance.

---

[117] See F Reynolds, 'The Ultimate Apparent Authority' (1994) 110 *Law Quarterly Review* 21.
[118] [1986] AC 717.
[119] [1986] AC 717 at 731.

In practice, a general requirement that the third party must check with someone who has actual or ostensible authority to bind the company to the contract in question is far too vague to achieve an efficient assignment of risk. The additional costs resulting from such uncertainty might even be enough to undermine the economic rationale for assigning a particular level of risk to the third party on the basis that the third party is the least-cost-avoider. The cost for third parties of bearing a risk of invalidity is increased by uncertainty as to what is actually required to avoid it. The cost includes any adverse effects on the third party's relationship with the particular agent if, for example, the third party can only achieve certainty by obtaining reassurance about the agent from those at the top of the company's management hierarchy.

5.2.3 The Economic Cost of not having a Reliable Reference Point

The case law applying the Diplock approach shows how condition (2) imposes an excessive burden of risk on third parties unless it is mitigated by focusing on the broad issue of whether it was reasonable in the circumstances for a third party to rely on a particular reference point rather than on the narrow issue of whether the third party relied on a representation made by someone with authority to bind the company.

British Bank of the Middle East v Sun Life illustrates the uncertain nature of the risk that the Diplock approach has assigned to third parties.[120] This case concerned the enforceability of undertakings (relating to the repayment of loans which the third party had made to another party) given on behalf of an insurance company, which was involved in both the life assurance and mortgage finance businesses. The company had a complex structure, being divided into regions and sub-divided into branches. Each branch had a 'branch manager' and there could be one or more 'unit managers' within each branch. Only authorised officers at the company's administrative headquarters had the actual authority to approve contracts for life assurance or mortgage finance. The agent, who had signed the undertakings given to the third party, was a unit manager at the company's 'City' branch. However, the third party did not rely on this agent as having the necessary authority, but wrote to the City branch, addressing the letter to the 'General Manager', asking for confirmation that the agent did have the authority to give such an undertaking under his sole signature. The branch manager of the City branch replied to the third party confirming this.

The House of Lords held that the third party could not enforce the undertakings against the company. The third party had relied upon the representation from the branch manager about the agent's authority and

---

[120] *British Bank of the Middle East v Sun Life* [1983] 2 Lloyd's Rep 9 (HL).

it was therefore this representation that had to satisfy condition (2). In his judgment, Lord Brandon held that because the branch manager did not have the actual authority to give the undertakings, it followed 'necessarily' that he did not have the actual authority to represent to the third party that the agent had the authority to do so. He also held that the branch manager did not have ostensible authority to make the representation.

Lord Brandon based his conclusion in part on the fact that there was no evidence of any conduct from which it might be inferred that branch managers did have this authority. In particular, limiting the actual authority of branch managers and other agents dealing directly with the public appeared to be a standard managerial arrangement for insurance companies. Lord Brandon also attached significance to the letter that the third party had sent to the City branch:[121]

> [The third party] was indicating clearly that the confirmation which he sought was confirmation by some person in the top management of [the company], who, by reason of his status, could be relied on to state correctly in reply the scope of [the agent's] actual authority ... [The reply] was not, as the [third party] would have it, a case of [the company] holding out [the branch manager] as having its authority, express or implied, to answer the letter in the way which he did; it was rather a case of [the branch manager], without knowledge or permission of [the company], holding himself out as having such authority.

The burden on the third party in order to remove the risk of invalidity was therefore to go beyond the City branch and find someone at the company's head office with the authority to give the undertakings.

This decision can perhaps be justified on the basis that, given the general practice in the insurance business, the form of the branch manager's representation was suspicious, inasmuch as it stated something that the third party might reasonably have been expected to realise was incorrect. The special circumstances of the insurance industry might also be relevant. It is arguable that insurance companies face an unusually high risk of loss from agents dealing directly with customers in this kind of situation since they could act against the interests of the company.

The House of Lords did not explore the question of whether the branch manager should be treated as having the authority to make reliable statements of fact and thus act as a reliable reference point for third parties of the kind in question. It did not consider whether it was reasonable that the only reliable reference point for third parties should be the company's headquarters. The House of Lords did not therefore consider the cost implications for third parties in general of not being able to rely upon the statements of branch managers and of not having any relatively low-cost

---

[121] [1983] 2 Lloyd's Rep 9 at 17.

means of removing the risk of invalidity. That does not necessarily mean that a third party in this kind of situation should not have to bear any risk of invalidity, but there should be a good reason to justify the costs of this risk

5.2.4 *The Agent as a Reference Point*

In *Armagas v Mundogas*,[122] the House of Lords addressed the question of whether an agent lacking actual and ostensible authority to make a contract might nevertheless have authority to make statements of fact about it. This was an unusual case in which there was found to have been a fraudulent conspiracy between the company's agent and the broker who acted as agent for the third party.[123] The company had sold a ship to the third party and the agent had purported on behalf of the company to lease it back with a three-year charter-party.[124] The agent, who had the title of 'vice-president (transportation)' and was its chartering manager, had informed the third party that he had obtained approval from the company's board for the charter-party. The third party argued that the agent had ostensible authority to communicate the company's approval to the contract and that it could therefore enforce the charter-party against the company.

In the Court of Appeal, Robert Goff LJ held that the agent's authority to make representations and statements of fact was limited to contracts that he had ostensible authority to make.[125] His ostensible authority to make contracts stemmed from the usual authority associated with his office and Robert Goff LJ held that it would have needed an express representation from those in charge of the company's management to give the agent ostensible authority to communicate the fact that the company had approved a contract that was beyond the scope of his usual authority.[126]

The House of Lords agreed with the Court of Appeal's decision. Lord Keith held that a third party could not rely upon the agent having 'ostensible general authority' to make a particular contract (arising from his appointment to an office or the like) where the third party knew that the agent's actual authority was limited so as to exclude contracts of the type at issue.[127] The third party would therefore have to show a representation

---

[122] [1986] AC 717.
[123] The judge had found that only the company's agent had been fraudulent and that a member of the company's top management had known about the transaction at issue. The Court of Appeal overruled these findings, holding that both agents had been involved in the fraud and exonerating the company's top management: [1986] AC 717 at 727–28.
[124] The third party had in fact entered into two charter-parties for the ship with the company, one for three years (the contract at issue) and the other for one year only, which they were told the company needed for 'internal reasons'. The company's top management only knew about the one year charter-party.
[125] [1986] AC 717 at 732.
[126] *Ibid.*
[127] *Ibid* at 777, citing *Russo-Chinese Bank v Li Yau Sam* [1910] AC 174 (PC).

conferring 'ostensible specific authority' sufficient to override the limitation, but Lord Keith said that 'such cases must be rare and unusual'.[128]

Lord Keith viewed the third party's argument that the agent had ostensible authority to communicate approval of the transaction as in effect an
argument that the agent had 'ostensible specific authority'. The third
party argued that the agent's own statement that he had obtained
approval for the transaction should have been sufficient to support an
increase in the agent's ostensible authority. In the circumstances, it would
have been unreasonable to expect the third party to obtain direct confirmation from the company's top management, 'particularly in view of the
shortness of time'. However, Lord Keith said that an extension of the
agent's ostensible authority could only be supported by some additional
representation from the company's 'responsible management' and that a
representation from the agent himself would not be sufficient.[129] He said
that the fact that the third party faced practical difficulty in obtaining confirmation from the company's top management was 'irrelevant'.[130]

As regards the general proposition that there was a conceptual difference between having authority to make a contract and having authority
to make statements of fact about an agent's authority to make a contract
or whether a contract had been approved, Lord Keith agreed with the
remarks of Robert Goff LJ to the effect that this could produce 'extraordinary distinctions in practice' and would be 'a most surprising conclusion'.[131]
He did not reject the possibility, but noted that it would be 'a most unusual
and peculiar case'.

As with the *Sun Life* case, the decision in the *Armagas* case can be justified on its overall merits. The charter-party was unusual in a number of
respects and the circumstances were suspicious enough to have put the
third party on inquiry. Robert Goff LJ agreed with this suggestion, but said
that it was irrelevant because the agent lacked ostensible authority in any
event.[132] However, the courts' interpretation of condition (2) in the Diplock
approach adds weight to the view that it imposes an unfair and inefficient
burden on third parties, particularly if arguments based on the onerous
nature of the burden placed on third parties are dismissed as 'irrelevant'.

5.2.5 *The Agent as a Reliable Reference Point*

In cases where the merits much more obviously favour the third party, the
courts have been prepared to recognise a distinction between having

---

[128] *Ibid.*
[129] [1986] AC 717 at 778.
[130] *Ibid.*
[131] [1986] AC 717 at 779.
[132] *Ibid* at 734.

authority to make a particular contract and having authority to make reliable statements of fact. Such cases also reveal more clearly the burden that the second condition of the Diplock approach places on third parties.

The point was raised in *Egyptian International v Soplex* because the agent had told the third party that in London 'one signature is sufficient'.[133] The company had argued that this amounted to self-authorisation. The Court of Appeal found that the conduct of the company's board amounted to a representation of authority sufficient to cover the contract, but Browne-Wilkinson LJ declined to rule out the possibility that the agent could have given himself ostensible authority through having the authority to make representations. Browne-Wilkinson LJ found support for this proposition in the judgment of Greer LJ in the *British Thomson-Houston* case, in which he had remarked that a third party should be able to rely upon someone to represent the company,[134] and of the endorsement of this by Pearson LJ in *Freeman & Lockyer*:[135]

> The identification of the persons whose knowledge and acquiescence constitute knowledge and acquiescence by the company depends upon the facts of the particular case ... An interesting passage, showing that the agent himself may make the representation which binds the company, is to be found in the judgment of Greer LJ in the *British Thomson-Houston* case ...

The point arose quite starkly, however, in *First Energy v Hungarian International Bank*.[136]

In *First Energy*, the third party had been in negotiations with the senior manager of the Manchester branch of the company, a subsidiary of a foreign bank, for a substantial loan facility. The senior manager had informed the third party that he had no authority to sanction a loan facility and the company had done nothing to suggest that he might have such authority. Following discussions and some interim arrangements, the senior manager wrote to the third party enclosing documentation and indicating that if the third party signed this documentation and returned it with certain other documents, the loan facility would be provided. The third party returned the documentation as requested, but the company refused to make the loan, arguing that the senior manager had acted without authority.

At first instance, the judge had found that the letter from the senior manager amounted to an offer, which the third party had accepted, and that the senior manager had ostensible authority to communicate the offer on behalf of the company to the third party. The Court of Appeal's approach to the issue of ostensible authority and the application of the

---

[133] [1985] 2 Lloyd's Rep 36 at 42.
[134] [1932] 2 KB 176 at 182.
[135] [1964] 2 QB 480 at 499.
[136] [1993] BCC 533 (CA).

Diplock approach is clear from the observations with which Steyn LJ began his judgment:[137]

> A theme that runs through our law of contract is that the reasonable expectations of honest men must be protected … if the prima facie solution to a problem runs counter to the reasonable expectations of honest men, this criterion sometimes requires a rigorous re-examination of the problem to ascertain whether the law does indeed compel demonstrable unfairness.

The company relied upon Lord Keith's judgment in the *Armagas* case to argue that it could not be bound by a contract when the only support for the agent's ostensible authority to make it was a representation that he himself had made.

Steyn LJ noted that Lord Keith had not ruled out the possibility that an authority to communicate approval of a transaction might arise. In the *First Energy* case, the agent's authority to make statements of fact would be a general ostensible authority arising from his office as senior manager at the relevant branch rather than a specific authority. He also noted Browne-Wilkinson LJ's observations in the *Soplex* case and the case law he had cited in support:[138]

> This line of authority reveals a tension between two conflicting principles. The first is that the shareholders of a company should be protected against hasty and ill-considered transactions entered into by the company. The second is that third parties who deal with companies in good faith ought to be protected. The *Royal British Bank v Turquand* line of cases represents an intensely pragmatic and serviceable resolution of the competing considerations in particular situations.

As well as achieving a pragmatic resolution of such a conflict, the indoor management rule also tended to strike an efficient balance between these competing interests because of the flexibility of the concept of being 'put on inquiry'.

Steyn LJ said that there would be circumstances in which an agent could generate his own ostensible authority:[139]

> It seems to me that the law recognises that in modern commerce an agent who has no apparent authority to conclude a particular transaction may sometimes be clothed with apparent authority to make representations of fact. The level at which such apparent authority could be found to exist may vary and generalisation will be unhelpful.

---

[137] *Ibid* at 533.
[138] *Ibid* at 543.
[139] [1993] BCC 533 at 543–44.

In concluding that the agent did have such an apparent (or ostensible) authority in this case, Steyn LJ took account both of the agent's status and of the implications for the third party if it had not been able to rely on the agent to represent the company:[140]

> [The] idea that [the third party] should have checked with the managing director in London whether [the company] had approved the transaction seems unreal. This factor is, of course, not decisive, but it is relevant to the ultimate decision.

Evans LJ also emphasised the significance of this factor:[141]

> As Staughton J said in *Armagas*, any other conclusion would be 'a triumph of logic over common sense' ... If [the company] were correct, it would mean that the [third party was] bound to seek confirmation from the [company's] head office in London, which would defeat the apparent object of appointing a senior manager in charge of [the] office in Manchester so that local business men could deal with him there.

The *First Energy* decision is difficult to reconcile with the strict logic of the Diplock approach as applied in the *Sun Life* and *Armagas* cases, but it is defensible in terms of meeting the parties' reasonable expectations and thus accords with the principle of security of transaction. It is also justifiable in terms of economic efficiency since the company in such a scenario is the least-cost-avoider, especially given the burden that third parties would face if they could not rely upon an agent of such seniority as a source of information about the company and in effect to represent the company to them.

5.2.6 The Continuing Uncertainty in the Law

The *First Energy* decision involved a manipulation rather than a fundamental revision of the Diplock approach, so it cannot be assumed that the courts will follow the Court of Appeal's lead in this respect. In particular, it is hard to reconcile with the judgments of the House of Lords in the *Sun Life* and *Armagas* cases.

In a case where the merits are less obviously with the third party, the courts may well revert to the strict doctrinal logic of the Diplock approach. In *First Energy*, the Court of Appeal came close to compressing the Diplock approach into one overriding question of whether it was reasonable in the circumstances for the third party to be able to rely on the agent to speak authoritatively on behalf of the company or whether, on the contrary, it

---

[140] *Ibid* at 544.
[141] *Ibid* at 547.

was reasonable to expect the third party to take some further course of action to ensure that the agent had actual authority to bind the company. Such compression would reproduce the flexibility of the indoor management rule, but with the added encumbrance of having to work around the notional requirement that the agent's ability to make a contract on behalf of the company must be founded on a binding representation of authority.

5.3 The Representation must have induced the Third Party to enter into the Contract

5.3.1 *The Need for Reliance*

A third party can only enforce an unauthorised contract against the company if he made or entered the contract in reliance on a representation that satisfies the other conditions. This is a necessary condition of the company's liability since the binding representation of authority operates as a form of estoppel.

In his analysis of corporate agency in *Rama v Proved Tin*,[142] Slade J. noted that ostensible authority had also been referred to as "agency by estoppel" and said that three ingredients were necessary to establish an estoppel, namely (i) a representation, (ii) a reliance on the representation, and (iii) an alteration of position resulting from such reliance. The second and third of these ingredients have both been subsumed into condition (3) of the Diplock approach. It is not necessary for third parties to prove any detriment beyond the fact that they have entered the contract and thereby exposed themselves to liability under it. The fact that the company can ratify the contract and enforce the contract against the third party despite the agent's lack of authority is therefore significant in enabling third parties to rely upon this form of estoppel.[143]

Condition (3) provides the starting point for a third party who has to establish an agent's ostensible authority in order to enforce a contract. A third party must first identify a suitable representation of authority and prove that he relied upon this when he entered into the contract at issue. If he cannot prove this, then it is irrelevant that there might have been a representation that would have satisfied the other conditions. In *Cleveland Manufacturing v Muslim Commercial Bank*,[144] for example, Robert Goff J held that a claim based on ostensible authority could not succeed because the third party (a bank) had not provided any evidence to show that it had relied upon a representation of authority. The third party had made a

---

[142] [1952] 2 QB 147 at 149.
[143] For a discussion of the divergences between ostensible authority and other forms of estoppel, see Bowstead & Reynolds at 8–029.
[144] [1981] 2 Lloyd's Rep 646.

payment to an intermediary (a shipping agent) that the third party was in fact obliged to make to the company. The third party had done this in the mistaken belief that the intermediary was acting as the company's agent and had been authorised to receive the payment for the company. The evidence showed that the third party had not done this pursuant to (and thus in reliance upon) any representation of authority that might be attributable to the company, but had simply made an incorrect assumption about the agent's role.[145] The third party was therefore still liable to make the payment due to the company.[146]

5.3.2 *A Third Party's Suspicion may negate Reliance*

A third party may also face difficulty if he questions the authority of the agent or seeks confirmation from elsewhere since this would imply that the third party was not prepared to rely on any representation of authority that had already been made. In the *Sun Life* case, for example, once the third party had sought confirmation of the unit manager's authority to give the undertakings, it could no longer claim to have relied on the agent's status as a unit manager or on his actual role in the company's affairs. Instead, it could only claim to have relied upon the subsequent representation made by the branch manager in response to its enquiry. In the event, this would probably not have made any difference to the outcome of that case.

Also, where a third party claims to have relied on a representation of authority made in response to a request for confirmation, the representation would have to be judged in relation to the suspicions that led to the request and as a response to that request. In the *Sun Life* case, the House of Lords attached significance to the fact that the third party appeared to have tried to direct its query about the agent's authority to the highest level of management, but had merely received a response from the branch manager, and to the fact that the branch manager had responded by stating as a fact something that the third party had already indicated that it did not believe to be correct.

In this kind of situation, the qualification to the indoor management rule, namely that the third party could not rely upon a presumption of regularity if he had been 'put on inquiry', may be relevant, although this concept is not an explicit aspect of the Diplock approach.

5.3.3 *Actual or Constructive Knowledge Negates Reliance*

A third party who knows or has notice that an agent lacks the actual authority to make a particular contract cannot rely on the agent having

---

[145] [1981] 2 Lloyd's Rep 646 at 650–51.
[146] The shipping agent had gone into insolvent liquidation after receiving the payment.

ostensible authority.[147] The third party's knowledge that the principal has not in fact consented to the agent making the contract in question contradicts and undermines any external impression that such consent has been given. As with an estoppel, a third party cannot rely upon a presumption that something is the case if he knows that it is not in fact the case.[148] In such a case, the agent could only have ostensible authority if there has been a representation of authority that takes account of and overrides the agent's knowledge.[149]

One complicating factor in this context is the extent to which a third party should be prejudiced by constructive as well as actual knowledge. In relation to the indoor management rule, the courts treated a third party put on inquiry as having constructive knowledge of the information that an inquiry would have revealed. Constructive knowledge is therefore flexible and depends on the circumstances that put a third party on inquiry and what the third party should have found out from making a satisfactory inquiry. It seems likely therefore, as has already been noted, that the idea of a third party being put on inquiry by unusual or suspicious circumstances also features in the Diplock approach and that it is relevant to the third condition.

It was argued in relation to the indoor management rule that the idea of a third party having constructive knowledge on the basis of being 'put on inquiry' and having a duty to make further inquiry provided a flexible means of enabling risk to be shifted to the third party if and insofar as the third party is the least-cost-avoider. In chapter five, it was seen that the idea of constructive knowledge has performed a similar function in relation to a third party recipient's potential liability for knowing receipt. In this context, the courts have evolved a flexible test whereby liability depends on whether, in all the circumstances, the third party behaved unconscionably in proceeding with a transaction without making further inquiry.[150]

In *Criterion Properties v Stratford*,[151] the Court of Appeal held that the test of unconscionability developed for knowing receipt should also be used to determine the ability of a third party to rely upon the ostensible authority of a company's board to approve a contract after it had found that the board had exercised its power to enter the contract for an improper purpose. This test could also be used to determine a third party's constructive knowledge and thereby its ability to rely upon the ostensible authority of subordinate agents.[152] Whether it would be unconscionable for a third

---

[147] Bowstead & Reynolds, Art 75.

[148] *Russo-Chinese Bank v Li Yau Sam* [1910] AC 174 (PC); *Armagas v Mundogas* [1986] AC 717.

[149] *Armagas v Mundogas* [1986] AC 717.

[150] *BCCI v Akindele* [2001] Ch 437 (CA).

[151] *Criterion Properties plc v Stratford UK Properties LLC* [2002] EWCA Civ 1883.

[152] See generally D Fox, 'Constructive Notice and Knowing Receipt: An Economic Analysis' [1998] *Cambridge Law Journal* 391.

party to rely upon an agent's ostensible authority should depend on the same factors that it was suggested should put a third party on inquiry for the purposes of the indoor management rule. These factors would include the relative status of the agent in the company's management hierarchy and the third party's scope for taking further action without incurring a burden that would be disproportionate to the risk of loss to the company.

In this way, the idea of constructive knowledge could provide a flexible adjustment of the Diplock approach that would ensure greater security of transaction for third parties and ensure that third parties would only have to face the risk of invalidity where they were clearly the least-cost-avoider. However, if the third condition of the Diplock approach were to be adjusted in this way, it would call into even further question the current formulation of the first two conditions.

5.4 The Company has the Capacity to enter into the Contract and to Delegate the Necessary Authority to the Agent

In so far as this condition reflects the common law doctrine of ultra vires as expressed in the *Ashbury Railway Carriage* case,[153] it has now been overridden by section 35 of the Companies Act 1985. Neither a company nor a third party can call the validity of a contract into question on the basis that it was beyond the scope of the objects clause and therefore void for lack of contractual capacity. In chapter five, it has been shown that the objects clause also sets an overall limit on the powers of the company and thus on the actual authority that could be vested in the board or any other corporate agent. Section 35A, rather than section 35, addresses this effect. Also, other provisions of a company's constitution may set limits on the powers of the company, on the actual authority of the board to exercise the powers of the company and on the power of the board to delegate authority to other corporate agents.

At common law, the doctrine of constructive notice, meaning a third party's deemed notice of a company's constitution and other public documents, limited the ability of a third party to enforce a contract that involved any violation of such provisions of a company's constitution, whether the third party sought to rely on the indoor management rule or on ostensible authority. In the Diplock approach, condition (2) as well as condition (4) maintains the doctrine of constructive notice since no one can have actual authority to make a representation of authority where that authority would be in breach of the company's constitution.

However, condition (2) must now be read subject to section 35A, which provides that the board's power 'to authorise others' to bind the company

---

[153] (1875–75) LR 7 HL 653.

is 'deemed to be free of any limitation under the company's constitution'. If a third party could show that they relied on a representation of authority from the board such as the appointment of an agent to an office, then he should be able to enforce a contract on the basis of ostensible authority despite any violation of the constitution. Nevertheless, the third party would have to establish the conditions necessary to rely upon section 35A, which were analysed in chapter five, and would be subject to the qualifications attached to that provision. The third party might therefore have difficulty if the ultimate representation supporting an agent's ostensible authority had been made by an inquorate board or by the company's shareholders. Also, if the third party were subject to section 322A, the contract would be voidable in any event.

6 THE ABOLITION OF THE DOCTRINE OF CONSTRUCTIVE OR DEEMED NOTICE

The Prentice Report had recommended that the doctrine of constructive notice should be abolished and the Companies Act 1989 purported to do this. Section 142 provided that a new section 711A should be inserted in the Companies Act 1985, which included the following provisions:

(1) A person shall not be taken to have notice of any matter merely because of its being disclosed in any document kept by the registrar of companies (and thus available for inspection) or made available by the company for inspection.

(2) This does not affect the question whether a person is affected by notice of any matter by reason of a failure to make such inquiries as ought reasonably to be made.

Section 711A was never enacted. This was probably due to the fact that the new system governing the registration of charges affecting companies set out in the Companies Act 1989 was never implemented. The wording of section 711A was unsatisfactory given the continuation of the existing registration system.

The Company Law Review recommended that the abolition should be carried out in the next Companies Act.[154] The 2002 White Paper included the following provisions in draft clause 17:

(1) Subsection (2) applies for the purposes of any question whether a transaction fails to bind a company because of lack of authority on the part of the person exercising (or purporting to exercise) the company's powers.

---

[154] See chapter one at n 60 for further details of the DTI's Company Law Review, which delivered its Final Report in 2001, and of its various reports and the 2002 White Paper.

(2) For those purposes the board of directors of a company shall be deemed to have authority to —

(a) exercise any power of the company; and
(b) authorise others to do so;

and this applies regardless of any limitations in the company's constitution on the board's authority ...

(7) Subsection (2) does not apply in relation to a power of the company which this act requires to be exercised otherwise than by the board.

(8) Without prejudice to subsection (2), in determining any question whether a person had ostensible authority to exercise any of a company's powers in a given case, no reference may be made to the company's constitution.

This would remove the doctrine of deemed notice rather more emphatically than the Companies Act 1989 would have done since there is no overt reference to the abolition being subject to the third party's duty to make reasonable inquiries.

7 CONCLUSIONS AND REVIEW

The Diplock approach, with its roots in the general law of agency, is less flexible than the indoor management rule and less suitable for achieving an efficient balance between the interests of companies and third parties and for ensuring that their respective reasonable expectations are given effect. The concept of ostensible authority in the general law of agency reflects a fundamental doctrine that principals should not be bound to contracts unless they have somehow manifested their consent to being bound and thereby assumed the associated risk. The doctrine of ostensible authority is not, however, compatible with the realities of corporate organisation that can make it difficult and burdensome for a third party to find a reliable reference point. In reality, a third party may have to make do with the assurances of the agent himself or a readily accessible superior. It also arguably fails to take full account of the artificiality inherent in attributing consent to a fictitious legal personality. A company can only make representations through the agency of others and only if they act in compliance with the terms of its constitution. In any event, unlike a human principal, none of those who can purport to speak or act as the company faces the risk of unlimited personal liability for the agent's actions.

It is arguable that a company that operates through a network of agents (or rather the shareholders benefiting from the activities of such a company) should be treated as accepting a general level of risk in relation to the activities of its agents, rather like the general level of risk that partners face in relation to the activities of their fellow partners. This risk should only be shifted onto third parties in situations where the third party is the least-cost-avoider. Moreover, the burden shifted onto third parties should be limited to the extent that they are the least-cost-avoider and should not be left open-ended.

The *First Energy* case can be viewed as reflecting a more efficient approach, but it is far from clear that it has gained general acceptance. In determining the circumstances in which the third party is the least-cost-avoider, the factors discussed in chapter two should be taken into account. It should be recognised that companies have other devices that enable them to reduce their agency costs and to contain the danger presented by agents acting without actual authority. In particular, companies can reduce these costs by employing better quality agents and adopting high quality systems of governance to supervise and control the activities of their agents.

It should also be recognised that, unless the overriding rule of attribution achieves an efficient allocation of risk, companies may have an incentive to limit the actual authority of their agents so as to maximise their scope for repudiating contracts that later prove onerous even though this may be ultimately harmful to the interests of companies in general. As regards the overriding rules of attribution applicable to subordinate corporate agents, the indoor management rule is not entirely satisfactory, but has much greater intrinsic flexibility than the Diplock approach. It would be more conducive to achieving an efficient specification of the overriding rule.

In any event, a major deficiency of the English law governing corporate agency is that there are no prescribed levels of authority for corporate agents, not even for directors. Further, there is no standard terminology for identifying a corporate agent with a prescribed level of authority. This creates a high degree of uncertainty for third parties dealing with corporate agents. It is arguable that prescribed standards or at least prescribed terminology could contribute towards improving efficiency in this area. In effect, this would equate with the kind of regulation necessary to overcome other problems involving asymmetric information.

7

Contracts Involving Self-Dealing

1 INTRODUCTION

1.1 The Meaning of Self-Dealing

THIS CHAPTER WILL focus on the law governing the validity of contracts (and other transactions) involving 'self-dealing'. A contract involves self-dealing, for the purposes of this chapter, if the third party is a director of the company or is a person with whom a director of the company has a connection of some kind. The significance of self-dealing is that the director's involvement or interest on the other side of the contract represents a potential threat to the company. However, the presence of self-dealing in a contract can trigger special legal consequences even though the affected director does not participate in the company's decision-making concerning the contract. As noted in chapter 1, the European Court of Justice has confirmed that the European First Directive on Company Law ('the First Directive'),[1] which required that third parties in general be protected from the risk of invalidity due to any constitutional limits on the contractual power of a company's board of directors, does not apply to contracts involving self-dealing.[2]

The circumstances that may amount to self-dealing will be explored in the next section of this chapter, but it covers a wide range of possibilities from direct involvement as third party to having a remote or indirect interest in the third party as a shareholder or creditor. The third party may not even be aware that a director of a company has the kind of interest that constitutes self-dealing. *Salomon v Salomon* provides some good examples of self-dealing.[3] Aron Salomon was the *de facto* managing director of the company that he formed to take over his business, although no board was formally appointed. He was third party to the company's purchase of his business and to the debentures issued by the company in part payment of the purchase price. Later, the company issued replacement debentures to a Mr Broderip to secure an advance that he had made to Salomon personally.

---

[1] EEC/68/151.

[2] *Cooperative Rabobank v Erik Aarnoud Minderhoud* (Case C–104/96) [1998] 2 CMLR 270.

[3] *Salomon v Salomon & Co* [1897] AC 22. See generally R Grantham and C Rickett (eds), *Corporate Personality in the 20th Century* (Oxford, Hart Publishing, 1998) ('Grantham & Rickett').

The *Salomon* case illustrates the potential danger to a company from self-dealing, which justifies the stricter level of regulation. The business it had bought later failed and the company ended up in insolvent liquidation. Although the business had been sound at the time of its purchase, the price paid by the company was viewed as excessive.[4] As Lord Macnaghten put it,[5] the price 'represented the sanguine expectations of a fond owner rather than anything that can be called a businesslike or reasonable estimate of value.' However, the fact that the purchase of the business and the issue of the debentures involved self-dealing did not in the event affect their validity.[6] The House of Lords treated the company's shareholders as having approved the transactions and, as will be seen in this chapter, that is one way of ensuring the validity of a contract involving self-dealing.

The *Salomon* case also illustrates the difficulty of protecting companies from the danger posed by self-dealing without undermining the benefits that such contracts can provide. Contracts involving self-dealing are essential to companies and cannot simply be prohibited. If their regulation is to improve efficiency, it should not be so onerous as to exceed the potential benefits. The kind of connection between a director of a company and a third party that constitutes self-dealing can also be a source of information about the third party and reduce the company's information costs. It may enable transactions to take place that would otherwise be prohibitively costly.[7]

Although Salomon's business eventually failed, it was sound at the time of purchase and the transaction could have worked out to the company's benefit. Salomon was probably better placed than most to judge the business and the associated risks. To improve efficiency, therefore, the goal of regulating self-dealing should not be to minimise the danger that it poses, but to maximise the net overall benefit that it may yield.[8]

1.2 The Legal Significance of Self-Dealing

It may not be readily apparent that a contract involves self-dealing and this is a potential problem for third parties since the presence of self-dealing means an increased risk of invalidity. The presence of self-dealing in a contract may in fact affect its validity at three levels. At the first level, a

---

[4] At first instance, Vaughan Williams J called the price 'exorbitant', although Lord Watson said that that was 'too strong an epithet': [1897] AC 22 at 36–7. Lord Davey said that the price was not 'so excessive as to afford grounds for rescission': [1897] AC 22 at 57.

[5] [1897] AC 22 at 49.

[6] The House of Lords rejected an argument that the purchase could be rescinded on the grounds of fraud.

[7] See, for example, *Framlington Group v Anderson* [1995] BCC 611.

[8] See A Griffiths, 'Section 317 and Efficient Self-Dealing: What Should an Interested Director be required to Disclose?' [1999] *Company Lawyer* 184.

company's constitution may make special provision for contracts involving self-dealing in the provisions that determine the actual authority of its board and other agents. For example, the interested director may be barred from voting on a contract involving self-dealing and from being counted in the quorum at a board meeting.[9] Or the constitution may provide that the company's shareholders must approve certain contracts involving self-dealing. Special regulation requires this to be done for certain contracts in any event.[10]

At the second level, the presence of self-dealing may weaken or even bar a third party's ability to rely upon an overriding rule of attribution. As noted in chapter 5, the statutory provision applicable to contracts made or approved by a company's board is subject to a special qualification where the third party is a director or falls within other designated categories and this qualification covers a wide range of contracts involving self-dealing.[11]

At the third level, there are special rules of law that govern the validity of all contracts involving self-dealing. These rules can be viewed as 'overriding rules of non-attribution' since they apply even where the company's board or other agent would otherwise have the actual authority to enter the contract.

1.3 The Law Governing Contracts Involving Self-Dealing

In the nineteenth century, once it had become possible for joint stock companies to adopt the legal form of corporations through registration,[12] the law came to view their directors as analogous to trustees.[13] They were treated as trustees of the company's property and subject to fiduciary duties when exercising the powers vested in them. It is a longstanding principle of equity that trustees and other fiduciary agents who are invested with discretionary powers of management are subject to a duty of good faith to exercise their powers in good faith in the best interests of their beneficiaries, this being the company in the case of directors.[14] Furthermore, they must not put themselves into a position where this duty

---

[9] See, for example, Companies (Tables A to F) Regulations 1985 SI 1985/805, Table A ('Table A'), reg 94.

[10] See, for example, Companies Act 1985, ss 319 and 320.

[11] Companies Act 1985, s 322A.

[12] See chapter 1.

[13] See, for example, *Lands Allotment Co* [1894] 1 Ch 616 (CA). The law has not always been consistent in this respect: see, for example, J Hill, 'Changes in the Role of the Shareholder' in Grantham & Rickett. See generally L Sealy, 'The Director as Trustee' [1967] *Cambridge Law Journal* 83.

[14] *Re Smith & Fawcett* [1942] Ch 304 (CA); *Charterbridge v Lloyds Bank* [1970] Ch 62; *West Mercia Safetywear v Dodd* [1988] BCLC 250 (CA); *Re Pantone 485* [2002] 1 BCLC 266.

of good faith may come into conflict with their personal interests or with a duty that they owe to someone else.[15] As Sir Robert Megarry V-C said in *Tito v Waddell*, 'equity is astute to prevent a trustee from abusing his position or profiting from his trust: the shepherd must not become a wolf'.[16]

This principle has been applied strictly and its consequences are triggered regardless of whether fiduciary agents in fact allow any conflicting interest or duty to prevail over their duty of good faith.[17] The principle is analytically distinct from the duty of good faith, although it serves to reinforce that duty in circumstances in which it is likely to come under pressure. It does not, however, place fiduciary agents under an absolute duty to avoid situations of conflict, although it is often expressed in such terms.[18] If it were to have this effect, then many arrangements that are essential to modern commercial life would become impossible. Instead, the beneficiaries of a fiduciary agent's discretionary powers can mitigate the consequences of the principle provided that the agent makes full disclosure to them of the relevant facts.[19]

The principle of equity therefore has the same effect as the kind of regulation that has been termed 'procedural' or 'reflexive'.[20] Such regulation achieves its goals indirectly, through the behaviour that it encourages the

[15] In *Plus Group v Pyke*, Sedley LJ said that the standard expression of the long-standing principle of equity as that 'a fiduciary must not place himself in a position where his duty and his interest may conflict' should be amplified to reflect the fact that 'an objectionable position is not only one in which duty conflicts with interest but one in which duty conflicts with duty or interest with interest': [2002] EWCA Civ 370 at 86.

[16] *Tito v Waddell (No 2)* [1977] Ch 106 at 240–1. See also *Re Thompson's Settlement* [1986] Ch 99.

[17] *Keech v Sandford* (1726) Sel Cas Ch 61; *Ex parte Lacey* (1802) 6 Ves Jun 625; *Ex parte Hughes* 6 Ves Jun 616; *Ex parte James* (1803) 8 Ves Jun 337; *Aberdeen Ry v Blaikie* (1854) 1 Macq 461; *Farrar v Farrars* (1888) 40 Ch D 395; *Bray v Ford* [1896] AC 44 (HL); *Silkstone & Haigh Moor Coal v Edey* [1900] 1 Ch 167 (CA); *Wright v Morgan* [1926] AC 788 (PC); *Regal (Hastings) v Gulliver* [1942] 1 All ER 378 (HL); *Boardman v Phipps* [1967] 2 AC 46 (HL).

[18] In *Movitex v Bulfield* [1988] BCLC 104, Vinelott J presented the principle in terms of a legal disability that triggers certain consequences without placing directors under a duty to avoid incurring them. This provides a basis for explaining the apparent conflict between s 310 of the Companies Act 1985, which renders void any provision in a company's constitution exempting directors from liability in respect of 'breach of duty', and enabling articles that authorise contracts and other transactions involving self-dealing, such as regulation 85 of Table A: see also J Birds, (1976) 39 *Modern Law Review* 394 and J Parkinson, [1981] *Journal of Business Law* 335. However, it seems clear that a duty of full disclosure underlies the principle of equity in addition to the duty of good faith and that Vinelott J's view of the legal nature of the principle is not sufficient to explain the discrepancy: see R Cranston, 'Limiting Directors' Liability: Ratification, Exemption and Indemnification' [1992] *Journal of Business Law* 197 and P Davies, *Gower and Davies' Principles of Modern Company Law* 7th ed (London, Sweet & Maxwell, 2003) ('Gower & Davies') at 396–7. The proposed statement of directors' duties pursuant to the Company Law Review will, however, remove the discrepancy. See chapter 1 at n 60 for further details of the DTI's Company Law Review, which delivered its Final Report in 2001, and of its various reports and the 2002 White Paper.

[19] See, for example, the judgment of Upjohn LJ in *Boulting Bros v ACTAT* [1963] 2 QB 606 (CA) at 634–640.

[20] See S Deakin and A Hughes, 'Economic Efficiency and the Proceduralisation of Company Law' (1999) 3 *Company Financial and Insolvency Law Review* 169 at 175–6.

regulated parties to adopt in order to avoid its impact. Here, the likely impact of the principle of equity is not to penalise or prohibit contracts that involve self-dealing, but rather to encourage fiduciary agents to make full disclosure about their conflicts of interest.

Early statements about the principle suggest that it originated to ensure the candour of trustees, given the impossibility of discovering for certain whether or not the terms of a contract had in fact been influenced by a conflict of interest.[21] This would explain the rigidity of the principle, which applies regardless of how reasonable the terms of a particular contract appear to be.[22] Lord Eldon stated the rationale of the principle of equity as follows:[23]

> [The doctrine] is founded on this; that though you may see in a particular case, that [the trustee] has not made advantage, it is utterly impossible to examine upon satisfactory evidence in the power of the Court, by which I mean, in the power of the parties, in ninety-nine cases out of a hundred, whether he has made advantage, or not ... if he chooses to deny it, how can the court try that against that denial?

In *Aberdeen Railway v Blaikie*,[24] Lord Cranworth LC applied the principle to company directors and held that it did not matter whether or not the interested director participated in the company's decision making because it was his duty 'to give to his co-directors, and through them to the company, the full benefit of all knowledge and skill which he could bring to bear on the subject'.[25]

The principle of equity is reflected in two distinct rules that apply to company directors, namely the 'no conflict' rule, which penalises self-dealing, and the 'no profit' rule, which penalises secret profits and the

---

[21] *Ex parte Lacey* (1802) 6 Ves 625; *Ex parte Bennett* (1805) 10 Ves 381. In the United States, Cardoza CJ held that '[u]ncompromising rigidity has been the attitude of courts of equity when petitioned to undermine the rule of undivided loyalty by "disintegrating erosion" of particular exceptions ... Only thus has the level of conduct for fiduciaries been kept at a level higher than that trodden by the crowd': *Meinhard v Salman* (1928) 249 NY 456 at 464. The strictness of the rule can also be supported on other policy grounds. On its 'prophylactic' role, see P Birks, *An Introduction to the Law of Restitution* (Oxford, Clarendon Paperbacks, 1989) at 332–3. See also M Christie, 'The Director's Fiduciary Duty not to Compete' (1992) 55 *Modern Law Review* 506 at 508.

[22] *Aberdeen Ry v Blaikie* (1854) 1 Macq 61 and *Transvaal Lands v New Belgium* [1914] 2 Ch 488 (CA). See also F Reynolds, *Bowstead & Reynolds on Agency* (London, Sweet & Maxwell, 2001) 17th ed ('Bowstead & Reynolds'), Art 46.

[23] *Ex parte Lacey* (1802) 6 Ves 625 at 627. See also Lord Eldon's reference to 'the impossibility of knowing the truth in every case' in *Ex parte Bennett* (1805) 10 Ves 381 at 385–6 and the endorsement of his statement by Knight-Bruce V-C in *Benson v Heathorn* (1842) 1 Y & C Ch 326 at 342–3.

[24] (1854) 1 Macq 461.

[25] *Aberdeen Ry v Blaikie* (1854) 1 Macq 461 at 473. See also *Benson v Heathorn* (1842) 1 Y & C Ch 323, *Costa Rica Railway v Forwood* [1901] 1 Ch 746 (CA) and *Transvaal Lands v New Belgium* [1914] 2 Ch 488 (CA).

exploitation of company property for personal gain.[26] The proposed codification of directors' duties pursuant to the Company Law Review subdivides the no profit rule into two distinct duties relating to 'personal use of the company's property, information or opportunity' and 'benefits from third parties' respectively.[27]

In the context of agency, the no conflict rule has been stated as follows:[28]

> Where an agent enters into any contract or transaction with his principal ... he must act with perfect good faith, and make full disclosure of all the material circumstances, and of everything known to him respecting the subject-matter of the contract or transaction which would be likely to influence the conduct of the principal or his representative.

In the case of companies, a company can relax the no conflict rule and mitigate its consequences either through its shareholders operating by ordinary resolution or through the terms of its constitution in the form of an 'enabling article' permitting self-dealing. Company constitutions invariably do contain an enabling article and they are invariably subject to an express condition that the interested director must make full disclosure of the conflicting interest to the company's board of directors.[29] This requirement of disclosure to the company's board is backed up by an express statutory duty to declare the interest at a board meeting.[30]

The general principle of equity is supplemented by further special regulation aimed at specific kinds of contract or other transaction involving self-dealing set out in Part X of the Companies Act 1985.

1.4 The Economic Significance of Regulating Self-Dealing

The goal in regulating self-dealing is therefore to ensure full disclosure of the conflict of interest by penalising a failure to do so rather than to prevent

---

[26] The evolution of the distinct no conflict and no profit rules is analysed in R Flannigan, 'The Fiduciary Obligation' (1989) 9 *Oxford Journal of Legal Studies* 285 at 299 and in M Christie, (1992) 55 *Modern Law Review* 506 at 509–513. The no conflict rule has also been termed the 'self-dealing rule'. For trustees, the underlying principle of equity has also given rise to a distinct 'fair-dealing rule' which Sir Robert Megarry V-C has summarised as follows: 'if a trustee purchases the beneficial interest of any of his beneficiaries, the transaction ... can be set aside by the beneficiary unless the trustee can show that he has taken no advantage of his position and has made full disclosure to the beneficiary, and that the transaction is fair and honest': *Tito v Waddell (No 2)* [1977] Ch 106 at 240. See also on the distinction between the self-dealing rule and the fair-dealing rule, *Re Thompson's Settlement* [1986] Ch 99 and G Moffat, *Trusts Law Text and Materials* (London, Butterworths, 1999) 3rd ed at 352–7.
[27] See the 2002 White Paper, Draft Clauses, Schedule 2, general principles 5, 6 and 7.
[28] Bowstead & Reynolds, Art 47(1). The burden of proof is on the agent to show that he acted in perfect good faith and after full disclosure: Art 47(2).
[29] See, for example, Table A, reg 85.
[30] Companies Act 1985, s 317(1).

its occurrence. This may be difficult in cases where a third party is unaware of the interested director's failure to disclose a conflict or even that a conflict of interest exists.

The economic significance of self-dealing is that it increases the risk of loss from the economic 'agency problem' discussed in chapter 2 and therefore burdens companies with additional 'agency costs'. This provides an economic rationale for including procedural regulation targeted at self-dealing in a company's constitution. Also, where a corporate agent approves a contract without having the actual authority to do so and the contract involves self-dealing, it is more likely that the third party is the 'least-cost-avoider'.[31] This provides an economic rationale for varying the applicable overriding rules of attribution to target transactions that involve self-dealing and subject them to special treatment. However, such variations should take account of whether or not the third party (if not a director) should have been aware of the relevant conflict of interest.

To minimise the adverse impact of self-dealing, regulation should take account of its benefits as well as its costs and seek to establish an optimal balance. A conflict of interest may, for example, provide a valuable channel of information between the company and the third party. This may reduce transaction costs and enable certain transactions to take place that would be prohibitively costly otherwise. There is recognition of this double-edged aspect of self-dealing in the nineteenth century case law on the no conflict rule. In *Imperial Mercantile Credit Association v Coleman*, Lord Hatherley noted:[32]

> [Shareholders may] think that in large financial matters of this description it is better to have directors who may advance the interests of the company by their connection, and by the part which they themselves take in large money dealings, than to have persons who would have no share in such transactions as those in which the company is concerned.

If the regulation of self-dealing is to promote efficiency, it must strike a balance that maximises the company's overall gains from its directors. Procedural regulation, which permits self-dealing subject to disclosure, can strike this balance provided that the costs of disclosure are minimised.

Compulsory disclosure as the basis of regulation can also benefit companies by encouraging the flow of information from directors to their companies. As was seen in chapter 2, stimulating flows of information can generate benefits in terms of dynamic efficiency. This has been suggested

---

[31] See chapter 2 on the 'least-cost-avoider'.
[32] (1871) LR 6 Ch 558 at 568. See also Lord Herschell's remark that it 'might sometimes be to the advantage of the beneficiaries that their trustee should act for them professionally rather than a stranger' in *Bray v Ford* [1896] AC 44 at 52 and the judgment of Upjohn LJ in *Boulting Bros v ACTAT* [1963] 2 QB 606 at 634–640.

as an economic explanation for the very strict application of the rule of equity that penalises undisclosed secret profits.[33] Thus, the practical effect of the rule penalising secret profits is not to prevent directors from making them, but to encourage directors to disclose their opportunities for doing so. If directors were not to have such a strong incentive to disclose, they would have a private incentive to conceal such opportunities so as to maximise their personal gain. This might lead them to conceal opportunities even where their company would be able to exploit the opportunity much more effectively and generate a greater overall gain. The private incentive would produce an inefficient outcome.

The inflexibility of the rule of equity therefore counters a potentially inefficient incentive to conceal information. Even in cases where it could be argued that a company would not have pursued (or would not have been able to pursue) a particular opportunity even if it had been disclosed,[34] there might still have been a gain from encouraging directors to disclose rather than conceal information about them. A director acting alone might not, for example, be the best judge of how to exploit an opportunity most effectively. However, to maximise the potential gains from disclosure, the costs of doing so should be minimised. This means having a clear and precise obligation of disclosure, preferably to a readily accessible body.

1.5 Disclosure in a Unitary Board System

The unitary board system limits the scope for achieving an efficient regulation of self-dealing. The factors noted in chapter 3 concerning the shortcomings of a company's body of shareholders as an active organ of governance are relevant here as well. Receiving and responding to the disclosure of information about a conflict of interest entails managerial decision-making.

For public companies, it is unrealistic to expect the body of shareholders to engage in active decision-making about conflicts of interest. This requires managerial expertise and specialised knowledge of the company's affairs as well as the ability to take a decision (as opposed to approving or rejecting a submitted proposal). In practice, a company's board is the body best suited to this kind of decision-making, despite the risk that a director's colleagues may not be ideal scrutinisers of conflicts of interest. Additionally, as the Law Commission and the Company Law

---

[33] See S Deakin and A Hughes, (1999) 3 *Company Financial and Insolvency Law Review* 169 at 182. See generally R Cooter and B Freedman, 'The Fiduciary Relationship: Its Economic Character and Legal Consequences' (1991) *New York University Law Review* 1045.

[34] As, for example, in *Regal (Hastings) v Gulliver* [1967] AC 134 (note) and *Industrial Development Consultants v Cooley* [1972] 1 WLR 443.

Review have recognised, there are problems of confidentiality in involving shareholders in matters of managerial decision-making.[35]

1.6 The Structure of the Law

The above economic considerations provide some explanation of why the regulation of self-dealing in general has focused on prompting disclosure to the board of a company. As well as the special rules of equity, Part X of the Companies Act 1985 has imposed additional regulation for specific contracts and other transactions involving self-dealing that pose an enhanced risk of harm to a company. Part X includes a mixture of prohibitions, limitations on the power of the board and disclosure requirements. These are subject to a mixture of civil and criminal sanctions. Some of the provisions are directed at particular types of contract, such as service contracts and loans to directors.[36] Others are directed at the scale of the transaction, in particular the special rules governing substantial acquisitions or disposals of assets.[37] For listed public companies, there are more stringent regulations for transactions involving self-dealing.[38]

Although it has some economic logic, this area of law has been criticised for its complexity and lack of coherent structure.[39] The Company Law Review noted that Part X had developed in a piecemeal fashion in response to 'particular abuses and scandals of the day' and has described its provisions as 'complex and somewhat incoherent'.[40] When the Company Law Review was set up, the Law Commission (in conjunction with the Scottish Law Commission) had already embarked on a review of this law and made recommendations for its overhaul and reform.[41] It

---

[35] See Completing the Structure at 4.16 and Final Report at 4.9.

[36] Companies Act 1985, ss 319 and 330–344 respectively.

[37] Companies Act 1985, s 320.

[38] UK Listing Authority, *Listing Rules* (London, FSA, 2003) ('the Listing Rules'), chapter 11. If a transaction involves a 'related party' and the relative value is five per cent or more, then the shareholders must give their prior approval by ordinary resolution. Further, the related party and any 'associates' should abstain from voting. See further below.

[39] See, for example, R Cranston, 'Limiting Directors' Liability: Ratification, Exemption and Indemnification' [1992] *Journal of Business Law* 197 and A Tunc, 'A French Lawyer Looks at British Company Law' (1982) 45 *Modern Law Review* 1 at 6–7. This has also been a theme in the relevant case law: see, for example, *Hely-Hutchinson v Brayhead* [1968] 1 QB 549 (CA), *Guinness v Saunders* [1990] 2 AC 663 (HL), *Lee Panavision v Lee Lighting* [1991] BCC 620 (CA), *Cowan de Groot Properties v Eagle Trust* [1991] BCLC 1045, *Runciman v Runciman* [1993] BCC 223 and *Neptune (Vehicle Washing Equipment) v Fitzgerald* [1996] Ch 274.

[40] Developing the Framework at 3.86.

[41] Law Commission, *Company Directors: Regulating Conflicts of Interests and Formulating a Statement of Duties* (Law Commission Report No 261, Scottish Law Commission Report No 173, The Stationery Office, London, 1999) ('the 1999 Report'). See generally, M Andenas and D Sugarman (eds), *Developments in European Company Law: Volume 3/1999: Directors' Conflicts of Interest: Legal, Socio-Legal and Economic Analyses* (London, Kluwer Law International, 2000) ('Andenas & Sugarman').

made some use of economic analysis to review the law and to inform its proposals.[42] The Company Law Review has largely, though not entirely, endorsed these.[43]

2 IDENTIFYING CONTRACTS INVOLVING SELF-DEALING

2.1 Defining a Conflict of Interest

For a third party entering into a contract with a company, it is important to be able to identify whether or not the contract does involve self-dealing. If the third party is also a director of the company, it clearly does. If the third party is not a director, it may be hard to tell because there is no precise definition of what kind of interest is sufficient to trigger the legal consequences of this classification.

For some of the provisions in Part X of the Companies Act 1985, the matter is straightforward. The third party must fall into a designated category of person for the provision to apply. Thus, the third party must be a director of the company or of its holding company or a 'person connected' with such a director (this including a company with which the director is 'associated') for sections 320 (substantial property transactions) and 322A (contracts in excess of the board's powers under the constitution) to apply.[44] However, section 317, which imposes a general duty on directors to declare their interest in any contract involving self-dealing at a board meeting, refers to 'a director who is in any way, whether directly or indirectly, interested in a contract or proposed contract with the company'.[45] This statutory duty does not concern third parties who are not directors since non-performance does not of itself affect the validity of a self-dealing contract. The risk of invalidity arises from any failure to comply with an enabling article relaxing the no conflict rule.[46]

---

[42] See the 1999 Report at 16, 31 and 83–111. See also J Lowry and R Edmunds, 'Section 317: Injecting Rationality into Directorial Disclosure?' in Andenas & Sugarman.

[43] See Developing the Framework at 3.62, 3.86–3.89 and Annex C, Completing the Structure at 4.8–4.21 and Final Report at 4.9 and 6.8–6.16.

[44] S 346 of the Companies Act 1985 defines these terms.

[45] S 317 implies that a director may be interested in a transaction indirectly through membership of another 'company or firm' or through 'a person who is connected with him' as defined in s 346 of the Companies Act 1985: see s 317(3). The no conflict rule covers a conflicting fiduciary duty, for example as a trustee or as a director of another company: see *Transvaal Lands v New Belgium* [1914] 2 Ch 488; *Boulting v ACTAT* [1963] 2 QB 606 and *Lee Panavision v Lee Lighting* [1991] BCLC 575. In *Cowan de Groot Properties v Eagle Trust* [1991] BCLC 1045, Knox J held that the interest of a bare trustee did not amount to a conflicting interest since such a trustee did not owe duties, but left open the question of whether a director is interested in a transaction if he is a creditor of another party.

[46] *Hely-Hutchinson v Brayhead* [1968] 1 QB 549; *Guinness v Saunders* [1990] 2 AC 663 at 697, per Lord Goff; *Cowan de Groot v Eagle Trust* [1991] BCLC 1045 at 1113.

A third party who is not a director also has a good reason to ensure that there is compliance with the enabling article permitting self-dealing and with any related procedural restrictions on the power of the board to make such contracts. Enabling articles invariably reflect the statutory duty under section 317, although not necessarily in identical language. The current version of Table A, for example, states that the interested director must have 'disclosed to the directors the nature and extent of any material interest of his'.[47]

As regards procedural restrictions, regulation 94 of Table A, which excludes the interested director from voting and being counted in the quorum in most instances, simply refers to 'a matter in which he has, directly or indirectly, an interest or duty which is material and which conflicts or may conflict with the interests of the company'. However, the key factor in each case must be whether the contract would be subject to the no conflict rule.

2.2 The Ambit of the No Conflict Rule

The case law on the no conflict rule has not developed a precise definition of what amounts to self-dealing in this context, although it does provide some guidance. A contract does involve self-dealing if a director has a beneficial interest in the third party, for example as a shareholder,[48] or owes a duty to the third party as a trustee or director.[49] It has been held that the no conflict rule applies even where a director has a small shareholding in the third party.[50]

In *Rolled Steel v British Steel*,[51] which concerned the giving of a guarantee and related security to the third party, there was self-dealing because a director of the company (who voted in favour of the contract and whose presence made the board meeting quorate) had a beneficial interest in the company whose liability to the third party was being guaranteed by the company. This director was also personally liable to the third party as a guarantor of the same liability.

---

[47] Earlier versions of Table A made an explicit reference to compliance with the statutory duty. Thus, regulation 84(1) of Table A in Schedule I to the Companies Act 1948 permitted self-dealing but stated that the interested director 'shall declare the nature of his interest at a meeting of the directors in accordance with s 199 [the predecessor of s 317]'. The discrepancy between the subsequent version and the wording of s 317 resulted from a revision of Table A to reflect a proposed but unimplemented revision of s 317. This followed a recommendation of the Jenkins Committee that the duty relate to 'material interests in contracts, whether or not any such contracts come before the board of directors': see the Law Commission's Consultation Paper preceding the 1999 Report (Law Commission Consultation Paper No 153; Scottish Law Commission Consultation Paper No 105, The Stationery Office, 1998) ('the 1998 Consultation Paper') at 83–6.

[48] *Costa Rica Railway Co v Forwood* [1900] 1 Ch 756 and [1901] 1 Ch 746 (CA).

[49] *Transvaal Lands v New Belgium* [1914] 2 Ch 488.

[50] *Todd v Robinson* (1885) 14 QBD 739 (CA).

[51] [1986] Ch 246 (CA).

In *Cowan de Groot v Eagle Trust*,[52] it was argued that a contract should be treated as voidable under the no conflict rule because a director of the company was a creditor of the third party. This director thus had a personal interest in the third party's solvency that might conflict with the company's interest in entering the contract on the best possible terms and he had failed to disclose this interest. Knox J indicated that this would not necessarily be sufficient to constitute self-dealing.[53] In any event, he held that if the third party had no notice of the director's failure to disclose the conflicting interest, he would still be able to enforce the contract under the indoor management rule.[54]

2.3 The Company Law Review

The Company Law Review has recommended that the obligation on directors to disclose a conflicting interest should be limited to 'material' interests. The Law Commission had already raised the question of how, if at all, the concept of materiality should be defined if the statutory duty were to be limited to 'material' interests.[55] It recommended that 'immaterial' interests should be excluded and that these should be defined as ones that would not give rise to a 'real risk of an actual conflict of interest'.[56]

The Company Law Review favoured a less restricted view of materiality and canvassed a proposal that an interest should be disregarded if the director (or third party) could prove that the board could not reasonably have felt constrained in its decision if it had been aware of the interest.[57] This would place the burden of proving immateriality on the interested director or the third party. Further, the test of materiality should be 'an objective one of what could reasonably have been expected to have swayed the board'.[58] The Company Law Review found wide support for restricting the duty in this way, but 'less consensus on the difficult question of how materiality is to be defined'.[59] It therefore recommended:[60]

---

[52] [1991] BCLC 1045.

[53] See Knox J's judgment in *Cowan de Groot Properties v Eagle Trust* [1991] BCLC 1045 at 1116–117. In an Australian case, *State of South Australia v Marcus Clark* (1996) 19 ACSR 606, the fact that a director of the company was also a director and shareholder of a major creditor of the third party was held to constitute a conflict of interest and to give rise to a duty to disclose it.

[54] *Rolled Steel v British Steel* [1986] Ch 246; *Cowan de Groot Properties v Eagle Trust* [1991] BCLC 1045. See the analysis of the defences available to such third parties in R Nolan, 'Enacting Civil Remedies in Company Law' (2001) 1 *Journal of Corporate Law Studies* 245 at 264.

[55] The 1998 Consultation Paper at 94–5.

[56] The 1999 Report at 87–1.

[57] Developing the Framework, Annex C at 11.

[58] *Ibid.*

[59] Completing the Structure at 4.11.

[60] *Ibid.*

[T]he test should be whether the interest could objectively have been reasonably regarded as material by the directors concerned, [meaning] that an interest could only be regarded as not material if the director could show that the board concerned could not reasonably have regarded it as being so.

3 THE EFFECT OF SELF-DEALING ON THE POWER TO MAKE CONTRACTS FOR COMPANIES

3.1 Actual Authority

3.1.1 The Special Nature of the Power to Award Remuneration

As well as precluding secret profits, the 'no profit' rule prohibits directors from receiving any remuneration for their services.[61] As with the no conflict rule, the practical effect of this prohibition is to encourage compliance with a formal procedure whereby it can be avoided. The bar on remuneration can be overridden by an ordinary resolution of the shareholders or by the board in accordance with an enabling article such as that in regulation 84 of Table A. Such compliance is therefore a precondition of the validity of any contract or other transaction concerning the remuneration or reward of a director and of any amendment to an existing contract.[62]

The decision of the House of Lords in *Guinness v Saunders* confirmed the importance of complying with the requisite procedure.[63] The power of a company's board to award remuneration to its directors does not stem from its general powers of management. The board cannot therefore delegate this power unless the enabling article expressly authorises it to do so. In the *Guinness* case, the board of a public company made a general delegation of its powers to a committee of three directors charged with the conduct of a takeover bid for another company. This committee purported to award one of its members a substantial bonus for his contribution to the success of the bid. The House of Lords held that only the board of the company had the actual authority to approve this bonus, but that it had no power to confer the necessary authority on the committee.

The payment was therefore void for lack of authority and was recoverable by the company in full. A contract or other transaction relating to the remuneration of a director that has not been properly authorised is void. It can only acquire validity if the company ratifies it by acting through a body that does have the necessary authority. This legal effect is different

---

[61] *Hutton v West Cork Railway* (1883) 23 Ch D 654 (CA); *Guinness v Saunders* [1990] 2 AC 663 (HL).
[62] *Runciman v Walter Runciman plc* [1993] BCC 233.
[63] [1990] 2 AC 663.

from that resulting from the no conflict rule, which merely renders a contract voidable at the instance of the company.[64]

The House of Lords in *Guinness* also ruled that the underlying rule of equity prohibiting remuneration meant that the director had no basis for claiming payment on a *quantum meruit* basis.[65] Directors should therefore ensure that their company's board (or its shareholders) approves a service contract or any other arrangement relating to their remuneration.[66] Directors should also ensure that the board observes all procedural restrictions on how it operates, including any special ones relating to self-dealing, since failure to do so would mean that it was not the board that approved the contract.[67]

The *Guinness* case can be contrasted with *Runciman v Walter Runciman plc*,[68] which concerned the validity of the extension of a director's term of office from three to five years. The company's board had not made this extension formally at a board meeting, but Simon Brown J found that all the directors of the company had known and acquiesced in the decision. Accordingly, it was the board, rather than just those directors actively involved in the decision, that had approved the extension. The extension was therefore not void, although its validity was still subject to the no conflict rule.

The significance of the distinction drawn in the *Guinness* and *Runciman* cases is that a contract made with actual authority, but in breach of the self-dealing rule is not void but voidable. The contract has legal effect, but the company has the right to rescind it. This right is subject to certain bars, which may affect the remedies available to the company or even deny the company any remedy at all.[69]

3.1.2 Other Special Limits Affecting Actual Authority

A company's constitution may subject the making of contracts involving self-dealing to more stringent limitations and restrictions than other contracts. In theory, the fact that a third party is a director of the company, or a party in which a director has an interest, might be expected to

---

[64] This distinction was crucial in the *Guinness* case since the company had brought summary proceedings to recover the payment and therefore had to show that the director had no arguable basis for resisting a claim for repayment in full. If the payment had been found merely to be voidable, then the director would have been entitled to argue that the company's right to rescind the payment was barred on the basis that the company could not make counter-restitution for the services he had provided: see especially the judgment of Lord Goff on this point. See also P Birks, 'Restitution Without Counter-Restitution' [1990] *Lloyd's Maritime and Commercial Law Quarterly* 330.

[65] The House of Lords also refused to award the director an equitable allowance, although it did not rule out this possibility entirely.

[66] Statute sets certain limits on the power of the board to award remuneration to directors or approve their service contracts: see Companies Act 1985, ss 311–3 and 319.

[67] *Smith v Henniker-Major* [2002] EWCA Civ 762. See generally chapter 5.

[68] [1993] BCC 233.

[69] See further below.

reduce the risk of a contract being made without authority. In practice, having a connection to the company may not help a third party where the overall boundaries of the board's actual authority are hard to discern, as in *Re Torvale Group*,[70] or where the scope of an agent's actual authority has to be discerned from the conduct of the company's board over a period of time, as in *Hely-Hutchinson v Brayhead*.[71]

A company's constitution may place special limitations or procedural restrictions on the board's actual authority to approve contracts involving self-dealing. Thus, regulation 94 of Table A provides that a director cannot 'vote on any resolution concerning a matter in which he has, directly or indirectly, an interest or duty which is material and which conflicts or may conflict with the interests of the company' subject to certain limited exceptions. Further, regulation 95 provides that where the interested director cannot vote, he cannot be counted in the quorum present for the relevant resolution.[72]

A company's articles of association can diverge from the model prescribed by Table A. It is open to those drafting enabling articles not only to permit self-dealing, but also to permit an interested director to vote on the contract and to be counted in the quorum. In that case, the constitution would not set any special restrictions on the board's authority to make or approve such a contract. However, the standard requirement in enabling articles that the interested director must declare or disclose his interest at a board meeting does not operate as a limitation on the board's authority to make such contracts. Otherwise, contracts made in violation of this requirement would be void for lack of authority rather than merely voidable under the no conflict rule.[73]

The terms of a company's enabling articles must be carefully construed to see the precise basis on which its board is authorised to approve a contract involving self-dealing. In *Rolled Steel v British Steel*,[74] for example, the Court of Appeal held that the required declaration of interest in this case operated as a precondition of the interested director's ability to vote on a resolution approving the contract and to be counted in the quorum. The director's failure to do so meant that the contract had not been duly authorised by a quorate board so that the third party would only have been able to enforce the contract by relying upon the indoor management rule.[75]

---

[70] [1999] 2 BCLC 605. See chapter 5.

[71] [1968] 1 QB 549 (CA).

[72] Such a provision in effect prevented the board from having the power to make a contract in which most of the directors were interested in *Grant v UK Switchback Railway* (1889) LR 40 Ch D 135.

[73] *Hely-Hutchinson v Brayhead* [1968] 1 QB 549; *Runciman v Walter Runciman* [1993] BCC 223.

[74] [1986] 1 Ch 246 (CA).

[75] [1986] 1 Ch 246 at 282–4. The third party had not in fact pleaded reliance on the indoor management rule. The Court of Appeal held that it should have formally raised the issue since the company would then have been able to challenge the third party's right to rely upon the rule by showing that the circumstances of case were such as to put the third party under a duty to make further inquiry.

3.2 Breach of the Directors' Duty of Good Faith

As was seen in chapter 3, the board of a company must not only observe the limits of its actual authority, but must exercise its powers in accordance with the directors' duties. These duties apply also when directors exercise powers vested in or delegated to them in their own right. Other corporate agents are subject to similar duties. Breach of duty poses less of a threat to the validity of a contract, but a third party's potential liability for knowing receipt can undermine its ability to enforce or rely upon the validity of a contract involving a breach of fiduciary duty.[76] And where a contract involves the exercise of a power for an improper purpose, a third party must be able to rely upon an overriding rule of attribution.[77]

Where a contract involves self-dealing, this may increase the third party's vulnerability to liability for knowing receipt. The courts may be more willing to find that those acting for the company acted in breach of their general duty of good faith.[78] If the courts find that there has been such a breach, they may then be more willing to find that the third party knew of the breach of duty or that it would be unconscionable for the third party to be able to rely upon the validity of the contract. Their general duty of good faith requires the directors of a company (whether acting as the board or in some other capacity) to exercise their powers in what they believe to be the best interests of the company.[79] Although this duty entails more than a lack of bad faith or conscious dishonesty, it does not set an objective standard and only requires directors to direct their minds to the proper goal. Lord Wilberforce has stated the courts' approach as follows:[80]

> [It] would be wrong for the court to substitute its opinion for that of the management or indeed to question the correctness of the management's decision, on such a question, if *bona fide* arrived at. There is no appeal on merits from management decisions to courts of law: nor will courts of law assume to act as a kind of supervisory board over decisions within the powers of management honestly arrived at.

Thus, in *Runciman v Walter Runciman plc*,[81] where a company challenged the validity of the extension of the notice period in a director's service contract by two years on the basis that it had been made in breach of the

---

[76] See chapter 5.
[77] *Criterion Properties v Stratford UK Properties* [2002] EWCA Civ 1883.
[78] *Neptune (Vehicle Washing Equipment) v Fitzgerald (No 2)* [1995] BCC 1000 at 1017; *Colin Gwyer v London Wharf* [2003] 2 BCLC 153 at para 76.
[79] *Re Smith & Fawcett* [1942] Ch 304 (CA); *Re W & M Roith* [1967] 1 WLR 432; *Charterbridge Corp v Lloyds Bank* [1970] Ch 62; *Bishopsgate Investment Management v Maxwell* [1993] BCC 120.
[80] *Howard Smith v Ampol* [1974] AC 821 at 832 (PC). See also *Colin Gwyer v London Wharf* [2003] 2 BCLC 153.
[81] [1993] BCC 223.

general duty of good faith, Simon Brown J held that the company would have to show that the decision was one which no reasonable director could possibly have concluded would be in the interests of the company or that there was evidence to cast doubt on the directors' good faith in making the extension.[82]

Contracts involving self-dealing may therefore be scrutinised to ensure that those directors acting for the company have complied with their general duty of good faith. In the *Runciman* case, the interested director was not involved in the company's decision-making. Where an interested director is involved in the decision-making, and especially where he or she is the company's only decision-maker, the courts are likely to scrutinise the contract even more carefully.[83]

4 SELF-DEALING AND THE OVERRIDING RULES OF ATTRIBUTION

4.1 Section 35A of the Companies Act 1985

A director who is also third party to an unauthorised contract in which he or she has acted as the company's agent may not be treated as a 'person dealing with a company' for the purposes of section 35A.[84] Also, the presence of a conflict of interest could make it easier for a company to prove that a third party was not dealing with it 'in good faith' and thereby prevent the third party from being able to rely upon section 35A.[85] It would be relevant to determining whether or not it would be unconscionable for the third party to be able to enforce the contract or rely upon its validity.[86]

Apart from affecting a third party's entitlement to rely upon section 35A, the presence of self-dealing is likely to trigger section 322A. If a third party to an unauthorised contract otherwise caught by section 35A is a director of the company or of its holding company (if any) or is a 'person connected' with such a director or is a company with which such a director is 'associated', then section 322A qualifies the third party's ability to rely upon section 35A to ensure the contract's validity.[87] Section 322A renders

---

[82] [1993] BCC 223 at 234–5. He applied the general statement of the duty in *Palmer's Company Law* (London, Sweet & Maxwell, 1992) at 8.508.

[83] *Zemco v Jerrom-Pugh* [1993] BCC 275 (CA); *Neptune v Fitzgerald (No 2)* [1995] BCC 1000.

[84] *Smith v Henniker-Major* [2002] EWCA Civ 762. A majority of the Court of Appeal held that the third party in this case, who was also the chairman of the board and the sole director present at the relevant board meeting, could not rely upon s 35A. They did not indicate how wide a range of directors beyond this would be similarly disabled. See chapter 5 on the conditions of s 35A.

[85] This condition operates as a proviso inasmuch as the third party is presumed to be acting in good faith unless the contrary is proved: see chapter 5.

[86] *BCCI v Akindele* [2001] Ch 437 (CA); *Criterion Properties v Stratford UK Properties* [2002] EWCA Civ 1883. See chapter 5 on how a third party's potential liability for knowing receipt equates to a lack of good faith in this context.

[87] Companies Act 1985, s 322A. See chapter 5.

the contract 'voidable at the instance of the company'. Section 322A(5) sets limits on a company's right to avoid a contract or other transaction, providing that it cannot do so if:

(a) restitution of any money or other asset which was the subject-matter of the transaction is no longer possible; or

(b) the company is indemnified for any loss or damage resulting from the transaction; or

(c) rights acquired bona fide for value and without actual notice of the [board's exceeding its powers] by a person who is not party to the transaction would be affected by the avoidance; or

(d) the transaction is ratified by the company in general meeting, by ordinary or special resolution or otherwise as the case may require.[88]

Further, section 322A(3) provides that, whether or not the company avoids the contract, the third party is also liable:

(a) to account to the company for any gain which he has made directly or indirectly by the transaction; and

(b) to indemnify the company for any loss or damage resulting from the transaction.

For third parties who are not directors of the company, section 322A(6) gives them a defence to the personal liability under section 322A(3) if they show that at the time of contracting they did not know that the company's board was exceeding its authority.

Third parties therefore have good reason to check whether or not they are within the scope of section 322A and, if they are, to ensure that their contract is made in accordance with the terms of the company's constitution. As noted in chapter 5, the Company Law Review has recommended that third parties within the scope of section 322A simply be denied the ability to rely upon the proposed replacement for section 35A.[89] If the statutory provisions were to be reformed in this way, a third party unable to rely upon the provision might nevertheless be able to rely upon a common law overriding rule of attribution.

4.2 The Indoor Management Rule

In *Morris v Kanssen*, the House of Lords held that a third party could not rely upon the indoor management rule because he was also a director

---

[88] See further chapter 3 on the different ways in which the company's shareholders have to exercise their power to ratify actions beyond the limits of the board's contractual power.
[89] See 2002 White Paper, Draft Clauses, clauses 17(5) and (6).

of the company.[90] Even where a third party is not a director, the presence of a conflicting interest may be relevant in determining whether the circumstances were such as to put the third party on inquiry and prevent the third party from being entitled to rely upon the rule. In the *Rolled Steel* case,[91] for example, a company executed a guarantee (and a debenture as security) for a debt owed to the third party by another company. A director (and majority shareholder) of the company giving the guarantee was also a director and controlling shareholder of the company with the debt that was being guaranteed. This director had also given a personal guarantee for this debt, increasing the conflict of interest. The third party appointed a receiver and manager to enforce the security and the receiver paid out the sums due to the third party under the guarantee.[92] The company later challenged the validity of the guarantee and debenture and sought to recover the sums paid out by the receiver.

In its defence to the company's claim, the third party failed to plead until a late stage in the proceedings that it would rely upon the indoor management rule to overcome the board's lack of actual authority. The Court of Appeal held that the third party had lost its right to invoke this as a defence since it involved a plea of mixed law and fact. Thus, although the third party had been entitled to invoke the indoor management rule, the company would then have been entitled to claim that the circumstances were such as to have put the third party on inquiry and to adduce evidence to that effect. The Court of Appeal held that it could not therefore be taken for granted that this third party would have been able to rely on the rule because it was arguable that its knowledge of the director's conflict of interest should have put it on inquiry.[93]

It is arguable that a third party's knowledge of a conflict of interest and of the implications of this conflict should be key factors in determining whether or not the third party should be entitled to rely upon the indoor management rule. In *Cowan de Groot v Eagle Trust*,[94] however, in which it was argued that a transaction involved self-dealing because a director of the company was also a creditor of the third party, Knox J held that this fact alone would not preclude the third party from being able to rely upon the indoor management rule. He said that the circumstances had not put the

---

[90] [1946] AC 459. See also *Howard v Patent Ivory* (1888) 38 Ch D 156. However, note the doubts expressed by Roskill J in *Hely-Hutchinson v Brayhead* about the ambit of the ruling in *Morris v Kanssen*. This is discussed below in relation to ostensible authority.

[91] [1986] 1 Ch 246 at 282–4.

[92] By this time, the third party had been taken over by the British Steel Corporation ('BSC') and the receiver made the payments to BSC as the third party's successor in title.

[93] See also the judgment of Browne-Wilkinson LJ [1986] 1 Ch 246 at 307 and the judgment of Brennan J in the High Court of Australia in *Northside Developments v Registrar-General* (1990) 64 ALJR 427.

[94] [1991] BCLC 1045.

third party on inquiry.[95] He distinguished the case from the *Rolled Steel* case on the basis that the Court of Appeal had ruled that the third party had attempted to plead the indoor management rule at too late a stage and so had not actually ruled that the third party must have been put on inquiry.[96]

4.3 Ostensible Authority and the Diplock Approach

Where a third party is a director of the company, it is not clear whether the House of Lords' ruling in *Morris v Kanssen* that the third party cannot rely upon the indoor management rule also precludes the third party from being able to rely upon a corporate agent's ostensible authority. In *Hely-Hutchinson v Brayhead*,[97] Roskill J held that a third party, who had only recently been appointed as a director of the company, could enforce an indemnity on the basis of ostensible authority. The agent who had executed the indemnity on behalf of the company was another director, who acted as *de facto* managing director, but he did not have actual authority to bind the company. Roskill J expressed doubt that the House of Lords' judgment in *Morris v Kanssen* meant that a third party who is a director must necessarily be treated as having constructive knowledge of the actual authority of the company's agents and could never rely upon their ostensible authority.[98]

However, the Court of Appeal in *Hely-Hutchinson v Brayhead* upheld Roskill J's decision on different grounds. The Court of Appeal held that the director in fact had implied actual authority to bind the company to the contract in question. The issues of whether the third party had been put on inquiry or had constructive notice of the agent's authority were therefore irrelevant to its decision. The Court of Appeal judges declined to express a view on whether a director could ever enforce an unautho-rised contract on the basis of ostensible authority.[99]

Whether or not a third party to an unauthorised contract that involves self-dealing is a director of the company, the main barrier to its entitlement to rely upon the corporate agent's ostensible authority is the third party's actual or constructive knowledge of the agent's lack of authority. As was seen in chapter 6, such knowledge undermines the third party's claim to have relied upon a representation that the agent did have the necessary authority to bind the company. In *Criterion Properties v Stratford*,[100] the Court of Appeal held that the board of a company had exceeded their actual authority by making a contract for an improper purpose. The court held that the third party could

---

[95] [1991] BCLC 1045 at 1117.
[96] *Ibid.*
[97] [1968] 1 QB 549.
[98] [1968] 1 QB 549 at 564–5.
[99] [1968] 1 QB 549 at 584–5 (Lord Denning), 588–9 (Lord Wilberforce) and 594–5 (Lord Pearson).
[100] [2002] EWCA Civ 1883.

enforce the contract if it could show that it was entitled to rely upon the board's ostensible authority to make it and treated this entitlement as negated by its potential liability for knowing receipt. On this basis, it held that the third party would be entitled to rely upon the validity of the contract unless this would be unconscionable in all the circumstances of the case.[101]

Where a third party is also a director of the company, it is arguable that this is a relevant factor in determining whether it would be unconscionable for him or her to rely upon a contract's validity or whether he or she should be deemed to have constructive knowledge of the agent's lack of actual authority. In the case of a third party who is not a director, the nature of the link with a director of a company should be a relevant factor. In effect, the issue of constructive knowledge in this context is analogous to the issue of whether or not a third party has been 'put on inquiry' for the purposes of the indoor management rule.

5 THE ADDITIONAL LAW GOVERNING THE VALIDITY OF CONTRACTS INVOLVING SELF-DEALING

The no conflict rule and the various provisions of Part X of the Companies Act 1985 may undermine the validity of a contract or other transaction with a company involving self-dealing even where the contract has been duly authorised or the third party is entitled to rely upon an overriding rule of attribution. These provisions therefore create an additional risk of invalidity for third parties dealing with companies beyond that which might result from an agent's lack of actual authority.

The requirements of this additional law can be summarised as follows:

(1) Section 317 obliges the interested director in relation to any contract involving self-dealing to declare the interest at a board meeting. Failure to do so exposes this director to a criminal sanction, namely an unlimited fine.[102]

(2) A contract involving self-dealing is also voidable by the company under the no conflict rule unless

   (a) it is approved or ratified by the company's shareholders, subject to full disclosure of the conflicting interest;[103] or

   (b) the company's constitution includes an enabling article and the interested director declares or discloses the interest to a board meeting and complies with any other conditions of the enabling article.

---

[101] [2001] Ch 437. See now [2004] UKHL 28, which is discussed in chapter 5.
[102] Companies Act 1985, s 317(7).
[103] *Re Cape Breton* (1885) 29 Ch D 795 (CA); *NW Transportation Co v Beatty* (1887) 12 App Cas 589 (PC). And note the comments of Upjohn LJ in *Boulting Bros v ACTAT* [1963] 2 QB 606 at 636–8 on the importance of full disclosure.

(3) For contracts involving the acquisition from or disposal to the company of non-cash assets above a specified value and where the third party is a director of the company or of its holding company or a 'person connected' to such a director (this including a company with which the director is associated),104 then the contract must first be approved by an ordinary resolution of the company's shareholders (or, as the case may be, of the shareholders of its holding company) pursuant to section 320.

(4) If the contract is of a particular type covered by Part X of the Companies Act (if, for example, it is a service contract, or concerns a payment made to a director, or involves a loan or similar kind of arrangement for a director or a person 'connected with' a director, or involves dealing in a share option in the company) then it is subject to the relevant restrictions, limitations, conditions or prohibitions set out in the appropriate section of Part X.

This chapter will focus on those provisions that have general application to contracts involving self-dealing. It will first examine the requirement that the interested director must disclose or declare his interest in any contract involving self-dealing to a meeting of the company's board, which stems from items (1) and (2) above. It will then examine the special regime for large acquisitions or disposals imposed by section 320.

As indicated in chapter 1, this book will not examine the various provisions of insolvency law that may affect the validity of contracts made with companies and the additional risk that these provisions pose to third parties.[105] However, as was noted in chapter 3, in addition to these provisions, the courts have established that the interests of a company that is insolvent (or virtually insolvent) are no longer to be identified with those of its shareholders, but instead with those of its creditors.[106] This shift of focus has an impact both on the content of the duties of directors towards such a company and on the complementary powers that are normally exercisable by the company's shareholders.[107] This is relevant to some of the law governing the validity of contracts involving self-dealing.

In particular, it has therefore been suggested that shareholders may lose their power to approve or ratify transactions caught by section 320 if a company is insolvent at the relevant time and it has been held that they cannot do so informally under the unanimous consent rule.[108] The same

---

[104] See s 346 of the Companies Act 1985 for the definition of these terms.

[105] On these provisions, see R Parry, *Transaction Avoidance in Insolvencies* (Oxford, OUP, 2001) and J Armour and H Bennett (ed), *Vulnerable Transactions in Corporate Insolvency* (Oxford, Hart Publishing, 2003).

[106] *West Mercia Safetywear v Dodd* [1988] BCLC 250 (CA); *Colin Gwyer v London Wharf* [2003] 2 BCLC 153.

[107] *West Mercia Safetywear v Dodd* [1988] BCLC 250.

[108] *Walker v WA Personnel* [2002] BPIR 621. See R Goddard, 'The *Re Duomatic* Principle and Sections 320–322 of the Companies Act 1985' [2004] *Journal of Business Law* 121.

reasoning should, in principle, apply to the shareholders' power to ratify a transaction involving self-dealing and thereby ensure its validity in relation to item (2) above. This issue will therefore be examined in a later section of this chapter.

6 THE REQUIREMENT TO DECLARE OR DISCLOSE AN INTEREST IN A CONTRACT INVOLVING SELF-DEALING

6.1 The Legal Significance of the Disclosure Requirement

A distinction can be drawn between contracts to which a director of the company is also the third party (a direct interest) and those in which a director has an interest in or other kind of link with the third party (an indirect interest). Third parties who are directors must formally declare their direct interest in the contract with their company at a board meeting both to avoid a criminal penalty under section 317 and to ensure that the contract is not rendered voidable under the no conflict rule.[109] Third parties who are not directors of the company must rely upon the relevant director to declare the indirect interest formally at a board meeting to ensure the validity of the contract pursuant to an enabling article.

Neither section 317 nor the no conflict rule is conditional on the interested director being actively involved in the company's decision-making process.[110] The Company Law Review expressed the view that the obligation to declare an interest should not arise in cases where the interested director is not aware of the interest and has not been involved in any way in the company's decision-making process. The Review canvassed a proposal to this effect,[111] which received strong support. However, the Company Law Review later accepted the view that there would be scope for abuse unless the director was obliged to declare an interest once he or she became aware of it.[112] The Company Law Review also recommended that failure to disclose an interest should entitle the company to civil remedies in respect of the transaction, which would be analogous to those flowing from the no conflict rule.[113] However, it took the view that where the interest is indirect, the third party should not be liable 'unless knowingly a party to the unlawful transaction'.[114]

---

[109] *Hely-Hutchinson v Brayhead* [1968] 1 QB 549; *Runciman v Walter Runciman plc* [1993] BCC 223; *Neptune (Vehicle Washing Equipment) v Fitzgerald* [1996] Ch 274.
[110] *Aberdeen Ry v Blaikie* (1854) 1 Macq 461.
[111] Developing the Framework at 3.62 and Annex C at 15.
[112] Completing the Structure at 4.14.
[113] Developing the Framework, Annex C at 18.
[114] *Ibid*. The Company Law Review canvassed a proposal that that there should be a codification of civil remedies for breach of directors' duties to complement the proposed codification of directors' duties: Completing the Structure at 13.71. In particular, it invited comments

Third parties who are not directors can be further categorised according to the nature of their link with a director of the company. Thus, if the third party is a company or other entity controlled by the interested director or a nominee of the interested director, then the courts are likely to pierce the veil and identify the third party with the director.[115] This identification may also expose the third party to a liability to account to the company for any profit or to compensate it for any loss in accordance with the no conflict rule.[116] If, however, the interested director is merely a shareholder in the third party, the courts will not identify them and the company will not, without more, be allowed to rescind the contract.[117] In one case, where the interested director was a creditor of the third party and the third party had no actual or constructive knowledge of the director's failure to declare his interest, it was held that the third party could rely upon the indoor management rule to enforce the contract against the company.[118] In effect, the interested director's failure to avoid the no conflict rule was treated in the same way as if the company's agent had lacked actual authority. This approach achieves a result in line with that advocated by the Company Law Review.[119]

6.2 The Significance of the Disclosure Requirement's Having Two Legal Sources

In the Court of Appeal's decision in *Hely-Hutchinson v Brayhead*,[120] Lord Wilberforce indicated that failure to declare a conflicting interest whether

---

on a paper by Richard Nolan, which proposed an approach based on s 322 of the Companies Act 1985. Following the response to this proposal, the Company Law Review noted that 'this is a difficult area and one which will require considerable further thought' and that there are numerous areas where 'important policy decisions need to be taken'. It recommended that 'the codification of civil remedies for breach of directors' duties be given further detailed consideration by the DTI, with further consultation before any possible inclusion in the Bill': Final Report at 15.28–15.30. See also R Nolan, 'Enacting Civil Remedies in Company Law' (2001) 1 *Journal of Corporate Law Studies* 245, which reproduces the discussion paper.

[115] *Silkstone & Haigh Moor Coal Co v Edey* [1900] 1 Ch 167 (CA); *Re Thompson's Settlement* [1986] Ch 99; *Movitex v Bulfield* [1988] BCLC 104 at 122. See R Nolan, (2001) 1 *Journal of Corporate Law Studies* 245 at 264.
[116] *Cook v Deeks* [1916] 1 AC 554 (PC); *CMS Dolphin v Simonet* [2001] 2 BCLC 704 at paras 98–105.
[117] *Farrar v Farrars* (1888) 40 Ch D 395 (CA); *Re Thompson's Settlement* [1986] Ch 99 at 114–115.
[118] *Cowan de Groot v Eagle Trust* [1991] BCLC 1045 at 1116–117, per Knox J. See also R Nolan, (2001) 1 *Journal of Corporate Law Studies* 245 at 264, who states that 'the transaction will be upheld if the transaction can be shown not to involve improper behaviour by the director', applying *Farrar v Farrars* (1888) 40 Ch D 395 and noting *Hickley v Hickley* (1876) 2 Ch D 190.
[119] See above.
[120] [1968] 1 QB 549 at 589. As Lord Goff later noted in *Guinness v Saunders*, the judgment in the *Hely-Hutchinson* case was given by 'an exceptional Court of Appeal consisting of Lord Denning MR, Lord Wilberforce and Lord Pearson': [1990] 2 AC 663 at 697.

direct or indirect renders a contract involving self-dealing voidable at the instances of the company. The statutory duty expressly provides that it does not prejudice 'the operation of any rule of law restricting the directors of a company from having an interest in contracts with the company' and thus preserves the effect of the no conflict rule.[121] Apart from this, there is no overt connection between the two legal sources of the requirement to declare an interest, save where an enabling article expressly incorporates the statutory duty. This lack of a clear relationship can be confusing where the wording of the enabling article diverges from that of the statutory duty.

The current version of Table A permits self-dealing provided that the interested director has 'disclosed' to the company's board 'the nature and extent of any material interest of his'.[122] This might be taken as a reassurance to third parties in general that the validity of a contract cannot be undermined if there proves to be a minor conflict of interest that has not been disclosed by the relevant director, although the director would still face the possibility of a criminal sanction under the statutory duty. Harman J held in *Lee Panavision v Lee Lighting* that the proviso to the enabling article should still be treated as reflecting the statutory duty:[123]

> [T]he whole thrust of the Act and the specific requirements for disclosure must be read into [Table A, reg 85] … the desirability of applying uniform tests causes the whole tenor of the statutory procedure under section 317 to be imported into [reg 85], so that when [reg 85] requires a director to disclose his interest but makes no specific provision as to when, how or to whom the disclosure should be made, that word 'disclosed', which is a wide and general word, must be read in the light of the closely analogous proposition in section 317.

The Court of Appeal in *Lee Panavision* based their decision upon other grounds and did not therefore make a ruling on this particular point of interpretation.

There was alleged to be a conflict of interest in the *Lee Panavision* case because the directors who approved the contract were subsequently given an indemnity by the third party against any personal liability for breach of duty that they might have incurred in making the contract.[124] Harman J held that the directors would have been aware of this indemnity at the

---

[121] Companies Act 1985, s 317(9).

[122] Table A, reg 85. Earlier versions of Table A did make an explicit reference to compliance with the statutory duty. Thus, reg 84(1) of Table A in Schedule I to the Companies Act 1948 permitted self-dealing but stated that the interested director 'shall declare the nature of his interest at a meeting of the directors in accordance with s 199 [the predecessor of s 317]'.

[123] [1991] BCLC 575 at 583.

[124] The Court of Appeal found that the directors had exercised their power to make contracts for an improper purpose: see further chapter 3.

time when they entered into the contract. The Court of Appeal expressed doubt about this finding and indicated that it would have been reluctant to find that the contract was voidable on this ground, given that the interest was common to all the directors and thus known to all the directors:[125]

> I would hesitate to hold that such apparently technical non-declaration of an interest in breach of section 317 has the inevitable result, as to which the court has no discretion, that the [contract] is fundamentally flawed and must be set aside if [the company] chooses to ask sufficiently promptly that it be set aside.

This appears to oversimplify the consequences for the third party of a finding that a contract is voidable.

However, the Company Law Review's proposal that the statutory duty should be limited to material interests and that a third party should not, without more, be penalised for a director's failure to declare an indirect interest, would remove the apparent discrepancy between the statutory duty and enabling articles.[126]

6.3 Complying with the Disclosure Requirement

A director of a company must declare any interest in a transaction with the company at a board meeting. It is irrelevant that the interest is obvious, as when a director is the third party. It is also irrelevant that the other directors of the company already know of the conflicting interest so that the declaration would not be disclosing any new information to them.[127] Further, the declaration of interest must be a formal event at a board meeting and cannot be inferred from the fact of the directors' prior knowledge of the interest.[128]

Hence, directors must declare their interest in their service contracts, or in amendments to their service contracts.[129] The one exception to this stringent insistence upon formality is that section 317 permits directors to declare in advance an indirect interest as a member of another company or of a firm or through 'a specified person who is connected with him' by means of a general notice.[130] Such a general notice is deemed to be a sufficient declaration of any interest in any contract made with such a company, firm or person.[131]

---

[125] [1992] BCLC 22 at 33, per Dillon LJ, who delivered the unanimous judgment of the court.
[126] See above.
[127] *Hely-Hutchinson v Brayhead* [1968] 1 QB 549; *Runciman v Walter Runciman plc* [1993] BCC 223.
[128] *Runciman v Walter Runciman plc* [1993] BCC 223.
[129] *Ibid.*
[130] Companies Act 1985, s 317(3). A person 'connected with' a director for this purpose is defined in section 346 of the Companies Act 1985.
[131] *Ibid.*

The Court of Appeal in *Guinness v Saunders* held that a formal act of disclosure would put the company's directors on notice of the interest and would give them the opportunity to reflect on their priorities: [132]

> Assuming it were true that all members of the board knew about the payment, that does not alter the fact that the requirement of the statute that there be a disclosure to a 'meeting of the directors of the company' (which is a wholly different thing from knowledge by individuals and involves the opportunity for positive consideration of the matter by the board as a body) was not complied with.

Lightman J also emphasised the procedural value of a formal declaration in *Neptune (Vehicle Washing Equipment) v Fitzgerald*,[133] which presented an extreme example of self-dealing. Here, the third party was also the sole director of the company. Anticipating his imminent removal from office, this director had arranged his own dismissal from office and authorised a payment of substantial compensation. The company sought to recover the payment, claiming (among other grounds) that it should be set aside under the no conflict rule. The company even argued that a sole director could never comply with section 317 because there could not be any 'meeting of directors' as required by that section. Since an inability to comply with section 317 would involve an irredeemable breach of the statutory duty, Lightman J held that a 'meeting of directors' should include a sole director in this context.

However, Lightman J held that even a sole director must make a formal declaration of his interest in a transaction involving self-dealing:[134]

> Where a director is interested in a contract, the section ensures that three things happen at a directors' meeting: first, all the directors would know or be reminded of the interest; secondly, the making of the declaration should be the occasion for a statutory pause for thought about the existence of the conflict of interest and of the duty to prefer the interests of the company to their own; third, the disclosure or reminder must be a distinct happening at the meeting which therefore must be recorded in the minutes of the meeting under section 382 [of the Companies Act 1985] and clause 86 of Table A, reg 86 … .

Whilst a strict insistence on procedural formality might be justifiable in relation to the interested director, it is less defensible where the third party is not a director. For an indirect interest, some flexibility is required to take account of the nature of the conflicting interest and of the third party's scope for identifying it and ensuring that the relevant director complies with the disclosure requirement.

---

[132] [1988] 2 All ER 940 at 944, per Fox LJ.
[133] [1995] BCC 474.
[134] [1995] BCC 474 at 480.

It is arguable that the law governing the implications of a director's failure to comply with the enabling article already provides the means for mitigating the impact on third parties who are not controlled by the interested director so that they do not face an unreasonable risk of invalidity.[135] However, it would be preferable to make this clear and to remove the uncertainty on this point.

The Company Law Review has proposed that the stringency of the disclosure requirement should be relaxed by enabling interested directors to show that their fellow directors were already aware of the relevant interest and also that sole directors should be excluded from the requirement altogether.[136] On the latter point, the Company Law Review canvassed a proposal that sole directors should be required to disclose a conflicting interest to the shareholders, but acknowledged that there could be practical difficulties with such a requirement.[137] The responses to the proposal pointed out that the shareholders in a company with a sole director already have the option of appointing an additional director so that disclosure can be made to the board in the usual way.[138] They can also amend their company's articles to require that a sole director declare any conflict of interest to the shareholders.[139] In effect, if the shareholders in such a company do not exercise these options, they can be viewed as accepting the resulting risk. The Company Law Review therefore proposed that the disclosure requirement simply not apply to sole directors.[140]

The 2002 White Paper did not include any specific proposals concerning the disclosure requirement and, in the proposed codification, the duty of directors in relation to a contract or other transaction involving self-dealing is specified in terms that are sufficiently flexible to leave open the precise detail of the eventual reform:[141]

A director of a company must not —

(a) in the performance of his functions as director, authorise, procure or permit the company to enter into a transaction, or
(b) enter into a transaction with the company,

if he has an interest in the transaction which he is required by this Act to disclose to any persons and has not disclosed the interest to them to the extent so required.

---

[135] *Cowan de Groot v Eagle Trust* [1991] BCLC 1045 at 1116–117.
[136] Developing the Framework, Annex C at 11.
[137] Final Report at 4.9.
[138] *Ibid.*
[139] *Ibid.*
[140] *Ibid.*
[141] 2002 White Paper, Draft Clauses, Schedule 2 para 5.

6.4 What Must a Director Disclose to Satisfy the Disclosure Requirement?

6.4.1 Inadequate Disclosure

It is possible that an interested director may declare the existence of a conflict of interest, but not reveal certain information that those acting on behalf of their company would find useful in settling the terms on which the company enters into the contract. This possibility raises the question of what information an interested director must reveal in order to satisfy the disclosure requirement. This may be governed by the terms of the enabling article. Table A, for example, includes a proviso that the director should disclose 'the nature and extent' of the relevant interest.[142]

A particular declaration or other act of disclosure might therefore be open to challenge as inadequate for not revealing the true nature or the full extent of the director's interest. It is also worth noting the position in the general law of agency:[143]

> An agent may not put himself in a position or enter into a transaction in which his personal interest, or his duty to another principal, may conflict with his duty to his principal, unless his principal, with full knowledge of all the material circumstances and of the nature and extent of the agent's interest, consents.

Where the third party is not a director of the company, the consequences of the interested director making an inadequate disclosure should be the same as for not making any disclosure at all.

Inadequate disclosure is likely to remain an issue when the requirement is reformed to implement the proposals of the Company Law Review. These are premised on the basis that the essential requirement will still be to disclose 'the nature and extent' of the director's interest in a contract.[144] In particular, the Company Law Review made the following recommendation:[145]

> We also suggested that disclosure should include disclosure of the nature and extent of the interest (which was unanimously supported, subject to matters of detail) and asked whether there should be an exception permitting confidential interests not to be disclosed, or a rule which required, in the case of a conflicting confidentiality obligation, that the director should merely declare that he had an interest and then be debarred from

---

[142] Table A, reg 85.
[143] Bowstead & Reynolds, Art 46, citing *Bray v Ford* [1896] AC 44 at 51. See also Bowstead & Reynolds at 6–055–6–062.
[144] See Developing the Framework, Annex C at 11, 12 and 17.
[145] Completing the Structure at 4.16.

participating in the decision. The great majority preferred the second option, which we adopt.

6.4.2 Liability for Inadequate Disclosure

There is case law to suggest that a mere declaration of the existence of a conflicting interest or even of the nature of the director's interest in a contract involving self-dealing is not necessarily sufficient to avoid the consequences of the no conflict rule. The point has arisen in relation both to disclosure made to a company's shareholders when seeking ratification of a contract involving self-dealing and to disclosure made to the board pursuant to an enabling article.[146]

In *New Zealand Netherlands Society v Kuys*,[147] which concerned a claim by an incorporated society against its secretary under the no profit rule, Lord Wilberforce for the Privy Council observed that there must be 'full and frank disclosure of all material facts', but found: [148]

> [The society] was quite unable to point to *any matter* relevant to the establishment of the newspaper or *which, had it been disclosed, could have affected the society's decision* that, on the facts found, had not been disclosed by [the officer]. (emphasis added)

In *Liquidators of Imperial Mercantile Credit Association v Coleman*,[149] a director had declared that a firm in which he was a partner would receive a commission in respect of a transaction that the company was entering. However, he had not declared the unusually large size of the commission. In the House of Lords, Lord Chelmsford addressed the issue of whether the company's directors would have entered into the contract if they 'had been fully informed of the real state of things' and whether they ought to have done so with that knowledge given their fiduciary duties to the company.[150] He held that the interested director should have disclosed the full amount of the commission and that the director's firm was liable to refund its profit accordingly.[151]

In *Gray v New Augarita Porcupine Mines*,[152] a director reached a settlement agreement with his company in which, among other things, he was released from his outstanding liabilities to the company, including any

---

[146] See, for example, *Costa Rica Railway v Forwood* [1901] 1 Ch 746 (CA) at 765 and *Boulting Bros v ACTAT* [1963] 2 QB 606 (CA) at 636–7.
[147] [1973] 1 WLR 1126 (PC).
[148] [1973] 1 WLR 1126 at 1131–132. See also the judgment of Lord Jauncey for the Privy Council in *Adams v R* [1995] BCC 376 at 386.
[149] (1873) LR 6 HL 189.
[150] *Ibid.*
[151] *Ibid.* See also the judgment of Lord Cairns at 205.
[152] [1952] 3 DLR 1.

arising from the misuse of the company's funds or for making secret profits. However, the director did not reveal the full extent of his potential liability and was released on terms that proved highly favourable to him. The Privy Council held that, whilst the director was not liable for fraud or deceit,[153] he had not disclosed the nature of his interest because he had not revealed to his colleagues that to settle with him on these terms 'was to release him from liability at a price that was singularly favourable to himself.' In effect, the nature of Gray's interest in the proposed agreement consisted of the fact 'that he stood to gain so much by the transaction: and only he at the time had the means of knowing how much'.[154]

As to how much detail a director in this situation is required to disclose, the Privy Council in *Gray* held that there was no precise formula and that it must depend in each case upon the nature of the contract or arrangement proposed and the context in which it arises. Referring back to the *Imperial Mercantile Credit* case, Lord Radcliffe said that when it was material to the judgment of those acting for the company that they should know the extent of the interested director's gain from a transaction, 'then he must see to it that they are informed'.[155]

6.4.3 The Limits of the Required Disclosure

The *Imperial Mercantile Credit* and *Gray* cases establish that an interested director must disclose full details about his likely gain from a transaction involving self-dealing in his declaration of interest where this information has a direct bearing on the merits of the transaction from the company's point of view and would thus be crucial to the decision on whether entering it would be in the company's best interests. In effect, by withholding this information, the interested directors in each case ensured that a decision was taken which was not in the company's best interests and which they knew was not in the company's best interests.

However, by avoiding a precise formula and relating the extent of the required disclosure to the facts of the particular case, this case law leaves some room to accommodate the Company Law Review's recommendation that a director should be able to avoid having to disclose confidential interests provided that he was debarred from the company's decision-making process.[156] Such a facility might be an essential prerequisite for many beneficial transactions to take place at all and would therefore be justifiable in terms of economic efficiency.

However, it is also possible to imagine circumstances in which it would not be reasonable, indeed would be unconscionable, for a director to be able

---

[153] *Ibid* at 10–12.
[154] *Ibid* at 14.
[155] *Ibid*.
[156] See above.

to remain silent by standing aside from the company's decision-making. A director might know that a transaction is not in the company's best interests and might also know that his colleagues would probably fail to protect the company's interests properly in the decision-making process. Depending on the precise nature of the director's role in the company, it might be reasonable to expect him to give the company the benefit of his superior knowledge and expertise and not allow him to opt out.

There is Australian case law to suggest that opting out and staying silent can constitute a breach of duty, depending on the circumstances of the case, but it has achieved this through the director's duty of care rather than by linking it to the disclosure requirement. In *Permanent Building Society v Wheeler*,[157] the Supreme Court of Western Australia held that the chief executive of a building society could not absolve himself from his duty to exercise reasonable care and skill in relation to a potentially harmful transaction by making a declaration of interest. He had a duty to ensure that the other directors appreciated the potential harm inherent in the transaction and to point out steps that could be taken to reduce the possibility of that harm. He could not avoid that duty 'by, metaphorically speaking, burying his head in the sand'.[158]

Again, in *Fitzsimmons v R*,[159] the Supreme Court of Western Australia (Court of Criminal Appeal) indicated that the content of the duty would vary according to the facts, with disclosure of the interest being a minimum requirement in this respect, but held that an interested director could not rely on the existence of a duty of confidentiality or the like to another party as entitling him to withhold material information about a transaction from his company in breach of this duty.[160]

6.5 The Legal Effect on a Contract of a Failure to Comply with the Disclosure Requirement

6.5.1 *The Company's Right to Avoid the Contract*

When a contract involving self-dealing has not been ratified by the company's shareholders or been made in compliance with an enabling article, the company can avoid it in accordance with the no conflict rule. This is

[157] (1994) 14 ACSR 109.
[158] (1994) 14 ACSR 109 at 160, per Ipp J. See also *State of South Australia v Marcus Clark* (1996) 19 ACSR 606, but note the lower standard indicated in *Centofanti v Eekitimor Pty* (1995) 15 ACSR 629. See generally R Baxt, 'The Duty of Care of Directors—Does it Depend on the Swing of the Pendulum?' in I Ramsay (ed), *Corporate Governance and the Duties of Company Directors* (Centre for Corporate Law and Securities Regulation, University of Melbourne, 1997).
[159] (1997) 23 ACSR 355.
[160] *Ibid* at 358 and 362–4.

essentially the same legal effect that section 322A of the Companies Act prescribes for certain unauthorised contracts involving self-dealing,[161] but the effect derives from general principles of equity.

A transaction that is liable to avoidance or 'voidable' rather than being void has legal effect, but its validity is subject to the company's remedy of rescission. However, the courts may not permit the company to exercise this remedy in certain circumstances. Lord Blackburn reviewed the law governing the right to rescind (or to elect to avoid) a voidable contract in *Erlanger v New Sombrero Phosphate Co*[162] His statement of the law still provides the main source of guidance.[163] Lord Blackburn indicated that rescission is no longer available in the following circumstances:

(1) The company has elected not to avoid the contract.[164]
(2) An innocent third party has acquired an interest in the property before the company makes its election.[165]
(3) There has been unreasonable delay or delay amounting to acquiescence.[166]
(4) There cannot be *restitutio in integrum* and the parties cannot be put in *statu quo*.[167]

6.5.2 An Election Not to Rescind

Such an election can presumably be inferred from the company's conduct and does not necessarily require an express declaration to that effect. Lord Blackburn held that as long as the company had not made an election, it retained the right to determine it either way.[168]

6.5.3 An Innocent Third Party

This refers to someone who acquires an interest in property that has passed under a contract involving self-dealing and reflects equity's general protection of a *bona fide* purchaser without notice. However, when the third party to such a contract is not a director of the company and is independent of the

---

[161] And the effect that s 322 of the Companies Act 1985 prescribes for contracts made in violation of s 320: see further below.
[162] (1878) 3 App Cas 1218 (HL) at 1277–283. This concerned a contract between a company and its promoters.
[163] See Lord Goff's reference to this as the 'most familiar statement of the law' in *Guinness v Saunders* [1990] 2 AC 663 at 697–98. See also the judgments of Simon Bown J in *Runciman v Walter Runciman* [1993] BCC 223 at 233–4 and of Clarke LJ in *Craven Textile Engineers v Batley FC* [2001] BCC (CA) at paras 27–32.
[164] (1878) 3 App Cas 1218 at 1278.
[165] *Ibid.* Lord Blackburn cited *Clough v The London and North Western Railway Co* (1871–2) LR 7 Ex 26 at 34–5.
[166] (1878) 3 App Cas 1218 at 1278–279.
[167] *Ibid*, citing *Addie v The Western Bank* (1866–9) LR 1 Sc 145 at 165.
[168] (1878) 3 App Cas 1218 at 1278.

director's control (and would not, in effect, be a 'person connected with' a director for the purposes of section 322A), then such a third party could also be treated as an innocent third party provided that they did not have actual or constructive notice of the facts giving rise to the company's right of rescission. The Company Law Review has recommended that such innocent third parties be protected from the civil law penalties.

In any event, from the perspective of such a third party, the interested director's inability to rely upon an enabling article or to procure the ratification of the contract by the company's shareholders is essentially the same problem as that presented by a lack of actual authority on the part of the company's agent. Therefore, as Knox J indicated in *Cowan de Groot v Eagle Trust*,[169] the third party should be able to enforce the contract against the company if it can rely upon an overriding rule of attribution. This would include section 35A, the indoor management rule and the doctrine of ostensible authority.

6.5.4 *Unreasonable Delay or Acquiescence*

Lord Blackburn referred to the general principle of equity that those who seek relief should use 'due diligence' after there has been 'such notice or knowledge as to make it inequitable' to delay. In the context of self-dealing, this would be the time at which the company had actual or constructive knowledge of the facts giving rise to its right to rescind.[170] Further, any change in the position of the parties or in the state of the relevant property would count against the company if it occurred after it had notice or knowledge of its right to rescind.[171]

Lord Blackburn found further guidance on this point from the judgment of the Privy Council in *Lindsay Petroleum v Hurd*.[172] This had indicated that the overriding consideration should be whether it would be 'practically unjust' to allow the company to rescind either because the company had effectively waived its right to do so or because it would be unreasonable to allow the company to rescind in the circumstances of the case.[173] Lord Blackburn held that two circumstances would always be important in judging the balance of justice or injustice in allowing the company to rescind, namely the length of the delay and the nature of the acts done during the interval.[174]

Lord Blackburn held that, in the case of a company, account had to be taken of the practicalities of taking action where, as in the case before him,

---

[169] See above.
[170] Identifying a company's knowledge for this purpose means attributing to it the knowledge of its agents in accordance with the principles discussed in chapter 5. See generally Bowstead & Reynolds, Art 97, and at 8–207–8–216 and *El Ajou v Dollar Land Holdings* [1994] BCC 143 (CA).
[171] (1878) 3 App Cas 1218 at 1279.
[172] (1873–4) LR 5 PC 221.
[173] (1878) 3 App Cas 1218 at 1279, quoting from the Privy Council's judgment in *Lindsay Petroleum* (1873–74) LR 5 PC 221 at 239.
[174] (1878) 3 App Cas 1218 at 1279.

the company's shareholders would first have to change its board.[175] On this basis, a company should not be deprived of its right to rescind on account of delay unless the delay had been excessive.[176] In *Runciman v Walter Runciman*, however, where the company sought to rescind the extended notice period in the director's service contract after it had been taken over by new controllers,[177] Simon Brown J held that Lord Blackburn's comments about the significance of delay in the case of a company had to be viewed in the context of the overriding consideration of 'whether the balance of justice or injustice is in favour of granting the remedy or of withholding it'.[178] In that context:[179]

> If then one poses the simple question: what does the balance of justice require in the present case, I am left in no doubt whatever as to the proper answer … To hold in these circumstances that what was at most a merely technical breach of a statutory duty of disclosure should render that variation unenforceable would to my mind involve the most patent injustice.

6.5.5 Impossibility of Restitution

Lord Blackburn said that it was clear 'on principles of general justice' that there must be *restitutio in integrum* as a condition of rescission. Whilst a Court of Equity could not award damages, it could, in rescinding the contract, take account of profits and make allowance for deterioration:[180]

> And I think the practice has always been for a Court of Equity to give this relief whenever, by the exercise of its powers, it can do what is practically just, though it cannot restore the parties precisely to the state they were in before the contract.

This condition has proved a significant barrier to the rescission of contracts involving self-dealing. In *Hely-Hutchinson v Brayhead*,[181] the Court of Appeal held that the indemnity given to the director was voidable because he had not declared his interest in it at a board meeting, but that it would be impossible for the company to make restitution to the director since he had already acted in reliance on the indemnity. If the company wished to avoid the contract, it must be 'totally avoided' and that could no longer be done.[182]

---

[175] *Ibid* at 1280.
[176] *Ibid* at 1282.
[177] See above at n 68.
[178] (1878) 3 App Cas 1218 at 1279, cited in [1993] BCC 223 at 233–4.
[179] [1993] BCC 223 at 234.
[180] (1878) 3 App Cas 1218 at 1278–279.
[181] [1968] 1 QB 549.
[182] [1968] 1 QB 549 at 594, per Lord Pearson. See also the judgments of Lord Denning MR at 586 and of Lord Wilberforce at 591.

In *Guinness v Saunders*,[183] the House of Lords found that the payment of special remuneration to the director was void for lack of actual authority and that therefore the company could recover the payment in full in summary proceedings.[184] However, Lord Goff noted that if, as the Court of Appeal had found, the only vitiating factor had been the director's failure to declare his interest in the payment at a board meeting, then the payment would have been voidable not void and the company would have had to establish its right to rescind in the circumstances:[185]

> The contract had to be rescinded, and as a condition of rescission [the director] had to be placed *in statu quo*. No doubt this could be done by a court of equity making a just allowance for the services he had rendered; but no such allowance has been considered, let alone made, in the present case.

In *Craven Textile Engineers v Batley FC*,[186] the Court of Appeal noted Lord Blackburn's reference to the court's doing 'what is practically just', but emphasised that this did not give the court a general discretion to do what seems fair and just in all the circumstances.[187] A company would not be entitled to rescind a contract if full restitution was impossible, but in determining whether or not this was the case, the court would consider whether it could do 'what is practically just to restore the parties to the position which existed before'.[188]

7 SPECIAL REGIMES UNDER PART X OF THE COMPANIES ACT 1985

7.1 Contracts Involving an Enhanced Risk of Abuse

The general regulation of contracts involving self-dealing through compulsory disclosure to board meetings reflects the need to balance the risk of the company's interests being threatened by the conflicting interest against the benefits that such transactions are likely to generate and the practical difficulties of bringing the company's shareholders into the decision-making process. It represents a reasonable compromise within the constraints of the unitary board system of governance.

Nevertheless, there are sub-groups within the general class of contracts involving self-dealing for which more rigorous safeguards than disclosure to fellow board members are necessary. Part X identifies some such

---

[183] [1990] 2 AC 663.
[184] See above at nn 63–6.
[185] [1990] 2 AC 663 at 698.
[186] [2001] BCC 679.
[187] [2001] BCC 679 at para 30.
[188] *Ibid.*

sub-groups for special treatment. For example, there is a relatively high risk of abuse in the making of loans or the extending of credit to a company's directors and relatively little benefit to be derived from permitting such transactions. Part X contains a detailed set of provisions aimed at such transactions based on a general rule of prohibition, subject to limited exceptions.[189]

The Company Law Review, whilst expressing the hope that it might be possible to simplify the specification of these complex provisions, followed the Law Commission in accepting that prohibition can be justified as the most efficient means of combating abuse in this area of self-dealing. It therefore rejected suggestions that the regime be replaced with a scheme based on compulsory disclosure.[190] However, it recommended that transactions approved by the shareholders be added to the permitted exceptions in this regime.[191]

7.2 Directors' Remuneration

Part X of the Companies Act also contains provisions regulating directors' service contracts and payments to directors.[192] These set a broad boundary around the power that an enabling article can vest in a company's board in this respect in order to overcome the no profit rule.[193] Vesting the power to award directors' remuneration in the board means that directors can determine their own remuneration. This has long been recognised as giving rise to a risk of abuse, given the obvious personal interest of directors in maximising their remuneration.[194] The risk is greater in companies in which the shareholders cannot exercise effective control over their board, especially public companies. Even where directors are not directly involved in the decision-making concerning their own remuneration, there is still a risk that those who are involved may be influenced more by their sense of a common interest or feelings of personal loyalty than by their duty to ensure the best possible terms for the company.[195] And all directors can be viewed as forming a network, which has a collective interest in establishing the highest possible 'going rate' of remuneration.[196]

---

[189] Companies Act 1985, ss 330–346.
[190] See Developing the Framework, Annex C at 28–30 and Completing the Structure at 4.21.
[191] *Ibid.*
[192] Companies Act 1985, ss 311, 312, 318 and 312.
[193] See above.
[194] See generally W Bishop and D Prentice, 'Some Legal and Economic Aspects of Fiduciary Remuneration' (1983) 46 *Modern Law Review* 289.
[195] See generally J Parkinson, *Corporate Power and Responsibility* (Oxford, Clarendon Press, 1993), chapter 7.
[196] *Ibid.*

It has, however, proved very difficult to find an effective and efficient mechanism for combating this risk of abuse. The key problem is that decisions about remuneration require managerial expertise and the shareholders cannot operate as an effective organ of management unless they are small in number.[197] The Cadbury Report recognised that it would not be practical to remove responsibility for settling directors' remuneration from the board:[198]

> The Committee has received proposals for giving shareholders the opportunity to determine matters such as directors' pay at general meetings, but does not see how these suggestions could be workable. A director's remuneration is not a matter which can be sensibly reduced to a vote for or against: were the vote to go against a particular remuneration package, the board would still have to determine the remuneration of the director concerned.

In practice, for those companies where the risk of abuse is greater, the shareholders can only be invited to endorse a pre-negotiated set of terms put before them. Moreover, in reaching their decision, the shareholders are likely to need guidance from the company's directors and to rely on this unless it is clearly against their interests. Reform of the law governing directors' remuneration has therefore been limited and targeted at listed public companies. Thus, the Combined Code requires 'remuneration committees' of independent non-executive directors to make decisions concerning remuneration.[199] And the Directors' Remuneration Report Regulations 2002 require that a report be produced in a specified form and submitted to the shareholders for approval.[200]

As regards the general regulation of self-dealing, directors' service contracts and any other transactions concerning the payment or remuneration of directors, including amendments to service contracts, are subject to the disclosure requirement.[201] The Company Law Review has recommended that they should be excluded from this requirement, at least where the director's interest is an obvious one.[202] Payments to directors by way of remuneration may be substantial, but they are payments for the provision of services rather than assets. They are not therefore subject to section 320 of the Companies Act 1985, which will be considered in the next section.

---

[197] See chapter 3.
[198] See *The Report of the Committee on the Financial Aspects of Corporate Governance* (London, Gee, 1992) ('the Cadbury Report') at 4.43. See also *Directors' Remuneration: Report of a Small Study Group* (London, Gee, 1995) ('the Greenbury Report'), *Final Report of the Committee on Corporate Governance* (London, Gee, 1998) ('the Hampel Report') and DTI, *Directors' Remuneration* URN 01/1400 (December 2001).
[199] *The Combined Code on Corporate Governance* (Financial Reporting Council) (as amended with effect from 1 November 2003).
[200] SI 2002/1986. See further on the regulation of directors' remuneration, Gower & Davies at 402–5.
[201] *Runciman v Walter Runciman plc* [1993] BCC 233.
[202] Completing the Structure at 4.12.

It is, however, open to those drafting a company's constitution to set a limit on the board's actual authority to authorise the remuneration of directors.

8 SECTION 320 OF THE COMPANIES ACT 1985

8.1 Substantial Property Transactions

Section 320 identifies a relatively large sub-group of contracts involving self-dealing and subjects these to a special regime whereby the company's shareholders must be brought into the decision-making process. It applies to contracts, or rather 'arrangements', concerning the acquisition or disposal of 'non-cash assets' above a specified threshold value. Section 320 prohibits companies from entering into any contract within its scope without first obtaining the approval of their shareholders. Section 321 makes some exceptions to the general rule, in particular intra-group transactions and arrangements entered into by a company in liquidation (other than a members' voluntary liquidation).[203] The Company Law Review has endorsed the Law Commission's recommendation that section 320 should be qualified to make it clear that a company is not prohibited from entering a contract within its scope if the contract is conditional on the shareholders giving their approval.[204]

Section 322 provides that any arrangement entered into by a company in contravention of section 320 'and any transaction entered into in pursuance of the arrangement (whether by the company or any other person)' is to be voidable at the instance of the company.[205] Section 322 subjects the company's right to avoid any such transaction to certain conditions (in effect, it places bars on the company's right to rescind) that broadly equate to those set out in section 322A.[206] Further (as with section 322A) section 322 makes the third party to any arrangement entered into in violation of section 320 liable to account to the company for any resulting profit and to indemnify it against any resulting loss or damage.[207]

8.2 The Rationale of Section 320

8.2.1 *Additional Protection for the Shareholders*

Section 320 gives third parties to potential contracts within its scope a good reason to ensure that the company's shareholders are formally consulted

---

[203] Companies Act 1985, s 321(2).
[204] Developing the Framework, Annex C at 26.
[205] Companies Act 1985, s 322A(1).
[206] Companies Act 1985, s 322A(2).
[207] Companies Act, s 322A(3). This liability arises regardless of whether or not the transaction is actually avoided by the company: s 322(4).

about the contract and that it is one they are likely to approve. Where the company is a private company, it may be relatively straightforward to comply with this requirement, as long as those responsible for organising the contract are aware of the need to consult the shareholders.[208] Where the company has a large number of shareholders or is a public company, the requirement is likely to prove onerous and to entail significant expense and delay. However, listed public companies are subject to more stringent regulation in any event inasmuch as their shareholders must give their prior approval by ordinary resolution to a 'related party transaction' with a 'relative value' of five per cent or more. [209]

For larger companies, section 320 is likely to operate as a disclosure requirement inasmuch as the shareholders are likely to look to the board to explain the merits of the contract from the company's perspective. The burden entailed by this procedure has to be weighed against the increased risk of loss associated with a contract involving self-dealing. The unitary board system does not facilitate any lower cost alternative that would provide an equally effective check on the risk of abuse. The Listing Rules also have to accommodate this deficiency of the unitary board system in the continuing obligations that they impose on listed public companies in respect of major acquisitions or disposals in general. They require that shareholders be notified formally of transactions with a 'relative value' of five per cent or more and that their prior approval be obtained for contracts with a 'relative value' of 25 per cent or more.[210]

The case of *British Racing Drivers' Club v Hextall Erskine* provides a cautionary tale about the impact of section 320, which also illustrates its purpose.[211] The company entered into a contract for the purchase of a half share in a motor dealership at a price of almost £6 million. This represented a diversification into a new line of business at a time when that business was in recession. The chairman of the company's board was a director of and a major shareholder in the vendor. He was also a director of the company's holding company. Section 320 therefore prohibited this contract unless the shareholders (or rather 'members' in this case) of the

---

[208] In *British Racing Drivers' Club v Hextall Erskine* [1997] 1 BCLC 182, the company's solicitors had advised that the company entering the relevant transaction did not need to obtain the consent of the shareholders of its holding company.

[209] See the Listing Rules, chapters 10 and 11. These specify a number of financial ratios for calculating the 'relative value' of a transaction depending on its nature and subject matter (comparison of gross assets, comparison of profits, comparison of turnover, consideration for the transaction compared to the company's market capitalisation and comparison of gross capital). A 'related party' includes a director of the company or a shareholder with at least ten per cent of the voting rights or an 'associate' of either of these. The related party and any associates must abstain from voting on the transaction. Penalties for breach of these rules include censure of the directors or the company and suspension or cancellation of the listing.

[210] The Listing Rules, chapter 10.

[211] [1997] 1 BCLC 182.

holding company gave their approval.[212] The chairman's involvement in the third party might have been a useful source of information, as noted above, and might have provided reassurance about the transaction if it had been revealed to the members. However, in this particular case, it was highly unlikely that the members would have approved the contract if they had been consulted beforehand and the board wished to conceal it from them. The members had not been asked to approve the contract beforehand and they refused to ratify it afterwards.

The company paid a price for the half share in the dealership that proved to be excessive and it made a large loss when the contract was eventually unravelled.[213] It did seem likely that the company's board had been swayed and its commercial judgment skewed by the chairman's interest and involvement in the third party. In his judgment, Carnwath J explained the purpose of section 320 and noted its relevance to the case in point:[214]

> The thinking behind [section 320] is that if directors enter into a substantial commercial transaction with one of their number, there is a danger that their judgment may be distorted by conflicts of interest and loyalties, even in cases where there is no actual dishonesty. The section is designed to protect a company against such distortions. It enables members to provide a check. Of course, this does not necessarily mean that the members will exercise a better commercial judgment; but it does make it likely that the matter will be more widely ventilated, and a more objective decision reached.

In *Re Duckwari*, Nourse LJ endorsed this view of the purpose of section 320, referring to 'the evident purpose' of section 320 as being 'to give shareholders specific protection in respect of arrangements and transactions which will or may benefit directors to the detriment of the company'.[215]

The fact that the third party is also a director of the company (or its holding company) or a person connected with a director should reduce the commercial risk (in terms of delay) that might otherwise result from having to consult the shareholders.[216] Given the nature of the transactions to which section 320 applies and the fact that third parties should have little doubt as to whether it applies to them or not, there is an economic case for placing this additional burden on this category of third party in order to protect the company's interests.

---

[212] The holding company was in fact a company registered by guarantee with roughly 500 members. Many of its members were involved in the motor trade.
[213] It could not be rescinded since restitution was impossible. A settlement was reached with the third party and the interested director whereby the shareholding was bought back at a much lower price.
[214] [1997] 1 BCLC 182 at 198.
[215] [1999] Ch 253 at 264. See also *Micro-Leisure v County Properties & Developments* 1999 SLT 1428; [2000] BCC 872 (Outer House).
[216] See generally chapter 3 on this process.

The Company Law Review endorsed the Law Commission's recommendation that section 320 should continue in substantially its current form.[217] In particular, it has supported the view that the approval of shareholders must be obtained for transactions caught by section 320 and that it should not be possible to substitute for the shareholders' approval the approval of the board, or the approval of 'independent directors', or a process whereby shareholders are notified of the transaction and do not object, or the report of an 'expert' that the transaction is fair and reasonable.[218]

8.2.2 Section 320 and the Unanimous Consent Rule

As was seen in chapter 3, it is possible for the shareholders of a company to exercise their powers informally, provided that they do so unanimously.[219] Where this is possible, it saves the time and expense (and reduces the attendant risk) of convening a general meeting.

Section 320 in effect gives shareholders a statutory power over contracts within its ambit. In the case of such statutory powers, the unanimous consent rule does not necessarily enable procedural formality to be overridden.[220] It depends on whether 'the purpose and underlying rationale' of the statutory power is just to protect the shareholders or goes further than that and, for example, is designed to protect the company's creditors as well.[221] The judgments in the *British Racing Drivers* and *Duckwari* cases have established that the purpose and underlying rationale of section 320 is limited to protecting the company's shareholders and that procedural formality is not therefore necessary.[222] This suggests that shareholders can approve a contract for the purposes of section 320 informally.[223]

It has, however, also been suggested that the unanimous consent rule should no longer apply to contracts subject to section 320 when a company is insolvent.[224] This is because it has been established that when a company is insolvent or on the verge of insolvency, the 'interests of the company' are no longer to be identified with the interests of the shareholders alone, but that the interests of the company's creditors intrude

---

[217] Developing the Framework, Annex C at 26.
[218] *Ibid.*
[219] *Re Duomatic Ltd* [1969] 2 Ch 365; *Cane v Jones* [1980] 1 WLR 1451; *Multinational Gas v Multinational Gas Services* [1983] 1 Ch 258 (CA); *Euro Brokers v Monecor (London)* [2003] EWCA Civ 105.
[220] See R Goddard, 'The *Re Duomatic* Principle and Sections 320–22 of the Companies Act 1985' [2004] *Journal of Business Law* 121.
[221] *Wright v Atlas Wright (Europe)* [1999] 2 BCLC 301 (CA). See also *Precision Dippings v Precision Dippings Marketing* [1986] 1 Ch 447 (CA) and *BDG Roof-Bond v Douglas* [2000] 1 BCLC 401.
[222] See R Goddard, [2004] JBL 121 at 124–6.
[223] *Re Conegrade* [2002] EWHC 2411.
[224] *Demite v Protec Health* [1998] BCC 638; *Walker v WA Personel* [2002] BPIR 621. See generally R Goddard, [2004] *Journal of Business Law* 121.

and displace them.[225] This affects the nature of the directors' duty to exercise their discretionary powers in good faith in the best interests of the company. It also means that the shareholders lose their power to ratify any actions of the directors that are in breach of the duty of good faith.[226]

In the context of section 320, a company's insolvency may not just affect the unanimous consent rule. It is arguable that the intrusion of the creditors' interests affects the shareholders' power to validate a contract that is subject to section 320, whether it is exercised informally or at a general meeting. It is also arguable that the directors' duty to express an honest opinion in advising the shareholders on how to exercise their power of approval would have to take account of the intrusion of the creditors' interests.[227] In any event, if the company goes into administration or liquidation, the validity of a contract subject to section 320 and approved by the shareholders could still be affected by the additional remedies available under the Insolvency Act 1986. Thus, the contract might be treated as a 'transaction at an undervalue' or as a 'preference' and set aside accordingly.[228]

8.3 The Conditions that Trigger Section 320

8.3.1 The Statutory Conditions

Section 320 is triggered when:

(1) A company enters into an 'arrangement' with a director of the company or of its holding company (if any) or a 'person connected with' such a director as defined by section 346;
(2) The arrangement is for the acquisition of one or more 'non-cash assets' by the third party from the company or by the company from the third party.
(3) The value of the non-cash assets is:[229]

    (a) not less than £2,000; and
    (b) more than £100,000 or (if less) ten per cent of the company's 'asset value'.

---

[225] *West Mercia Safetywear v Dodd* [1988] BCLC 250 (CA); *Colin Gwyer v London Wharf* [2002] EWHC 2748. See V Finch, 'Directors' Duties Towards Creditors' (1989) 10 *Company Lawyer* 23. See further chapter 3.

[226] *West Mercia Safetywear v Dodd* [1988] BCLC 250; *Fulham FC v Cabra Estates* [1992] BCC 863 (CA).

[227] *Rackham v Peek Foods* [1990] BCLC 895; *Crowther v Carpets International* [1990] BCLC 460.

[228] Insolvency Act 1986, ss 238 and 239. See also *Re Conegrade* [2002] EWHC 2411, in which Lloyd J held that a transfer of property to the company's directors (who were also its shareholders) had been validly approved under s 320, but nevertheless constituted a preference under s 239 of the Insolvency Act.

[229] These thresholds were set by the Companies (Fair Dealing by Directors) (Increase in Financial Limits) Order 1990 (SI 1990/1393), art 2(a) with effect from 31 July 1990.

8.3.2 An Arrangement

This point arose in the *Duckwari* cases,[230] which concerned an arrangement whereby one company took over from another a contract for the purchase of certain property. In *Re Duckwari (No 2)*, Nourse LJ held that 'arrangement' includes agreements or understandings having no contractual effect:[231]

> Further, there is no misuse of language in describing a transaction contemplated by such an agreement or understanding as one which is entered into 'pursuant' to it.

8.3.3 Non-Cash Assets

This means any property or interest in property other than cash, 'cash' including foreign currency.[232] Further, the acquisition of a non-cash asset includes 'the creation or extinction of an estate or interest in, or a right over, any property and also the discharge of any person's liability, other than a liability for a liquidated sum'.[233] The provision of services is therefore outside the scope of section 320 and it does not contribute to the regulation of directors' remuneration. The Company Law Review, following the Law Commission, has recommended that it should be made clear that section 320 does not apply to covenanted payments under service contracts or to *bona fide* payments by way of damages for breach of contract or by way of pension for past services.[234]

The *Duckwari* cases also addressed the issue of what constitutes non-cash assets for the purposes of section 320. The third party, which was also a company, had entered into a contract to purchase a freehold property for £495,000 and had paid a deposit of £49,500. One of the company's directors was also a director and shareholder of the third party. The company took over the contract from the third party and paid the balance of the purchase price to the vendor. It received the transfer of the property and paid the amount of the deposit to the third party. The company's shareholders had not approved the transaction and the property subsequently declined in value.

In *Re Duckwari (No 1)*,[235] Millett LJ rejected an argument that there had been a novation of the original contract and had thus been no direct

---

[230] *Re Duckwari plc (No 1)* [1997] 2 BCLC 713 (CA); *(No 2)* [1999] Ch 253 (CA); *(No 3)* [1999] Ch 268 (CA).
[231] [1999] Ch 253 at 260.
[232] Companies Act 1985, s 739(1).
[233] Companies Act 1985, s 739(2). This wording is repeated in the 2002 White Paper: Draft Clauses, clause 224.
[234] Developing the Framework, Annex C at 26.
[235] [1997] 2 BCLC 713.

arrangement between the company and the third party. He held that there was no evidence to support this view and that there was an arrangement between the company and the third party, namely an assignment or a simple 'taking over' of the third party's rights and liabilities. However, he indicated that even a novation would have amounted to an arrangement between the company and the third party since the third party would have had to give its consent.

Millett LJ held that the third party had transferred an asset to the company and that this asset could be described in two ways with equal accuracy: first as the benefit of the purchase contract and secondly as the third party's beneficial interest in the freehold property. By either description, the company was acquiring 'property or any interest in property other than cash' and thus acquiring a non-cash asset.

8.3.4 *The Value of the Non-Cash Asset*

This may be crucial to ascertaining whether or not a particular contract is caught by section 320. In practice, the consideration paid by or to the company provides the principal point of reference in this respect. However, section 320 merely refers to the 'value' of the non-cash asset or assets without specifying how this value is to be determined in the event of a dispute. In the case of a disposal by the company, the transaction should be caught by section 320 if the value of the assets can be shown to exceed the requisite threshold even though the amount of the consideration does not. This does depend on the view that assets have an objective value that can be ascertained and used as a reference point whether the company is acquiring or disposing of them.

A Scottish case, *Micro-Leisure v County Properties & Developments*,[236] addressed the argument that the value of the asset to the particular purchaser should be taken into account for the purposes of section 320. The asset at issue was a strip of land and the purchaser was the owner of an adjacent area of land with development potential. The combined land had much greater development potential and thus a much higher cumulative value. If the value of the strip of land sold by the company were to be calculated as a proportion of this enhanced cumulative value, then its disposal would be caught by section 320. Lord Hamilton noted the lack of prescribed criteria for valuation in section 320:[237]

> The absence of definition suggests, in my view, that Parliament intended the value of the non-cash asset to be determined, having regard to the statutory purposes, in the context of the particular circumstances of the transaction or arrangement.

[236] 1999 SLT 1428; [2000] BCC 872 (Outer House).
[237] 1999 SLT 1428 at 1430.

For guidance on this statutory purpose, he had noted the judgment of Carnwath J in *British Racing Drivers* and also Nourse LJ's reference in his judgment in *Re Duckwari (No. 2)* to 'the evident purpose' of the provision as being 'to give shareholders specific protection in respect of arrangements and transactions which will or may benefit directors to the detriment of the company'.[238] Accordingly, Lord Hamilton held that the enhanced value of the asset to the particular purchaser was a relevant factor:[239]

> Otherwise, not only would the director be acquiring the strip at an advantageous price but the company would be failing to take advantage of the known circumstance that its property could on sale to a particular purchaser realise a significantly higher price than its value treated in isolation.

On this basis, the enhanced value would represent 'the true market value or worth' of the asset and this should provide the reference point for the purposes of section 320.

Even valuing an asset by reference to consideration may not be straightforward where, as in the *Duckwari* cases, the company is acquiring an asset that is not easy to specify in isolation from a wider arrangement of which it forms part. In *Re Duckwari (No 1)*, the Court of Appeal held that the value of the non-cash asset acquired from the third party was the amount of the deposit. The company acquired the third party's rights under the contract (or its beneficial interest in the freehold property) and these rights entitled it to be credited with the amount of this deposit when paying the outstanding purchase price to the vendor. The deposit therefore provided the reference point for assessing the value of the rights acquired from the third party given that the company could only acquire the freehold property itself by paying the outstanding purchase price and discharging the unpaid vendor's lien.

Millett LJ rejected the third party's argument that the value of the asset acquired from the third party should be treated as nil on the basis that the company was in fact liable to pay the purchase price in full. He also rejected an argument by the company that the value of the acquired asset should be treated as equivalent to the full purchase price of the freehold property and held that, in acquiring the property, the company in effect acquired two assets: first the right to call for the transfer of the property from the vendor (subject to payment of the balance of the purchase price), which was acquired from the third party in exchange for paying it the amount of the deposit; and secondly the extinction of the vendor's unpaid lien in exchange for paying the balance of the purchase price, which in effect was acquired from the vendor. This point might have proved critical

---

[238] 1999 Ch 253 at 264.
[239] 1999 SLT 1428 at 1430.

to the relevance of section 320, but in the event the amount of the deposit was a few thousand pounds higher than ten per cent of the company's asset value and the section still therefore caught the transaction.

8.3.5 The Company's Asset Value

This is the value of a company's net assets determined by reference to the accounts prepared and laid in respect of the last preceding financial year in respect of which such accounts were so laid. However, where no accounts have been prepared and laid before the time when the arrangement was entered into, the company's asset value is the amount of its called-up share capital.[240]

8.4 Consequential Liability under Section 322

The company's right to avoid or rescind a contract for breach of section 320 is subject to conditions that broadly reflect the equitable bars on rescission and the equivalent provisions in section 322A. Further, as with section 322A, the third party and the directors of the company who authorised the arrangement or transaction on behalf of the company face personal liability to account for any profit and to indemnify the company for any resulting loss or damage.[241] There is a link between the two consequences in that one condition of avoidance provides that the company cannot avoid the arrangement or transaction if it 'has been indemnified in pursuance of this section by any other person for the loss or damage suffered by it'.[242]

In *Re Duckwari (No 2)*, the Court of Appeal had to consider how much of the loss that the company claimed to have suffered it could recover through its right to an indemnity. Nourse LJ started by noting that section 320 is a prohibition on the board and constitutes a statutory limit on the contractual power of a company's board. Exceeding this limit is therefore equivalent to a breach of trust.[243] If section 322 had not provided specific remedies, the company would have been entitled to recover compensation that would have restored it to the position it would have been in if the transaction had not taken place. Where the company realised an acquired asset at a loss, it would be entitled to recover that loss.

However, it was argued that although the company had suffered a loss in realising the freehold property, this was not a loss 'resulting from' the transaction but rather from the subsequent fall in its market value. Nourse

---

[240] Companies Act 1985, s 320(2).
[241] Companies Act 1985, s 322(5), however, provides that a director is not liable 'if he shows that he took all reasonable steps to secure the company's compliance' with s 320.
[242] Companies Act 1985, s 322(2)(a).
[243] [1999] Ch 253 at 262–3.

LJ held that he would not construe the right to an indemnity in such a restrictive fashion, given the purpose of section 320 and the remedy that the company would have but for this specific right.[244] In particular, he said that it would be hard to see the rationale in denying the company its remedy of rescinding the contract in the event of an indemnity being paid to it if the indemnity were to be restricted in the way that had been suggested. However, in a further judgment, Nourse LJ held that the company's right to an indemnity against its loss did not extend so far as to cover the borrowing costs it had incurred in order to finance the acquisition.[245]

9 CONCLUSIONS AND REVIEW

There is an economic case for treating contracts involving self-dealing differently from contracts with companies in general in the rules of law governing their validity. Companies face a specific risk of loss from the conflict of interest, which increases the benefits of having stricter rules of attribution and exposing third parties to a greater risk of invalidity. Also, the relatively narrow range of contracts affected by the stricter rules reduces the costs for third parties in general. It is also arguable that the kind of connection between a director and a third party that constitutes self-dealing should reduce the costs of having to comply with stricter rules, such as the commercial risk that accompanies delay.

This chapter has shown that the stricter regulation of contracts involving self-dealing takes effect at three levels. First, these contracts are usually treated differently in the terms of a company's constitution governing the actual authority of a company's board and other corporate agents. Secondly, the presence of self-dealing is relevant to the operation of the overriding rules of attribution governing the validity of unauthorised contracts. Thirdly, contracts involving self-dealing are subject to additional regulation that may affect their validity. In particular, they are subject to the general disclosure requirement, which ensures that those acting for the company are formally notified of the conflicting interest and should therefore have full information as to the potential risk to the company.

The special regulation of contracts involving self-dealing has to be flexible in order to take account of the variety of ways in which a company's directors might have an interest in a contract and the fact that a third party might not be aware of the conflict. In particular, the regulation has to be flexible enough to draw a distinction between third parties who are directors or who are controlled or influenced by directors and third parties who are independent of the directors interested in them. There is such

---

[244] [1999] Ch 253 at 264.
[245] [1999] Ch 268.

flexibility in the terms of the various overriding rules of attribution and in the impact of the additional regulation. Thus, contracts made in violation of this regulation tend to be voidable rather than void.

The special regulation of contracts involving self-dealing also has to work within the limitations of the unitary board system and the fact that there is no special organ for monitoring a company's board other than the body of shareholders. The scope for simply reducing the actual authority of the board is constrained by the deficiency of the body of shareholders as an active organ of management and the limited role that it can realistically be expected to play in the case of companies with large numbers of shareholders, especially public companies. This deficiency is reflected in the fact that the general regulation of contracts involving self-dealing is procedural, requiring formal disclosure of the conflicting interest to the board. Further, those transactions where there is the greatest risk of abuse are simply subjected to a general prohibition.

Within these constraints, the regulation of self-dealing can promote economic efficiency by striking a balance between combating the increased risk of loss to companies and the fact that as a general rule contracts involving self-dealing are likely to be beneficial. This economic rationale is reflected in the fact that the relevant law has evolved to impose procedural regulation focused on the board. It is also reflected in the insistence of the various rules of equity on strict compliance with this procedural regulation and their penalising failure to do so, even where a company might not be able to establish that it has suffered any harm as a result of the non-compliance. There is an economic logic in this approach since compliance is not an onerous burden.

One factor that increases the cost of compliance is a third party's lack of awareness of the need for compliance. This may be due to ignorance of the conflict of interest. It is not necessarily reasonable to expect due compliance by a third party who is not a director or someone closely connected to a director. This factor is, however, accommodated inasmuch as the consequences of non-compliance vary according to the nature of the affected director's interest in the third party.

The main deficiency of the law governing contracts involving self-dealing, apart from the shortcomings of the unitary board system, is its complexity. Its insistence on procedural formality can also seem absurd in some contexts, especially since it is backed (in theory) by criminal sanctions. It is, for example, hard to justify the fact that a director who fails to declare an interest in his or her own service contract at a board meeting is committing a criminal offence and liable to an unlimited fine. The recommendations of the Company Law Review, building on the earlier work of the two Law Commissions, will do much to remedy this deficiency.

Index